American Journey

AMERICAN JOURNEY
The Times of Robert Kennedy

Interviews by Jean Stein

Edited by George Plimpton

Harcourt Brace Jovanovich, Inc.
New York

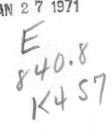
First edition

ISBN 0–15–191070–7

Library of Congress Catalog Card Number: 73–78867

Printed in the United States of America

Contents

Introduction

American Journey is an example of a relatively new genre in publishing—the use of oral history as a form of communication. Using new techniques, this book is itself perhaps an innovation within that form.

Oral history (nearly 400 such projects are under way at this writing) has been largely thought of as the collecting of interview transcripts for storage in archives in order to provide historians with research material. Somewhat less common is the use of these interview transcripts as a literary form—in which the raw transcripts are edited, arranged, and allowed to stand for themselves without intervention by the historian. True, a few examples have proved successful, both critically and commercially. Of the sociological studies, Oscar Lewis's books, particularly *La Vida* and *The Children of Sánchez*, should be mentioned; so should Jan Myrdal's *Report from a Chinese Village*, Ronald Blythe's *Akenfield*, and certainly *Lay My Burden Down*, B. A. Botkin's study of slavery as recounted by ex-slaves, which, as a WPA project of the thirties, was an important forerunner of oral history as a form of literary convention.

A compendium of oral-history publications would also include both dialogue and interview books. *Dialogues of Archibald MacLeish and Mark Van Doren* is an example of the first category. Among a number of books in the second are *Felix Frankfurter Reminisces*, Studs Terkel's *Division Street: America* and *Hard Times* (which are sociological studies but depend partly on the question-and-answer technique), the Robert Craft interview collections with Igor Stravinsky, the *Writers at Work* volumes on the craft of writing, and the collected *Playboy* interviews.

American Journey is an innovation in the field in that for the first time the authors attempt to subject oral history to the narrative process, in which a succession of voices describe events in the chronology of a man's life in a form that could be called "oral narrative."

The structure of the book is relatively simple: the oral accounts of two journeys are recalled. The first consists of reminiscences of Robert Kennedy's funeral-train trip from New York to Washington. Interviews were held not only with those aboard, but also with people from the immense crowds that came to stand along the railroad tracks. This provides the framework of the book, the cradle upon which the other journey—Robert Kennedy's life story as recalled by his associates— is set. The original plan of the book was to interview only those standing by the tracks and those invited aboard the train—close Kennedy friends and associates (it was William Walton who mentioned, "You could tell the story of Robert Kennedy by telling the story of the people on the train"). But while it was tempting to stick to such aesthetic niceties, it was felt that the need to include particular aspects of Kennedy's career, and to get different points of view, required going to outside sources. To ease the reader's journey through the book, each voice is identified once within each chapter with his profession as of June 1968.

A word about procedure. Over the course of two years, 347 interviews were conducted, many running to as much as forty pages of transcript. Advertisements were placed in local newspapers along the train route asking for interviews with those who felt they had something to offer.

The interviews were edited and the selected contents broken down into approximately fifty categories, with perhaps as many as fifty different references to a single topic—"Robert Kennedy and the Cuban missile crisis," for example. These various monologues were then spliced together chronologically to give a sense of narrative flow and, always, to keep the spontaneous quality of the spoken word. Editorial intervention was restricted solely to the placement of the material, so that there are no voices other than those of the interviewees.

Obviously, there are certain disadvantages to presenting history in this fashion. The historian, working in a more usual way, can mold his source material to suit his purpose; he can remove discrepancies; when there are any gaps, he can conjecture; he can supply his own narrative and descriptions. On the other hand, the editor or historian working in oral narrative must allow the voices to speak for themselves. And the voices are sometimes disparate and contradictory, or repetitious, and prove difficult to link. If there are differences of opinion or fact, these cannot be explained editorially. Furthermore, the material must come from interviews in which the interviewee is often guarded, or has forgotten, or cannot resist the improvement of hindsight, or presents his view in a leaden manner that does not transcribe well and must be discarded, however knowledgeable it is. Often, people who should be interviewed refuse; or their own spoken words, without the formality of literary conventions, startle them to the extent that they do not allow the transcript to proceed into print.

The concept of *American Journey* was not to give a solid historical representation of an era. The technique used is occasionally almost the kaleidoscopic "flicker" technique of films, in which a series of quick images of considerable variety provides an effect of wholeness. The success of such a technique obviously relies on the quality of the voices themselves—and the important compensation in putting together this particular oral history was that Robert Kennedy had surrounded himself with remarkable people, both friends and associates, who talked as if inspired—with candor and insight, and humor especially—whatever the nature of their relationship with him. Indeed, the freshest, most informative material seemed to come less from the public figures than from those for whom being interviewed must have been a novelty, the women particularly: Ann Buchwald, Kay Evans, Helen Keyes, and others. Their evidence is unfettered, and it has translated well to the printed page. It is their contribution—rather than that of the public figures, who are more reserved, less personal, and tend to the general rather than the explicit—that shows this oral-history technique at its best.

The purpose of this book, however, was not to extend the possibilities of such techniques, but to record the impact of Robert Kennedy on the turbulent decade of the sixties. The train was a provident focal point. It not only brought together his associates for the last time, but the effect of that slow journey to Washington on those who watched it, either on television or along the railroad tracks, was a profound one. Kate Haddad (a granddaughter of Franklin Delano Roosevelt) says in her interview what so many others echo about the effect of Robert Kennedy and the symbolic catharsis of that train trip: "I hope it did something to all those people. I hope that I will never be the same either, that my life will . . . perhaps it's too much to say 'take a different turn,' but perhaps my life will have a newer kind of meaning than it did before. It sounds kind of pompous when you say it, but, boy, I hope all those people in the train and outside will never quite be the same. . . ."

J. S.
G. A. P.

June 27, 1970

Acknowledgments

The listing of acknowledgments below does not begin to suggest the support, the advice, and the many hours that generous pepole gave toward the making of this book. We are especially grateful to the following, who in a variety of ways did so much to assist us: Margaret Butterfield, Cynthia Conroy, Lorraine Cooper, Laura de Coppet, Ann Cuss, John Kenneth Galbraith, Dun Gifford, David Halberstam, Michael Harrington, Phyllis Jackson, Stanley Levison, John Lewis, Robert Minor, Willie Morris, Freddy Plimpton, John Seigenthaler, Gretchen Stewart, William vanden Heuvel, John Walker, Wendy Weil, Roger Wilkins, and Andrew Young.

We offer special thanks to the following people who gave interviews that, although they do not appear in this book for reasons of space, provided excellent background material: Samuel Adams, Mayor Thomas d'Alessandro, Karen Alleva, Tom Berkley, Richard Boone, Zeke Boyd, Benjamin Bradlee, Joan Bradon, Ann Brinkley, Sam Brown, Willie Brown, Jerry Bruno, David Burke, John Carlin, Kitty Carlisle, Olga Carlisle, Paul Carver, the Reverend William Sloane Coffin, Roy Cohn, Edward T. Cone, Tim Conway, Paul Corbin, Mr. and Mrs. Tom Corcoran, Walter Cronkite, John Curia, Jr., Richard Cardinal Cushing, the Reverend Sidney Daniels, Edward Delight, USN, Walter Dombrow, Richard Dougherty, John Douglas, Robert L. Douglas, Justice William O. Douglas, James L. Drake, David Dubinsky, Laverne Duffy, Mayor Thomas E. Dunn, Police Lieutenant Jack Eberhardt, Jane Eisenberg, John T. Fallon, Buffy Ford, Dall Forsythe, John Frankenheimer, Thomas Frost, Paul Fusco, Joe Garcia, Lieutenant General James Cavin, Colonel John Glenn, Dorothy Goldberg, Congressman William Green, Bertha

Greenfield, Senator Ernest Gruening, William Gruver, Ambassador Cherif Guellal, Charles Guggenheim, Elzbieta Halberstam, Chief Inspector Joseph Halferty, Marie Harriman, Bill Hartigan, John Herling, Mary Herling, Kalman Hettleman, James Jackson, Senator Jacob K. Javits, Gloria C. Johnson, John Johnson, Mireille Johnston, Brandy Jones, Kirby Jones, Dr. Julian, Alan King, the Reverend Bernard La-Fayette, Jr., Ruth Lehrer, John Lewis, Cliff Linedecker, Samuel Lloyd, Joe Loftus, Mack Lyons, Colonel Floyd Mann, Peter Marudas, John McCone, Kenneth McCormick, Ruth McGee, Patrolman Charles Mc-Groarty, Margaret McNamara, Robert Minor, Judge Francis X. Morrissey, Lieutenant N. E. Muffley, USN, William Murphy, Jacques Nevard, John Nolan, Jr., Anthony Nye, Lou Oberdorfer, Terry Olsen, Gordon Parks, James Peck, Charles Petero, Gary Peterson, Sidney N. Phelps, Wendell Pigman, A. Philip Randolph, Robert J. Regan, Walter Reuther, Police Commissioner Frank Rizzo, Ted Robinson, John D. Rockefeller IV, Nick Rodis, Warren Rogers, Walt Rostow, Dean Rusk, Bayard Rustin, Nicole Salinger, Philip Schaeffler, Tammy Scott, Lawrence Cardinal Sheehan, the Reverend F. L. Shuttlesworth, Judge Samuel Silverman, Benjamin Smith, Joseph Smith, Theodore Sorensen, Dr. Benjamin Spock, David Strauss, William Styron, Evan Thomas, Frank Thomas, Mary Ann Thomas, Stanley Tretick, Stewart Udall, Sander Vanocur, Manuel Vasquez, Robert Vaughn, Gore Vidal, Angelique Voutselas, Mary Warner, Warren Weiner, Justice Byron White, Roy Wilkins, Edward Bennett Williams, W. Willard Wirtz, Edward Wlazlowski, Presley Wood, Doris E. Wright, and Robert Young.

All the interviews and tapes made in connection with this book will be donated for inclusion with the papers of Robert F. Kennedy.

A number of people should be singled out for particular thanks: Gillian Walker, for her ideas and assistance throughout the project, especially at its conception; Arthur Schlesinger, Jr., for his encouragement since the book's inception; Burke Marshall for his forthright assistance in the final stages of the book's preparations; Bonnie Lefkowitz for her help, especially for her valuable critiques; Edwin Barber, our editor at Harcourt Brace Jovanovich, for his editorial advice and for his persistence and faith in this book; and to Barbara Shalvey, who worked tirelessly for two years as a researcher and transcriber, and in a few cases as an interviewer.

American Journey

SAUL STEINBERG, artist

The adventure: you left home and you were taken by your parents somewhere. The railway station was gloomy. It was completely perfumed with the inferno smell: the smell of sulphur, the smell of coal. The railway engine with two great mustaches of steam coming up the sides. They were obsolete American railway engines, sent to places like Rumania. I traveled second class, and then third class with peasants; crowded, panicky. The roofs were covered with people traveling . . . soldiers traveling on roofs, ducking when the tunnels came. The nights spent in trains, sleeping, leaning against someone's shoulder, taking a mouth harmonica and making a song. A whole community is established on a train. There is something very beautiful, very dramatic, and very erotic—this community of people going somewhere. And the constant fear . . . The train would stop at railway stations. You never knew how long it was going to stop there. One dashed for water, for . . . oh, classical comical scenes of natural necessities, let's say. Everybody dashing. No facilities on the train, of course. People talked . . . talked to each other, but they talked with the prophetic quality of people who have no future together. So that, occasionally, they said things that they didn't mean to say, or they looked the way they didn't mean to look. And this accidental quality brought in the same virtue of a temporary society. Two people meeting in a forest are just as close as two people in a railway compartment. It's the same dramatic situation of seeing somebody a long way before you meet him; you know that the social system is going to be established only when you meet . . . really when you pass by each other. A minimum of civility is done. You smile! You show peacefulness . . . peaceful intentions. You say, "How are you?" You salute. It would be horrible to meet in this loneliness and not salute.

3

Prologue

ANTHONY M. BOYSA, *fireman*

I was woken about eight o'clock in the morning. A crew dispatcher
from Newark called me. My number just came up. We work in rotation.
I live ten minutes from Sunnyside Yards, I had plenty of time. I got
there about 9:30. I dressed a little cleaner. They told us when they called
us up to dress special—but I didn't stay clean long. When you walk
through the aisles in the engine, you brush past all the motor casings. I
operate the boiler. All I did that day was to test it in the yard. We
wouldn't need it; it was hot enough that day. My engineer was dressed
up in a suit and white shirt and tie. That was unusual.

VINCENT EMANUEL, *electrician*

I just wore a business suit—a regular suit in case anything happened
and I had to stay overnight in Washington. They took a lot of precautions. Before we took the ride, we were investigated by the Secret Service.
They asked where we were born. As a matter of fact, I was born in Italy
and the fellow on the protect train behind us was born in Italy and the
fellow that rode the pilot train ahead of us—he was born in Puerto
Rico. So, there were all foreigners on the train. I left Italy when I was
one year old. We had to give date of birth, nationality and stuff like that.
I've been with the railroad forty-two years. Always with the Pennsylvania.
I started out as a water boy, taking water to the men that were working
on the tracks.

5

JOSEPH BELLINGER, *Penn Central food supervisor*

We had started stocking the train at Sunnyside Yards Friday morning at 9:00 A.M. We were two supervisors and two laborers and it took all day from 9:00 to 5:00 without a lunch break to load that train. A shortish man was calling the shots and he made some changes; he ordered more of the buffet than usual—for the dignitaries. The dignitaries could get a full meal if they wanted it—steaks, hamburgers, cheesecake—things of that caliber.

JOHN ELLIS, *campaign worker*

What kind of a railroad car would we have the casket in? How would we get the casket on the car? That was the kind of logistical problem we talked about with the Penn Central. First we talked about a boxcar. We were going to fit out a boxcar with air conditioning and try to fix it up so it wouldn't *look* like a boxcar. Then it was apparent that we couldn't use a boxcar because so many members of the family would want to be next to the casket during the train trip. Besides, there would be absolutely no visibility at all. We thought about a baggage car. That's what had been used for Franklin D. Roosevelt's funeral train. The casket was in the open door of a baggage car in the middle of the train, along with the flowers.

Finally we settled on a private car, an observation car, with a platform in the rear. Immediately inside the car from the rear platform there was kind of a parlor room which we decided to use for the casket; then there were some very small staterooms, and a dining room. We found out how large the casket was, and we got a car that had a window large enough for it to fit through. Actually, we had to take the window out in Penn Station to load the casket in.

Then we had a one-foot-high catafalque built—a little platform covered with black velvet—which the casket was to rest on. That was the sort of thing we went through with Robert Minor, the Penn Central guy. He just sort of sat down with us and we went through all the possibilities.

JOHN ROONEY, *funeral director*

Our problem was: What can you put on the outside of a railroad car that won't blow off? One man here suggested using magnolia-leaf garlands—magnolia leaves being very close to black. They okayed the garland. But later they said they wanted *green* laurel leaves—not magnolia. There was a real problem getting the laurel leaves at night. But they

6

were very insistent. We finally got a florist's warehouse, through Rialto Florists, a twenty-four-hour-a-day florist at Lexington and 57th Street, to open up for us. We paid more, of course. The garland itself was made by a florist on 85th Street and Madison Avenue—Christatos and Koster. They worked all night and decorated the train in the morning.

FRED DUTTON, *campaign aide*

It was the Kennedy family that decided on the funeral train back in California when Robert Kennedy still lived but it was apparent there was no hope. Ethel and Ted and Steve and Jean Smith and Pat Lawford were discussing the arrangements in one of the hospital rooms of the Good Samaritan, and the rest of us were waiting outside in the corridor. Ethel and Ted decided that the services should be held at St. Patrick's in New York, and the burial at Arlington. What do you do then? There were too many people to go by plane. So the train emerged out of necessity. Steve Smith transmitted the decision to those of us who were waiting outside.

PETER SMITH, *campaign worker*

We had taken over a nurse's desk and established a little command post down the hall. I'd say there were three of us who were fully operational: John Seigenthaler, Jerry Bruno, and I. We had been going for a full hard week in California and we couldn't stop. There were dozens of phone calls coming in with magic formulas to save the Senator. Some of them wanted me to take down magic-type hex words that were not English or any other recognized language, but were supposed to have some sort of curative effect. There were suggestions on what he should be fed . . . that herbs are the only way that you could cure this sort of thing. Onions and garlic had a lot to do with it. Most of them involved people going in and chanting these words, lying on the floor. A lot of it had to do with the position of our bodies in the room while we would be saying these words. I took them, half listening to what was being said. . . . After the first two or three, I began to realize that we were going to get them forever. Between these phone calls from all the people who had magic formulas to offer to save the Senator, and doctors to suggest, Jerry called John Nolan at Hickory Hill and told him we wanted a funeral train.

DUN GIFFORD, *campaign aide*

You force your mind to go through what has to happen. You just close your eyes and you think: funeral, church, flowers, music, seating, invitations, train. Okay. Put somebody with music. Put somebody with flowers. Put somebody with invitations. Put somebody with worrying about the Monsignors. Bang, bang, bang, bang, bang. Fortunately, there were enough people with enough experience working under severe pressure to be able to do it. And the *cars!* Think of the endless numbers of limousines which have to be arranged for, and . . . music. Someone has to cue the organist that Andy Williams is going to sing a song; he has to have the music; Andy has to tell him what beat. Just the *endless* details. We sat down around the coffee table in Steve Smith's office in the Pan Am building in New York and looked at one another; and okay, you know, it seemed very simple. We'd all done seating for conventions or rallies or whatever. We had a diagram of the church seating plan. So we looked at one another and said, "Okay. How many seats for the family? We'll put them up in the front in the right-hand side. Well, where's the family list?" Of course, there wasn't one. We had no idea how many seats, you know, the immediate family would take. We tried to add it up as best we could. We gave whatever it was—the three or four front pews—to the family. And then, "Well, how many people in the White House party?" Who knows about Lyndon Johnson? Is he going to bring the whole staff of the White House? Is he going to bring three people? So, we had to play around with that a little bit— trying to find out from the Secret Service how many people were coming from the White House. We did know exactly how many diplomats. Angie Duke had that so well organized; he was brilliant. Brilliant! So that was easy to block out. Then, how many people for the congressional delegation? Well, we got people out of bed in the middle of the night to find out if they were coming. And then how many close friends? How many close political associates? How many general seats? You have to set up people at the doors to say, "My God, that's the President!" He sits there, you know. "Who are you?" "Well, I'm the Lieutenant Governor of Illinois." "Well, have you got an invitation?" "Yes!" Well, you have to figure it out: is he a family friend? Where does he sit? We knew it was going to be very, very close.

GEORGE PLIMPTON, *author*
The preparations went on while we were coming back in the plane which was carrying Bobby to New York. It was odd that anyone could function. Yet I think as the earth fell away, so in a sense did that cloaking sense of depression and gloom. After we got ten or fifteen

8

minutes up in the air, the natural *esprit* of those people who surround Ethel and the Senator began to break out. People began to move up and down the aisle. Of course, many were still numb and exhausted, so a lot of people just tried to sleep. But when Ethel came through the plane, just as she was to do on the train, everyone saw that she was trying to put a face on all of this, and it gave them a release, I think, and they were able to start functioning. Work started on the funeral arrangements. I remember Dave Hackett—one of Bobby's closest people—came by with a yellow pad and asked us to put down as many people as we could think of with strong personal attachment to the Senator to stand watch—what was afterward called "the vigil"—over the coffin in the Cathedral. So that took one's mind off things. There was a lot of general conversation. We were all insulated . . . I mean with the sky outside. But then the insulation began to collapse as soon as the plane started down. We went through the clouds and at the first glimpse of the lights of New York . . . well, that was the end of conversation. It became so quiet you could hear the plane creak. We could see the lighted area where the plane was expected. When we got there, we filed off of the back of the plane. It was an awfully hot night. The lights were very bright, red police car beacons revolving. I particularly remember seeing Arthur Schlesinger, Jr., standing waiting for the plane. His face was puffed and utterly tragic. He's famous, as you know, for his bow ties. That night was the first time I'd ever seen him without one of those perky ties of his. He was wearing a long black knit tie.

GILLIAN WALKER, *theatrical producer*
Television floodlights and the sounds of an airport . . . the noises of technology; and then the crowds of people . . . the famous people standing waiting. André Meyer said that it seemed like a garden party. Everyone waiting for that plane to come; it was an *enormous* jet with all the incredible noise that a jet makes—screaming as it makes its landing— and the people moving up to it. You felt this enormous potentate was coming, or someone who had tremendous power. Everyone was there. All the power: the police cars, all the machinery of government there. Then with this enormous plane coming in . . . the impressiveness of that, and the concentration of everybody on this plane door which would open. And the door opened and all there was was a box! It was a very moving thing because it seemed that that was the end of everything . . . that was it. It was the end not in the sentimental sense, but just suddenly you saw the meaninglessness of power.

9

ALFRED FITT, *Assistant Secretary of Defense*

Robert McNamara leaped out of the car, dragging his wife after him. We walked to where the people had gathered under the big arc lights. It was hot, and muggy, and depressing. When the hoist was being raised at the front end of the plane where they were to bring the coffin out, Joan Kennedy was one of those riding the hoist—and I can remember the photographers, who were about ten or fifteen yards behind me, hollering, "Who's the blonde babe on the hoist?" Photographers are the same, I guess, the world around.

PETER SMITH

Many people were obviously there for political reasons, particularly since some of them were engaged in political struggles. Attempts were made to move them up close to the plane. For example, Mayor Lindsay was there. His aides wanted to move him up immediately to Mrs. Kennedy while the coffin was being loaded into the hearse. I told one aide in civilian clothes that nobody was going up. Then I saw a police captain say to a group of policemen, "Let's have six men to move the Mayor up." I went over to him and I said, "You're not moving the Mayor anywhere." Governor Nelson Rockefeller's aides tried to move *him* forward. We, again, had to physically restrain the people trying to move him. Two Secret Service men with him said, "You shouldn't be doing that to a man of his . . ." Well, I said, "This is what the family wants and this is the way it's going to be." That was the way it turned out. Lord, it was hot. It was like walking into a dark exhaust pipe, getting off that plane. It was humid and 85° and we all felt as if we were in heavy suits.

ALFRED FITT

I remember that Bob McNamara saw Jacqueline Kennedy and rushed to her; she wept briefly on his shoulder. Then we found the car. The Dillons and Mrs. McNamara were in back; this Army sergeant and McNamara and I were in front. It was a black Chevrolet sedan—in the midst of about twenty-five or thirty long black limousines. We tore off into the night with the cavalcade. I was struck by a lot of things during that whole period, but one of the most touching was the way people lined the expressways and the approaches to the expressways and the bridges overhead. I suppose it was about 9:30 or 10:00, and they were just standing there waiting to see Bobby Kennedy's hearse go by.

JOHN ROONEY

Mrs. Robert Kennedy insisted on riding in the hearse herself, which is highly unusual. I had been called Thursday morning by a priest at Good Samaritan Hospital in Los Angeles. I was told we would meet the plane at the airport, in the evening, and that I would be receiving instructions later. At the airport, we provided the hearse and five limousines. It was the first time I have ever experienced such a thing as someone riding in the hearse. Senator Ted Kennedy and Bill Barry were in there with her. Highly unusual. But we have to remember that this was such an emotional thing.

WILLIAM VANDEN HEUVEL, *campaign aide*

The long tour began into New York; solid crowds were lining the streets. One vivid impression I had was when the coffin was carried into St. Patrick's. The church was mostly dark, with lights along the aisles leading to the altar; the catafalque had been set up to receive the coffin. As we carried the coffin into the church, a woman, kneeling in prayer in the back pew, stood up and walked behind it. It was Mrs. Joseph Kennedy. She had been waiting and praying there instead of going to the airport. It was shocking suddenly to see this person, whose life had known so much tragedy, walking again behind the coffin of another murdered son.

DUN GIFFORD

We kept the vigil going all that night. Most of the time there were six men: three standing on either side of the casket. In the middle of the night, sometimes there were only four; and sometimes there were only two. But there were always people there.

ROGER HILSMAN, *university professor*

I was reminded of an obscure poem of Kipling's which is written from the point of view of one of the four soldiers stationed at each corner of the casket—I guess it was Victoria's . . . or Edward VII's—a poem where these soldiers stand with bowed heads; and he talks about the defeat of the thousands of people going by. What tore me a little bit was that when I stood the vigil I heard several people quite independently come up and touch the coffin and say, "Forgive us, Bobby" . . . just ordinary people coming up. What they meant, I don't know, but it was very poignant.

11

RONNIE ELDRIDGE, *political adviser*

I was in charge of the church Thursday night—the night that they came in from California. I was supposed to be in charge of, as Joe Dolan said, "the VIPs coming in." That was the incredible night. Nobody could get into St. Patrick's without the police and the Secret Service checking it with Mrs. Eldridge. It was really the first time I had spent any time in St. Patrick's. I didn't have a dark dress. Joe Dolan said, "You must go, but you have to look more funereal than that. God, it would help if you looked a little more *Catholic*."

So I came home, and the only dark dress I had was a wool dress. I put it on and went down to the church, and from the time that the family left until eight o'clock the next morning I was in charge. We put together the vigils. Teddy Kennedy had put the first group for the vigil together: Jerry Bruno and Fred Dutton and a lot of people who had been campaigning in California. Those of us who were handling the vigil were all Jewish, and we really didn't know what to do. Teddy's group kept standing and praying—this group that we hadn't expected to turn up. We thought *we* would have the first team of the vigil people; nobody quite knew how to replace them . . . and they all looked exhausted. Finally, Kevin McGrath said, "Just walk your six people up there in a line."

So we got the people in our first vigil, and they just walked up there, and the other people turned very neatly, and it was all as if it had been planned, you know . . . and they left. Our first vigil had Al Blumenthal and Myron Cohen and a lot of Jewish people, and I kept thinking, "If some of Bobby's people saw this they would have *fits*."

Bobby just would have laughed, really. At about three o'clock in the morning I was sitting in a pew thinking that this was really the final irony: this middle-aged, middle-class Jewish housewife from the West Side of Manhattan in this tremendous Cathedral with Robert Kennedy! I mean the whole thing was just incredible! By the time the next morning came, I was really quite tired. I stayed the next day in the Bishop's residence. It was fascinating. I had dinner in his kitchen, lobster thermidor or perhaps it was Newburg.

AL BLUMENTHAL, *New York Assemblyman*

Paul O'Dwyer came on his own, unasked, the first night of the vigil. He was ash white—the color of his hair. I wanted to cry all over again. Marcy O'Rourke stayed at St. Patrick's for sixteen hours, saying his rosary. He and Senator Ted Kennedy alternated for the first five hours.

12

I remember that at 3:00 A.M., and I had been up for three nights straight, I was so thirsty that I knew what it was like to be lost in the desert. Where to find a drink in St. Patrick's Cathedral at 3:00 A.M.? Finally, I said to Marcy, "I can't hold out. You have to help me." Marcy took me down all the back stairs and chambers—it was very scary; something I guess like the catacombs of Notre-Dame. I had a cold drink of water in the robing room. Then, on the way back to the main part of the church, in one of those back passages, Marcy said, "I could set up a meeting with a friend of yours here. Maybe you could discuss your abortion reform bill with him." I looked puzzled. He said, "Yes, Cardinal Spellman is buried right behind you."

RONNIE ELDRIDGE

It was a warm night and the side doors were open and the light shone in. Policemen were very nice. It was just very quiet. Then some hammering would break out. They were erecting scaffolding for the television. The people who stood vigil that first night were so different from the people who did it the next day. The groups were put together at the last minute, and they were young people. One of them, just wearing a shirt, sat in the back; he cried his eyes out. Somebody gave him a tie and a jacket, and finally he put them on and stood vigil for a while. And Geoff Cowan, who was working for McCarthy, and Paul Gorman, who was writing McCarthy's speeches . . . they all came. They're kind of radical kids, and they basically liked him.

ANN BUCHWALD, *family friend*

Friday morning we went right to the Commodore, where they had a press room set up in the East Ballroom. I looked and it sort of overpowered me because one has sort of childish, countrified ideas of a funeral and its preparation. Here were hundreds of people; the setup was exactly like the start of a campaign or an announcement of a great gala. I saw the coffee urns and the pots, and the fifty typewriters down one wall, and fifty down the other, and all the television sets and the telephones, and Frank Mankiewicz up in front at a little lectern, and the loudspeaker. I was thrown by it. Both Art and I just wanted to do something to say good-by to Bobby. This was so big and everybody was taking notes and it was as though something good were going to happen, instead of something sad. I think that's what threw me. And the questions were the same, and in the same voices that you hear at a press conference: Senator, when do you expect to do such and such? In this case, the questions were: Will the train stop? Will we have time for photos? What entrance do we take? How do we get in? What if we haven't gotten a telegram? Can three members of the same . . . ? You know. But all so awful! Frank was behind a lectern that said COMMO-DORE HOTEL. I made notes: fifty typewriters down the middle; thirty to fifty phones; two TV sets; 200 people—mostly men; coffee table and big urn—silver.

AL BLUMENTHAL

By the next morning we were in full gear. People came from all over the country to help with the funeral arrangements. I think there was at least one advance guy from every state where the Senator had cam-paigned. There was one guy who had quit his job as a teacher to work with us in Hammond, Indiana. He set up the phone operation, went to California to work, and then came to New York for the funeral and worked his head off for three days. It was that kind of a funeral because the people who set it up wanted to give him one last campaign. If there's one thing he liked, it was a well-put-together organization. And every-where I went I heard people saying, "He would have liked it this way."

WILLIAM WALTON, *artist, family friend*

We were all trained into emergency operations because of campaign-ing. We all had a common objective, and had worked together—so many of us—that we were able to put a very impressive public event together on short notice. I know that on the occasion of the President's funeral, the protocol people of London couldn't believe that it had been put together this fast. They said it would have taken them ten days to do it.

DUN GIFFORD

Teddy came in for a major review of where we were in the funeral arrangements, where the train people were, the church people, and the invitation people. He said, "Okay. How are we doing? Are we going to make it, or are we not going to make it?" Then, everybody would scatter again. Invitation people would go to their room, the vigil people to their room, and the train people to their room, and the Arlington people to their room. And you just would keep churning along.

CARTER BURDEN, *campaign aide*

At one point, my mother-in-law [Mrs. William Paley] appeared at the

14

Pan Am building headquarters with a big picnic basket full of sandwiches and beer and Cokes and so on for everybody. Some of the sandwiches were pretty exotic, like *pâté de foie gras*. I remember one guy picked up one of them and started eating it and said, "That's the best liverwurst I've ever tasted!"

DUN GIFFORD

We wanted to increase the capacity of the church by putting in chairs down the outer edges of each aisle. We were desperate because we had 4,800 people on our invitations list that we wanted to invite; and we only had like 3,100 seats. We went around and around with the Secret Service men, who were by and large very nice; but they were quite insistent that having the chairs in the aisle would cause a security problem. We asked, "Why? Why is it more of a security problem to have people sitting in the aisles than sitting in the pews?" They said, "Oh, well, it's easier to move people out of pews than out of the folding chairs, you know; and you just have to *understand* these things." We said, "Oh? Um-hum, um-hum. Yeah, okay."

So we had to prune the list down some more. The biggest problem with the Secret Service was: Where was the President going to sit? And where was the Vice-President going to sit? We were very prepared to have them both sit in the front row together, which was appropriate. The Secret Service said, "No. Can't be that way. They've got to be separate and apart, so they won't be in the same line of fire," and all that stuff. And around and around and around. So finally, of course, the President sat . . . you know where he sat. Very near the front. Second row, I think. They didn't want him to sit in the front row because it was too easy for somebody to reach over, walking by, and go bonk with a candlestick. So he sat in the second row, as I recall, and the poor Vice-President sat back underneath the scaffolding in the sixth row.

Then there was the problem from the Secret Service of what buttons to wear . . . the identification for people who had to move around. They were very reluctant to give out too many of these little buttons— with the stripes and the star-shaped things and all that jazz. Very secret codes. One hour, it would be a yellow thing; and the next, six hours later, it would be a red one. And the mystery was, "Who's giving them out? Where the hell can you get 'em?" Because you'd be happily marching around in there and doing your work and everything, and the next minute, you walk up, and the Secret Service man says, "I'm sorry. You can't go in." "What do you mean, I can't go in? I've been around here

15

for the last forty-eight hours." "Well, you don't have the right button. I'm sorry." "Well, I'm working staff . . . blah, blah." "You come see the superior." So, you get handed up the line, you know, until finally you get to a guy who says, "Oh, for Christ's sake, this guy's been here for forty-eight hours. Give him a pin, Willy." And you'd get your pin and go.

RICHARD DRAYNE, *campaign aide*

We had to take care of the reporters. I think we finally carved out 300 seats for the press in St. Patrick's and we were holding desperately to those, knowing that we were probably going to lose some of them to the people in the organization who were putting together other groups. We got a letter delivered from NBC and they said here's our list of people that we want accredited to St. Patrick's for the Mass. There were 111 of them. *One hundred and eleven*—we had 300 seats and one network wanted 111. The New York *Times* wanted fifty-four—I think they got three.

CARTER BURDEN

About five o'clock Friday morning, there was a big meeting with practically everybody who happened to be around at the time to cut down the master list. You can imagine how arbitrary it became because everybody was at the ragged edge. Nobody had had any sleep for two days. People came in and out. One or two people would read through these index cards and someone would say, "We can't have *him*." But Angie Novello, Bobby's secretary, would say, "Oh, yes, he played touch football last Thanksgiving." That kind of thing. About 7:00, Teddy came in after we'd got the list down to what we thought was barely manageable. He had obviously been up all night. We went over the lists. It was for Teddy to give the final approval to the lists so we could begin to get the invitations out. Teddy sat there for about an hour and added to the list, pulling names out of the air. For instance, he put down the name of some guy who had worked in Jack Kennedy's congressional campaign in 1952, a sailing instructor on the Cape.

Then, of course, began the rather morbid and patience-trying period when everybody and his brother started calling up and asked for tickets, or they were indignant that they hadn't received any, and so on. It was very difficult. It separated the decent people from the indecent rather rapidly.

16

AL BLUMENTHAL

Bill Haddad had devised the invitational-telegram system, but it became painfully clear almost immediately that the telegrams alone would never do. There were too many people who were not at home to receive their telegrams and who could not be located. So Jim Flug, Carter Burden, Kirby Jones, and Steve Smith decided there would be a ticket setup too. This is how we set up the physical distribution of tickets: From the Kennedy office in the Pan Am building I got the approved guest list, and the instructions—the code for who was invited where, and how the list could be modified.

Then at the Kennedy headquarters on 38th Street and Madison we set up a bull-pen operation with tables and enclosures. When people came in the front door, they were asked at the front table if they had received their telegrams. If a person had, he was told that the telegram was his ticket and that was all he needed. If he was not home to receive his telegram, he was sent back to tables broken down by sections of the alphabet. If his name was found on the approved list, he was given a 5 by 7 card with his name on it. It might say, "M&M Blumenthal, 2FT," which meant "Mr. and Mrs. Blumenthal, two tickets, classified 'friend,' including train." Then he went to still another table, where I was giving out the actual tickets, with the assistance of two girls and two men. If a person was not on the guest list, or if he was not invited on the train and he complained, he was also sent to my table. In back of me were tables with two people on direct phone lines to the Pan Am building to clear changes. At first I initialed all changes, but there were 300 to 400 of them, and I couldn't approve all of them myself.

I've never seen so many people driven to participate in anything in my life. Every person I knew called me. The political people in my district were driving me out of my mind when they found out I was running the ticket distribution. At least three county leaders called and said they had to have tickets for certain constituents.

People can be pretty awful. One broad was trying to steal tickets for two hours—even after she had her own. Then we discovered quite by accident that people were catching on to our system as well. They learned the code on the 5 by 7 cards and made their own. Husbands would change the "1" on their cards to "2" so that their wives could come. We did what we could. We changed the color of the card first. Then we tried changing from ball-point pens to red and green Magic Markers. We even had a special stamp.

We ran the ticket center through the night, right through until 9:00 A.M. the next morning, which was Saturday.

RON FOX, *campaign worker*

I helped with the ticket distribution. It was one of the ugliest things I've ever seen. As soon as I walked out of that headquarters, I wanted to forget what I'd seen. It was certainly not the side of human nature you want to remember. We were working all night Friday, since the invitation list came down in alphabetical parts. No matter how many tickets a person had, he simply couldn't understand why he didn't have more. A mayor, for example, would fly into New York and send his bodyguard to pick up his tickets. He'd want three or five tickets. And chances are he hadn't even supported the Senator. They acted as if they were fighting for tickets to get on the convention floor instead of going to a funeral —as if it were a political social happening, tantamount to that year's Truman Capote party. People felt that if they were excluded from the funeral, their political credentials would be questioned for the rest of their lives. They'd say things like, "How can my wife not be invited? She went sailing once with the Senator."

MILLIE WILLIAMS, *staff secretary*

I was on the switchboard at around 1:00 A.M. Thursday night, or Friday morning, when George Wallace's office called. An aide of Governor Wallace wanted a ticket for him. Then they called a second time—they wanted two passes this time: one for the aide and one for him. Then they called a third time for more tickets. Helen Schwarz was handling the invitation list so I referred him to her. He never did get his ticket. They should have known that the first thing people would say is, "What the hell is *he* doing here?"

ANGIER BIDDLE DUKE, *diplomat*

There is a man who claims to be the Biafran Ambassador. I ran into the same fellow at Martin Luther King's funeral. There *is* a representative of Biafra in the U.S., who is given by the Biafran government the rank of ambassador, but he is not recognized by our government. I don't know whether he's a public-relations fellow, a lawyer, or what . . . but he does exist, and he was, at that time, causing a certain amount of commotion because he would call and say he was the Ambassador of Biafra, and people would get confused. He got me on the phone and said, "What arrangements have you made for the diplomatic corps to

18

go to the church?" I said, "Proper arrangements." He said, "I'm the Ambassador of Biafra." I asked, "Where are you planning to sit, sir?" He said he would like to sit with the corps. I said, "The corps is restricted to those who have presented their credentials to the White House, but anybody who grieves and mourns the death of Senator Kennedy is welcome, I imagine." He could not sit in a diplomatic section, but if he wanted, I'd send him down to Steve Smith's office so they could give him a ticket. I never heard from him again and I don't know his name. The same thing happened at the Martin Luther King funeral; he wanted to get in with the diplomats at *that* time.

JOSEPH A. CALIFANO, JR., *special assistant to President Lyndon B. Johnson*

On late Friday, the President decided to go to the funeral. He talked a lot about not wanting to pre-empt the funeral and become the center of attention. That, in effect, resulted in his decision to take Mrs. Johnson and me.

We left his secretary in the helicopter in New York—she ordinarily would have gone to a funeral. The President would take just the minimum necessary. He was very sensitive about that. We went to the funeral, flew up and flew back that Saturday afternoon. We flew up from Washington in a Jetstar. Whatever airplane the President flies is Air Force One for the moment. And we flew from Kennedy Airport to Central Park at about 60th Street in a helicopter. Then we drove from Central Park to St. Patrick's. There was great concern about the President going to the funeral because the Secret Service had had so many bad reports. Fifteen minutes before the President arrived they picked up someone with a gun in his attaché case.

ALEX SMITH, *campaign volunteer*

I just sort of wandered into this incredible experience. I went to the Madison Avenue headquarters on Friday evening to see how I could be of any help. One of the people in charge asked me to take over from some of the people there as it seemed to him rather disorganized. I explained to him that it was okay with me but that many of the people performing functions there were rather impressed with their roles and would not readily relinquish their duties—particularly to someone who'd just wandered in from the street. He said he didn't really care, to go back and see what I could do. So I worked there that evening.

The next morning, the day of the funeral, I was working at the invitations control at the Pan Am building. It was very, very hectic. I had four tables surrounding me, with different phones, and on each table was the master invitations list, the supplementary list, the changes which were made or added to the master and/or supplementary list, and the train list with its accompanying supplementary list. God, I had just wandered in off the street! There were constant telephone calls from the headquarters on Madison and 38th. As the Kennedy people left Madison and 38th for the funeral services at St. Pat's, I became more and more responsible. I was called with questions ranging from Kennedy family luggage (it had been sent over to me) to problems as to how they should lock up headquarters. In addition to the telephone calls coming in every five seconds or so, people were being sent over, and outside there was a line of dozens of people waiting to try to obtain invitations from me. U.S. Senators they didn't recognize over at 38th Street were being sent over, as well as chauffeurs of people like Douglas Dillon trying to collect invitations for their employers. It was a mad scene. The staff and volunteers began to leave for the funeral. The only help I had was a young nephew of Larry O'Brien, who came over to get an invitation. I pressed him into helping me.

Around 10:45 A.M. or so, I received a frantic call from Nick Katzenbach's office at the State Department in Washington. They didn't have a copy of the people coming on the train, and those going to the funeral at Arlington. I told them I had all the lists, including last-minute changes, and that I would take a plane down as soon as possible to get the lists to them. Larry O'Brien's nephew and I started rounding up the ten different pieces of luggage and boxes which belonged to the Kennedy family which I simply had not had the time to deliver to the funeral train. Around 11:00 A.M., the switchboard operator called me and told me that Northeast Airlines had a special plane available at Marine Terminal at La Guardia and they would hold the flight until I got there with my lists and the Kennedy luggage to take it all to Washington. At the same time, she said she had the Secret Service on the line and they wanted to talk to someone "in charge." So I took the call. There wasn't anyone else. I was told very briskly that they had picked up someone at the church with a gun. Would I please come over immediately? I said okay. I rounded up all the lists for Washington. O'Brien's nephew, David, and I grabbed the luggage, boxes, and the tennis rackets and we rushed out with one of the policemen on duty helping us get a cab to the police precinct house.

Well, we arrived with the luggage, tennis rackets, boxes, and so forth really jamming that cab, and I told David to remain in the car with the stuff while I went inside. Waiting were more than a dozen reporters and radio and TV cameras. The desk sergeant insisted on knowing who and why I was there. I whispered very softly the reason. He couldn't hear. He said, "Speak up!" Well, I did. I said loudly, "I'm here about the man with the gun!"

Immediately the press were on me; they ran outside and surrounded David, who was with all the stuff in the cab. I ran outside. To every question being asked I answered, "No comment." I told David to do the same. Finally I went upstairs with some Secret Service people, FBI agents, regular police detectives, plainclothesmen—a whole gang of them. They told me what had happened. They showed me the gun this fellow, Gary De Dell, had on him, and they showed me who he was through a one-way mirror. I spent about twenty minutes explaining to them the method of operation and control of invitations, et cetera, the role played by the office I was working out of at the Pan Am building, and the role Madison Avenue had to play.

This man's name was not on the master list or the supplementary list. Therefore, the white (ordinary) invitation he had could only have been stolen or given to him at Madison Avenue by someone there without correctly checking and getting the okay from our office in the Pan Am building. I was told that he had said a "Susan Smith" had given him the invitation. Furthermore, he said he was a good friend of Jerry Bruno, Joe Dolan, Frank Mankiewicz, and others. This could not be ascertained by the Secret Service because they couldn't reach these people. They were on their way from St. Pat's to Penn Station.

So it was decided I would try to get to these people at Penn Station and ask them. We went downstairs with a Secret Service agent (I left David with a Coke upstairs) and left for Penn Station in a radio car. After a hair-raising trip crosstown, going all out with the sirens going up one-way streets, we arrived at one of the side entrances of Penn Station. There were thousands of people there and hundreds of policemen. There were two Secret Service agents with walkie-talkies waiting for us, and they ran ahead as buffers clearing the way. An agent from some *other* group tried to stop us. There was this quick, odd confrontation and he was pushed aside. By then there were a dozen agents, cops, and myself running through tunnels and stairs trying to reach the train which was just about to pull out. We arrived just as the train left. Well, that was that. The absolute order at that time was not to stop the train for anything. So we went into the office of the Pennsylvania Railroad and

21

tried to reach the train through the radio-telephone hookup. The connection was impossible. Then it was contemplated getting a helicopter to Newark or some place the train might stop. The whole purpose was to find Susan Smith and hold her. The control room at Penn Station was full of Secret Service men and FBI men. They were all very edgy. This scene of our running into the station was apparently seen on TV and created quite a stir with people around there not knowing what the devil was going on.

Then we raced back to the precinct house with the radio car. The press was there. I would not say anything except "No comment." They left rather disgruntled. I remembered the airplane at Marine Terminal. I had the police call and ask that it continue to be held for us.

Then I made a telephone call to Washington to Katzenbach's people to explain the delay. This telephone call to Washington on the precinct house telephone created a big mess with the captain. He was all upset about the bill. I gave him three dollars, which he flung back at me. There was a big argument between the special agents and the police—sort of comical in a way—about the bill and how it would appear on the books.

Finally, we took off in the Secret Service agent's car with all the boxes, the tennis rackets, and the luggage, et cetera, for the Marine Terminal at La Guardia. There was a tremendous amount of traffic on the East River Drive. The agent, who did not have a siren, was driving as fast as he could, honking people out of his way. We came up to another fast-moving convoy with a police car in front of a black Lincoln; we joined the convoy; apparently the police saw the license-plate symbol and realized who we were. We arrived at Marine Terminal with all the tires squealing. There were more agents waiting; there was a big Northeast 727 and a small Lear-type executive jet waiting in the area. The man in the black Lincoln in front of us turned out to be Richard Nixon. He boarded the small jet. We ran up the ramp of the 727 and discovered there were only two passengers aboard the plane—my wife, Sheila, who had flown from Boston to go with me to Washington, and Mr. Simon Chilewich, the co-chairman of Kennedy Citizens in Westchester.

David and I took all the boxes, luggage, tennis rackets, et cetera, up to the cabin and I had the stewardess get some cold towels for the Secret Service agent who had been with us most of the day. It was very hot. I sat back, after washing my face, and had a drink. We had a nice flight to Washington. During the flight, one of the stewardesses remarked that she had heard some noises in one of the Kennedy boxes we had. We opened it and found a couple of live baby chinchillas, which apparently belonged to one of Senator Kennedy's sons.

Anyway, we arrived in Washington and were met by both the Secret Service and Katzenbach's chauffeur. I had had enough of the Secret Service, so we opted to go with the chauffeur to Katzenbach's office at the State Department. There, I gave his aides the lists, which were promptly Xeroxed. We relaxed there and I took a quick shower. I don't know that Katzenbach would have approved of strangers using the shower in the bathroom at his office, but I did anyway. I needed it. I had had quite a time since wandering into headquarters to see if I could help. . . .

FRANK MANKIEWICZ, *press secretary*
I talked to that guy De Dell about a week afterward. He's all right. He didn't know he had a gun. He just took a briefcase. You know, some of his briefcases had guns in them, and some didn't. I mean, he's one of those gun fellows. He was a kind of hanger-on in the Syracuse office. Jerry Bruno knew him quite well. It was really pretty easy to get a ticket if you knew the names of a couple of people. They showed up, and what are you going to do? It was a question of making instant decisions . . . you know, saying, "Well, he's not lying. He is telling the truth. He should have a ticket."

GEORGE STEVENS, JR., *director, American Film Institute*
All that work, and to such ridiculous ends. You realized what was going to be buried was that capacity to marshal all of the strength, and imagination and skill to do a job. But the job was intended to be the running of the country, not simply to organize a funeral and a guest list and handing out tickets and a train to ride a coffin to a cemetery.

THE REVEREND THOMAS J. CONNELLAN, *priest*
There was a radical change that took place between the time they celebrated the funeral Mass in Washington for President Kennedy and the Mass for Bobby. The funeral Mass for the President in Washington was the grim funeral Mass in black, with all sorts of references to the Day of Wrath, to justice and retribution. It was also in Latin.

Mrs. Kennedy had said: "If there's one thing about our faith, it's our belief that this is the beginning of eternal life and not the end of life. And I want this Mass to be as joyous as it possibly can be." This jibed exactly with what the Church wanted done, what the Cardinal wanted done. The funeral itself stressed the Resurrection, the beginning of life. It was in English, and the vestments were violet instead of black.

ANN BUCHWALD

It was funny because the night before the funeral it started so sad that evening, with everybody in black and sitting around, and then all of a sudden, at the dinner table, in kind of waves, the tide coming in, all of a sudden there was laughter, and pretty soon it was just like any Kennedy party. Art said it was probably one of the gayest spots in New York that night. For instance, little Willy, who has two front teeth missing—Willy Smith, Jean Kennedy's son, he's about seven, I think—came into the dining room with his pet chameleon. It looks like a miniature dinosaur. Apparently he had never gotten over being awarded only a second prize at the Hickory Hill pet show which was held the month before and which Art judged, along with Rowland Evans and Phil Geyelin.

So Art said, "Bring it out and I'll see if it's worth a first prize. Maybe we missed it." So, out Willy comes and puts down right in the middle of the dinner table this five-inch-long, sort of miniature monster, all gray; and it *walked*; you'd swear it was made of stone, but all of a sudden it moved and it walked between the soup plates and over to the flowers.

Well, Art said, "Oh, it walks! I didn't know it walked! Of *course*, it gets the first prize." He said, "Take it over to Mr. Evans and see if he'll say it gets the first prize." Art wrote Willy Smith when he got home . . . they had a bunch of blue first-prize ribbons left . . . and he wrote a letter of apology, and sent Willy the first-prize ribbon.

Ethel arrived at 9:00. She wanted Andy Williams to sing "Ave Maria" at the funeral the next day, and the Monsignor wouldn't let her because . . . as a Catholic, I should *know* . . . I *think* "Ave Maria" is related only to happy times. It's a sort of joyous hymn, to be sung at First Communions, Confirmations, novenas, and such things . . . not anything to sing at a funeral. It would have been disrespectful to Bobby, really. That's what the Monsignor said. But he put his foot down so hard that Ethel got angry and she said, "All right. He'll sing the 'Battle Hymn of the Republic,'" which was one of Bobby's favorite songs. The Monsignor had to give in. She said, "I won! I won!" The argument, you know. Andy was going to sing *both* songs.

Well, Andy came in with a yellow legal pad, and he asked me if I knew any words to the "Battle Hymn of the Republic." I said, "All I know is 'Mine eyes have seen the glory,'" but I suggested that he look around and see; maybe the Smiths had a songbook, like most families have, you know, best-loved songs. Then I said, "Call a song store." Well, we realized it was too late. It was after 10:30. It was quite a problem. Nobody in this crowd had any idea of the words beyond, "Mine eyes have seen the glory." Well, it was John Glenn, finally, who looked it up in The Encyclopaedia Britannica, and found it, and then stood there squinting, because it was in very tiny print, reading it out loud while Andy took down the words: "Mine—eyes—have—seen" . . . on his yellow legal pad. Andy doesn't memorize very well. He was going to put the words on shirt boards—you know, the cardboards that come in your shirts—so he would have his own cue cards.

LEONARD BERNSTEIN, *conductor, composer*

After he died I had received a call from Jackie on the Coast. She said, "We're all sitting here"—meaning the family—"trying to figure out what would be the best music to do at the funeral; we naturally thought of you. You're the only one whose taste and judgment should dictate what goes on."

I said that was very flattering. When the President was killed—John Kennedy—in '63, a television memorial was mobilized. I don't know how we did it because we were all in such agony; but I did get the Philharmonic together with the chorus and soloists, and we performed Mahler's Second Symphony on CBS.

In this case, I didn't know exactly how to go about it. I had never worked with Monsignors before. I told her I would do everything I could. Immediately I got in touch with the people at St. Patrick's Cathedral. From the start I began to have a very difficult time. For one thing, they have only two Masses which can be sung—musical Masses. One is the one they did for the Arturo Toscanini service—a sort of dreadful, 19th century, pompous Mass which I told them I really didn't think was right. Didn't they have a Gregorian Mass that could be sung? A real authentic one, which is, you know, always the most moving. It turned out they had one Gregorian Mass which they sing at St. Patrick's—but it's not complete and it's not right for a Requiem Mass. There were all these problems.

Then I began to think what I could bring in, and I thought of the slow movement from Mahler's Fifth Symphony; I thought if I could get the strings of the Philharmonic together—all that's required is strings and harp—then I could fit them in some corner of the Cathedral and play that . . . which, in fact, we did . . . finally. That was arranged for. Then I began to think what should be sung. Naturally I thought about the Verdi Requiem . . . one passage from it in particular, the "Requiem" section of it, which would not require an orchestra but simply the mixed choir and one soprano solo. Oh, no. It was impossible because women are not allowed to sing in St. Patrick's. No woman has ever sung in St. Patrick's, nor could there be female voices in the choir. It turned out that they have a ten-voice male choir, which is all they could supply. You can't do any Verdi with that. I couldn't argue with them. I mean this is the tradition and I had no right to interfere in the proceedings of St. Patrick's.

I then got a call . . . while I was on the phone arguing all this with Monsignor X . . . and it was Jackie calling from the plane. The operator said, "You have a signal from the White House. One moment please." I asked Monsignor X to hold it a minute. Obviously it was a radio call from the plane relayed through the White House; there was Jackie on the phone with an amazing amount of background noise— chatting and carrying on. This was the plane that was bringing the body, and it seemed a very odd atmosphere. But then I bethought myself of Irish wakes and things like that, and I thought, "Well, you know, thank God they're all bearing up so well."

Jackie said, "I'm sitting here on the plane next to Ethel. She has certain wishes about the funeral." I told her what I had arranged so far, which was the Mahler, and she thought that would be beautiful. I told her I was having trouble with the other things, and she said, "No. You just insist. You just tell them that you are in charge. The family has given you this authority." I said, "Well, the Monsignor is on the other line and I've been trying to tell him that for a long time now, but I don't seem to be able to get . . ."

"Well," said Jackie, "Ethel's first wish is that the nuns from her old school, Manhattanville School, sing certain things that she remembers from her days there . . . from her youth: 'In Paradisum.' " I forget what else; there were two things that she wanted the nuns to sing. I said, "Well, how am I going to get them to allow nuns to sing if they won't allow any female voices?" She said, "You tell them that that's Ethel's wish. She would also like 'The Navy Hymn' to be sung."

There were a few other things. Some mention was made of Andy Williams. I said, "Well, I want to do everything possible to satisfy Ethel's wishes, but you did say that you would leave the musical choices to me; it does put me in an odd position if I . . ."

I went on like this because I suddenly found myself in the position of just relaying other people's wishes. Jackie said, "But you know it will make her feel so much better and bring her such comfort if she can have these things." I said I had to draw the line at Andy Williams. I just didn't see the point.

Well, we left it there, and I went back to Monsignor on the other phone and I told him the latest and he was horrified. He said, "It's out of the question. We can't do it. I recognize the position you're in; you're supposed to have authority on this. But we cannot have the nuns, and we cannot have the choir." It was a terrible mess.

Meanwhile, I had engaged the choir. They were rehearsing. A soprano soloist had been found. They were preparing and rehearsing all over the place. Still I didn't know whether they were going to be able to perform. The following day was the critical morning when these decisions would have to be made. I've forgotten exactly the sequence of events. I was supposed to get back to Monsignor Somebody Else, into whose hands it had been placed; they were passing the buck a lot, you know, at St. Patrick's.

When I called at nine o'clock I found that it had been settled. Jackie had gone to see Archbishop Cooke herself. That must have been at 8:00. She had simply gone and said, "This is the way it's going to be." He said, "Of course." She told me later that she had discovered Ethel had been there half an hour or so before she had come, which would make it 7:30 or something, and she had already settled the whole thing. These women are really Rocks of Gibraltar. People of enormous will and authority. Archbishop Cooke did not hesitate. The order was given, and all the Monsignors flew about their duties: the Requiem was in, and the sopranos were in and the Manhattanville nuns were in . . . who were marvelous, by the way, and they sang so beautifully. Andy Williams was out. "The Navy Hymn" was in—that was fine, and so was whatever the other things were. My two contributions were really Mahler and the Verdi; the other things were pieces that Ethel had asked for.

So the next day was the funeral itself. That day started very oddly. A telephone call came just as I was about to leave the house for the church. It was about 9:00. I was told not to go to the church until police detectives had arrived to take me there. There had been a threat on my life. On my life. That's all I needed at that point. I said, "Well, this is ridiculous. I mean, who would want . . . ?" "Well, it's probably a crank call," they said, "but we can't take any chances." I arrived at St. Patrick's surrounded by my detectives and plainclothesmen. I was greeted by an assistant manager of the Philharmonic, who had just learned to his amazement that Andy Williams was in the choir loft and had been there since 7:00 that morning.

I said, "Well, all right then. Let him be there. But what's he going to do?" Nobody knew. "When may we expect him to sing?" Nobody knew. This is just to give you an idea to what extent I was in charge.

Anyway, it was a beautiful service, as you remember. The Mahler part of it was made more beautiful by the Kennedy children's procession up to the altar carrying the Communion articles. It happened to the accompaniment of this ten-minute Mahler piece, which made it twice as moving. I didn't realize it was happening because I was busy in my corner conducting at the time, but when I saw shots of it later on television I saw people weeping all around. It's just a movement from Mahler's Fifth Symphony, but it's of particularly poignant intensity, just exactly the right music for the occasion . . . even, perhaps, too emotional. The Verdi also sounded very beautiful sung from the choir loft.

Then came, of course, the big surprise of the day . . . which was that suddenly, at the most unexpected moment, this voice issued from the choir singing the "Battle Hymn of the Republic." It turned out to be *the* smash of the funeral. I say this in my own disfavor because I would have done anything I could to avoid it—bad taste and all the rest. But, as it happened, being unaccompanied, this one lone voice coming from the choir loft, singing, somehow it was terribly moving. Partly because it was so unexpected; partly because it was so simple. For some people, it turned out to be the most moving part of the whole service. That doesn't make me a great arbiter of these matters. But it did turn out well . . . Andy Williams and all. I had no idea what he was planning. All I knew was that he was hidden in the choir loft and at any moment might break into song. So, between that suspense and the other thing of being surrounded by plainclothesmen, with the threat on my life, everything was full of suspense, which just added extra dimension to what was already a very tragic and emotion-laden occasion.

ELIZABETH HARDWICK, *author*

The whole American thing of his death . . . It was a real sort of ecumenical thing in the church, with the "Battle Hymn of the Republic" sung in that sort of pop style. It's not really a hymn. But they sing those hymns, at least in the South, with a tremendous amount of sort of semipop style. I was very moved by it. I think it was suitable to him. And what was it? Mahler, I think. That was terrific. Absolutely beautiful. Even the kind of eulogy that Teddy Kennedy read was different. You don't usually do that sort of thing in church. It was a wonderful sort of pop funeral in this big Cathedral.

THE REVEREND ANDREW J. YOUNG, *civil-rights leader*
In a black community, funerals are big social events. Back in the old days, in the country, blacks never took vacations. The only time they got to travel was going to funerals; it was traditionally a time when all of the people involved in the dead person's life sort of came together. And you had that feeling at St. Patrick's. It was a very representative segment of a society—with many people from minority groups who were down almost as part of the family. And that was probably quite appropriate. It is, well, kind of a trite thing to say, but it was probably one of the most democratic situations I've been in.

PETER EDELMAN, *legislative aide*
Cesar Chavez came with a couple of farm workers. Cesar had walked in with these people, and there wasn't a place to sit down. So he stood up. He didn't realize where he was standing, but he was standing directly in front of the whole section of Congressmen, blocking their view. You know, he didn't do it deliberately, but it was just such a nice touch.

RUTH BERLE, *family friend*
Milton had turned white in the church; he got on the bus to go to the train, but then he said, "I just can't." He was so upset, he just went home; a combination of everybody pushing around us; the press was standing on the pews—they were just awful; it drove him crazy; he was livid. Jackie Cooper finally took his Mass card and hit some girl who was standing on a chair. The general thing just upset him so. But when we got off the buses to get on the train, Rosey Grier took my hand in his and he held on.

GEORGE STEVENS, JR.
After church, I got into a car with my wife, Liz, and Dave Powers, and Rowly Evans, and Kay—a crowded funeral limousine—and we rode down Fifth Avenue, and I've never seen Fifth Avenue just barren of cars, and silent crowds on both sides of the street.
Dave Powers broke the silence by telling stories about Irish wakes.

29

He's absolutely irrepressible. He said President Kennedy was making a speech one time and he said, "Dave, can you give me a good wake story to tell to those people?" Dave told him the story of Wakes O'Sullivan, which he repeated to us as we were riding down Fifth Avenue to the train between all of these crowds of mourners. It's about this wake that goes on for three days, and the widow says to Wakes O'Sullivan—this guy who makes a profession of reading the obituary notices and showing up at wakes—"Wakes, what do you think of this one? Are you enjoying it?" And he says, "This is one of the greatest wakes of all time, Mrs. Murphy. In fact, I think you ought to put him on ice and keep it going for another two days." Dave is riding down Fifth Avenue telling this story. We finally had to ask him to stop because this was a day you didn't want to be riding down Fifth Avenue laughing. So we quieted down, and after a while somebody asked about the train ride, "What are we going to do for four hours on a train?" Dave Powers said, "Don't worry about that. You'll be wishing it never ends."

LUCY JARVIS, *television producer*
When I got on the train I was so upset that I got up and said to Pierre Salinger, "I don't think I can go through with this. I just can't go down to Washington. I don't think I can cry any more, or feel any more. I just don't think I can do it." He looked at me and said, "Lucy, if you don't take this ride, you will probably miss the most emotional and the most impressive experience of your whole life. If you don't go, you will never forgive yourself because you'll hear about it and you'll read about it, and you will feel that it was the last experience you wanted to share and you will have not shared it." So I went back and sat down in my seat.

1

JUNE 8, 1968
PENN STATION, NEW YORK CITY . . . 1:03 P.M.

VINCENT EMANUEL, *electrician*

They had two locomotives on the funeral train; I was on the second one. That's procedure with the railroad when they have a heavy train; in case one goes sour, they have another one. They were both working, both pulling . . . they had couplings in between so one engineer could operate the two engines just like a subway car. I was on the second car with the Secret Service man. He introduced himself—Mr. Kellerman. He is in the William Manchester book about John F. Kennedy because he was in the fatal car in Dallas. He was going to watch from the right side of the locomotive. We began chatting about different things, like this was the first time he'd been on a locomotive and this was one trip he didn't like. Neither did I, to tell you the truth, on account of it was a funeral train.

GILLIAN WALKER, *theatrical producer*

While waiting to start, I was impressed with the kind of sterile atmosphere of the train—very aware of the steel, and the glass, and the sort of sterility of the inside of the train, the people in their little black dresses looking very tidy and almost unhuman. Their hair was done very nicely, and their faces looked very composed. Somehow it all seemed as if everyone had turned out for an Antonioni movie. There were these steel carts that went down the aisles with sandwiches, these closed steel boxes, and these seemed to be part of the unreal interior. It was very silent in the beginning; nobody talked; it was very hushed and very cool because of the air conditioning.

31

ANTHONY M. BOYSA, *fireman*

The train started late. We expected a slight delay. It was delayed all right. No one had the slightest idea that all those people would be along the route. We got going about one o'clock, and we came out of the tunnel on the Jersey side. The people were standing along the tracks and on the factory roofs. I didn't know what they were doing there at first.

JOHN KENNETH GALBRAITH, *economist*

If you were burying Ronald Reagan, you would obviously want to do it with an airplane; but if you are going to bury Robert Kennedy, his people live along the railway tracks.

MILTON GWIRTZMAN, *campaign aide*

There were people standing in the marshes in New Jersey, watching. I had the impression that it was almost two different worlds. When you looked outside and saw the emotions of the people standing beside the tracks, you got very drawn to the tragedy of the occasion; so you would leave that and turn back to the people in the car and almost forget the nature of the occasion.

RUSSELL BAKER, *columnist*

It was a Saturday afternoon; warm and kind of summery. Remember how warm it was? And all these people were out doing their Saturday things; it was sort of Saturday-afternoon America. But they ended up at the railroad track, and the reaction was kind of varied, as you'd expect. A lot of solemn people and a few carrying flowers and signs and what not. But it really impressed me to see America with its hair down on Saturday afternoon. It was like seeing the whole country. And what impressed me was, you know, we're not really a beautiful people. This is really quite apart from what the day was all about. The Kennedys, in a way, had this kind of grace and glamour that people loved or hated. They had beautiful people around them. And there, outside, were all the ugly people. Really, you know, all of us ugly Americans in our undershirts and our potbellies hanging over them; the women with their hair up in curlers. Everybody just looking dreadful and overweight and pasty. And they were all out there looking at this great symbol of what they voted for and what they cared about.

MICHAEL HARRINGTON, *author*

Aside from its own tragic aspects, it evoked all the other deaths I have ever known. I think Dylan Thomas' line is very true: "After the first death, there is no other."

So I could not face squarely and candidly what my feelings were. But as I looked out of the window of the train, I could see my own grief mirrored in other people's faces. And that was the experience that would threaten my composure.

SYLVIA WRIGHT, *reporter*

I didn't talk to anybody on the train. But I thought people shouldn't be saying, "Why are all those horrible people out there along the tracks, staring? Those scavengers!" I heard Jack Paar say, "Those scavengers all come to stare, and don't give the Kennedys any privacy."

He was wrong. The people *needed* some tangible proof that it really had happened and really was true. When we rode from St. Patrick's Cathedral to Penn Station, I thought, "Isn't it incredible? Thousands of people lining Fifth Avenue in the streets of New York, ten and fifteen deep, to watch Greyhound buses roll by!" But I understood that. It made it official. There was a police car with a flashing red light; and then they got to see a hearse and black limousines in order, and buses rolling by in order. Something had indeed happened. It was their way of touching it and believing it! You know, people always have said how terrible that Jacqueline had to be there and see her husband shot, and have him in her lap. But I think how terrible if she had been in Washington, and the last she had seen was a whole, healthy man running off across the lawn to the helicopter; then she's supposed to believe that man is dead because somebody said so! But she saw it happen, step by step, and her mind was able to adjust slowly; when he fell in her lap, she saw what might be. So that by the time they got to the hospital, she already was aware of the possibilities. . . .

I think it's selfish to say that people shouldn't come to stare. I can even see why they want to go and stare at Jackie or Ethel, and snoop in their privacy by looking under their veils. They want to see, are you okay? are you a real person like me? are you okay? People don't mean to be rude. They mean to care.

CHARLES QUINN, *television correspondent*

You'd see a man standing way off in the distance, saluting; you'd see another man standing with his hand over his heart; or a fire truck on top

33

of a knoll with four or five firemen with their hands over their hearts, and the little light going around and around. And the girls on horseback; and the boats . . . all those bridges we passed over and those dozens of boats bobbing up and down in the water, and the people just watching. The American flags; the fireboat named the *John F. Kennedy*, with the people on it saluting. . . .

LOUIS COLLINS, *fireboat captain*

We had no permission from the powers that be. Still, we are allowed fifteen minutes away from quarters by boat without having to notify our chiefs. So we took it upon ourselves to do it. We're at the foot of Center Street on the Passaic River. We have a little house there for an office and a bunk room. We're all Catholic, all four of us, and we thought it would be a nice gesture. The train bridge is only five minutes down the river. I'm the acting captain. The other three are firemen. The fireboat is called the *John F. Kennedy*. The city council got together and decided it would be nice to commemorate the Kennedys' name. We have thirteen and one-half miles of waterfront to cover—loose boats and barges to retrieve, and drownings and lost bodies, and we go dredging and all that. We have three turrets that we use to put fires out, and some thought we should put water out—that is, turn on the turrets—but I said no, that they'd take it for a celebration if we did that. They'd get the wrong idea. So we just stood in silence when the train went through. That's all. We saluted the train. We couldn't see very much inside, naturally. We said at the time that it must have been a very sad ride for them because there were so many of the family there. We didn't put anything in the log about it. After all, it wasn't official. We were out there a half-hour or so. It's always nice on the river. There's always a breeze.

CARTER BURDEN, *campaign aide*

I think it was Bill Walton who said, "You know, you could tell the story of Robert Kennedy by telling the story of the people on this train."

K. LeMOYNE BILLINGS, *family friend*

I don't think there was anyone on the train who had known Bobby for a long time who didn't think back and consider the early times, and what it was that made him the sort of person he turned out to be. His father had so much to do with it.

34

Every father, I guess, wants to instill in his children certain things to make them successful and good citizens. This is what a father *wants* to do, but so few know how, and so many do it badly, unmeaningly. Mr. Kennedy was somehow able to do it right . . . not to spoil his children and yet not to make them resentful with his strictness. He was able to follow a very fine line . . . make them want to improve themselves and please him, and he did this without undue force. He did it with love, and yet with strictness.

I was around that house as I grew up, and I was conscious of the fact that he didn't like his children not to win. Now, this didn't mean that they'd be *punished* if they didn't. But they knew it would be disappointing to him. He watched, you know, all their races, all their competitions, and he was interested in every single thing they did. He was always on hand. I was there a lot from the time I was fifteen years old. I was never in his house when Mr. Kennedy wasn't there.

I'm sure Mr. Kennedy never slapped a child in his life. But his eyes would just take you right out the window. You could tell when he was not happy; he didn't have to say anything. Some of his children inherited those eyes. Pat Lawford certainly has them, and so did Bobby. Young Bobby has said the same thing about his father—that he could tell by his eyes exactly how he felt.

The meals were more like forums, really, with Mr. Kennedy leading the discussions. There was no frivolity, but they were always exhilarating and fun. Mr. Kennedy purposely avoided any discussion of business at the family meals. He had made enough money not to need to make any more; he saw no reason for them to do what he had done.

When Mr. Kennedy wasn't there, it was just a normal family talking about everyday matters. But when he was there, it was something! He would always take the opposite point, no matter what it was. He always encouraged his children to argue with him . . . and he never encouraged them to agree with him. He *never* wanted them to agree with him. That's why the President really had such a good relationship with his father. All this talk about the President being influenced by his father is crazy because he was raised *not* to be.

Kathleen got into the table conversation a lot right at the beginning. She was, of course, close to Jack and Joe's ages. She was bright and on the ball. She was like Jack in many ways and very much the favorite of the father at that time. Bobby, of course, was much younger, and therefore was *slower* to join in. He was quieter, and he took longer to develop; but it was always all there. Bobby just suddenly grew up to what he had obviously been all along, but which hadn't been recognized. Mr. Kennedy found he had another able son, which I don't think he had realized at first.

ROBERT LOWELL, *poet*

I got him on his father once. His friend Tom Johnston was there. He'd been at the Yale Drama School. I asked, "If you were to cast Robert Kennedy for a role in Shakespeare, what would you choose?"

Tom Johnston said, "Henry the Fifth."

I said, "That's a very trite choice; he's too much like Henry the Fifth. Why don't you cast him as Falstaff?"

Bobby just sort of glared at me in a rather friendly way, and he said, "Why would you cast me as Falstaff?"

I said that Henry the Fifth isn't a very good person to be cast as; after his terrible invasion of France, he married a French princess. Five years later he was dead of fever in Paris, leaving a son who was murdered by the English and an occupation force of Englishmen which was ousted and destroyed by Jeanne d'Arc.

Then he said this extraordinary thing. He went to his bookshelf; there was a three-volume set of Shakespeare there; he got out the Histories, read that deathbed speech from *Henry IV* when the king talks about how he came to his crown, how he had prepared the way of succession for his son; "Henry IV, that's my father," he said.

Now, that seems like an absolute *non sequitur*. But I think it's very profound. I never tried to figure out what it meant, but now I think I know. He meant he had a very difficult career coming from this difficult, but very elevated forebear who made it possible. And he really *was* cast in this role of Henry the Fifth, not altogether a desirable one—as I had pointed out to him—and perhaps a doomed one. That's over-interpreting it. The whole point was that it was sort of intuitive, and things were left undisentangled.

FRANKLIN D. ROOSEVELT, JR., *business executive*

From everything I saw, he was a great father. He didn't leave a stone unturned to encourage his boys and make it possible for them to participate in sports. I don't think he really understood their intellectual development, and I don't think that mattered so much. I think what he was after was to encourage them to have a tremendous competitive instinct in anything they did. He encouraged them to have a feeling that they had to win; that there was no point in being second best . . .

36

and I think they all had this, in a way, in varying degrees. Jack originally wanted to be a professor, an intellectual, but when Joe died—young Joe, in a plane explosion in World War II—Jack realized that he had to get out and compete. The family's obligation to be in public life really was then his obligation, and he managed to change himself so that he could meet that obligation.

As for Bobby, I just have a vague recollection of a rather small kid with a lot of spunk.

MARY BAILEY GIMBEL, *family friend*

He mostly stood on one foot with the other toe resting on top, his head a little bit down, looking out from underneath his forelock. Dave Hackett was his best friend then and afterwards. Hackett was the hero of our school, captain of teams and those things. Bobby was shy and whimsical and a little bit solitary. So their school roles were different, but their friendship lasted. Years later I remember driving over one of those bridges in Washington. Bobby was Attorney General then and we were riding in one of those long black shining cars that transport officials. Bobby said, "Dave can't remember where it was I got ahead of him," liking to tease him about the days when Hackett was the star of football, hockey, and baseball, and Bobby was a little bit obscure.

DAVID HACKETT, *family friend*

I used to go to Catholic Church with him; he used to come to my church and I used to go to his. I remember going to his at school when we were about seventeen. There was no altar boy, and the priest said he needed somebody. So Bobby just got up and became an altar boy. He would move into those situations where most of us would not. I think if anybody got in trouble, he would just instinctively move right into it, whereas most people are too afraid or embarrassed.

I think everything he did was very difficult for him. Athletics for him —which he loved—were always difficult. Studies, the same thing. And also, I think, with his social life. But he just persisted in all those things. But I don't think he ever had anything easy.

K. LeMOYNE BILLINGS

He was smaller than his brothers; I think he was conscious of his height—because his two older brothers and his younger brother were all over six feet. He had a large, well-developed torso, but his legs were short. This is probably the reason why he took such a terrific interest in competitive sports—constantly trying to improve himself and be better than the bigger guy. He's the only one of the Kennedy brothers who made his letter in football at Harvard. He just was tenacious about everything he did.

KENNETH O'DONNELL, *family friend*

I'd just come back from the service in 1945. Bobby was at Harvard on the Navy V 12 program; I was playing football, and so was he. He was in a sailor suit; I didn't know who he was from Adam, but we were thrown together in that he had a very unfortunate experience with the coach, just as his brother Joe had before him . . . like all of us, we don't like our coaches, I suppose. My brother, who was captain of the Harvard football team, and I also had had the same difficult experience, and that's how we really got together—because of a mutual dislike of someone. Frankly, the football team was not very good; most of those who would have been playing football in their senior year were still in the service; most of the squad was younger than I was by two or three years, and Bobby was one of that group. I didn't pay much attention to him as a football player; we were waiting for the regulars to return the next year.

But he was tough then, and I respected his perseverance and guts. I didn't realize he was Ambassador Kennedy's son until about six weeks after we had become friendly; I read in the Boston *Post* one day that Ambassador Kennedy's son had done very well in one scrimmage.

I was always interested in politics and history. My father was a football coach, and football came first, but I was interested in politics. I had known Ambassador Kennedy by reputation, and had not thought very highly of him politically; he was an isolationist, and I had been very pro-Roosevelt, which he was not—at least in the forties. That was the first real relationship with Bobby—that we began to talk about politics; by the end of the first year, we had become very close friends. He took me home a couple of times. He got me going with the Ambassador. The second or third time I was in the Kennedy house, he outlined the framework of an argument and got his father launched into a dissertation which I disagreed with totally. I disagreed with Ambassador Kennedy throughout our whole association. Although I respected him, he never cared too much for me. His ideas and mine were very contrary. I didn't say anything because I was a guest in the house, and I wasn't that rude as yet. Bobby said, "Dad, now that you're all done, I want you to know that Kenny absolutely, *totally* disagrees with you, don't you, Kenny?" I laughed nervously, and the old man laughed like hell. We had our confrontations, but he was always a gentleman.

In 1946, Bobby began to meet other kinds of people—people who didn't give a damn who he was. For Bobby Kennedy the choice of friends could have been very simple . . . he was obviously one of the more desirable *social* types . . . I mean, all the girls would like to have gone out with Robert Kennedy. He was a handsome boy then, and very wealthy and from a well-known family; he was much more well known in the Boston social set then he was in ours. But he made his choice very clearly from the beginning. He was invited to every so-called fraternity—we don't have fraternities at Harvard, but they have clubs, which are probably more social, and he was invited to join almost all of them. I think he joined one, and one of the big complaints about Bobby Kennedy comes from that crowd—that he joined but only went there once in his life. He had made a very clear decision about the fellows he wanted to be with—a very irreverent, disinterested group of fellows just out of the service after three years. They had been all over the world. One fellow who hung around with us was a fighter pilot in China who'd just come back after serving with General Chennault; there was another fellow, a Russian major, who had been three years in the infantry and lost his arm. They were all two, three, four, sometimes five years older then he was. At first they didn't like him very much. They didn't want to pay any attention to him; they didn't think he was that good a football player, and they thought he was just a rich kid who happened to be hanging around. But after about six months, he became one of the group, and they stayed with him all his life. Most of them were ushers at his wedding. We used to kid about them. They were so big that they couldn't get down the aisle side by side. We had a party the evening before, a bachelors' party at the Harvard Club in New York, at which everyone got in very good shape. John Kennedy was there, he was a Congressman then, and he agreed that he had never seen such an outrageous, irreverent group of characters in his life. They wouldn't buy their morning suits, or whatever you wear at a wedding, because they cost too much. We were all living on $75 a month, so we said to hell with it, we're going back to Boston; we don't want to *go* to the wedding. Bobby ended up paying for them. The in-laws, the Skakel family, were horrified by all of his friends, not so much the father, who loved the fellows and joined right in with the fun, but the mother. She couldn't understand where Bobby got these characters that were around him, who all weighed 250 pounds, and were Greeks, Armenians, Italians.

K. LeMOYNE BILLINGS

The relationship between Bobby and his brother Jack became extremely close during the political years. Up until the time of the first senatorial race in 1952, the age gap was quite big. They were really different generations. When a kid is sixteen and his brother is twenty-five, the relationship isn't the same as when it's twenty-seven and thirty-six.

All of the Kennedys were very close; as siblings they were brought up to be close . . . nothing very unusual. But this close relationship that the President had with Bobby at the time of his death really didn't have the opportunity to blossom until the time they were thrown together politically. It really began, I believe, in Jack's senatorial race. Things weren't going well, and Bobby came in and managed the entire campaign, even though he had never had any experience of that kind before. It became immediately obvious that he was an excellent administrator; he had all these abilities that had been latent. He became one hell of a good campaigner. These mutual *political* experiences, along with the natural brotherly love that already existed, brought them together.

KENNETH O'DONNELL

The first I heard about Jack running was from Bobby. He had graduated from Virginia Law School and gone to work in the Department of Justice, under a fellow named Jim McInerny, who is now dead. And that was the time when the Reconstruction Finance Committee was under tremendous fire for corruption, and also the Internal Revenue Service, and many of the Internal Revenue Service directors were being indicted. Bobby was up in New York, working on the investigations there—his first real assignment. About that period, he called me, knowing how much I liked politics, and he told me that his brother, John Kennedy, was going to run in Massachusetts, either for the Senate or for Governor, he didn't know which, since it depended on what the then Governor did. He asked me if I would go to work for his brother. That was December of 1951. I worked for John Kennedy until about April. The campaign began as an absolute catastrophic disaster. His father had come up and associated himself with elder statesmen who knew nothing about the politics of that day and age. He had not been in Massachusetts for twenty years. But he was such a strong personality

40

that nobody could—nobody *dared*—fight back. I was too young, and I had never been in a campaign. The Ambassador didn't think I knew anything about politics. I might have been a good football player, but he thought that was about the extent of my ability; in the other fellows he had no confidence. The only time the campaign got any direction was when John Kennedy, who was then a Congressman in Washington, was able to get up to Massachusetts to overrule his father.

So we were headed for disaster. The Congressman and I had a big argument one day, and I told him that the campaign could only be handled by somebody who could talk up to his father; nobody had the courage to, and *I* certainly didn't have the qualifications, and it just wasn't going to work unless Bobby came up: he knew enough about Massachusetts; he had a lot of friends, and the *big* plus was that he could talk to his father. So John finally told me to call him—angrily, I might add, because nobody likes the bad news of politics. So I called Bobby, and got him in New York, and *he* was very angry. He was right in the middle of an investigations case; he enjoyed it; he loved what he was doing, and he said to me, "I don't know anything about Massachusetts politics; I don't know any of the players, and I'll screw it up and . . . I just don't want to come." So I said, "Unless you come, I don't think it's going to get done."

About a week later, he called me on the phone and said, "I'm coming up; I've thought it all over, and I suppose I'll have to do it." But I mean he was the most unhappy fellow that you ever saw in your life. But after he got to Massachusetts, he put it together. It was difficult because nobody felt his brother was going to win; the politicians were hanging around because they figured that Joe Kennedy was going to spread a lot of money around and that would be helpful to everybody; that was their only interest in John Kennedy. It was a rough campaign, and Bobby Kennedy put it together. He realized he didn't know all about politics; he listened when he should have listened, he was tough enough to handle his father, and he was tough enough to handle the organization. They all had total confidence in him; he worked twenty-four hours a day, and all of the guys who worked for him are still here today, and they're Bobby Kennedy guys. The politicians up there didn't like him because he didn't do what they told him to; he built an independent organization because we all agreed that that was the only way to do it; whatever we suggested, he always stood up for us, even when we were wrong and made mistakes; and he could stand up to his father, and he could stand up to the powers when we didn't have that

41

capacity; until he came, we didn't have really any muscle. He supplied it, which began the controversy about his ruthlessness.

HELEN KEYES, *administrator, John F. Kennedy Library*

At the start he stepped on toes. He alienated labor in Massachusetts because he didn't know who anyone was. You know the sort of brusque manner he had. The head labor leader in Massachusetts came into headquarters one night; he was just hanging around, which politicians do around headquarters. Bobby came by and said, "If you're not going to work, don't hang around here." You just don't say that to the head of the AFL-CIO in Massachusetts! Bobby didn't like hangers-on in politics. He liked doers. He had very good judgment and yet, because he was young, he blew a lot of things. Bobby was very abrasive, as he always was with certain people. And yet he hopped right into it, the way he did with everything. He was in his shirt sleeves all the time. He'd do anything. He'd lug cartons and seal envelopes. He couldn't speak very well then. We never even used him as a filler. He had that little stammer.

K. LeMOYNE BILLINGS

He was always working in areas where he was weak, which was so exhilarating to watch, because Bobby was constantly striving to improve himself—every year he grew a little bigger. His older brother was a born natural speaker who never had to take a lesson in his life. Bobby was naturally a poor speaker. I remember when he came back from an extensive tour of Russia with Justice Douglas. They had gone to places where Americans had not been allowed to go before—places that were opened up especially for the Justice. He came back with a lot of ideas and a lot of pictures. It was the first time that he had really done any photography, and he took some *really* good pictures—and he came back with a *hell* of a story. But he just couldn't express himself well at that time. He was one of those guys who just don't naturally do well when they're speaking in public. I heard him in Palm Beach, and I heard him in Washington . . . and both were terrible. But he kept doing it. And I absolutely *know*, without ever being told this . . . I can just see Bobby going to a professional speaker for help, and I can see him talking in front of mirrors, and working far into the night on his speeches. I just can see him doing that. That's the man! That's what he would have done! That's what he would have done in any area where he was weak. He didn't end up being the greatest speaker in the world—he never was as good as his brother—but he ended up being a very decent and a very *honest* one; one that came through with great integrity. He was able to learn how to express himself as he really was, and he accomplished this in the same way he did everything else . . . by hard, tenacious work.

CHARLES BARTLETT, *journalist*
He was always on the telephone. You'd hear Bobby, "Yes, Dad. Yes, Dad." It was a tremendous campaign. There was nothing left undone.

DAVE POWERS, *curator, John F. Kennedy Museum*
There was no job that he wouldn't do. I remember one time in 1952, on the bridge running from North Station to Charlestown, the fellow that was the campaign secretary in Charlestown was having difficulty getting a big ELECT JOHN F. KENNEDY SENATOR sign up. We had a ladder that just barely reached it. Here's Bobby standing on the top rung of the ladder. The only people I had ever seen that high were firemen. And there he was, banging those nails in to elect his brother Senator.

HELEN KEYES
I don't know what would have happened without him. At the beginning we were skeptical. Polly Fitzgerald and I had been working our heads off. We had five or six of those big receptions for ladies. Bobby and Kenny O'Donnell came on the scene when we were having one in Fitchburg. They proceeded to tell us we were doing everything all wrong. Jack had been out of his mind with joy because at the first one in Worcester we had gathered 5,000 ladies; the next one we had about 7,500. He thought they were the greatest thing in the world, but these two *experts* arrived and told us they were terrible. They said the hall was filled with Irish Catholics who were going to vote for Jack anyway, and we had just better get some Polish ladies or some French ladies, or something like that, or the whole thing was a waste of time. We were heartbroken. No one had ever said a mean thing to us in our whole lives. At every one of the receptions from then on, Bobby would stand by the receiving line to see what the ladies' names were as they went by. He'd wait, and there would be *one* Irish lady, and he would come over and say, "Mrs. McCarthy just walked through. Are you *ignoring* everyone else?" He was just really teasing us. But by the end, we had organized about thirty-five of these receptions, and we had entertained about 75,000 women at them. Of course, that's the vote by which Jack won the election, so Polly and I claimed full credit. Finally Bobby wrote

each of us a note and said that we were right and he was wrong and the little old Irish ladies did vote and it did count.

JOHN SEIGENTHALER, *campaign aide, editor,* Nashville
   Tennessean

The night before the election, they have a traditional place in the South Boston area where the candidate always closes his campaign. But there's another place, called Mattapan, which is a Jewish community just outside of Boston . . . and they were having a rally there in a very small hall. It was not clear who was going to go. Bob and Ted and Jack, all of them had said, "Well, I'll *try* to make it."

As it turned out, they *all* wound up there. The hall was just packed with people—they'd come to see Jack Kennedy. They had a brass band up front. Teddy was up there. So was Bob. Foster Furcolo—he was the Governor of Massachusetts—and his wife were there. All the Democratic politicians were there. We'd been there about five minutes, and Jack Kennedy came in. A fellow named Robert Murphy, who was the Lieutenant Governor, was making this speech. Murphy was one of those fellows who have absolutely no terminal facilities in speechmaking. One long crescendo built into *another* crescendo. He knew that the featured speaker of the evening was Jack. But he just couldn't turn off. He'd say, "And furthermore, I'm telling you people . . . ," and he'd go on with it. We sat and waited, maybe ten minutes, maybe fifteen minutes, and he was still pouring it on. Finally, in sort of a sweat, he began to wind up his speech, and he said to that audience, in which there was *nobody* that night who was not Jewish: "Furthermore, I'm telling you that if you go out and bring home the Democratic Party tomorrow, the Democratic Party is going to bring home the bacon for you for the next four years." That's the way he ended. I mean it was like . . . peeing in the punch bowl. The place was just like a graveyard, and then somebody started to clap. And then nobody clapped. And then two or three people clapped, and somebody started to laugh. The poor master of ceremonies got up and said, "Ladies and Gentlemen, I'd like to introduce the next Senator from Massachusetts, the Honorable John F. Kennedy."

You just couldn't imagine a situation worse for a politician. Well, he walked up to that microphone and he said, "Ladies and Gentlemen, everything that has been said and everything that *could* have been said in this campaign *has* been said." And they roared! He said, "So, I'm not going to make a speech. Instead of that, the brothers Kennedy are going to sing a song." He said to the bandleader, "Do you know 'They're

44

Breaking Up That Old Gang of Mine'?" The other brothers got up, and they started singing. This was the first time I ever realized that Bob Kennedy couldn't carry a tune in a bucket. I mean I sang songs with him all around the world—Japan, and Jakarta, and Berlin. He just can't sing! But Teddy and the President carried him, and they did very well. When they got through with "They're Breaking Up That Old Gang of Mine," they had everybody in the hall singing with them, literally turning it into a great rally.

KENNETH O'DONNELL

I remember that once the election was over and JFK was elected Senator, that was it. John Kennedy went to Washington; he wasn't going to be involved in Massachusetts politics; Bobby packed his bag. We went down to the Cape to celebrate the victory, those of us who had been most involved, and we sat in the Ambassador's living room and talked; and out on the lawn we played football . . . it was late November. The Senator had gone on a vacation. It was really difficult to realize what a great victory it had been. Though we look at Massachusetts as a Democratic state, in fact we're not. The Democrats had not elected a United States Senator in Massachusetts since the twenties. Nobody in the Democratic Party ever cared who was Senator. No one could afford that kind of a contest. Everybody was sure Kennedy was going to get defeated; after all, Eisenhower was on the ticket. The night of the election, the Boston *Globe* announced that Kennedy had lost, so it was that kind of a contest. Obviously, we thought the world was our apple that night, and we were sitting there, and Mr. Kennedy said to Bobby, "What are you going to do now? Are you going to sit on your tail end and do nothing now for the rest of your life? You'd better go out and get a *job*."

2

VINCENT EMANUEL, *electrician*

I tell you, it was really something to sit there all the while, just keeping your head out of the cab window, looking at the crowds. I seen people running all over! They were running toward the train. They tried to touch the train as it went by. People are crazy! They are. They're crazy! They'd *touch* it! A lot of people waving. A lot of people crying. I seen *nuns* from all around with signs like REST IN PEACE, ROBERT and I'LL PRAY FOR YOU. A lot of nuns! All along the road. I seen one fellow there with a gun! He was like he was on guard. He didn't have the gun up to his shoulder. It was a rifle. I was going to attract the attention of the Secret Service man on the other side of the cab, but I figured he was harmless . . . which he was. He just stood there at attention on my side of the train. This was in Jersey.

JOSEPH BELLINGER, *Penn Central food supervisor*

I'll tell you that the people who weren't on the train missed something I truthfully think will never be seen again. The tracks were lined with more people than I've ever seen. Many of them were putting coins on the track for souvenirs. Every rosebush within a mile of the tracks was plucked bare. Everyone had a rose or a banner. They were throwing roses at the train. I wish you could have seen the ones with the roses who stood right by the track. They would take the rose, put it right on the track, and let the train roll over it so they would have a souvenir. People were praying. The men had their hats off. They were crossing themselves. It wasn't curiosity. It was paying respects to someone they

46

dearly loved. The signs read, WHO WILL BE THE NEXT ONE? and WE HAVE LOST OUR LAST HOPE. These were signs the colored had. It was mostly whites that had the signs that said, GOOD-BY BOBBY and WE STILL LOVE YOU.

CHARLES HARBUTT, *photographer*

They were people in a very precise way. It was not just people undifferentiated, but the people we think of when we talk about Norman Rockwell tableaux. Because from the train you could see all those types. You would see the people that had just walked to the tracks from playing their Little League ballgame. At one point, we passed a recreation basin, and all the yachts were drawn up and people were caught in mid-drink, with the beer can halfway to their lips—the whole business of the true American out enjoying his weekend. What you got were tableaux of America, all drawn to this dingy site of the railroad tracks. There was one great hippie who was dressed in Indian clothes, and he was waving the *British* flag, and you know, it was beautiful . . . because turned on, he was *still* drawn to come out. Two men pouring cement, you know. They had dumped a wheelbarrow, and there was a big pile of cement. The man that was supposed to be raking it was looking, and the man that had dumped it, *he* was looking. All stopped because of the train. Another part of the Norman Rockwell character of it: we passed one little town where the train station was really no more than a bus shed. About four people could comfortably sit in it—somewhere in the middle of New Jersey. Lined up in front of it were the police chief in his uniform, the Mayor, the fire chief in his uniform, the head of the American Legion in his uniform, and one or two other people who were obviously the most important people in this little town. And then down from that, down on the tracks or on the grass along the station—I guess it was actually gravel—were the people. And you felt like you saw the whole town and their elected officials, you know, but there were only maybe twenty people there. It was fantastic because you didn't need any more, you know. You had the whole town coming out, and it was almost like the Fourth of July. The suburban family in Bermuda shorts standing on the tailgate of a station wagon, all waving flags. At one point, a Cadillac had stopped. I doubt it was chauffeur driven. But a big black Cadillac was stopped; the people inside didn't roll down their windows—it was a hot day and they had air conditioning on—but they sat and watched. And a lot of gulfs . . . America is a lot of gulfs. I think part of what Bobby was doing was working in them. We passed a plant—a modern

47

plant out in Jersey someplace—and, very carefully, the executives in their white shirts were standing several yards away from the workers in their overalls.

SONNY FOX, *television performer*
I remember going through one station and a lady standing on a platform and tossing a bouquet, stiff-armed. She missed the train by a good thirty feet, and the flowers just lay on the tracks . . . on an adjoining track as we sped by. But she wanted to reach out and make a connection.

FRED PAPERT, *advertising executive*
Those people standing along the railroad track were saying, in effect, "We really cared . . . not just about Robert Kennedy but about the country. We care what's going on. We want to get involved." I felt that people were holding their kids up and saying, "You look at Robert Kennedy, and that's the way you should lead your life. You should decide what matters to you, and then pursue it." He was always pursuing—right from the beginning.

K. LeMOYNE BILLINGS, *family friend*
After he helped get his brother elected to the Senate, he had to think of his own career. He had *lots* of frustrations in his Hoover Commission job; he wasn't at all happy. He had decided to dedicate himself to the government, and he hadn't found his niche, and didn't know where he was going to find it. This made him, at that time, an unhappy, angry young man.

That was the period when many people formed their ideas about him—people who didn't know him, who met him in Washington at parties and sometimes found him antagonistic and argumentative; it was because he was frustrated inside. He was filled with so many things he wanted to do, but he felt he wasn't accomplishing anything. He was getting nowhere. He just didn't see his future. He wanted to be involved in something where he could contribute! He felt he was marking time in the Hoover Commission job. I know he had great admiration for President Hoover—the whole Kennedy family did, including Mr. Kennedy. Bobby had a great admiration for him as an administrator. But he didn't feel his job there was of importance. And then, on top of that

48

his father was a member of the commission, and often it isn't the happiest situation—to be working for one's father.

RUSSELL BAKER, *columnist*

It was apparent that he really wasn't very happy in those early days. He was very ambitious. I said to him, "Why don't you run for Mayor of Boston?" He looked stunned at the suggestion. This was long before it was apparent that even his brother Jack was going to run for high office. But I felt, you know, he was obviously going to go someplace in politics. The naïveté of my suggestion—Mayor of Boston! It just overpowered him.

KENNETH O'DONNELL, *family friend*

Then he took the job that ultimately hurt him. He went to work for what turned into the McCarthy Committee; he didn't know Joe McCarthy from a cord of wood; he went to work for a fellow named Francis Flanagan, who had been in the Justice Department with him and who was then counsel for the committee. He worked there until the confrontation on the Army-McCarthy hearings, when he resigned and joined the minority as legal counsel. That was where he first met Joe McCarthy.

Even the supposed links between Joe Kennedy senior and McCarthy are exaggerated. It is alleged he contributed to McCarthy's campaign, and I think the documents are probably correct. But I think it was natural that Joe Kennedy, who had been so assaulted by the press himself—and who had the kind of personality that would react—would think Joe McCarthy was being unduly put upon and come to his assistance.

I used to tell Bobby what I thought of Joe McCarthy on the telephone, and at the other end there'd be silence. That was our normal relationship. After a while he'd say, "He isn't that bad, but I agree, you know— but . . ." And he kept defending his pasha. Bobby had the greatest capacity for the underdog. He thought that there were unfair aspects to the criticism of the Senator. If he had a weakness, *that* was his weakness—whenever somebody was in real trouble or was being unfairly treated, then he was for him, whether the issue involved him or not.

When they got to the Army hearings, I used to talk to him twice a week. He was really upset. He still personally didn't dislike Joe McCarthy, for reasons which escape me; but I never met Joe McCarthy, so I'm not a judge of that. But Bobby was incensed at the way they were treating witnesses; he was incensed at the Cohn-Schine investigations, and he thought they had lost all sense of direction; and he wanted *out*, without any question. So he quit, and that was the end of it. He did so quite independently.

ROBERT LOVETT, *banker*

The first time I met Robert Kennedy was during the McCarthy hearings. He had accompanied his father to the airport, and he introduced us. I remember riding up to New York on the plane with Joe Kennedy, saying, "That's pretty tough company he's traveling with," having in mind particularly McCarthy, for whom I had absolutely no use at all, and young Cohn, who seemed to be about as unpleasant a character as one could find in a day's march. Joe said, "Well, put your mind at rest about that. Bobby is just as tough as a bootheel."

PETER MAAS, *author*

A lot of people told me that Senator Joe McCarthy was personally a very affable fellow to be around. I remember Senator Stuart Symington telling me that after they had had a go-around in the Army hearings, with McCarthy viciously attacking Symington, he met McCarthy in an elevator and got slapped on the back as if they belonged to the same Kiwanis Club. McCarthy wanted to be great friends. One evening, Bob and I were having dinner, and I said, "How could you . . . I just cannot understand how you could ever have had anything to do with Joe McCarthy." He said to me, "Well, at that time, I thought there was a serious internal security threat to the United States; I felt at that time that Joe McCarthy seemed to be the only one who was doing anything about it." And he said, "I was wrong." So that was that. I think that's where Jack Newfield is right in calling him an existentialist politician . . . if you accept that definition of existentialism where a man defines himself in his own experience.

ALICE ROOSEVELT LONGWORTH
  (*Mrs. Nicholas Longworth*)

I had been invited several times to Mrs. Cafritz', and this time I accepted. I had been out of town, and got back in time to dress for dinner. A white orchid—one of those orchids that have already gone brown around the edges—had arrived, accompanied by a message: "Senator McCarthy shall come for you at 7:00 to escort you to Mrs. Cafritz' dinner." I thought Mrs. Cafritz had figured it out: Elderly single lady, venerable, interested in politics; a Senator must escort her. I didn't want any part of it. I thought that when he arrived, I'd have the maid tell him that I had my own car and would see him there. But that would have been too rude. I heard the bell when he arrived, and I looked over the banister and said how kind he was and how thoughtful Mrs. Cafritz was, but that I was going out in my own car. He gave the impression of being in a black cape that he had thrown dramatically over one shoulder. At the dinner, I was seated between him and Bob Hope. You'd be glad to have someone like Joe McCarthy on your side if you were in a big row or street fight. I think he'd throw paving stones very well— awful things. After that dinner, whenever we met, he'd say, "How's my blind date?" And I was so weary. Was it possible to exchange these yokel civilities? Then he said, "Now, I'm going to call you 'Alice.'" And I said, "Oh, no, Senator McCarthy. You're *not* going to call me 'Alice.' The men who collect the trash call me 'Alice,' and the policemen on the block and quite a number of various people call me 'Alice.' But you are not!" I think I was excessively mean to him, but he had the approach that in the Longworth family we call the easy manners of the perfect jay. So, from then on, I never really saw him at all.

K. LeMOYNE BILLINGS

His relationship with Joseph McCarthy was different than with Roy Cohn. He didn't admire McCarthy, but he rather liked his personality. I think that he was sort of interested in what made McCarthy tick. He was very much *against* the whole McCarthy method. He was completely against the way McCarthy operated. The only time I saw them together was after McCarthy had been censured. McCarthy was not only a very broken man but a very sick one. I remember his wife was the one who carried most of the conversation. Bobby was sorry for him, although he felt he had got what he deserved. This is an example of Bobby's compassion. It was typical of him to go and see somebody in trouble.

In 1956, with the Democrats controlling the majority, Bobby was appointed counsel for the majority on the McClellan Committee. At last he was in a position to make a real contribution. I think he was entirely responsible for many of the great successes of the McClellan Committee during that period. He was certainly responsible for exposing the operation of the Teamsters Union. He felt that something should be done about any system giving such power to any man to be used the way

Hoffa used it. His contributions to the McClellan Committee were enormous. He was no longer frustrated. He wasn't the angry young man any more.

WALTER SHERIDAN, *campaign aide*

From '57 to '59, we worked at an unbelievable pace. Other congressional committees had looked into the Teamsters Union, but they'd all been fixed. He wasn't about to be fixed; he meant business.

He had interviewed me for a job going up the stairs on his way home. He hired me just going up the steps; it was so typical because most of my conversations with him since then were while walking up steps, or riding in cars or up and down elevators, or going to airplanes—because he was always on the move. I worked with him on the McClellan Senate Rackets Committee for four years.

Senator John Kennedy was on the committee, and the two of them were a match for anybody. It was all very exhilarating and worthwhile. You grow up with idealistic ideas, but you realize more and more that you can never get them into action. All of a sudden the things you had thought should be done *were* being done, and *could* be done, because this man felt strongly enough to do something about them. Even during lunch hours—you gobbled a hamburger when you could and kept going. We made cases during lunch hours just by making the right call at the right time. There was a case in Pittsburgh where we had information that a trucking company was paying off a fellow named Barney Baker, one of Hoffa's right-hand men, a big 280-pound fellow. During lunch hour, Bob Kennedy said to me, "Go and call this guy from the trucking company." So I did and hit him cold, out of the clear blue sky, "Did you pay money to Barney Baker?" The guy was so stunned at getting a long-distance call with a direct question, he said, "Yes." Then Carmine Bellino and I went out and verified everything in the books; a couple of days later, the fellow was in testifying how he paid off Barney Baker.

Bob Kennedy always used the direct way . . . "Call him." So you learned a lot about directness and aggressiveness. He was terribly honest in his approach. People don't really know how to cope with pure integrity . . . and this is what he had. First, they thought he was some young rich kid—they could manipulate him and he'd go away; but as time went by, they saw that not only could they not do anything with him, but he *wasn't* going to go away. His brother was obviously going to be a candidate for President. They tried every political trick in the books . . . like

52

hiring Jake Arvey from Chicago as their lawyer, calling in the political guy who would say to Bob, "If your brother wants to be President, he's going to need our support. Why don't you call this off?" Whenever they'd go to John Kennedy, he'd say, "Go see Bob." They'd go to Bob, and he'd throw them out.

I think the Hoffa thing had a great deal to do with the "ruthless" term. The vendetta idea came up and was vocalized by a lot of the liberal press. Paul Jacobs, out on the Coast, was one of the main sources of information about Jimmy Hoffa when we started the McClellan Committee; yet he ended up writing an article four years later for the *Reporter* magazine that was very critical of Bob Kennedy and me; it was called "The Extracurricular Activities of the McClellan Committee."

But "ruthless" isn't the right word. The word is "determined" or "persistent" or "aggressive," and he was that. They say he saw things in black and white. He did—because, to a certain extent, that's the way things are. He was intolerant about several things. He was completely intolerant of dishonesty, particularly in somebody he trusted; he'd much rather you say "I don't know." But, if you tried to kid him—and people tried to kid him along the way because they do that all through life—well, you just couldn't kid him because he'd pin you down.

ALEXANDER M. BICKEL, *lawyer, educator*

As counsel to the McClellan Committee, the dominant impression was one of the single-minded prosecutor. Civility is a word that can describe what we expect of the ideal prosecutor, and that seemed to me to be lacking. The congressional investigative power is a kind of wild horse in the American constitutional system—justified and tolerated because of the need of Congress to inform itself in order to legislate. The congressional committee is a sort of star-chamber court that calls people in and punishes them—whips them with publicity—punishes them with a sanction of publicity. He seemed to engage in punitive expeditions. In more than one instance, the purpose of calling witnesses and the manner of questioning them gave fairly blatant evidence of purposeful punishment by publicity rather than fulfillment of the function of informing Congress. Now these things aren't separated by any bright line. It's a matter of surmising it out of the record and of imputing the motive to the questioner.

CHARLES BARTLETT, *journalist*

He did fight. He just wouldn't let go. In 1955, I got a lead that Harold Talbot, then the Secretary of the Air Force, had been running a management-personnel concern in New York. I talked to Bobby about doing a sort of joint investigation, which we did. He used the committee's facilities, and I used what *I* could, and we pulled together the fact that Talbot had continued to operate this management-advisory firm even though he was Secretary of the Air Force; he was, in fact, doing some soliciting for this firm from his official position. Bobby was persistent in that. He just bird-dogged him. We finally got to a hearing, which was highly dramatic because there was not a Senator who supported what we were doing, because they were all very fond of Mr. Talbot. But Bobby kept pressing. It was only Bobby's persistence that made a success of the hearings, which finally broke in such a way that the President had to request Mr. Talbot's resignation. I got a Pulitzer Prize out of it, but Bobby's slice of the Pulitzer Prize was tremendous.

MURRAY KEMPTON, *journalist*

When he began investigating labor racketeers, he came to New York with the McClellan Committee and called me up and asked me to come to see him, under the illusion that journalists know something about crime. We had a sort of inconclusive conversation, I think. But the Kennedys had a way of asking direct, pertinent questions . . . just cutting to the heart of it. All of his people have this ability.

CLAYTON FRITCHEY, *columnist*

He gradually became a more open person. In the days when I first knew him, when he was on the Senate Committee, he played things very close to the vest. A feeling about him then, which was not without justification, was that he was not warm or open; he gave the impression of being tough, somewhat suspicious, skeptical—if not cynical; he tended to look at people in a way that was a little forbidding.

MURRAY KEMPTON

One of the minor things that I miss the Kennedys for is that if you went to committee hearings and you were bored, as one often can be in open committee hearings, the Kennedys had great *bones*. Bobby had the kind of handsomeness that is as attractive, I think, to men as it is to women—the kind of handsomeness that is not remotely offensive to men. Their bones were just, you know, out of this world.

54

PIERRE SALINGER, *campaign aide*

I heard they were going to look into labor racketeering. In October of 1956, when I was a reporter, I was doing a three-part series of articles about Jimmy Hoffa and Dave Beck for *Collier's* magazine. I went down to find out when they were going to have their first hearings, so that I could time the publication of my articles along with that. I had been working on the Teamsters for a lot longer than they had, at that time, and I had a great deal more stuff. It was a nice counterpoint.

What I remember most about that meeting with Bob was that it turned out not to be an interview at all, because he spent all the time asking me what I knew.

CLARK MOLLENHOFF, *reporter*

Jimmy Hoffa had rehabilitation programs in the Teamsters Union for ex-white slavers, ex-robbers, ex-thieves of various types. There were priests and ministers around the country who thought Jimmy Hoffa was the greatest thing in the world because of this; but when you examined the program, you saw that Jimmy wasn't rehabilitating them, he was merely making them high labor officials, and using them for thievery and thuggery for *his* benefit.

MURRAY KEMPTON

I remember one day coming to his office during one of these hearings; and he had a letter—an anonymous letter signed "A Friend"—which had some information in it. He said to me, "You know there's something very curious I've learned. If you get a letter typed on stationery, seven paragraphs in length, and signed by somebody, you can be absolutely sure it's a lie. But if you get a letter which says, 'I saw Jimmy Hoffa take $300 from somebody in a bar in 1947,' signed 'A Workingman,' it's always true."

FRANK GIFFORD, *sportscaster*

They had a big investigation going on. They parked this old, beat up Chevrolet right in front of P.J. Clarke's. Everybody jumped out. As we walked into P.J.'s, Bobby turned around and said, "Who's going to stay with the secrets?" Apparently, they had all these briefcases, you know, all this big investigation sitting in the trunk of the car . . . I mean, I'd never been around that kind of a scene. They were talking about digging

55

up a field or something, looking for some money that somebody had embezzled or something.

WALTER SHERIDAN

What they were actually digging for was a woman—a reporter from Joliet, Illinois, who had disappeared . . . presumably killed and secretly disposed of for exposés she had written about labor racketeers in Joliet. Jim McShane, who was working on the committee then and later became Chief U.S. Marshal, went with Bob to the Joliet prison, where an inmate said he knew where this woman was buried. He sounded very convincing. Bob and Jim got the warden to let this fellow out, and they went to a field where the woman was supposed to be buried. They started digging, and pretty soon the farmer who owned the land came out to check on them. The prisoner told McShane to be careful because he thought the farmer knew about the woman being buried there. So McShane, who was a great double-talker, told the farmer they were on an official state metallurgical survey. The farmer seemed to fall for it. He disappeared, and they went back to their digging. Nothing turned up. Finally, the prisoner said, "Well, I was mistaken." He had got the spot wrong, but *now* he recollected, and he knew *exactly* where the body was. So he took them to a new spot, and they started their digging all over again—Bob pitching right in with them—until they looked up, and there was the farmer coming over the hill. And he's got these three big fellows with him—I think they were his sons. So at that time they decided they had had enough of it. The prisoner was just stringing them along. He'd had his afternoon outing. Bob took it in stride. He saw the humorous side of it. When you've been had, you've been had. They did an awful lot of digging.

MURRAY KEMPTON

I remember Ed Williams once said about Hoffa that he was a man who liked to jump out of buildings . . . you know, jump out of the third floor, the fourth floor, the fifth floor; finally, from the thirty-second floor, he would bust up when he got to the ground. Life, to him, was a war.

Bob, who had an underlying distaste for the kind of people his father used to buy, recognized the devil in Hoffa . . . something absolutely insatiable and wildly vindictive. With the older guys, like Dave Beck and Frank Brewster, I think Bob felt that they were just self-indulgent and rather weak men, certainly as far as the sins of the flesh were concerned. But he recognized in Hoffa a general fanaticism for evil that could be thought of as the opposite side of his own fanaticism for good . . . and, therefore, involved direct combat. Hoffa and Kennedy had feelings about each other of an intensity that can scarcely be described. There is a story—possibly apocryphal—that certainly fits the temperament and the passions of the two men. The Teamsters, just before Dave Beck's fall, constructed a headquarters in Washington that some people called "The Palace," but which persons with slightly more baroque sensibilities tended to think of as an example of American Warehouse Marble, early fifties . . . where Hoffa had an office from which he could glare across at the McClellan Committee offices in the old Senate Office Building. It was Hoffa's custom to work quite late. When he left, he never turned the light off. He explained the reason for this: if Bob left to go home, and he saw Hoffa's light on, he would immediately say to himself, "I'm not going to go home any earlier than that bastard." There was in both of them a passion for the other's discomfort.

ANGELA NOVELLO, *personal secretary to Robert Kennedy*
Cye Cheasty was a retired Navy man working in a law firm in New York. He had been approached by one of Hoffa's men to get a job on our committee and get information about our investigation of the Teamsters, and report back to Hoffa. Cye Cheasty said he'd think about it, and he immediately came down and conferred with Bob and Senator McClellan and told them the situation. So they made him a double agent.

Then the FBI caught Hoffa with Cye Cheasty handing him some committee papers. He was brought to trial with Edward Bennett Williams representing Hoffa, and Cye Cheasty represented by the government. We were determined that Hoffa get his just due. I'll never forget the day that the jury came out and gave their verdict. Cye Cheasty called me and said, "Angie, you won't believe this, but Hoffa was acquitted."

We were all sick. I wrote a note to Bob, who was in the midst of conducting hearings; he just looked at the note, put it aside, and went right on. We were all so depressed because Hoffa, we thought, seemed obviously involved; we were dreading the moment when Bob would come in. He came into the office and caught the mood; he looked around and said, "Come on, now. Let's get to work. We have a lot of work to do.

No sitting around." And that was it. It wasn't the end of the world as far as he was concerned.

BUDD SCHULBERG, *author*

I was asked to do the screenplay of *The Enemy Within*. That was the book about his years on the McClellan Committee fighting Hoffa. It was a film project in the early sixties. I flew up from Mexico City to come to dinner at the house in Virginia. I was told he wanted to kind of size me up. I had said, "Well, that goes both ways."

That night, I started to like him. He was there with his children. He was pretty much surrounded by his team at dinner. During the soup, Bob suddenly asked me what I thought of his book. I said I liked it a lot. If I hadn't, I would not have come. Then he asked, "Well, was there anything that you didn't like about it?" I said, "Yes, as a matter of fact, there was one chapter that I really didn't care much for."

I could feel someone kicking me under the table. It was Jerry Wald, the Hollywood producer who was going to do the film. He was literally kicking me in the shins.

Bob said, "What was that?" I said, "It's the chapter about how hard everybody worked on the staff—how they got up at night, and worked all day and all night." I said, "Frankly, that left me a little cold because, you know, as a taxpayer I just would expect you to all work hard. I work pretty hard. So it didn't really send me so much." Well, I got a little static from some of the people around the table.

The film of *The Enemy Within* fell through, basically because the large studios were scared of offending people who are the fairly powerful force in this country—the big labor racketeers who are tied in with the underworld and the Mafia and deeply involved in the entertainment business. It was just simple old-fashioned fear. That was something you didn't associate with Bob.

PETER MAAS

Of course, Hoffa was finally indicted. Robert Kennedy moved on to things that were infinitely more important. Jimmy Hoffa, just on a scale of importance, was far down the pike, just the way Roy Cohn was. Roy Cohn was running around screaming that Bob Kennedy had a vendetta against him. Nonsense. Some years ago, I wanted to do a Roy Cohn story. I remember asking Bobby what was happening on the Roy Cohn investigation. Bobby turned around to Ed Guthman and said, "Well, what *is* with Roy Cohn?" I mean it was something he didn't even think about any more. It was the same with Hoffa. When Bob was counsel for the McClellan Committee, Hoffa was very important to him because he symbolized in a personal way *all* the corruption and the ugly power that Bob was against. Of course, they personally detested each other. That triggered a lot. They had these personal confrontations. He felt Hoffa was a bad guy. But, as I say, in subsequent years, he became involved in much more positive things.

CHARLOTTE CURTIS, *journalist*

It had the artistic elements of a *Grand Hotel* or a *Ship of Fools*. Because everyone was isolated. As a reporter, when you cover a charity ball, it's true that everybody who is anybody, let's say, is *in a* ballroom; but they're in a ballroom for a very short period of time; some people come late, and some go home early. But at this event, everybody got on at the same time and nobody could get off until the end, you see, and it was so long. And then the juxtapositions: I was sitting with Pam Turnure Timmons and her husband at one point; we were having lunch and a drink beside the window. Here were these people standing on the side of the platforms in tears and looking in at you eating lunch! But that's part of the Irish wake—you can't cry for nine hours.

JOSEPH ALSOP, *columnist*

There was always that ludicrous mixture of heartbreak and how do you get your sandwiches? That's always true. It always happens when people who love someone very much who's gone are necessarily gathered together; they have to go on nourishing themselves and deciding whether to have another drink.

But it wasn't really like a wake at all. One had the feeling that the clan had lost its chieftain and was going to bury him. It must have been medieval. You could almost divide people into non-clan members, people who had come along for the show; and the members of the clan like myself, who had some kind of independent existence; and then the people who worked for Bobby but, nevertheless, had some kind of independent existence all the same; and then the unfortunate people, whom I won't name, who really had lived through Bobby in a rather parasitic manner, whose independent existence had come to an end. It was the funeral of the Irish chieftain. I can't think of any previous example of it. Why I must have received a dozen, to my mind, supremely silly letters from outwardly perfectly intelligent people, saying that now that Bobby's gone, the only thing we can do is run Teddy for President. It was exactly as though now that O'Neill is gone, O'Neill's son is the only possible chieftain of the clan. It is not at all the normal thing in America, let me tell you.

FRANK MANKIEWICZ, *press secretary*

An interesting cultural thing was happening on the train, because you really had three different groups, in terms of religious culture. The Irish were drinking and having a sort of wake, which is fine, and they were just as grief-stricken, and probably more so, than anyone else. Then you had the Protestants, who weren't quite sure, I think, how to act. Somewhat disapproving, I believe they were, of the people who were having a good time, and feeling that since what was going on in the train was probably just an extension of the funeral, they should act funereal. And then the Jews, who respond on occasions like this with far more show of grief.

I'm not suggesting, now, that any of these three groups felt any more or any less grief than anyone else. But the people were responding in a rather primitive, cultural way: the Irish were having a wake, the Protestants were at a funeral, and the Jews were weeping and carrying on—they'd have torn their clothes if they'd thought of it—looking out the window and empathizing with the people outside, weeping for the full eight or nine hours. The Protestants sort of sat stiffly and consoled each other. The Irish drank. Everybody was in a real splendid sort of communion.

MICHAEL HARRINGTON, *author*

One particular aspect of the train ride that stood out was its Irishness. Before my own father died, I had always detested the Irish wake; I had thought it an incredible and vulgar irrelevance to have a social situation—in effect, almost a party—over a dead body. Then I discovered through my own experience that there's a profound wisdom in that Irish tradition.

At the time of death, relevant things are exactly what you don't want to confront. Irrelevant things are a distraction, and that ridiculous idea of sitting around a room with people drinking and talking politics—which has certainly happened at all the Irish wakes I've ever been to—is really a decent strategy for dealing with an intolerable fact. Even the telling of dirty jokes—by the priests themselves at some Irish wakes—is, in some way, an affirmation of life in the presence of death.

I felt that mood on the train. There were quite a few people who were drinking fairly heavily. I was involved in some political conversations where it was almost as if no one had died. It was almost as if we were not *on* that train. We were talking about the future, and that was the point—this marvelous Irish tradition of irrelevance. It became even more pronounced, it seemed to me, as the trip wore on; as the train delayed and delayed.

At the wake in *Finnegans Wake*, everybody is drinking and kicking up a storm, and eventually there's so much shoving and pushing that some of the whisky splashes on Tim Finnegan. He rises from the dead at his own wake, which is a very Irish conception.

The whole thesis of *Finnegans Wake* is, in a sense, the fall and rise—the Resurrection—of Ireland. It is everything from Adam and Eve, to the future, to the life going into the sea. But there is this profound Irish tradition of gaiety as contrasted, for example, to the "Sitting Shiva," where the old tradition is more the rending of garments; the wailing at the direct emotional confrontation with grief.

BUDD SCHULBERG, *author*
All the liberals and the backsliding Protestants were in terrible shape. You could just go down the aisle and pick them out. For those who have trouble about a concept of Paradise, it's much harder and all these strong men like Rosey Grier were messes. I think it's a sublime faith. I would look at someone and say, "Gee, I didn't realize he was Catholic." You see they felt that Bob was in Paradise.

HELEN KEYES, *administrator, John F. Kennedy Library*
The thing that I resent the most is the way that the train was written up by some of the press as a sort of rollicking Irish wake. The whole point is that if there *is* gaiety and laughter at an Irish wake, it's simply because this is what we believe: that when people die they go to heaven; so rejoice! The press missed that whole point. They made it sound as though people were crying and then decided to laugh to bolster up their spirits. I believe that Bobby is in heaven, so I'm not

going to waste any tears on him. God put us on this earth. He never said it was going to be easy; it isn't easy—it's a trial period, and if you succeed then your reward is heaven, so rejoice!

GERALDINE BROOKS (*Mrs. Budd Schulberg*)
I've never been exposed to that kind of courage before. I found people who were just going along with their daily life, trying to make everyone else feel at home; there was no self-pity, no self-indulgence. And I said, "God, I wish I had that kind of faith." We're Jewish. I said, "I swear to God, if I could convert today 1 would." It was such a godsend to me. You could look around and absolutely *see* which of those people were strong Catholics.

DAVE POWERS, *curator, John F. Kennedy Museum*
The men in those old Irish wakes would be in one room and the women in another. Only the Irish understand that sort of thing. There were the great wake-goers like Wakes O'Shaughnessey. That was his name—Wakes. The Boston *Post* was the paper that everyone in Charlestown used to read in those days; it's not published any more. But the *Post* had tremendous death columns, and Wakes O'Shaughnessey would look at them.

It would give the names. You'd see a name like Patrick McLaughlin, and it would list where he came from originally . . . "County Cork," it would say. Charlestown was the town where everyone lived, but still it would say "County Cork."

In those days, you'd be considered a heathen if you used a funeral parlor. The Irish would say, "The house was good enough for Pat when he was alive, and it's good enough for him now." So wakes were held in the tenements. All the relatives would come for miles. The people in the tenement like the Sullivans on the first floor, the Murphys on the second, and the Doughertys on the top . . . or the McLaughlins . . . well, they would do the cooking and everything. The whole house would be turned over to the wake. Often, on a hot night, they'd be on the rooftops. In the old Irish wakes, they would keep it going until the friends and relatives that lived the farthest distance would be there. Sometimes it meant three nights, or four nights.

Now, of course, your Irish wake has become more sophisticated. They've moved from the tenements to the funeral parlors with the air conditioning. And that's why the funeral parlors today are much better.

63

Because these people in the old days, at the end of three or four days, would be practically dead themselves!

Anyway, Wakes O'Shaughnessey would look at the paper. He'd go, "Oo-ooo, this will be a wonderful time," and he'd be the first one there and the last one to leave. On the third day, the widow would say, "Oh, you must have been Pat's greatest friend! You're the first one here every night, and the last one to go." Then, sort of letting him in on a secret, she says, "You know, it's a funny thing—Pat had some relatives who are not quite as Catholic as I am, and they're talking about having him *cremated*. What do you think we ought to do?"

And so Wakes O'Shaughnessey said, "Why don't you *stuff* him and keep the party going? It's a corker!"

ARTHUR SCHLESINGER, JR., *historian*

Dave Powers knows more about wakes than I do, but it did seem to me very much like a wake. That mixture of grief and hilarious reminiscence. The Irish wakes always seemed to me a marvelous thing. This one was really a wake on wheels. I was aware of the tremendous sense of that kind of fortification in sorrow through seeing and talking to people who also loved the man who died, who were there for their own reasons, who represented jarring notes. I chiefly remember long talks with people like David Harlech and Kenny O'Donnell and Dick Goodwin. I said to O'Donnell, as we were looking out the windows, I said, "Marvelous crowds." To which he replied gloomily, "Yes. But what are they good for now?"

KENNETH O'DONNELL, *family friend*

He asked me to go to the 1956 Democratic Convention with him. He and I flew out to Chicago, and we arrived—that great well-oiled Kennedy organization, two young fellows that had never seen a convention before in their lives—to find a headline in the paper that one of those being considered for Vice-President of the United States was Senator John Kennedy. This is about three days before the convention began. We got off the plane and went to the Ambassador East. The manager took us up to the penthouse. Peter Lawford rented it by the year, and Bobby Kennedy was so horrified that anybody would rent something that they didn't live in, he wouldn't stay there . . . I was, perfectly willing to stay there. He said no, and went down and rented a room and stayed there.

64

We had a bit of a campaign for John Kennedy. They had a floor fight, and Bobby and I ran around like a couple of nuts and tried to make believe we were busy. But, I mean, who could you talk to? It was just a joke; we didn't know two people in the place. It was John Kennedy by himself. He didn't like Estes Kefauver, and he had captured the enthusiasm of the galleries and the delegates, and they wanted to nominate him. He would have been nominated, in my judgment, but the board broke, and I think there's no question they stole it, which is good. They had a tote board—which computes, you know—and you'd be watching it, and it would go up to X number of votes. Kennedy was something . . . twenty-eight votes away, and the board broke down, which means somebody pulled the plug on the board.

I was having a hot dog, standing with Senator Albert Gore, whom I didn't know, and he didn't know me. A young lady who was the publisher of a very influential newspaper in his state said, "If you don't go for Estes Kefauver, that's the last for you." Gore walked back, and I walked with him—crazy things at conventions—and we went up to Governor Frank Clement. And while I was standing right there, he said to Governor Clement, "Governor, we've got to switch." Clement said, "Yes, I think you're right." Gore said, "Yes, we're going for Estes." Clement said, "Estes! Are you crazy?!"—he couldn't stand Kefauver. Gore said, "No, but that's it," and then he whispered in his ear.

I stood and listened while they were whispering—I didn't hear the whispers—but the next thing I knew Tennessee was signaling the switch. Mr. Rayburn recognized Tennessee, and Tennessee shifted from Gore to Kefauver, and then all the delegations began to follow suit. At the time, California was switching to Kennedy, which would have put him over the top without any question. So there's no question in my mind that there was an arrangement made. Bobby and I went over to see Senator Kennedy. He was angry; Bobby said to him, "You're better off than you ever were in your life, and you made the great fight, and they're not going to win. You're going to be the candidate the next time."

HARRISON SALISBURY, *assistant managing editor*, The New York Times

During Stevenson's presidential campaign, the first thing I noticed about him was that he seemed to be so isolated from the rest of the Stevenson group, who were all terribly enthusiastic and working night and day for Adlai. Bobby always seemed to be on the fringe of the

65

crowd someplace. He was always watching what was going on. I began to hear from the Stevenson people that they were pretty miffed at the way they were not getting any support from Kennedy. It suddenly occurred to me that what Bobby was doing was observing how a campaign is run from the inside, noting every possible detail for future use, when he would be running one for his brother.

I used to go and sit with Bobby and talk to him; there's always lots of free time, you know, in a campaign, and he was never busy. He made no bones about what he was doing. He was very interested in the mechanics of the campaign. What struck me about him was that he was very young and quite aloof, really, and self-contained, and he didn't miss a single thing. The questions he asked were always very much to the point—about things that would directly concern him and his brother. His whole interest was concentrated in that fashion. It seemed to me he had very few friends in the campaign entourage. Nor did he try to make friends with these people, although later on many of them came over and joined the Kennedy group; I mean the Schlesingers, Dick Goodwin, and all the rest of them were with the Stevenson group at that time.

But Bobby was not interested in them. He wanted to know exactly how you run a campaign, and what mistakes you make and what you didn't make. I remember one time in particular: instead of being back at the end of the train watching the people greet Stevenson, Bobby was tired that day and he just sat on the railroad tracks . . . and I sat down with him, and we had a long talk about running the campaign. He was talking about what the candidate *ought* to do . . . practically all the things that Stevenson didn't do. Stevenson tended to lock himself up in a compartment when he was traveling, and spend all his time working over his speeches. He wouldn't spend time sitting with his aides and assistants, working out strategy for, say, how you're going to take over Ohio. He would fiddle with his speeches, or have somebody else redraft something. That was where all his interest and concentration was. Bobby was not interested in that at all. That was something the speechwriters could take care of and you would map out in advance; you'd know your territory well enough so that you'd know in advance what kind of speeches you were going to make; you shouldn't bother with written-out speeches for each campaign experience. If the candidate would have certain topics that he would talk about informally, he'd have a special group writing down this kind of material. He was absolutely right about this. When they came to set up the campaign four years later, this is exactly the way it operated. I had the feeling after the Stevenson campaign that Bobby knew every single thing there was to know about a campaign. He just squeezed all that absolutely dry.

WILLIAM BLAIR, JR., *general director, The John F. Kennedy Center for the Performing Arts*

I remember one time we were campaigning through Connecticut, and Bobby was in car number nine or ten. As we approached the Massachusetts line, he was moved up to car number one with Adlai Stevenson. I said, "We don't want to hear any more complaints about your position in the parade." He laughed about that and said, "Well, I suppose I'll be dropped back to the last car when we leave Massachusetts." He respected Stevenson a lot, but they were never very close—which was too bad, but neither's fault.

HARRISON SALISBURY

He calculated very accurately what the political odds were. He was confident that Stevenson could not win the election. This was the reason why he didn't get out and try to rally the Catholic groups, many of whom were stirred up because Stevenson was divorced, and his former wife was making a certain amount of trouble at that time . . . and this all had come into the campaign. He wasn't going to use up any Kennedy political capital helping Stevenson, because it was a lost cause. If he didn't use it up, he'd have it available for his brother four years hence, and he was perfectly objective about this. You could say he was cynical or ruthless. These are the adjectives that have been so often applied to him; but I never thought that this was a real cynicism or ruthlessness. It was simply a facing up to the reality of the situation, and then drawing perfectly logical conclusions. But the conclusions always centered around his brother and the future of the Kennedys. This was the core of his whole existence.

JOHN KENNETH GALBRAITH, *economist*

Four years later, he was running his own brother's drive for the presidency. Working with him, I remember my feeling of great age. Abraham Ribicoff and I were the only two of the whole Kennedy convention staff that Bobby in the 1960 campaign referred to as "sir." Yes, I remember that vividly. We met every morning in the Kennedy headquarters at the Biltmore Hotel, and reviewed the day's activities. This was perhaps the first time that I had seen Bob at close range, because I was not terribly active that year in the primaries. I had been away. First of all, I was struck by the real skill with which he distributed the day's duties, and the insistence that he had on the *substance*, rather than the form, of the work. Politicians are often content to talk with somebody as distinct from *convincing* somebody. Bob's question was never, "Did you talk with him?" but always, "Did you get him? Did you get his support?"

I was struck by his complete freedom from illusion as we went over the delegate position. Each morning, we had a roll call of the states as to who was for Johnson, who was for Hubert Humphrey, who might be leaning toward Stevenson, and who was for John Kennedy. Bob never wanted good news; he wanted the precise and accurate estimate. Very often, somebody seeking to cover up some delinquency might say, "Oh, I'm sure we are going to get so-and-so many votes from Iowa." Bob would shake him down and bring him back to the truth. He had a quality that he shared with his brother; both had been in politics long enough to be suspicious of its baroque rhetoric. They both disliked it. They cut through this to the hard common sense of any political situation, without any feeling that they were destroying the conventions that other politicians cherished. I think, perhaps, this had something to do with their both coming from Massachusetts. In Massachusetts, the baroque tendencies of politics reach a ridiculous level, and they probably were especially contemptuous of it.

ARTHUR SCHLESINGER, JR.

One of the many misconceptions about the Kennedys is that they were highly organized, systematic planners; that, for example, Robert Kennedy had a great nationwide organization, and a timetable, and everything was being methodically worked out, and he was making decisions in '67 and '68 on the basis of what would happen in 1972. A total misconception. The Kennedys were not very good. They had no belief in the value of long-term planning. They were brilliant improvisers, *i.e.*, in any particular situation, they could move in and mobilize resources in a series of *ad hoc* actions. I was very much involved in Robert Kennedy's 1964 campaign. It was such a confusion that I remember asking whether he could conceivably have been the man who ran the allegedly well-organized presidential campaign of 1960. He said, "Well, that wasn't so hot either." He said, "If you win, your campaign is always regarded as brilliantly designed; if you lose, it's always regarded as incompetent."

68

HELEN KEYES

Bobby never had any idea of what problems people had in just living. He would call and expect you to drop everything. He called me on a February night from Wisconsin (this was the '60 campaign) and said, "I want you to come out here as soon as you can and stay until the primary election is over." I said, "Gee, Bobby, I don't know. I teach school. I don't know if I can. Probably you'd have to speak to the Superintendent of Schools." He said, "Oh, fine, I'll do that." I said, "All right." He said, "Can you come out tomorrow?" Right after he finished talking to me, he called the Superintendent of Schools. When I got to school the next morning, I had a message that my classes had been covered, and off I went. I arrived in Milwaukee. I went to the hotel to check in, and Angie Novello met me and said, "You're to fly to Wausau"—which could have been Warsaw, Poland, for all I knew— "and meet Bobby."

So I got in a private plane—I was never so frightened in my life. I hate flying more than anything in the world—and I arrived in Wausau, where I saw Bobby for ten minutes. He said, "Now, this is what I want you to do. There are five districts we know Jack can't win—the third, the fifth, the ninth, the tenth, and the twelfth. We're not going to bother scheduling him in person there very much, but we're going to try with the girls." He said, "Pat and Eunice and Jean will be coming for two weeks, at different times, and I want you to schedule house parties for each one of them; they're to do nine each a day, three in the morning, three in the afternoon, three in the evening. So start right here, set some of these functions up here." He left.

If you have a job and you want to get it done, and you don't care *how* it's done, send Paul Corbin out to do it—but just understand you can never send him back to the same district. He adored Bobby. His house had very high ceilings, and when you got in, there was a photograph of Bobby—it must be five by three feet—with lights shining on it. The darnedest thing you ever saw in your life! You wouldn't believe it. He became a Catholic, and Bobby was his godfather. I said to Bobby, "You need Paul Corbin in the Catholic Church like you need leprosy." And he said, "Now, Helen, he's sincere." And I said, "He is like fun. He wants to be a Catholic because *you're* a Catholic." He said, "Well, who cares? If he gets something out of it, and he's been through all the instruction and all." Bobby had the weirdest godchildren in the whole wide world.

Anyway, Bobby let us loose there in Wausau, Wisconsin. The confidence he displayed was just unbelievable. He gave you a job and presumed that you'd do it. If I had called him and said, "Bobby, I *can't* get nine people in Stevens Point to give house parties for the girls," he would have said, "Well, why can't you?"

So I stayed and I tramped around that strange state. We had lists of Democrats. We didn't know whether they were for Humphrey or Kennedy. Paul Corbin would say, "You're a Democrat?" and the person would say, "Yes." Corbin would ask, "You for Humphrey or Kennedy?" and they'd say, "We're for Humphrey." "Why? Is it because Kennedy is a Catholic?" And they'd say, "Well, that's part of it." Then Paul would say, pointing at me, "Well, this lady's a Baptist from New England, from Boston"—I kept expecting to be struck by lightning for denying my faith—"and *she's* for Kennedy."

Then my line would be, "Would you have some ladies into your house to meet Peter Lawford's wife, Pat, the candidate's sister?" One of his series was being rerun on television, so everyone there knew who Peter Lawford was. We offered everyone Peter Lawford's wife, and then we'd run in one of the other sisters, Jean or Eunice, and say, "Oh, well, Pat just had such a busy schedule!" The girls were terrific!

Can you imagine wandering around the way we did? I mean there were fifteen of us out there—I didn't know a soul when I went there. Two days before the election, Bobby called me and said, "Well, now you'll have to come to West Virginia." I said, "You'll have to call the School Committee." He called the School Committee, and we left on the *Caroline* for West Virginia in a blizzard.

WILLIAM WALTON, *artist, family friend*

The campaign in West Virginia in 1960 was the first time that he had ever moved through the houses of the poor and examined the way that they lived. Unless you have been a social worker, the upper-middle-class person isn't likely to see the way the poor live. Of course, his sympathy for such people had existed before. That is not something you acquire suddenly, on the road to Damascus. For him, West Virginia was a particular kind of watershed; it had something to do with the quality of the state and the people, who were terribly open and friendly.

Bobby's early speeches were hardly set speeches. We would arrive at the tipple of a coal mine just as the shifts were changing; and he would just walk up to them in a simple, direct way and say, "My name is Bob Kennedy. My brother is running for President. I want your help." And then he would stand with them . . . they, all black with coal dust, and his hands black from shaking hands. He'd discuss the issues of their wages, their village conditions, and Social Security, and education. He would seldom make a speech in the real campaigning sense. His personality came over very well in this intimate face-to-face kind of thing. They dug him. They'd kid him, but he would kid back.

FRANKLIN D. ROOSEVELT, JR., *business executive*

We wound up winning by seventy per cent. It was quite clear to everybody that the Kennedy family spent an enormous amount of money on television, radio, newspaper ads; a very large and expensive staff . . . as compared with Humphrey's campaign, which really was poorly financed. He traveled around the state in a bus. We had all kinds of speakers, airplanes flying people around. . . . Oh, my gosh, it was a real production. Of course, Hubert Humphrey pulled out right after that; he withdrew. That really left it up to Lyndon Johnson at the convention . . . because Jack went on to win the rest of the primaries, right on through the Oregon primary, the California primary. Then it was up to Lyndon Johnson to try and stop our bandwagon.

WILLIAM WALTON

The West Virginia primary in 1960 was the first time I picked up the close connection between Hubert Humphrey and Lyndon Johnson. But it was an odd one. Hubert was the candidate, and theoretically LBJ had nothing to do with this primary; but in small town after small town, the leading town banker would lean back after a few minutes and say to me, "Well, you'll never guess who called me yesterday. Senator Johnson called me up, and he's for Humphrey!" It happened in town after town after town. But the interesting thing was that Johnson, though he had access to great campaign funds, never cut them loose in sufficient quantity to allow Hubert to stage a really good campaign. It was a poor-man's campaign. If Johnson had really wanted him to win, he would have given him money. We could only assume that he didn't want him to win; that he wanted to fight Kennedy himself . . . which he did in the convention.

JACK CONWAY, *labor official*

The thing that always flashes back in my mind is the meeting twelve hours or so following the successful nomination of Jack Kennedy and the decision to pick Lyndon Johnson as the vice-presidential candidate. It was at this meeting that Jack Kennedy indicated that he was in this very difficult bind because there was a special session of the Congress—a seven-week session—that was to take place between the convention and the election. Lyndon Johnson, as the Majority Leader, was in the driver's seat, and he could give Kennedy a lot of trouble and hurt the campaign if he were sulking. Kennedy felt that the least he could do—and *should* do in this situation—was to offer the vice-presidency to Lyndon. Frankly, he didn't think Johnson would take it, but in the process of making the gesture, it might solve some of the emotional problems. I turned to Robert Kennedy, who was not too far from me, and I said, "Bob, don't do it. Because if you offer it to him, he'll take it. And if he takes it, it'll ruin everything that we've done."

MURRAY KEMPTON, *journalist*
The whole thing sounded like a street quarrel. He had that look on his face. I remember one of the reporters at the Democratic Convention in 1960 saying, "Whenever you see Bobby Kennedy in public with his brother, he looks as though he showed up for a rumble."

CHARLES BARTLETT, *journalist*
We were at Marian Davies' house. While Lyndon was being nominated for the vice-presidency on the floor, Bobby was directing it from there, staying in touch with Larry O'Brien. The nominating was going on; the liberals had been pacified. Nobody was very cheerful, and Bobby was the least cheerful, I'd say. The sun was going down and all of Bobby's children were sort of in a big fountain out in front. Mr. Kennedy was in a velvet smoking jacket, standing in the doorway in a very grand manner with his hands behind his back. It was at this point that Mr. Kennedy said, "Don't worry, Jack. Within two weeks they'll be saying it's the smartest thing you ever did." He wasn't going to share this anguish of Bobby's.

JESSE UNRUH, *Speaker of the California Assembly*
Actually, the Democrats really didn't want to use Lyndon very much in the presidential campaign. In addition to that, Lyndon himself did not like to come to California. He never did—and still doesn't—understand California politics, and is very uncomfortable in this state. One story sticks in my mind that illustrates how close the Kennedy family was, and what great confidence John Kennedy had in Bobby as a campaign manager. When he made his last swing before the election, we had bought statewide television time for a thirty-minute speech. We

had a controversy over who should introduce him. I wanted to bring Lyndon Johnson out to introduce him, again trying to get the vote that I thought we were losing. Bob was insistent that we use Stevenson. We argued for two or three weeks. Finally, naturally, Bob, the national campaign manager, won over the state campaign manager. Stevenson came out. I'll never forget when John Kennedy got off the plane that morning. I got in the car with him to take him to his first speech, at the University of Southern California, and he said, "Well, Jesse, who's introducing me tonight?" I said, "Stevenson." He said, "Stevenson!" And a short couple of expletives accompanied that. He said, "Who made *that* decision?" I thought, "Boy, here's a chance to sort of stick it to Bobby a little bit." So I said, "Bobby." And without one minute's hesitation, John Kennedy said, "He must have had a good reason." That was the end of it.

CORNELIUS RYAN, *author*

I had been sent up to Hyannis Port with Charles Henderson to make preparations for election day. Senator John Kennedy arrived at the little airport early that morning, and later I saw him on the terrace at the back of his house along with Jackie. His face was drawn. He looked strained and tired. He sat down on a bamboo chaise longue, and he pulled a blanket up around his chin. It was quite nippy. His father came across at that point wearing a gray flannel suit with a monogram on the left breast pocket. He seemed very fit. Instead of nervously awaiting every scrap of news, Jack Kennedy launched into a big discussion with me about World War II and my books. He began to talk about the merits of General Rommel as a commander and about the invasion. I remember he asked me, If Rommel had not left his headquarters in Normandy to visit his wife in Germany, could the invasion have been stopped? I replied that it would not have made any difference, though our casualties might have been higher *had* he been present.

Across the lawn at his own house, Bobby Kennedy and his staff had set up a command post in the breakfast room. Occasionally, Bobby would come out and walk along the lawn down by the sea, in deep concentration, and then he'd come back in again. He seemed to have the ability to separate himself from what was going on around him. A couple of times during the day, people threw a ball around on the lawn. Peter Lawford was hunched up in a great big sheepskin coat, sitting there on the terrace. Everybody was tense. When the message came in that said Hawaii had gone for Kennedy, there was a great hurrah, and

Teddy stood up and said, "And you fellows all thought I was doing nothing else in Hawaii but lying on the beach!"

Then, late that evening there was the first premature announcement on TV that Nixon was coming to the microphones, possibly to concede. I was standing with Pierre Salinger and Jack Kennedy. He was wearing gray slacks and carrying a sports coat with a gold silk lining with horses' heads imprinted on it. He was carrying that in his right hand, and in the other a paperback that I believe was called *Sayings of Great Presidents*. Suddenly he said to Salinger, "Is there any more milk?" As we waited for Nixon to say something, here was Senator Kennedy asking for milk! I went back into the kitchen, opened the refrigerator, but all I could find there was a bottle of beer. I opened that and gave it to him.

Bobby was in total command of the situation. He was very crisp. Curiously, one of the strange things I noticed was that there was very little communication between Jack and Bobby. Jack would come into the breakfast room and stand with his back against the wall, just listening. Bobby would be at the far end of the table surrounded by telephones. There were calls from political leaders all over the country. Bobby would say, "How are things going there?" He had that particular Massachusetts twang in his voice, which always seemed to me . . . when he got tensed up . . . terribly pronounced.

It was quite an evening—because you've got to remember we won that election by a gnat's eyebrow!

CHARLES BARTLETT

Jack wanted Bobby in the Administration . . . I don't think he knew exactly where. I think it was the father more than anyone, it seemed to me, who really felt he should be in the Justice Department . . . that Bobby should be the Attorney General. Obviously, it wasn't Jack's initial thought, because he offered it first to Abe Ribicoff, who turned it down.

I think Bobby was a little apprehensive. My concern for him was that he would be thrust into the middle of the desegregation controversy; that he was not a diplomat in any sense, and that he would aggravate the strains of the desegregation thing and suffer from it . . . become a negative figure in the public eye. He had so little instinct for politics, and was so direct in his approach to things and so impolitic much of the time. I had the feeling that JFK wanted to have Bobby go into the Defense Department at maybe the second or third level, and let him slowly take over.

74

At that point, the father came in with the Justice Department. Bobby didn't seem very happy about it. We talked. I said, "It seems to me you'll have some problems." Bobby said, "Well, maybe you'd like to call Dad." I said, "No. I *wouldn't* like to call Dad." Then I got a call from Jack saying, "Lay off this thing. It's all settled." So I never mentioned it to him again. But I must say that from the day he went in, I don't think he ever enjoyed anything more.

PETER MAAS, *author*
I asked President Kennedy, "Well, why appoint your brother as Attorney General? Everybody says he has never been in a courtroom and he has no legal experience." President Kennedy wheeled around and said, "Well, an Attorney General doesn't have to be a lawyer, he doesn't have to ever be in a court. An Attorney General is supposed to run a department of some 30,000 people, and it needs a hell of a manager, and my brother is the best manager I've ever had and the best one that I know of—and *that's* why he's going to be the Attorney General."

4   SOUTH STREET, NEWARK,
NEW JERSEY

CHARLES FERRIS, *U.S. Senate aide*

There was one incident that really got to me. This big obnoxious bloke demonstrated an insensitivity that really hurt. I never wanted to swing at someone so badly. As he looked out the window and saw this middle-aged, well-dressed man fall to his knees, he remarked: "Look at that crazy fool, falling to his knees." I made it a point to find out who he was. He was one of those New York socialites who was there not because Bobby meant anything to him but because being there was the thing to do.

JEFF GREENFIELD, *campaign aide*

There were a lot of people there who said to themselves, "Here I am, an important person, because I'm on the train." You know, wow! The kind of people who sit in on meetings and bowl their way into conferences because they want to be there; they have nothing to say or do or contribute—the kind of people, I suppose, who drink all the liquor and eat all the food and really don't know why they are there. I didn't mind people who talked with each other and were happy to see each other. You don't sustain eight solid hours of extreme emotional anguish. We're not Eastern people. It's just not the way people function, particularly not the way people function from that environment. But I think anybody who cared had his own moments of very quiet reflection.

BURT GLINN, *photographer*

You go down that train, and all the people that you would see and

76

all the people that you knew. . . . You realized how many strands were in this incredibly strong rope that Robert Kennedy had woven.

ANTHONY LEWIS, *chief of the London bureau,* The New York Times

First, I thought it was an awful idea that he became Attorney General. I couldn't believe it. When Bill Lawrence wrote a piece for the New York *Times* from Florida, saying that Bobby was going to be Attorney General, I thought how terrible that was. I had this image of him as a very brash young man with no experience in the law, no particular ability, a short temper, and no understanding of the things that I cared about in the law . . . which were respect for people's rights. But what made me begin to feel differently was his choice of assistants at the Department of Justice. When he became Attorney General he picked such outstandingly good people: Burke Marshall, Archie Cox, and Nick Katzenbach.

He did one or two things out of sheer kindness or sense of fitness. I recall that someone I knew very well was a career lawyer in the Justice Department—Philip Ellman, who had been in the Solicitor General's office for many years and was an excellent man. Well, Robert Kennedy had never heard of him, and Ellman certainly had never taken any part in politics. But people told Bobby that he was a good man, and Bobby arranged for him to be a Federal Trade Commissioner. That was, I thought, quite exceptional.

RAMSEY CLARK, *Attorney General of the United States*

In my opinion, Bob Kennedy could have been a disaster as the Attorney General. Human nature is such that many people were prepared to think, Well, we're just stuck with the kid brother here, you know. What's he ever done? Why is he Attorney General? He was just barely thirty-five years old. I suppose the average Attorney General of the United States had been twenty years older than that. Must have been. He had never practiced law.

But he had advantages. He had been in the Department, of course. His sister Eunice had been in the Department. Eunice Kennedy Shriver. And Sarge, her husband, had been in the Department. That's where they met. Eunice came in 1945 or '46 as adviser on juvenile delinquency to my father when he was the Attorney General. They used to call them "dollar-a-year people." What it meant was that they were volunteering their services for an important job; a lot of good will existed in the Department because people remembered that.

In addition, two or three people who had been Bob's roommates at Justice had moved up into high positions. They knew him and remembered him as a young lawyer, and carried good will. Oren Waterman was a roommate of Bob's, and he'd moved up to be about the third-ranking official in the Internal Security Division. That made a difference . . . because he was a bridge to all the old lawyers in the Department.

Even so, it could have been a disaster . . . because if Bob hadn't been aggressive, and if he hadn't been effective . . . well, who knows? He *had* to be better than anybody because there would be so much doubt about him. On the other hand, if it looked like he was trying to *prove* himself . . . why, that would have been bad.

So, he just had to come at it very hard and naturally. And that's what he did. Within a year, all that doubt and resentment, all those essentially jealous notions—What's this young guy ever done? Why should he be Attorney General?—were gone. I don't think there was a residue after a year. You couldn't live there and not know the place was alive.

His office epitomized his whole style of living. It was terribly busy, and somewhat cluttered; and there was an air of excitement and life about it. He was running between that office and several others—literally running in and out. That spirit captured the Department almost immediately. You know, a department is a great lethargic institution with thousands of people, very impersonal; generally people in direct personal contact with the Attorney General are very few in comparison with the total numbers. In fact, the personality of the Attorney General is irrelevant to most of the people. That's the sad fact about institutions, I guess.

But it became different. It really did. I've known the Department of Justice an awfully long time. I used to walk the halls as a kid—pre-teen-age, because my father had joined the Department as a lawyer when I was nine years old—and I'd come to sense the atmosphere and the mood of the place. It was a quiet and sleepy place until January of '61. I don't mean that it was not effective, but just that it was a quiet, impersonal, and uninvolved institution. Periodically, there were areas of great activity and effort. But really, before the spring of 1961, it was almost as if it was humming quietly . . . and then it came *alive*.

One of the first things that Bob started doing—he really shook up some of the old-timers—was just walking around the halls. My God, no Attorney General ever walked around the halls before! Every Attorney

General always rode down in that private elevator to his automobile; the only time you'd ever see him was when he'd be walking from the automobile to the door. That's true even of Assistant Attorneys General.

Well, Bob started walking the halls. He would go into doors. There is a little door on the second floor, right above the entrance where the cars drive through on the first floor, where there's a catwalk that goes around. This little office off the catwalk was assigned to a very fine lawyer. He was one of these quick people. He learned quickly. He had been bored with his work for a good many years, and he had been something of a problem for his supervisors. If he was given work, he would do it . . . and he'd want more. So Bob saw the door and walked in, and saw him sitting there with his feet on the desk, reading a novel. There was quite a scene! Bob said, "What are you doing reading that novel on government time?" or something like that. You know, Bob could get upset. The average fellow would have been very diplomatic about it, but Bob responded very naturally. This was government time; the Department of Justice had a very important mission . . . and here's a guy in working hours, office hours, sitting with his feet on the desk, reading a novel!

Over the next three years, about every six months, we'd be sitting there, and all of a sudden Bob would say, "What's that fellow doing now?" As a matter of fact, it was the best thing that ever happened to him. I guarantee you that in the next three years he had *lots* to do.

PETER MAAS, *author*

If there was one thing that turned me completely pro-Bobby, it was when I was doing a story about Igor Cassini, who was a society gossip columnist in New York. I had been working on it for a long time—and it was eventually revealed that Cassini was a secret agent for the Dominican Republic dictator, Trujillo. Cassini hadn't done too much for Trujillo yet, but he was making a lot of money, and he was on the verge of cashing in on his alleged friendship and access to the Kennedy family. When I'd tell people how much I liked Bob Kennedy, they'd say, "Well, you can forget it if you run the Cassini story, because the lead of the story involves Bobby's father; 'ruthless' Bobby'll get you for that." One New Year's, I think in '61, Cassini and Joseph Kennedy senior were at dinner, and Cassini brought up this thing about how the Communists were ready to take over the Dominican Republic, and so forth, and that President Kennedy's Administration should look into it. The upshot was that old Mr. Kennedy did intervene, and President Kennedy sent a fact-finding commission to the Dominican Republic headed by Ambassador Robert Murphy. So it was not small potatoes! Of course, the threat to Trujillo was not the Communists, but his own generals, who eventually knocked him off. But Cassini was responsible for the mission, and it made him look good to Trujillo. It was one of the first steps in fulfilling his contract.

Well, at any rate, I wrote this whole thing. I said, Well, God damn it! If that's the way it is and Bobby is going to get me, the hell with it. I'm not giving up the story. Then Audrey, my wife, said to me, "You ought to go down and tell him." I said, "I'm not going to do it! I'm not going to change a word." She said, "I didn't ask you to change a word, but you're a friend now, and it's better that you tell him than his hearing it from somebody else." So I thought about it for a day; I was really kind of edgy about the whole thing. I said, "All right. I'll do it." I called Ed Guthman and I said, "Look, Ed. I've got this nasty story coming out that involves some members of the Kennedy family." "Well," he said, "come right down."

So I flew down and walked into the office, and Bobby said, "Well, what's this all about?" I said, "Well, you know, I've just been doing a long piece on Gigi Cassini. . . ." I remember Bob almost half rising out of his chair, saying "No. No. We've looked through all that." There had been a lot of rumors about Cassini, but nothing that you could put your finger on. "There's nothing to it," he said. "Well," I said, "there *is* a lot to it, and the fact that the FBI looked into it doesn't mean they had the same motivation as if it was a *kidnaping*. Some of them probably wouldn't mind working for Trujillo *themselves*."

Well, I ticked it all off, and it took about an hour and a half. He sat there and didn't say anything at all. He sat there kind of hunched over in that big chair in that big room, with his chin on his fingers, that kind of traditional manner he had. So I finished. All he said was, "Thank you very much," and I left. I was still damn worried about what might happen to my story.

The next day we got a phone call from the FBI, and for the rest of that week, I felt like I was running a field kitchen for them. They had motivation now. *Three* sets of agents examined everything I had. This went on for about a week. I was impressed; but then I thought, Well, now they're going to foul it up somehow. It's all some kind of plot. I was a little paranoid; you're always a bit paranoid when you're doing this kind of thing anyway. Well, the upshot was, as we know, that Cassini was indicted; he faced conviction, so he pleaded *nolo contendere* he lost his column and his reputation. He got a suspended sentence and a fairly hefty fine. I was amazed that a guy like Bob Kennedy would do this. I was so used to fixes in covering politics that this was such an extraordinary thing. There were fifteen different ways his people could have fouled up the investigation or done something to have it thrown out of court. But it obviously never entered his mind.

ANTHONY LEWIS

One matter that I think insufficient attention has been paid to was the role he played on the issue of legislative districting—apportionment— which was argued in the Supreme Court while he was Attorney General. If it had been left to the Solicitor General, Archie Cox, or others, they'd have taken a rather cautious, technical, circumscribed, careful lawyer's view. Bobby felt strongly that the Court should take a forthright position.

NICHOLAS deB. KATZENBACH, *Under Secretary of State*

So many of the magazines said that Archie Cox had prepared Bobby's argument before the Supreme Court; this was not true. Archie did write an argument, but Bobby didn't like it and changed it very considerably from what the Solicitor General had proposed. Then he went over and over it, because he didn't want to use any notes.

BURKE MARSHALL, *attorney*

The case is called Grey against Sanders. It is an awfully important case—the question was whether the Constitution requires that congressional districts be apportioned so that basically there's one man, one vote. That is, you shouldn't have a district that represents 20,000 and another district representing 200,000 because, obviously, the man that lived in the district that represented 200,000 only had a tenth as much political power for his vote as the other man. It was an issue that there was a great deal of disagreement about. But Bob Kennedy was always clear in his own mind that equal protection of the law, and due process should require that everybody's vote for the state legislatures and for Congress be given equal weight. And that's the way the Court finally went.

It was *the* case he wanted to argue. I mean everybody said he wasn't a lawyer really, you know, and he always joked about that. He wanted to argue a case before the Supreme Court to show to himself and everybody else that he could do it. And the issue that he wanted to argue was that issue. There were lots of reasons for him not to. As I say, it was a terribly difficult issue and, politically, the wrong kind to get involved in —particularly for his future as a political force in the South, which was deeply affected by this issue. But he made a good argument. The Court didn't ask him any questions. If they had, they would have found out that he'd really gone into it awfully deeply. But when an Attorney General argues a case, the Court thinks, Well, here's the Attorney General, and he's a busy fellow—somebody wrote out an argument for him, and so we won't embarrass him by asking him questions that he can't answer. That would be a traditional way for the Court to treat an Attorney General. And that's the way they treated him. But there weren't any questions he didn't have an answer to.

THEODORE WHITE, *author*

I don't think you can judge a man by his intellectual capacity. I think you judge a leader by his capacity to use intellectuals. Intellectuals have spent their lives researching the thing they know all about . . . economics, or foreign affairs, or finance, or hysterectomies. They may know more about certain things than anybody else, but they can't tell you what to do. They are map makers. It's as if you had a Rand McNally chart tell you how to go to Chicago. A Rand McNally map will tell you the roads to Chicago, but you must decide whether you want to go there in the first place, or go by plane or by auto, or leisurely or fast. Bobby was a man who knew how to use other men. He had impeccable taste in men. There are certain guys who've got good taste in women; others have got good taste in men. Henry Luce had superb taste in the men he chose. So did Ed Murrow. Franklin Roosevelt had it. John F. Kennedy had it. Adlai Stevenson had it. By good taste, I mean using another man to do something you want to get done, and choosing the right man to do it. Who would have thought that mild, meek Burke Marshall would have turned out to be so effective a civil-rights leader? But he did. I *couldn't* see it when Bobby chose Burke Marshall. But Bobby saw something in Burke that none of the rest of us saw. And Burke went. That's good taste in men. Ed Guthman. Bobby's administration of the Department of Justice was first class! First class! So, I wouldn't characterize Bobby as an intellectual. I'd characterize him as something more important: the guy who can use intellectuals.

PETER EDELMAN, *legislative aide*

The law clerks on the Supreme Court used to have various famous people—mostly from the law—to lunch, and we would sit around and talk. Robert Kennedy was invited. We had never had anybody who was a political figure. He came and shook hands with everybody in the room, which I thought was strange because I didn't know people who did that sort of thing. I sat next to him, and during the whole conversation with this guy who I thought was a real toughie, he sat there with his hands absolutely shaking underneath the table, obviously not at all comfortable in the company of these young smart alecks. He was asked tough questions, and he answered them very well. He was particularly good on organized crime and on Hoffa, which we were all skeptical about. So I was quite impressed with him then. Arthur Goldberg had been telling us that he was a much better fellow than the press made him out to be. That was really the first time I ever saw him, and I just had that sort of fleeting, favorable impression.

ALEXANDER M. BICKEL, *lawyer, educator*

One immediately had the sense of a fellow who wasn't afraid of having able people around him and, indeed, of a fellow with a vision of public service that would have done anybody proud. So that was the first thing that one noticed. The rest came more slowly, because naturally, in an office like that, a record is made fairly slowly, and some of it isn't out yet. There were all kinds of decisions. There was the bail reform that was initiated; there was the ultimate attitude that the Department took on wiretapping, for example. His was essentially a proposal to forbid wiretapping, allowing it only in a very limited category of cases involving national security. People will tell you that all wiretapping is evil and that the record shows that Kennedy didn't believe that; he didn't . . . on the record. But I don't think the position of some civil libertarians, which is that wiretapping is all evil and there ought to be none of it, is a tenable one in a world where all men are not angels, unfortunately; all jails are evil too; we live in a real world, where we have to do certain things, and the best we can hope for wiretapping is that it be done decently and in a controlled fashion. In the Hoffa case, his tap on Hoffa's wires was legal and passed judicial muster.

PETER MAAS

He was appalled at the power of organized crime. What affected him most was the mob's ability to corrupt public officials. He became concious of this during the time he was counsel for the McClellan Committee. All these major racketeering figures appeared before the committee, and they all took the Fifth.

When he became Attorney General, he really became the first Attorney General in history who not only cared a great deal about this, but was knowledgeable about it—and could *do* something about it: he had a brother in the White House, which helped considerably, especially with J. Edgar Hoover. When Bobby first became Attorney General, he really thought he could work with Hoover, and he used a very interesting technique. Instead of saying, Why aren't you doing this, that, or the other thing about organized crime? he couched all his approaches to Hoover as if he assumed the FBI was already doing it: Can I have information on this, information on that?

Actually, the whole thrust of the FBI at that time was in matters of internal security. In New York City, over 400 FBI agents were tracking down Reds and infiltrating Communist organizations; only *four* were involved in organized crime, and that job consisted mostly of clipping newspapers. After three years, Bobby had it all switched around. Bobby was responsible in '62 and '63 for the passage of a whole series of anti-racketeering bills that gave the FBI and the other federal agencies much more jurisdiction than they ever had before, and the organized crime section of the FBI became an elite outfit.

RFK's problems were pretty much with the hierarchy at the top of the FBI—and not with the people in the field. I think he had a great admiration for FBI agents; I think his quarrel was really with Hoover.

One of the cornerstones of Hoover's reputation was stopping the Reds. He was very reluctant to give up the Communist menace, because people don't like to throw away a good thing. He'd taken a stance; that was Hoover's big thing. There probably were more FBI agents infiltrating than there were Communists in the party.

BURKE MARSHALL

The real problem that Bob had with Mr. Hoover, I think, was not on the FBI and civil rights; it was because Hoover tried to blame him for practices they had engaged in since at least Justice Clark's tenure as Attorney General—and maybe before that—namely, eavesdropping. Supposedly, the FBI would not institute a tap on telephones without authorization from the Attorney General. As far as I know, they lived up to that. But they also engaged in countless instances of eavesdropping that were illegal; instances that the Attorneys General—not just Kennedy, but his predecessors—were not asked about and did not know about. When their practices became public, in '65 or some time in '66, Hoover tried to blame that on Bob Kennedy.

PETER MAAS

Hoover many times pushed for a wiretap on Martin Luther King. There is a difference between a "bug" and a "wiretap." A bug is something that's put in your room and, at that time, there were no constitutional rules governing it; the FBI didn't have to get any authorization. Wiretapping is an interception of the communication of a telephone, which *is* covered vaguely by FCC regulations, and authorization has to be given by the Attorney General. Hoover had developed the information that one of King's advisers was a member of the Communist Party. So he was a "threat." Hoover kept pushing and pushing. Anyway, with all this pressure from Hoover, Robert Kennedy, as Attorney General, was in a difficult spot. Here, the head of the most respected law-enforcement agency in the world was saying that this associate of King's was practically in bed with the Kremlin. Hoover was, in effect, saying, If you don't authorize this order, you're endangering the country.

In any event, about a month before President Kennedy was assassinated, Bob signed a wiretap authorization. These wiretap authorizations are only good for six months, and then they have to be renewed. Bobby only signed one—six months. Then, the President's assassination. We know what happened to Bobby—the tailspin he went into afterward, and how he tuned out on everything. Okay. Now, time passes. All the way to the Cassius Clay trial on his draft refusal, when an FBI agent testified that there had been an unauthorized electronic eavesdropping on Martin Luther King's phone for *over four and a half years*; he specifically said "unauthorized." There was a big brouhaha about that. Then Hoover, himself, had an interview with a reporter in Washington, and he said that wiretap had been authorized by Robert Kennedy. He was trying to muddy the waters so it looked like Bobby, the ruthless Kennedy, was tapping the show. Hoover was the one who kept it on, of course, though the taps *never* showed anything about King following Communist orders.

ROGER WILKINS, *director of the Community Relations Service, Department of Justice*

I would just go along with what Ramsey Clark has said publicly: that Mr. Hoover just kept pushing Bob, pushing him and pushing him. Finally, Bob said okay. He said, "All right, just to prove to you that it's not true, I'll authorize the tap." My God, a man's privacy is almost sacred. You take away the privacy of the people in this country, and if people begin to talk on their telephones or in their bedrooms or in their

85

homes as if someday what they're saying is going to be a matter of public record . . . well, what have you got left? *What have you got left!?* Dr. King talked to me about that surveillance and I know he knew what they were doing. It troubled him deeply. You don't authorize a tap on somebody's phone just to prove to some other fellow that the guy's not subversive.

ANTHONY LEWIS
Bobby was always very collected about the J. Edgar Hoover business. I can't imagine *most* people reacting to a situation like that, where a supposedly subordinate official of government was totally insubordinate; and not only insubordinate, but nasty and tricky. Most people would be angry, bitter. Bobby always seemed to treat it as a piece of irony. He would say, "Think of that!" or "Look what he's done now!" with a kind of amused amazement. Of great distress to Bobby was Hoover's extraordinary attack on Martin Luther King. Bobby's reaction was, "Isn't it awful? But isn't it part of life? Isn't it terrible that I can't do anything about it?"

BILL BARRY, *campaign aide*
At the Justice Department party, Ethel spoke to J. Edgar Hoover. There was a little electricity between the two of them. On the way out she put in the FBI suggestion box: "Chief Parker of Los Angeles for Director of the FBI."

PETER MAAS
We have a terrible problem—and I'm paraphrasing essentially what Bobby said to me—that you have individual liberties on the one hand, and on the other, you have this really massive underworld operation utilizing every civil-liberty loophole for their own benefit.

RFK was striving to get some middle ground where you would have legalized taps and bugs with stringent controls, involving only certain areas of internal security, of organized crime, and certain specific crimes like kidnaping and murder, and to have these taps authorized on a high court level. But he felt that there ought to be really stiff penalties for people who misused taps. It's extremely dangerous, and I think he was conscious of that. He thought about it as much as anything when he was Attorney General . . . about attempting to reach some middle ground in the hope that, as imperfect as it might be, people couldn't just seize on every single loophole—and the best defense lawyers in the country defending Cosa Nostra chieftains, referring to Samuel Adams and the Constitution, and getting their clients off for immense fees. You can't be too repressive; but on the other hand, you can't have these people walking away with half the country . . . and they *are*. Murray Kempton wrote this piece in which he said the Mafia business was all junk . . . oh, a few dollars here, a few dollars there. What he fails to understand is that the Cosa Nostra is like any feudal society; only a few people at the top make all the money; the rest of them are just peasants. Certainly Kennedy was convinced about the corruption aspect of it. Another Congressman or Senator or whatever always turns up who's in the bag to the mob. And I think that that more than anything in the organized crime area motivated him.

McGEORGE BUNDY, *president, the Ford Foundation*
In many of these things, his function was to go prod and poke people into doing their best, and staying with the problem, and not giving up until we got a better answer. He was that kind of a terrier of a man.

CHARLES BARTLETT, *journalist*
The White House as an institution was sometimes in conflict with the Justice Department as an institution. Occasionally, some in the White House complained that Justice was too independent. For example, I tried to help the President when they got in that trouble with U.S. Steel on the steel price rise. After it was all over, U.S. Steel backed down. Bobby called me and wanted to indict a man I'd dealt with in New York who had been very instrumental in acting as an intermediary between the White House and the U.S. Steel Corporation. I said, "But, Bobby, you can't do that. This man is not a stockholder of U.S. Steel; he's not an official of U.S. Steel. He's just acting in the public interest, and he's trying to help with the problem." Bobby said, "Well, you settle it with Jack."
So I called the President, and told him about it. There was a long pause on the White House end of the line. He said, "You know, what this Administration needs more than anything is an Attorney General we can *fix!*"

ROOSEVELT GRIER, *former professional football player*
I kept thinking it was a fantastic day for campaigning. I thought, The Senator would love this crowd. I could just see him out making that speech. I'd love to have him talk to 'em. That's what I was thinking about. I'd say, "Oh, Senator, you got a crowd out here today. If you just tell them something, you can't miss." Every place we went there was a crowd. I was thinking that if he was out on the platform, he could stand up and say the words that would make everything all right. It'd be good. His kind of crowd.

MICHAEL HARRINGTON, *author*
The fact that the people who watched the train were so predominantly Negro is a function of the political geography of American cities. Negroes live in the areas adjoining the railroad tracks; middle-class and rich people normally don't.

Robert Kennedy, for some reason, had touched such a profoundly responsive chord in poor people. After all the assassinations—John Kennedy, Malcolm X, Martin Luther King, and now Robert Kennedy—I thought that among Negroes, in their grief, there was a desperate feeling that whenever a man in this country, black or white, speaks out for black people, he's shot dead. Certainly there was the feeling that the man who was the Negroes' candidate for President of the United States—no question about it—was no more. Negroes might really come to feel that with Robert Kennedy, they lost their last chance in the white community.

88

I really don't understand it fully. There are other politicians who had a record as good as Kennedy's. There are politicians who had been fighting for civil rights, in a sense, before Robert Kennedy really became concerned. But a part of it, obviously, was the fact that he was his brother's brother. John Kennedy had not done much for Negroes because of the slenderness of his congressional majority and the precariousness of his political position. Yet he is remembered in much the same way as Roosevelt is remembered—as a great savior and friend of the Negro people—and Robert Kennedy benefited from that.

PETE HAMILL, *columnist*

What the hell did he know about blacks? Nothing. He had some vague sympathies, I'm sure, for their plight. But he really learned after he became a Senator, and that was by going into the slums. I was with him one time here in Brooklyn, and we went into some *horrible* tenement that was one of the worst I've ever seen; there was a little girl with a mangled face all torn up. He said, "What happened to her?" The Puerto Rican mother explained that the rats had bitten her face when she was a little baby. That kind of thing is not Spiro T. Agnew . . . "When you see one slum, you've seen them all." That had to affect Bobby. It affected him the way most things did. He was outraged.

I think the blacks understood that he had learned not by going to the New School and looking at seventy-two Gunnar Myrdal charts to tell him about poverty. The blacks know when it's your mouth talking and when it's your heart talking. He learned viscerally. It's been a long time since we've had somebody who felt things in ways that were not just political or intellectual.

HARRIS WOFFORD, *educator*

It had been in May of 1960, before the convention, that Bob said, "I want you to come full-time and develop a civil-rights section of the campaign. I haven't known many Negroes in my life, and we just haven't paid much attention to this front." He said the family representative on this aspect would be Sargent Shriver. "He's the family man on this, and he knows all these things," was somewhat the way he put it. Shriver had been one of the founders of the Catholic interracial movement in the fifties and was considered the house radical.

I was helping Chester Bowles draft the platform. Bowles said,

"Obviously we've got Southerners on the committee, so we don't have a flaming civil-rights majority. But we'd better begin with a maximum plank. We'll draft the plank that says everything we can think of that we *ought* to do at the maximum, and we'll negotiate as much of it as we can."

So we wrote the maximum. Bob, who moved fast on things, had a session with us. We talked through the question of the civil-rights plank and concluded that the Kennedy delegates should be asked to support a strong plank. Then instead of really checking it out with us, when all the Kennedy delegates assembled for the morning meeting, Bob Kennedy got up and said to them—to our amazement—"And now, on the civil-rights plank our position is we go *all out* for the Bowles plank." I felt like saying, "Hey, wait a minute, the Bowles plank is beyond where you really want to go; we wrote it *expecting* it to be cut down." But he had said it, and got an ovation from the delegates. So Bob said again, "Just remember, all the way with the Bowles platform."

When I finally got to Bowles to tell him that the Kennedy word was out to support his *maximum* plank, he couldn't believe it. That's basically how we got this really superstrong civil-rights plank in 1960.

Two items, as I recall, that we felt we were bound to lose in bargaining were the powers we wanted for the Fair Employment Practices Committee, and also the elimination of the literacy tests.

The first test of the Kennedys' civil-rights feelings came when the Martin Luther King affair happened in Atlanta during John F. Kennedy's presidential campaign. There were two episodes. King was first arrested by Atlanta city police under Mayor Hartsfield. I called Morris Abram, who was then an attorney in Atlanta and a friend of Mayor Hartsfield, and said, "King's been in jail five days; and I'm supposed to be a civil-rights man for John Kennedy—and King's old friend—and I haven't been able to do a thing."

Morris said, "This is just the time to call because Mayor Hartsfield has just assembled the Negro leaders of Atlanta, and he's trying to find the right thing to do." I said, "Well, you just tell him to do something to get King out of jail. This is a scandal." He said, "Fine, I'm going right down, and I'll tell him what you said."

About two hours later, he called me and said, "Hold onto your hat. Mayor Hartsfield has just announced that in response to Senator John F. Kennedy's direct personal intervention, he has released Martin Luther King."

That was good for King and I thought was going to be all right for the campaign, but I guessed it was going to be the end of me with the Kennedys. Morris said, "Just a minute, here's Mayor Hartsfield." Mayor Hartsfield came on and said, "Harris. You get through to that young Senator friend of yours, and you tell him that old Bill Hartsfield has just delivered him the election on a silver platter. Please don't pull the rug out from under me. Now I know, Harris, I've run with this a little further than you intended but, boy, I needed a peg, and when you gave it to me, I swung on it." I said, "Well, you know, the Senator still doesn't know anything about this." He said, "I'd guessed that, but you can get through to him before the press does. Okay? I've only *just* announced it to the radio and television."

So I got through to Kennedy's group on the walkie-talkie out in Kansas or somewhere. I got through to Ken O'Donnell or Pierre Salinger, and I heard vile language for a few minutes. They finally got out a statement saying that one of Senator Kennedy's aides had called to inquire about Dr. King's constitutional rights, or something like that. So King was released, but then immediately he was rearrested by the little county court where he had been previously fined and given a suspended sentence for driving with an out-of-state driver's license. He was put in the county jail and sentenced to six months at hard labor. We tried to figure out what to do, how to get him out, what Kennedy should say.

At a certain point we had drafted a very strong statement for Kennedy to issue. The Governor of Georgia said, "Don't issue it and I'll get the son of a bitch out." Kennedy called me and said, "It's been agreed that I won't issue a public statement. The Governor will get King out. After all, we're interested in getting him out, not in making publicity." I said, "Fine." But they didn't get him out. Morris Abram, I believe, managed to get him moved to the state penitentiary, where he'd be safer. They moved him in the middle of the night. Mrs. King called me in near hysteria because she didn't know the reasons for his being moved. All she knew was that about four o'clock in the morning, they'd driven him into cracker country, 150 miles or so. And she was six months pregnant and terribly upset on the phone.

THE REVEREND ANDREW J. YOUNG, *civil-rights leader*
They put him, literally, in some kind of chained-up strait jacket, and put him in the back of a paddy wagon . . . and drove him there in the middle of the night. He didn't know where he was going. All because of a traffic violation.

HARRIS WOFFORD

After Mrs. King hung up, Louis Martin, my chief colleague in the civil-rights section of the campaign, and I were talking about what we were going to do. I said, "If these beautiful and passionate Kennedys would just lose their cool for once and show their passion, maybe Jack would do something like just calling her. He doesn't have to issue a public statement, but just call her and express his sympathy." Louis said, "That's the most beautiful thought I've heard. You don't know what that would do to her and people like me."

So I tried to get through to the Kennedy party but they wouldn't answer me. The last call they had gotten from me was such a surprise and so unpleasant that they probably didn't really want to talk to me again. Then Chester Bowles called on something else and I said, "Mrs. King really needs some word from afar that would encourage her. Why don't you call her?" I knew King admired Bowles. He said, "Wonderful. I'll call her, and as a matter of fact, I'll have Adlai Stevenson call her. He's here for dinner, and we'll both talk to her." I said, "That'll be wonderful; that'll help."

The next morning she called and said, "I bet you put him up to it." Still, she said, it was wonderful to hear Chester Bowles on the phone . . . that he really was concerned. "Nobody of any importance has called or talked to us."

She didn't mention Adlai. Bowles later said, "I tried my best to get Adlai to talk to her, but he said he just couldn't possibly . . . he'd never been introduced to her."

Later that morning, Sarge Shriver called. I said, "Look, I couldn't get through to your brother-in-law. But it's all right because Chester Bowles has already called Mrs. King." I kind of teased him. I'd basically given up the idea of getting through to Kennedy. But Shriver said, "Why do you think it's too late? It's a great idea."

He told me later that he drove out to O'Hare Inn at about eighty miles an hour, and the whole gang was there: the Senator, O'Donnell, O'Brien, Sorensen, Salinger—all of them. He said he knew if he brought it up and there was a committee discussion, nothing would happen. So he waited. Ted Sorensen went off to work on a speech; Pierre went out to the press, and finally only O'Donnell was there, and then *he* left. Shriver said to Kennedy, "I know you don't want to issue a public state-ment . . . but have you thought of calling Mrs. King?" Jack looked up and said, "That's a wonderful idea. Do you have her number?" Shriver dialed and got her. Jack was great on the phone.

The next thing I knew, Morris Abram called and said, "It's happened. Old Dr. King, Martin's father, who signed a Republican ad the week before for Nixon, has just come in and said, 'If any man will wipe the tears from my daughter-in-law's eyes, I'll vote for him, even though I don't want a Catholic. But I'll take a Catholic or the Devil himself if he'll wipe the tears from my daughter-in-law's eyes. I've got a suitcase full of votes—my whole church—for you to give to Senator Kennedy.'"

At this point, Bob Kennedy called Louis Martin and me in, and he lashed us back and forth. He said, "You bomb throwers probably lost the election. You've probably lost three states. From now on in, the civil-rights section isn't going to do another damn thing in this campaign."

Bob went on to New England. The next night, David Brinkley called me and said, "There's a crazy story coming over the wire that now a brother of the Senator has intervened, and called the Judge directly to get King released." I thought, Which brother? Ted wouldn't do it; he's in California and doesn't know anything about this whole thing. Shriver, they might mean . . . but Shriver would certainly call and talk to us before he did anything like that. As for Bob, well, he'd just conveyed his opinion on the whole thing. So I said, "It just can't be true, David." He said, "Well, we're going on the air in about ten minutes. Should I disregard this story?" And I said, "I just can't believe it."

So, he disregarded the story and, of course, it turned out to be true. It was Bob. Later that evening he called John Seigenthaler and told him that he had called the Judge that morning. John had asked, "After what you told Harris and Louis yesterday? What do you mean?" And Bob had told John, "Well, I couldn't get to sleep. I was so sore at that cracker Georgia Judge putting a decent American in jail and sentencing him to six months on a hard-labor gang for driving with an out-of-state driver's license, when it was actually because he was black and fighting for civil rights. I just got so mad that I got that Judge on the phone and said, 'Are you an American or not? If you're an American, you get that man out of jail.'"

JOHN SEIGENTHALER, *campaign aide, editor,* Nashville Tennessean

Bob called in. I said, "Guess what that crazy Judge in Georgia's done?" He said, "What's that?" I said, "He put out a statement saying you had called him and criticized him for arbitrary use of judicial power. He thinks you're a young whippersnapper sticking your nose into the judicial process of the State of Georgia. I told the press section of the National Committee that you didn't do any such thing as that and for them to issue a denial." A long pause on the phone. He said, "Well, I did. I came up on the airplane, and I thought about it. I had some reading to do and I couldn't do the work." You know, he frequently carried a big bundle of work, and even in those days, wherever he went, he carried this work with him. He said, "I thought about it and I kept thinking that it was so outrageous. When I got off the airplane, I'd made up my mind that somebody had to talk to that Judge."

RAMSEY CLARK, *Attorney General of the United States*
We came in with a high level of commitment to civil rights but probably started fairly slowly. The action tended to begin with the Freedom Riders early that summer of 1961. That presented very difficult challenges to new people who had just moved into office: What do you do? If it had happened in '58 or '59, and there had been an experience of departmental attitude toward it, you'd have a base of experience from which to make a judgment. But here, all of a sudden, we had this new phenomenon . . . and we had responsibility. The first thing we knew, Byron White and Bill Orrick had on these white helmets and were down in Montgomery and places like that with the Freedom Riders, and John Seigenthaler was getting knocked down and one thing and another. Different people had different reactions to the Freedom Rides. I would say the dominant reaction in the Department of Justice was: Why are they doing this? Why are they making so much trouble for us? Why don't they stay home?

I don't think there was any lack of sympathy for what they were trying to achieve as their ends. But there was real concern about the means—the risk. Buses were burned. We just didn't know what was going to happen. And we were terribly frightened that there might be physical violence and deaths. That was the chief concern. The other concern was: Does this make any sense? I mean, Is this the way to go about it to achieve an end? Some of us said, Why can't we litigate? Why can't we sue and accomplish all this? What is typical of actions of this type through history is that the people's sense of urgency was greater than leadership's . . . events kind of swept it away.

But I think you'd have to say from hindsight that leadership handled a very difficult problem very sensitively. We don't realize it so much any more, but public opinion was overwhelmingly against the Freedom Riders coming down from the North. They looked like troublemakers.

94

Why should they go all the way down there just to use a restroom that's been segregated, or a waiting room in a bus station? They seemed to be a kind of busybody. "That's not your place. You don't live down there."

National insensitivity to the denial of civil rights made the country think that this was a bunch of foolishness. Well, that made it difficult for the Department . . . and difficult for Bob. The President had won by a very slender margin. The South had given him electoral votes. And Bob was the brother of the President. He was so closely identified with the President that many people thought that what he did tended to involve the President to a higher degree than if some stranger had been doing it. In fact, I think it worked the other way. I think Bob became a lightning rod for the President, and drew away from him a lot of the antipathy that comes from doing your duty, particularly in the civil-rights area.

BURKE MARSHALL, *attorney*
At first, the Freedom Riders went through the South without much notice. But then in Anniston, Alabama, in early May, they were attacked and their bus was burned, and some of them were beaten. When they got to Birmingham, that happened again. Then nobody from the bus company would drive the bus from Birmingham to Montgomery. It stayed in Birmingham for a week, sitting there.

Bob Kennedy would say to the Greyhound representative, "Why can't you get someone to put guards on the bus?"

"Well, no one will do it. The union won't let them," and so forth.

"How many bus drivers do you have?"

He'd say, "Two thousand bus drivers," or whatever it was.

"You mean you can't get one of them to drive that bus?"

Bob didn't know this guy's name; he kept calling him "Mr. Greyhound."

Finally we made an arrangement with Governor Patterson and the bus company to get the damn bus moved out of Birmingham into Montgomery. But as soon as it got to Montgomery, the state protection withdrew and the Montgomery police turned it over to the mob; the Freedom Riders were beaten up—some of them very severely. John Seigenthaler went down there on behalf of Bob Kennedy, and he was beaten up. When this happened, we brought a lawsuit and got a court order. But unless you reoccupied the entire South, it was difficult to see how you could protect every bus that moved through. There was the question whether to let the buses go through Mississippi without the

Army protecting them. A lot of people said, Well, you can't do that. Then Senator Eastland and some people in Mississippi said, "We will see that those people are protected."

We decided to accept Eastland's commitment. It worked. There was a changing of the guard at the border between Alabama and Mississippi. The Mississippi Highway Patrol picked up the buses and escorted them through to Jackson, you know, with a whole lot of helicopters and press people. These people in the buses rode through Mississippi at ninety miles an hour. Absurd spectacle!

JOHN MAGUIRE, *educator*

In April of '61, I chanced onto Martin Luther King on a plane flying from Newark to Ithaca . . . to Cornell, where he was a visiting lecturer and I was a backup speaker. On that flight, he half seriously said, "We may need you some time. I've just come from a meeting with Robert Kennedy at the Justice Department. The civil-rights leadership has called his attention to the fact that the whole area of public transportation—particularly the use of terminal facilities in the South—could, by simply having the Interstate Commerce Commission reaffirm the language of its charter—which is pre-1896—avoid all the kind of litigation that went on for so long in the educational field." Robert Kennedy's reply, as Martin reported it, had been that the ICC was probably the slowest moving of all regulatory agencies, and that even if he appealed to them to do this, it would probably take three or four years of hearings. The civil-rights leaders were understandably angry at this response. The whole point of the meeting was premised on the fact that the Negro vote had elected John Kennedy. This was the first of the kind of positive responses they felt they should have.

Well, I said I'd help. So, we talked about that and the fact that Bayard Rustin and Jim Farmer of their group raised the possibility of putting together an interracial group that would use public buses and go down through the South and attempt to sit-in as a racially mixed group at lunch counters and use restaurant facilities and restrooms.

The next thing I read, like everybody else, was about the Freedom Rides. The fateful day came on Mother's Day in '61, when the Freedom Ride group attempted to go from Atlanta to Birmingham. They went on two buses. One was overturned and set on fire in Anniston, Alabama, about halfway; the other group got through to the Birmingham terminal where the police simply withdrew and let them be beaten mercilessly. At that point, it looked as if the experiment of the Freedom

Ride was over because the people were just in no shape to go on. Then the black students in Nashville began picking it up, coming from Fisk University—the group that eventually emerged as the real leaders. All through the week they tried, but were always repulsed and ferried in cars back to the Tennessee state line. They'd go back to Nashville and make another attempt the next day. Finally on Saturday, the word came through from the then Governor of Alabama, Patterson, to simply let them come on through. A huge crowd had gathered at the Montgomery terminal. They were allowed to pass through Birmingham on down to Montgomery. There, they were really beaten horribly. John Lewis was one of the people involved, and there are vivid pictures of him lying there with his head split, blood all over his face, with the Attorney General of Alabama, McDonald Gallion, down on his knees, reading an injunction to him. The poor guy was nearly unconscious. I believe that was the day that Robert Kennedy's friend John Seigenthaler had his head cracked as an observer for the Justice Department.

I was down celebrating a birthday with Bill Coffin, the Yale chaplain, and we were speaking very bravely, that if anything happened to the Freedom Riders, we would go down and keep this thing going, which was, in a way, real bravura because up to that point, no representative white clergy or teachers had gotten into it . . . except for people who were professional pacifists or Quakers or reconciliation people.

Martin was at Ralph Abernathy's house in Montgomery. So, we put in a call and said, "Martin, you remember in April when you said such and such?" "Yes." "Well, how would you feel about our coming?" He was marvelous: "Well, I don't want to put any pressure on you, but we need every bit of help we can get." Some kind of thing like that, which clinched it as far as I was concerned. I knew I had to go. So, the next day, there was a rally on the New Haven green in sympathy for the Freedom Riders. I remember quite vividly speaking on the green and ending up dramatically that the cars were waiting.

In our group we had a black law student, George Smith, who subsequently went with the Legal Defense Fund; a guy named Gaylord Noyce, who was then assistant to the Dean of the Yale Divinity School; David Swift, just turning fifty, marvelous kind of Lincolnesque character who was my chairman at Wesleyan. When I went in to tell him I was going, he quietly said, "Well, don't you need somebody to go with you?" I said, "Well, yeah. But I was going to see if some Young Turks around here would go." He said, "I think I'd better go." I always thought of him as a kind of pillar of convention in some ways. He said,

"But let me call Jane"—his wife—"and see what she thinks." So he called, and I thought, Oh, Lord. They'll have to have a long discussion over the phone. He called and said, "Jane. John's here. He's going on the Freedom Ride, and I think I should go with him. What do you think?" No more than thirty seconds had elapsed when he put the phone down and said, "Let's go." And I said, "Well, what did she say?" "She said, 'Be sure and take your glasses off and put them in your glasses' case.' "

I've always treasured that. Anyhow, the five of us—the Connecticut Five—made our way down on the plane; we got to the Atlanta airport, where we found two black students, Charlie Jones and Clyde Carter. They had just finished their term at Johnson Smith Seminary in North Carolina, and they were coming down also to join the Rides. We said, "Look. We've only got one black man with us—George Smith. Why don't you kind of come with us, and we'll cast lots together?" So then we were seven: four whites, three blacks.

In Atlanta we stayed at a place called The Waluhaje—a Negro apartment-motel. I was just chattering nonstop to belie my apprehensions; I was reminding the brethren that all these names meant something in Choctaw Indian. "Alabama" means "Here we rest." "Sylacauga" means "By the waters." "Tuscaloosa" means "At the head of the river." They asked me what "Waluhaje" meant in Choctaw. I said, "Well, I don't know. It's obviously a Choctaw name." I went up to the man at the desk. I said, "What does Waluhaje mean in Choctaw?" He looked at me. He said, "Man, that's just the first two letters of the last names of the four guys that built this place!"

I was totally discredited for my knowledge of the Deep South; whenever I would try to fill the brethren in with local color, they would say, "Ya, there goes that Choctaw again!"

After a news conference, at noon at the Ebenezer Church in Atlanta, the Kings' church, we went down to the bus terminal. The hostility was incredible! The people were just glaring at us as we boarded the bus in Atlanta. We really felt fairly safe in Georgia. They were hostile crowds, sullen . . . but standing quite a distance away when we would get down and take a rest stop. The State Highway Patrol accompanied the bus to the Georgia state line; then we really had the feeling we were being thrown to the wolves.

The towns in Alabama on the way to Montgomery were mill towns where one-third of the male population was free at any time for riot duty. The towns were organized around textile manufacturing, and the toughs in T shirts were out. In a couple of these towns, they came right to the bus with sticks in hand and beat on the side, "Come out, you Nigger-lovers!" Coffin, who was not a great exponent of nonviolence in those days, said, "By God, I wish I had my pearl-handled revolver." He had served on General Patton's staff during World War II, and had a vision of going out and shooting these guys. I had to keep reminding him of the spirit of nonviolence, and that furthermore, pragmatically, it would be very wise if he would sit down and not show his head in the window.

George Smith—this black student—all the time was studying for his exams at Yale . . . and he *never* looked up from his book, no matter how loud the commotion! They would beat on the bus with their sticks. So George Smith, throughout all this chaos, and in each town it got worse, was reading this law book, never looking up. . . . Finally, when we got there, I said, "George, what was the book?" The title was *Future Interests*, which is apparently a technical legal subject . . . but really was the whole point of this man being down there.

We arrived in Montgomery at about five o'clock. There had been such elaborate and continuous radio coverage . . . particularly that these whites from the North were there . . . that our movements were covered by commercial radio. It looked like the whole town had turned out. Between 3,000 and 5,000 people were circling the bus terminal when we arrived. It's in an indentation; it's down, almost like driving into a pit. I whispered to Bill, "I know how the early Christians felt in the arena."

We had arranged before we left Atlanta to be met at the bus terminal by Ralph Abernathy and Wyatt Walker, who would come in two cars and carry off the seven of us to Abernathy's home. Well, the military were all around: about 500 soldiers with bayonets, restraining an angry crowd and looking like they would love to have . . . you had the feeling . . . run us through with their bayonets. It was a torridly hot, sunshiny day, late May in Alabama. The sweat was just pouring down inside our suits. We lined up alongside this silver Greyhound bus like a rogues' gallery—seven of us spread out—and Abernathy nowhere in sight. We were out there about twenty minutes in this extraordinarily tense situation, with bricks occasionally being lobbed over, sort of trying to smile, and very frightened.

Finally the soldiers parted, and two cars, one of them an old Chevrolet, came in under a hail of rocks to pick us up. Ralph was driving the first one. The reporters, of course, were there, the TV cameras grinding away. As we got in the cars, a reporter ran up to Ralph and said, "Have you heard what Robert Kennedy, the Attorney General, has just said?" Ralph said, "No. I haven't been listening to the radio." He said, "Well, John Kennedy is in Vienna right now, holding these initial conferences with Khrushchev; he says that he urges you to stop the Freedom Rides, because he says that this kind of thing is embarrassing him in Vienna." And Abernathy's beautiful answer: "Well, doesn't the Attorney General know that we've been embarrassed all our lives?"

We went over to Abernathy's home. Abernathy's six-year-old son looked at Bill Coffin and asked, "White man, are you going to hurt me?" We had a great chicken supper, and talked, and collected ourselves a little bit. Robert Kennedy and Martin were in direct telephone communication. That was one of the interesting features . . . that Byron White, who was then a deputy of Robert Kennedy's, was down with Governor Patterson over at the Governor's Mansion, less than a mile from Abernathy's house. Here we were over at Abernathy's house, talking to Robert Kennedy in Washington . . . White and the Governor talking to Robert Kennedy . . . but no one would complete the third leg of the communications triangle and call over that one mile! We all had to go through Washington.

By about midnight, Robert Kennedy made a proposal to Martin King. It was that if Dr. King would call off the Freedom Rides, he would honor Dr. King's counterproposal *if* he could get a pledge from Governor Patterson that night, and within the next few days from the Governors of the other Deep Southern states, that at some predetermined time there would be desegregated use of terminal facilities. The stupid thing about Patterson was that he wouldn't agree to that. Oh, he wouldn't promise these Niggers anything! He actually talked that way. So, by about one o'clock in the morning, Martin came in and said, "Well, men. We've got a very simple decision here. We're not going to be able to work out an arrangement with the Attorney General; we're really just faced with the simple issue, Do you want to go on? . . . on to Jackson?" Before we could say anything, he said, "Let's just have a word of prayer about that."

I stood there and just wept. The black men got down on their knees . . . and one by one, the white men got down on their knees. A lot of silence . . . and then Ralph prayed and Martin prayed. Then Martin said, "Now, don't decide right now. You all go off by yourselves and talk about it yourselves. We don't want to put any pressure on you to do this." So we went in and talked, and we decided it was such a tense situation that we would vote secret ballot. It was simple: if you wanted to go on with it, put yes. That business about embarrassing the President really weighed heavily on us; I mean that really gave us pause. No question about it. So we went and slept on it a few hours, fitfully. We came back in the morning, and Dave Swift passed out the pieces of paper and we all wrote. The staggering thing when we counted them: seven yeses! It was just great. We all jumped around and hugged each other. So then we had to call the military, General Graham's office, to escort us back to the bus station to resume the journey.

We were arrested before we even got going. We got down to the bus station and bought our tickets to Jackson, expecting to go. Dr. King had that morning flown back to Atlanta. Ralph Abernathy, Wyatt Walker, Bernard Lee, and Fred Shuttlesworth took the seven of us down. We said, "Well, let's sit down and have a parting cup of coffee. If we're going to test this thing, let's test it now." Well, as soon as we sat down in the terminal and ordered Cokes or coffee, the Sheriff of Montgomery County swept in and put us all under arrest; we were plunked into the paddy wagon. People just cheered. There were great numbers of them ringing that bus station even though the city was under martial law. We were taken to jail, fingerprinted. In jail, we were segregated. The blacks had to go on one side, and we had to go on the other.

So there we were in jail. Later in court, as the case developed, the general was asked why he had arrested *us*. He'd let a racially mixed group go the very day of our arrival. He said, "I was so furious because I thought if I finally got that first bunch of roughnecks out, it would all be over!" His outrage was to suddenly realize that it was never going to be over! That there would *always* be somebody coming in and demanding this basic and simple thing just infuriated him . . . coupled with the fact that a number of our group were preachers. Why are they coming down here to preach to *me*?

By leaning out of the jail window, through the bars, I could point out to the guys the house where I was born. I had been born right there in Montgomery. It tickled them . . . very moving. My grandfather had been a jurist—Judge Merrill of Alabama—and his son, my mother's oldest brother, was on the Alabama Supreme Court. One of the ironies is that a year and a half later, he had to disqualify himself because he was ruling on a case involving his own nephew. I kept telling them about my Uncle Bud: "He'll come see us. I'm sure Uncle Bud will come down here." Well, Uncle Bud had *no* desire whatsoever to be identified with his erring nephew. . . . The guys with me told me that they thought Uncle Bud was like the historical Jesus: a lot of people *talked* about him, but they had never seen him with their own eyes. They really doubted there *was* an Uncle Bud. Months later, when we were down to one of the trials, I *forced* them to go by the Supreme Court building and *see* the name written up there: "The Honorable Pelham J. Merrill, Cleburne County Supreme Court Justice."

Of course, all this, being put in jail, had quite an effect on my family. The local stations were playing up this John Maguire, son of Dr. John Maguire, grandson of Judge Walter Merrill . . . and sounding absolutely incredulous that this nice Southern boy should have obviously flipped out and done this strange thing! And so the Baptist preacher . . . my grandmother later told me this . . . appeared on a hot May day in a black serge suit that he wore just for ceremonial occasions— principally funerals—and he said, "Mrs. Merrill, have you heard about your grandson?" She said, "Yes. Yes, I have." And then he said, "I came over to have prayer with you." He opened up his little book and began reading the office that you read when there's been a *death* in the family, as if literally I had died. I asked my grandmother why she didn't interrupt him. She said she was so perplexed herself at that point that she appreciated all of the consolation she could get: divine support and succor.

That was the way it was greeted. On one of our subsequent trips down to the trial in Montgomery, the Montgomery *Advertiser* had as its editorial one day: "The South has its Benedict Arnolds too." That day was Benedict Arnold's birthday. It started off: "Today in County Court of Montgomery County, one of our own Benedict Arnolds is back. . . ." It went into a little history of my background and said: "And so, John Maguire joins that despicable group of rebel turncoats: Tallulah Bankhead, William Faulkner, Tennessee Williams. . . ."

After it was all over . . . a few days after we got out of jail . . . we got to Atlanta at three o'clock in the morning to get a flight back to New York. We were the *only* people in the plane. As soon as we walked on the plane one of the stewardesses threw a pillow at us, and we got into this jolly, just insane, giggly pillow fight. We were slinging these pillows at the stewardesses and carrying on! Except George Smith. He just sat there reading his law books! Finally I said, "George, how come you're not getting in the pillow fight?" He said, "Ain't no black man goin' to throw a pillow at a white woman down here in the airport in Atlanta, Georgia!"

People often ask about the Freedom Rides: *Were* they a success?

All social historians of the movement of the sixties credit them with different things . . . released fresh energies, almost in sort of geometrical growth. But the important thing is that Robert Kennedy in April had said that even if he initiated hearings in the ICC the next day, he could not get the ICC to move for three or four years—that was his prediction. Because of the pressure of the Freedom Rides, they began hearings on August first; on September first, they made the decision that on October first all heating in buses would be without reference to race, color, creed, and all carriers would have to have that sign in the buses . . . in all the terminals, the "colored" and "white" signs had to come down at the fountains and at the restrooms. So here was a classic instance where the pressure of concerned people simply moved the government much faster—infinitely faster—than otherwise would have been the case.

PETER MAAS, *author*
I think Bob changed on the day that his administrative assistant—and now editor of the Nashville *Tennessean*—John Seigenthaler, got hit over the head in Montgomery. I was in his office right afterward. He was possessed by an enormous anger, but not so much physical as that he looked like he'd just been poleaxed *himself*. He took it as if he had been down in Montgomery himself and been hit.

Bob didn't change except through experience. I remember him talking about the civil-rights situation before that time, a few days after he had become the Attorney General, and he said no, he didn't anticipate too much trouble in this area. I asked him, thinking of Little Rock, "Do you think you'd ever anticipate the time when you'd have to send troops to the South?" He said no, he didn't. He felt men were reasonable.

RAMSEY CLARK
About a year after the Freedom Rides the Meredith case came up. It was an important part of the history of the early sixties . . . more than a footnote. Somehow, it seemed to epitomize the real immensity of the struggle: the legal, social and political, and finally, violent. . . . Guys like John Doar and Jim McShane and Burke Marshall and those great fellows had spent months on it . . . many months. The rest of us were doing our regular business until, I guess, Saturday, the 29th of September 1962. You could feel that what you had feared was coming—a real, emotional buildup down there—a feel of movement toward the University of Mississippi at Oxford.

BURKE MARSHALL

James Meredith decided, for his own reasons, that he was going to go to the University of Mississippi. Nobody in the government talked him into that. In fact, I was always told by Medgar Evers and by Thurgood Marshall, who was in charge of the Legal Defense Fund at that time, that they hadn't chosen Meredith as a test case. They had other things to do, and I doubt they thought that integrating Mississippi was the greatest idea. But, in any event, he wanted to do it, and it was his prerogative. Once he had decided, all sorts of things flowed from it. We didn't get really involved until the beginning of 1962. I told Bob Kennedy that Meredith was going to end up at the University of Mississippi, and he had better be prepared.

In the meantime, there were really outrageous legal proceedings going on, with the federal Judge in Mississippi isssuing the most extraordinary series of stay orders, all of them overruled by the Fifth Circuit during the summer of '62. The Justice Department intervened in the case because we wanted to get some sort of control over what happened, to influence what kinds of orders were issued to make sure that they were adequate and that the university officials in the first place, and the State of Mississippi secondly, understood . . . I mean so that even if they didn't accept it, at least they understood what their obligations were. They never did accept it. The university finally did, but the State never did.

NICHOLAS DeB. KATZENBACH, *Under Secretary of State*

Bobby's final words to me as I headed for Ole Miss—"If things get rough, don't worry about yourself; the President needs a moral issue."

RAMSEY CLARK

The decision was whether to go in with Meredith on Monday morning. That's when you usually register. We decided that we ought to go in on Sunday afternoon. So much of the risk of violence is really psychological; once you are in, the pressure dissipates and is released. We set up a command post in Bob's outer office on Sunday.

One of the things about that day was the long delay in moving the 101st Airborne, General Billingslea's group, stationed just south of Memphis. There was this *terrible* delay in getting them started after the marshals had been pretty much encircled there in front of the administration building, and tear gas had been used. We couldn't get the Army moving fast enough. We thought we were going to run out of tear gas for a long time there. If we had run out of gas, then there would have been no way of keeping the groups separated. If they had not been separated, there would have been real violence.

I was on the phone in Washington; twice Nick Katzenbach asked whether the marshals could draw their guns. I would ask Bob in the White House. We had open lines. We'd discuss the situation. The word both times was "No." Pretty hard decision to make in Washington. There had been a very violent night down in Mississippi, with two deaths already. Nick wasn't recommending it. The marshals wanted to. We all thought that unless there was a clear and present danger to life, pistols should not be drawn. Of course, a man had authority to draw his gun only if he was being fired directly upon, or for self-defense, or to save a life. The marshals' request was for purposes of appearance and to avoid potential assault, rather than an actual assault. And the decision was no both times. Bob said later . . . and I think he was right . . . that those were the most critical decisions and moments of the evening. You don't know what would have happened if they had drawn their guns. There's something very frightening about a pistol. Of course, the marshals were outnumbered four or five to one. To have them draw their pistols might have drawn fire from the rifles and the shotguns out in the crowd. . . .

JAMES MEREDITH, *law student*

A lot of troops were used to get me in the University of Mississippi. Really a lot of troops . . . I mean I don't think the Russians sent that many into Czechoslovakia. It seemed to me very clear that Bobby Kennedy was the main man in determining that these steps be taken. Had they not made the decisions they made, the course of my life would have been different. Bobby sent the marshals. He could have sent just two. His decisions kept me alive. I'm still here.

6

SAUL STEINBERG, *artist*

I can talk only about television and photography because, sitting and watching the train go south, this is what I saw, and whatever emotion comes with it is superficial . . . what's called a blackmail emotion, a *grand guignol* or TV emotion. The one simple fact was the railway engine coming at you, with one black eye in the center of it. This was the electric light, the lighted beam of the train, which on photography because of its brightness appears black. That's a photographic phenomenon. And there was something curious about this coat of arms—the shape of the front of the locomotive advancing, with this menacing black eye surrounded by white glimmer . . . which gave, of course, a mournful expression to this Cyclops. The train made its mournful whistle. It's always mournful and tragic and very appropriate. By comparison, the European whistle is hysterical, more high-pitched, and it's slightly comical. The American horn is nostalgic and sad, tragic.

STANLEY LEVISON, *attorney*

While the train was proceeding to Washington, we were watching it on television and, at points, listening but not looking at the screen. At one point I *heard* the commentator saying, "The people are lined up along the tracks . . . particularly black people. They have built bonfires for miles, and the train is proceeding within the parallel lines of bonfires." I called to my wife and said, "This is extraordinary. I expected something, but I didn't expect this!" Then, as she came in to listen, the

106

commentator concluded, saying, "And so, the train bearing the body of Abraham Lincoln reached Washington."

CHARLOTTE CURTIS, *journalist*
I wrote down some notes: "Outside it was sunny, and there were groups of adults and children among the wastes of New Jersey. It's seventy-four degrees, according to a thermometer on the Commercial Solvent." It must have been a company out there. "Passed Sherwin Williams paints with 'The Paint That Covers the World.' Newark. Slowly through Newark, but never stopping. Then there's a blast from the whistle—one long blast, then another. Women in that kind of universal gesture of horror: their hands over their faces."

IVANHOE DONALDSON, *fellow, Institute for Policy Studies*
Every once in a while the train would go under a trestle; and there, standing there all by himself, would be a cop . . . quietly standing and saluting the train. These guys didn't have to do that. Obviously, he was out there by himself, you know, he could be *sitting* for all he cared. But there he was. I remember seeing cops holding young children in their arms so that they could see the train clearly—oftentimes, black kids. I just thought, People can be so damn human sometimes, and so destructive at other times. I couldn't understand. I was trying to place the image of that cop . . . obviously moved, some of them crying, some of them holding children, some of them quietly by themselves a hundred yards from anybody else, saluting the train in the ultimate of privacy, you know, and not trying to be visible . . . and yet the image I have of cops, you know, well I couldn't correlate the two. That was the train ride for me. It was like Martin Luther King. It was trying to bridge the gap between the dream and reality. There was the dream, all along the train tracks. But yet, in the last car, in that caboose, was the reality.

RAMSEY CLARK, *Attorney General of the United States*
The Kennedys were sympathetic with Dr. King from the beginning. It was the same with Cesar Chavez. These men were in their earliest days, in the national sense, unpopular figures. We don't remember that today. Dr. King is generally revered in America today, but in 1960 and 1961 he wasn't. There was no real awareness of the civil-rights problems. The bus boycott seemed to most Americans an absurd and remote thing:

107

What are those people doing? Who needs the buses the most? The poor blacks. They don't have a car. How are they going to get from one side of town to another? Who are they really hurting by boycotting the buses? It was a mystery to people.

But before we came into the Department, there was a sympathy and an understanding and respect between the Kennedys and Dr. King, which translated into the Department of Justice's attitude quite quickly from the very beginning. I had no idea at that time that Dr. King was a great man. I just had no basis for thinking that. Now I think that he was one of the truly great men that the country has produced. The Kennedys knew that at that time.

STANLEY LEVISON

It's interesting to compare Joe Kennedy senior and Martin Luther King's father. Joe Kennedy was determined that his sons should attain political importance, and he put his vast wealth and his connections and prestige behind them. That can't be said for Martin's father. Martin's father didn't finance any of Martin's activities; nor did he have that kind of determination that Martin must get to the top. Indeed, for the first five years of Martin's public career, his father was urging him not to try to be a national leader. He finally gave up, realizing that Martin felt this was his destiny and he had to do it. But Daddy King never charted that kind of course for Martin. He accepted it. He adjusted himself to it. That's the difference I see between the two.

But it's interesting. Martin could be described as an intensely guilt-ridden man. The most essential element in the feelings of guilt was that he didn't feel he deserved the tribute he got. He was an actor in history at a particular moment that called for a personality; he had been selected as that personality. If he had been less humble, he could have lived with this great acclaim; but as it was, he always thought of ways in which he could somehow live up to it; he talked about taking a vow of poverty; getting rid of everything he owned—including his house—so that he could at least feel that nothing material came to him from his efforts. The fact is that when he died, the amount of material goods he left was *extremely* small for a man of such enormous public stature. Possibly the most valuable properties were derivative—the royalties on his speeches and written works. Other than that, he owned very little. Although he was often accused of having Cadillacs and a mansion, he never owned anything better than a Pontiac . . . and that was a very old one. He had a house . . . but the most impressive thing about it was the size of its mortgage.

Even the house troubled him greatly. When he moved from a very small house to one large enough to give his growing family some room, he was troubled by it, and would ask his close friends whether they didn't think it was too big. To him, it loomed as a mansion, and he searched in his own mind for ways of making it smaller. Martin found it difficult to live comfortably in his house because he had such a sensitive conscience and such a sense of humility. It comes from his whole background. He was born in what white people would call a middle-class family; but in black life, it's an upper-class family . . . at *least* upper-middle-class. His high-school graduation present was a convertible; for a black family, that's a very handsome kind of present.

So Martin was always aware that he was privileged; that he had enjoyed a better education by far than a Southern Negro can hope for; that through his education, his way had been very comfortable at all times . . . and this troubled him. He felt he didn't deserve this. One reason he was so determined to be of service was to justify the privileged position he'd been born into. He came out of college and almost immediately walked into national and international leadership—with the point of view that he had never deserved and earned the position. It resulted in a continual series of blows to his conscience, and this kept him a very restive man all his life.

THE REVEREND ANDREW J. YOUNG, *civil-rights leader*
There was always a strange kind of affection between Bobby Kennedy and Dr. King. While they didn't have a great deal of contact, King always felt that there was something very genuine about Bobby. He never thought that the Kennedys knew all the answers, or that they were, you know, born great. But he used to contrast the Kennedys and the Johnson Administration—that when you talked with the Kennedy Administration, they would listen and you would do most of the talking; when you talked with the Johnson Administration, you would listen and they would do most of the talking.

In some ways I avoided meeting Bobby deliberately, because I thought he was probably basically decent, but I had to avoid becoming a camp follower. Anyway, that's my idea with big political people. I guess I didn't want to get captured; the period was not one in history for black leaders to get overenthusiastic about any white politician. Our independence is a political and cultural necessity. But Bobby Kennedy was very easy to get enthusiastic about: he said all the right things; he had a way of coming through in a clutch.

JOHN SEIGENTHALER, *campaign aide, editor,* Nashville Tennessean

I wouldn't say they always agreed. Bob recognized the need for dramatic manifestations of civil-rights work, but also the need for a very basic and pragmatic approach to the political problem involved. When they got to talking about voting rights, for example, Bob would say to King, "You know, there are some areas in the South where Negroes are now permitted to register to vote, and a voter-registration drive would bring about a substantial increase in the number of Negroes who register to vote, and the result of *that* would be that some of the politicians wouldn't be so fresh in that area, if they knew they had to face up to that black vote. They don't vote."

King recognized that, but I think his emphasis was: Well, they *can't* vote in McCullough, Mississippi, and if we're going to arouse the conscience of the nation, we need to go to McCullough, Mississippi, where nobody is allowed to vote, and create a dramatic demonstration there so that people all over the country will recognize it.

Bob said, "That's fine. But don't overlook the fact that in Baton Rouge, Louisiana right now, where they *can* vote, there are only forty per cent of the black people registered, and if somebody would go in there and just give them a little encouragement, we'd have eighty per cent."

From where each was sitting, there was a slight shade of difference in their approach to problems. But each recognized the good faith of the other.

JOHN MAGUIRE, *educator*

They were going to picket the Justice Department. King started walking toward the building, and Robert Kennedy came bounding down the steps and got in line with them, and linked arms, and walked up the last hundred yards or so. . . . That sure does take the wind out of your sails! It's hard to preach to a man who's come down and got in line with you!

DR. VINCENT HARDING, *educator*

I remember Martin constantly being amazed at the naïveté, and—on some levels—the coldness of the analysis that was coming out of the White House. On the one hand, he really hoped that he could believe in people like Bobby; and on the other hand, a certain black wisdom told him that he had better not try to believe in them. Very often he talked about how *unfeeling* they seemed to be about the legal situation, and how hesitant they were to move in the situation.

MARIAN WRIGHT EDELMAN, *civil-rights attorney*
The whole thing was just *so* 19th century and just *so* uncontrolled and *so* without any law. If anything was going to survive in the community, the government had to take an active role. But, in fact, we couldn't get them to do it. Young organizers and community people would see horrible things, and call up friends in the Justice Department and say, "Do something," and meet the response of: "Call us back when somebody gets shot or the bomb actually goes off." If we got a tip that the Ku Klux Klan was going to plant a bomb, then obviously the instinct was to call the FBI and say, "Could you—ah—protect us?" But, you know, they'd say, "Sorry. Call us back when something happens." You know, "Thanks a lot!" In fact, a Justice Department lawyer was called the night of the Philadelphia slayings of Schwerner, Chaney and Goodman, when somebody *thought* this was going to happen, *had* a tip-off . . . and the lawyer just went back to sleep. This happened at least a hundred times over a two-year period, and it just didn't make for very good relationships.

As for the role that Bob Kennedy played as Attorney General, I am quite aware of his political problems. It wasn't Kennedy's fault; he was the symbol. Kennedy understood that the government was doing nothing. He perceived the impact of the disappointed expectations again and again. It resulted in SNCC going the way it went. Originally, the SNCC kids were the *most* idealistic, the *most* trusting; they really believed they could change the world . . . and yet to see the same kids five years later . . . !

I told Bob Kennedy a story that illustrated the relative issues. Not a nice story to tell . . . but it illustrated the whole point. It was written by a little kid in a Freedom School. The story was called "Cinderlilly"— about a little girl in McComb, Mississippi, who, every year, saw the big white folks downtown having a great big ball at the armory. Every year, the little girl would say, "I really want to go there." The mother would find some excuse. Finally the year came when Cinderlilly was just too big to be put off. The mother said, "All right. But you really can't go because you haven't been invited." So Cinderlilly says, "Oh, yes. I've got my invitation." She said, "I'll take the Fourteenth Amendment to the Constitution, and if that doesn't work, I've got the Civil Rights Act of 1964." The mother said, "But who's going to take you?" The little girl said, "Prince Charming, Bobby Kennedy, is going to take me!" (I almost cry every time I tell this story.) The little girl said, "I'm sure he's going to show up." So, sure enough, Prince Charming promised that he would take her to the ball. And the night came. She was very excited. But, at the last minute, Prince Charming called and said he couldn't come! The little girl was crushed. But she said, "I'm going to go anyway." And she took her Fourteenth Amendment and she pocketed her little Civil Rights Act of 1964, and went down to the ball. The doors were closed, but she could hear the music going on inside. She kept knocking. Finally, the doors opened; they looked at her . . . "Where's your invitation?" So she pulled out the Fourteenth Amendment and gave it to them. The doorman started laughing. He passed it around the room, and everybody started laughing. But the little girl had this other Act in her pocket. So she pulled that out and gave it to them. And everybody kept laughing and laughing.

The last scene of the little story is that the little girl was crushed, and just stood there crying.

I told Bob Kennedy that story. I said, "It's a cruel story. Prince Charming simply didn't show up!" He didn't say anything. But I couldn't think of anything better to tell him in the sense of how people felt about things at that point.

At that time, Kennedy was *not* attuned to what was going on in the black community. He really did *not* have the sense of outrage that eventually he did learn to experience in going to Mississippi, in going to California, in going out to Indian reservations.

Originally, the big thing that formed my first impression of the Kennedys was their choice of judgeships, the *fantastically segregationist* judges who were appointed to district benches in the South! How Burke Marshall could say, "I saw Judge Cox sitting there in the Justice Department, and he *promised* me he would uphold the law." I mean those of us who had been working in the South long enough, we know that kind.

But the point is that Robert Kennedy could say, "You're right," which I think was perhaps the most disarming thing. "Yeah, that was a bad decision, wasn't it?" You know. Or, "Yeah, we were lousy there, weren't we?" That ability to admit limitations and admit, "I would do things differently." To admit, "Maybe I wasn't as strong as I might have been," and that maybe Harold Cox was a lousy appointment.

DR. VINCENT HARDING

Again, what I *see* and what I *felt* I saw in both Kennedys was a tremendous gift of manipulation. There was, I think, a certain ruthlessness about moving after the things that they wanted. Though Bobby had this great empathy for the black situation, I feel about him basically the way I feel about Abraham Lincoln: that he was a good man, in the wrong sense of the word; he was a white man whose basic commitment was to the destiny of white America. He would deal with the black people in whatever ways were necessary to fulfill that destiny, as he saw it. But I don't think he had any of the kind of vision of, for instance, a very radical kind of person who would see that the future of America might well be in the hands of black people. Bobby was still a proprietor of the white liberal; clearly the liberal establishment of America was still, for him, a white-defined American society against which we were moving. And it seems to me he has to be placed always in that context. So I don't buy the stories of how deeply he knew black people. I think he was in some ways brutally political, but was wise enough and sharp enough to see the ways black people had to be dealt with if the system was going to be carried on. Just like Roosevelt saw the way that labor was going to have to be dealt with if the system was going to be carried on. The two probably fall very much in the same kind of category and probably, to some degree, played the same kind of role: the one with labor, the other with the black movement. So, if I were white, I would probably say, "All praises be to Bobby Kennedy for helping on some levels to keep things in order." But I'm not sure now how we're going to judge that in the future.

My feeling about the whole situation, from the University of Mississippi *through* '62 and '63, was that the basic problem both Bobby and Jack had was that they were in the American liberal tradition, trying to hold onto the basic structures of the society, trying to keep them in an essential order and unity while bringing about change within that. So they negotiated with the powers in Mississippi over the university situation, and they tried to keep the covers on in both Albany and Birmingham, trying to operate with that Southern white structure; essentially, they were trying to avoid a tearing of the fabric. Of course, my own feeling was that tearing was absolutely necessary for something real to take place.

BURKE MARSHALL, *attorney*

Then Birmingham in April 1963. Dr. Martin Luther King, for reasons which he stated in a letter from the Birmingham jail, a very eloquent letter, wanted to disturb the conscience of the nation and the conscience of the city of Birmingham and the state of Alabama through public demonstrations of what life was like for the Negroes in what he called "the most segregated city in the country—the toughest city," and that was Birmingham.

The demonstrations in Birmingham were about restaurants that wouldn't let Negroes in; some drugstores that let them in, but wouldn't let them sit at the lunch counter; stores where they did business, yet weren't allowed to work in. I mean they were banned from everything in that city—everything. And so those were the issues.

STANLEY LEVISON

There was a two-day meeting in Dorchester, Georgia, in which key members of the staff and board members of the SCLC met to analyze Birmingham, and assess the temper of the country, and decide whether this was an appropriate campaign with a possibility of success. It was decided that Birmingham—the largest, most grimly segregated city in the South—needed to be tackled, because if victory were won in Birmingham, the results would radiate across the South . . . as indeed they did.

But one of the factors that was carefully assessed was the role of the Federal Government. It was decided that there was a kind of tacit alliance between the Federal Government—the Kennedy Administration—and the civil-rights movement; that if the civil-rights movement could arouse the country and create the demand . . . that this Administration would hear it and respond. Unlike earlier Administrations, whose position was, We will not be influenced by demonstrations, *this* Administration indeed said it would be influenced by demonstrations; and, as the President's later addresses showed, he said that *because* of the events in Birmingham, we have to consider new legislation, which earlier they had said was impossible. It was a case of responding to what was going on in the streets . . . not ignoring it.

Perhaps the most dramatic moment in the Birmingham planning meeting was at the close. As one of the people there who knew the history of Birmingham and Bull Connor, I thought it would be useful to point out that Bull Connor had an ugly history with the labor movement, and had fought for years to keep it out of Birmingham . . . with the use of force and brutality and a variety of other devices employed to defeat

114

what was then a powerful movement; we were not *as* powerful as the labor movement had been in its organizing days. Consequently, we had to realize that we were facing a rough adversary with much less power in our hands than the earlier movements. Then Martin said, "I want to make a point that I think everyone here should consider very carefully and decide if he wants to be with this campaign." He said, "There are less than a dozen people here assessing the type of enemy we're going to face. I have to tell you that in my judgment, some of the people sitting here today will not come back alive from this campaign. And I want you to think about it."

BURKE MARSHALL

Well, in a sense, there was no way of getting at those problems through law; and, at the same time, everybody looked to Bob Kennedy to cure these problems. There was no way. I mean a lot of people at that time, Northern black people, thought that the way to cure it was to send in the Army. In fact, we talked to the Army. Of course, the Army would have stopped all the demonstrations. So, the Army wasn't any solution. It would have acted as a symbol of federal power, but it wouldn't have made a difference.

The only way we had to get at the problem was through trying to find acceptance by both sides. Of course, Kennedy was disliked. He was the subject of the cartoons and the columns and the editorial comment to the people who ran the newspapers and the radio stations; and to the people in the streets and the politicians down there, he was the source of trouble . . . not the source of the solution. So we tried to act as a sort of mediator while the white people that ran the city of Birmingham realized that they had a stake in making a change that was inevitable anyway. In making an accommodation that was acceptable to Martin King and his people, there would be a symbolic change, at least, that meant something for the future.

But at the start, there was nothing. The politicians in Birmingham were not in a position to make any sort of accommodation with Martin King. They wouldn't talk to him. They wouldn't talk to anybody that *would* talk to him. They talked to a few Negro lawyers who had been active down there for years, but they wouldn't talk to Martin King. Somebody had to bridge that. We got groups together that would talk to each other . . . store owners, who had a stake because they were being boycotted and losing money; politicians, who had a stake because it was costing the city an awful lot of money; people that owned real estate, who had a stake because it was ruining the values of real estate in Birmingham; the law-enforcement people, the police chief, and particularly the sheriff, who had a stake because their men were on duty twenty-four hours, and were underpaid and quitting, and so forth. You'd try to bring those personal interests home to these people. The problem was getting them to realize how really easy it was, from their point of view, to make a gesture that would, for the time being, deal with their problem; how easy it was just to open a lunch counter . . . two or three jobs, basically; they could accept that. That was all that Martin King really was wanting to prove. He wasn't trying to work a revolution, not an overnight revolution. He wanted recognition of what was right and what was unfair. And, once he got that in a way that was public, then that was enough.

Martin King had planned to start a protest movement in Birmingham *earlier* in 1963. At the time there was a series of citywide elections going on, and some of the white people we were in touch with took the position that these elections would change Birmingham from the Bull Connor kind of city government it was into a better city government. Protests would affect the elections adversely. Martin King thought there was something to that, and he delayed his protest once or twice. Then in April or May, although those arguments still existed to some extent, he concluded that he shouldn't delay any more, and he started leading these protests; they grew into massive street protests, and the reaction from the city government and from Bull Connor was predictable . . . and outrageous. The country got mad, and there was a great deal of support from the Negro population in Birmingham and around the country for the protests.

I went down at that time because it was such a matter of strong concern. I called up Martin King, and I couldn't get him; I talked to Wyatt Walker, or somebody down there. I said that we thought they should put off the demonstrations. It was in a motel, and I thought to myself then—and I still think that it is true—that the Birmingham police, through the motel switchboard, were listening to everything I said to Wyatt Walker; and that in the ensuing days and weeks, the fact that I'd made that call and had that kind of conversation under those circumstances, with the Birmingham police eavesdropping, gave me a standing of credibility with the white people in Birmingham that I couldn't have gained in any other way.

We had a series of meetings on a marathon basis with different groups. There were groups that would meet with each other; and then there were groups that would meet with some people and not with other people; and then there were groups that wouldn't meet. The white political leaders and business leaders, generally speaking, wouldn't meet with Negroes; none of them would meet with Martin King or Fred Shuttlesworth or the identified leaders. Some of them would meet with what they called "the local people," as against what they called "the outsiders."

DR. VINCENT HARDING

I have a constant recollection of Burke Marshall sitting off in a corner with his arms folded, and so-o quiet; in fact, I hardly remember him ever saying anything in the whole session . . . looking like a Mr. Chips who had come to town.

THE REVEREND ANDREW J. YOUNG

I thought that the Justice Department did a tremendous behind-the-scenes job of pulling the Birmingham community together. The country in 1963, I think, could have gone either way. Either there could have been a response to nonviolence in the creative, nonviolent manner that Martin had designed and the Kennedy Administration supported. Or there could have been a rejection and frustration. Birmingham was in such a state, then, that either the black or the white community could have gotten out of hand any minute.

That was when Bull Connor used dogs against demonstrators. Nobody was really bitten . . . I think one guy was scratched up by a dog, but not to the point where it was a serious wound. Nothing more than a tetanus shot was needed. But we brought one or two men, who had had their clothes torn off and were scratched, to tell what happened to the crowd in the church. Then we thought about it very logically. People were angry and upset. But I asked the congregation, "How many people have ever been bitten by dogs before?" And about half the people sort of half raised a hand; they'd had some kind of attack with dogs . . . if nothing but a dog biting them on the ankle while riding a bicycle as children. I asked, "How many played baseball?" and, "How many have been hit in the head with a bat?" I guess a good percentage had. We just forced people to stop to think about it . . . that a lot of veterans of both World War II and Korea had taken risks in fighting essentially for freedom for white people . . . and to compare the dangers and risks they ran to the gain for black people. I said, "Well, if you ran this kind of risk to fight for somebody else's freedom, why aren't you willing to run the risk of facing dogs and possibly billy clubs, when you did that as a child, you know, just for kicks? Isn't it worth being bitten for freedom?" And with that, everybody marched outside, and not one person was bitten by a dog. The animals were more human than the segregationists.

ROGER WILKINS, *director of the Community Relations Service, Department of Justice*

Dr. King finally got school kids to march—black school kids. Bob's line was: "Well, I don't approve of that. It's a bad thing to have children marching. Shouldn't use children." Well, I was furious! I wrote him a note. The point I made was that those kids, marching up and down those Birmingham streets, were learning more about their own human potential and their own ability to affect their own destinies and their own communities than they *ever* learned in those doggone schools! One day on the picket line was worth maybe a semester in school. He answered and said, "That's very interesting, Roger, but after all, the children can get hurt." My own judgment was that the psychic damage that those schools and those conditions were causing those kids was much, much more serious than any fire hoses . . . than injuries that could be inflicted by any fire hoses or dogs!

THE REVEREND ANDREW J. YOUNG

It was always a very touchy situation. But Bobby Kennedy, Burke Marshall, and Joe Dolan . . . they did some phenomenal things. They used a very creative and imaginative approach to slowing problems and tensions that was almost para-governmental. . . . Maybe politics functions this way all the time. Up to that point, settlements in civil rights had involved the courts, or some kind of presidential order, or something very official. But now you began to get a kind of unofficial, personal reconciliation with both whites and blacks, which was very new. I began to get an appreciation for that way of working with people, rather than with principles and laws and truths. Going through a period of great tension and social stress, he was very much the diplomat. And I began to like that.

BURKE MARSHALL

Jimmy Baldwin came out to Hickory Hill for breakfast one day just after the Birmingham agreement. He and Bob Kennedy had a rather good conversation about the cities. We were driving back to the Justice Department—the three of us—and Bob asked him, "Can you find some

118

people who can tell me what the government can do?" So Baldwin said, "Yes. I know just the people."

We had the meeting soon afterward at the Kennedys' apartment in New York. Well, there were *some* people there that knew something about the problems of the cities in terms that were translatable into money, and legislation, and political action—particularly, Kenneth Clark, and Edwin Barry from Chicago. But nobody else had any experience or knowledge that was translatable in those terms, which is what Bob was looking for. They were actors and artists. As a result, the meeting had no purpose in terms of what we'd come for; it ended up basically as, "Well, you don't understand." "Well, *you* don't understand either"—charge and countercharge, rather than any conversation.

JAMES BALDWIN, *author*

I felt there was a way to talk to him, to reach him. When we were in the car he said, "Why don't you get a couple of your friends together. I'm going to be in New York tomorrow, and maybe we could meet and talk." So I said okay, not quite realizing what I'd gotten myself into. I called up a few friends. The bunch of people I knew are fairly rowdy, independent, tough-minded men and women. About a dozen of us were there—Lena Horne, Kenneth Clark, Lorraine Hansberry, Ed Barry. Then there was Jerome Smith, with whom I'd worked in the Deep South—a black student who had been very badly beaten. He happened to be in New York seeing a doctor. He set the tone of the meeting because he stammers when he's upset. He stammered when he talked to Bobby. He said that he was nauseated by the necessity of being in that room. I knew what he meant. It was not personal at all. If you'd been in Birmingham and on those highways and in those jails waiting for the Justice Department or the FBI to act, you'd be nauseated too. Bobby took it personally and turned away from him. That was a mistake because when he turned toward us . . . the reasonable, responsible, mature representatives of the black community, Lorraine Hansberry said, "You've got a great many very accomplished people in this room, Mr. Attorney General. But the only man you should be listening to is that man over there."

It got worse. Bobby didn't understand what we were trying to tell him; he didn't understand our urgency. For him it was a political matter. It was a matter of finding out what's wrong in the twelfth ward and correcting it . . . like packages or whatever the kids wanted in the twelfth ward, giving it to them and everything would be all right. But what was wrong in the twelfth ward in this case turned out to be something very sinister, very deep, that couldn't be solved in the usual way. Bobby didn't understand that. And our apprehension of his misunderstanding made it very tense, and finally very ugly. If we couldn't make the Attorney General of the United States, who was a fairly young and intelligent man, understand the urgency of the black situation, there wasn't any hope at all. You know? There were several highlights. I asked Jerome if he would take up arms in defense of America. I'll never forget Jerome's face. He said, "Never! Never! Never!" This got through to Bobby. It didn't surprise me that Jerome would not take up arms. I was surprised that Bobby was surprised. He didn't understand how anybody could feel that way about his country. We tried to indicate that if you were black it was very easy to feel that way; in fact, it was almost inevitable.

DR. KENNETH CLARK, *psychologist, educator*
It really was one of the most violent, emotional verbal assaults and attacks that I had ever witnessed. Bobby became more silent and tense, and he sat immobile in the chair. He no longer continued to defend himself. He just sat, and you could see the tension and the pressure building in him. Harry Belafonte, more than anyone else, tried to move in in a personal, protective way; he tried to intercede in terms of raising personal contacts, such as swimming in the pool with the Kennedys, and things of that sort. He tried to bring a human, social thing into it, but nobody paid any attention to that. It didn't work. The rest of us came right back to the issue. And it went on for hours—about three hours of this kind of searing, emotional interaction and confrontation. The point we were trying to put over was: Look. The Kennedys have a tremendous amount of credit with the American people. This credit must be used by them. You and your brother must use this credit to lead the American people into an awareness and understanding of the nature of this problem, and what has to be done.

Specifically, it was suggested that Jack Kennedy should make not only just public announcements but a dramatic gesture, such as taking a child and leading him into a desegregated school, or going to the University of Alabama and saying, "This is the law of the land." Bobby kept saying, "No. This would be senseless. This would be phony." We were saying: Not phony.

This was the abrasive clash here: our insisting that the crisis demanded extraordinary acts, and Bobby retreating and saying no, and occasionally coming back and saying . . . well, implying . . . that we were ungrateful; that we were insatiable, et cetera. It was *the* most dramatic experience I had ever had.

JAMES BALDWIN

Then Jerome said, "You shouldn't be worried about the Communists or America's foreign enemies . . . because the real dangers in America are inside . . . right here."

He was explaining he didn't know how much longer he could remain nonviolent, how much longer he could take being beaten and spat on. It was a very hard thing to ask a people to endure. He finished up by saying, "When I pull the trigger, kiss it good-by."

Lorraine Hansberry said that she understood what Jerome was talking about, the difficulty of being a Negro man, but she was very proud of Negro men and she wasn't worried because they had done really beautifully, all things considered. She said, "But I am very worried about the state of a civilization which produces that white cop standing on that Negro woman's neck in Birmingham." And she stood up, and she said, "Thank you, Mr. Attorney General." She walked out. And we followed her. And that was that.

DR. KENNETH CLARK

We left convinced that we had made no dent or impact on Bobby. In fact, my personal judgment was that we had widened the gap. Whatever rapport had existed before was disrupted; it may very well have been that Bobby Kennedy was more antagonistic to our aspirations and goals than he was before, because the clash was so violent.

But then at the end of May, Vice-President Johnson gave that Gettysburg talk and in June, Jack Kennedy gave that famous civil-rights speech of his, which contained many of the same ideas. So our conclusion that we had made no dent at all was wrong.

My own reactions to Bob Kennedy continued to be dominated by that experience. I had left there feeling that this man was an extraordinarily insensitive person, extraordinarily loyal to his brother; he personalized issues that did not seem to me to be understood by personalization; I did not leave there feeling that he was a racist, by any means; I felt the way Lorraine and Jim felt . . . that he did, in fact, represent about the best that white America had to offer, but this was tragic because he did

121

not have empathy. There was no sensitivity on the part of Bobby as to the basic problems and issues. I felt it was a question of sensitivity. For example, Bobby said somewhere in that crisis of confrontation to the whole group: "My brother is President of the United States, the grandson of an immigrant," et cetera. "You should understand that this is possible; that in the next fifty years or so, a Negro can be President." Well, this was the last thing to say to the group . . . particularly at that time. Jim Baldwin said, "You know, my family has been here for generations. . . ."

JAMES BALDWIN
After that I think he was always a little mad at me . . . which is kind of sad, but understandable. He was confronted, however untidy it may have been, by so many disparate types . . . yet united. What really connects Lena Horne and Jimmy Baldwin? It must have looked weird. What connected all of us to that student? No one had ever heard of him; he didn't sing or dance or act. Yet he became the focal point. I think that threw Kennedy. That boy, after all, in some sense, represented to everybody in that room our hope. Our honor. Our dignity. But, above all, our hope. We can't afford our black boys being beaten half to death. We can't afford it.

DR. KENNETH CLARK
I changed. I did not become an avid Bobby Kennedy devotee or fan, but I respected the complexity of the man. I saw in a larger perspective how this came out of the impasse; he probably did a double take somewhere. I first interpreted it as his being bludgeoned by his brother into rethinking that we might have had a point. But I later felt that maybe he did some serious rethinking on his own. I don't believe that Bobby Kennedy was an angel in any way. But I do think that our original judgment . . . in that meeting . . . might have been overharsh and severe. Had he lived, he really would have demonstrated a rare combination of courage, clarity, and concern about the same issues that concerned me.

JOHN DOAR, *president, Bedford-Stuyvesant D & S Corporation*
After Birmingham, it was unacceptable to him that Congress would not pass legislation. I remember that he insisted in a conference with President Kennedy and Vice-President Johnson that until Congress acted and passed legislation, the situation was just unacceptable to an American civilization . . . to this country.

BURKE MARSHALL

He met with virtually every Senator, including the Southern Senators, within a period of two weeks, with virtually *all* members of the House of Representatives, except for those from the Southern states. There was no point in talking to them. That was one avenue of approach—with the Congress directly. Secondly, he organized a series of meetings in the White House in which the President participated, and the Vice-President, the Secretary of State, Luther Hodges, and other members of the Cabinet—which were designed to bring this problem to the attention of the leaders of various groups in the United States and tell them that they had to help solve it. The groups were educators, lawyers, business people, church people, labor people, and a number of others; there must have been ten, twelve, fifteen meetings of that sort . . . all, again, within a space of three or four weeks. And then thirdly, he urged President Kennedy, against the advice of many people in the White House and many political advisers, to take the civil-rights issue on a moral, personal basis, to the country. President Kennedy did so in a speech in June, right after the business at the University of Alabama with Governor Wallace.

DR. VINCENT HARDING

They had this way of gathering together different groups and running a pitch to them about how much we need your help, and this kind of thing. It was a very funny scene, though, because I got this telegram saying: "The President of the United States would like you to come to Washington to talk about matters having to do with civil rights," or something like that. I said, "Wow! I finally made it! Here, the President is calling me. I'm going to take my wife along with me too."

So when I got there, I found this *mass* of people who had also been called by the President to give him advice on what he should do. That sort of quieted me down a little.

John Kennedy spoke to us first. He said he was bringing us together to tell us about what *he* was trying to do as far as the bill was concerned; that he wanted and needed our support. Then Bobby spoke. Rose, my wife, and I talked about this later on, and we talked about it again after they were both assassinated. Our feeling was that something got a little bit more beneath the surface where Bobby was concerned; John Kennedy was a harder surface to get through; Bobby indicated more the physical emotion . . . you got the sense that you could get your hand on a person. He was speaking before a group of a hundred, a hundred and fifty people. I remember he said something about how *he* felt he would respond if he were a black person at this particular time; on a certain level, I had the feeling that he was serious in trying to say how he would feel as a black person, even though I thought that at certain levels it was really impossible for him to do more than *want* to feel that. People asked them questions. Ralph Abernathy got up and made a very ceremonial kind of statement about, Oh, Mr. President, we are . . . blah, blah, blah.

I wanted to say some things a good deal more critical because I *was* critical of the way both of them were dealing with the situation. But it was clear that we really hadn't been brought there for dialogue.

ROGER WILKINS

Marian Edelman and I had come from a meeting one day; we were walking down the street in New York and she said, "You're pretty much anti-Bob. Why?" And I told her why. Among other things, I told her at that time about the tap on Dr. King's phone; she was the only one I ever told that to. Marian said, "Well, Roger, when he came down to Mississippi, I thought, Oh, well, it's just a bunch of guys coming down for publicity. But he did things that I hadn't done. He went into the *dirtiest, filthiest, poorest* black homes, places with barely any floor, and only potbellied stoves; and he would sit with a baby who had open sores and whose belly was bloated from malnutrition, and he'd sit and touch and hold those babies." She said, "I didn't do that! I didn't do that! But he did. And I saw that compassion, and I saw that feeling, and I saw how he was learning." And she said, "That's why I'm for him." There lies the great tragedy. We've lost that compassion, that understanding, that capacity to grow.

JOHN MAGUIRE

Having watched the pilgrimage of Robert Kennedy . . . I think at first he had no more special sensitivity of this problem than his brother did; they just had essential liberal attitudes, but no real feeling for it at all. I think the clubbing of John Seigenthaler was the first opening— when he began to see how vicious outraged whites could be.

For John Kennedy, Oxford with Meredith really was a turn for him. The night of the Meredith thing . . . it was the first time a President had talked about race in America as a moral problem. Eisenhower always refused when pressed, and said he would not get into the morality of it; he was just going to speak about this as a legal problem. So it was a great turn when John Kennedy first came out on the night of the Meredith episode and said, "This is a grave moral problem" . . . and then he was lost.

Then came Robert Kennedy's journey. Oxford. Birmingham. The meeting with James Baldwin was crucial. Then, certainly that trip to Mississippi, that whole succession of trips that came close together: Indian reservations. Cesar Chavez . . . but particularly that fact-finding trip to Mississippi, where he saw hunger and those bloated-bellied babies.

I remember asking Martin Luther King about Robert Kennedy once, when I was driving him along . . . he was speaking in Connecticut . . . and he said, "Umm, I believe he's comin' around. I believe he's comin' around."

7

THE REVEREND RALPH ABERNATHY, *civil-rights leader*

I went back to the last car to express my condolences. When I got there, Mrs. Jacqueline Kennedy said, "Oh, Reverend. Thanks for coming in." She said, "You'll be able to help us lift this. It should be elevated so that the crowds of people watching the train might have the chance to see it." They weren't seeing anything because the casket was on a very beautiful stand that wasn't more than six or eight inches off the floor. So we got some chairs and set the casket on them. That was the experience I will not forget—lifting his body. In any funeral, the most important persons are not those who read the scriptures or pray the prayers, or even deliver the eulogy. They are the pallbearers. When I die, the people who carry my body I want to be the dearest of friends that I have in the world. I was not an official pallbearer for Robert Kennedy, but at least I lifted the weight of his body when he could no longer lift it.

CARTER BURDEN, *campaign aide*

As I came to the glass-paneled door to enter the small sitting room where the casket lay, they were just practicing folding the flag. John Glenn was instructing them. When they finished, I went into the room. Impressions are never what you expect; I suppose I expected a very somber, solemn scene . . . and, indeed, in many ways it was. But in many ways it was just the opposite. The casket was raised up so that it could be seen through the window, and all around the ledge just beneath window level were paper cups and Coke cans and half-eaten sandwiches and overfilled ashtrays. Just like the remnants of an ordinary picnic. It was a room that people had been living in—the family had been waiting out the long afternoon like everybody else on the train—eating and drinking Cokes and talking and laughing. It jarred me at first.

When I came in, most of the family were out on the back platform; only Ethel was there, sitting beside the casket. It was the only moment, then or since, that I saw her cry. She sat there, immensely still, and hunched over in a plain straight-backed chair. She had a rosary in her hands, and her head was resting against the casket.

ART BUCHWALD, *columnist*
The coffin itself was on chairs. And it was not just the honor of standing vigil. You literally had to *hold* the coffin so it wouldn't fall. I was sort of embarrassed to stay in that compartment because Teddy was there, and Pat, and Jean; and they were talking. I didn't know what to do. So I went out on the platform where the children were. And that was the first time, being on the train, that I really had a feeling of what was going on outside the train. Inside the train, you couldn't hear anything. But on the platform, you could hear the cheers, and the people crying. At several places along the way, I noticed kids running out after the train would go by and picking things up off the rail. I asked one of the Kennedy kids what that was about. They said that people were laying things on the rails, and then the train ran over them, and they were souvenirs. They were medals or money, I guess, or coins.

DAVID BRINKLEY, *television commentator*
When Robert was Attorney General in his brother's Cabinet, *Time* magazine ran a cover story that concluded he was the second most powerful man in Washington, which is probably true. A day or two after that, he was at the White House talking to his brother, the President, who said, "Bobby, I see by *Time* magazine that you're the Number Two man in town. Well, that means there's only one way for you to go, and it ain't up!"

K. LeMOYNE BILLINGS, *family friend*
Bobby and Jack had very different personalities, and really different interests outside of politics, outside of their work. And really different senses of humor; their closeness really was based on their political work.

127

RICHARD NEUSTADT, *educator*

He differed from his brother, it seems to me, in lots of temperamental ways. Jack Kennedy was a much more eighteenth-century character; he was cool; he was so self-disciplined; he certainly wasn't a *cold* man—people who thought that were wrong—but he was a man who mistrusted passion. Bob trusted passion more. My impression of Bob the last year was that he was getting wrier, which is a quality his older brother had so markedly; wrier, funnier . . . funnier about himself . . . and perhaps the beginnings of some of that detachment. Jack was always standing off looking at himself; Bob never used to do that, but was standing off looking at life with a more ironic tone in the last year or so than he ever had before.

He was terribly impatient with institutions. I'm sure part of his public response had to do with that impatience in him. He even had an accord with the Northern blue-collar workers who afterwards turned to Wallace. The kind of frustration that turns people to Wallace is frustration based partly on fear of the black; but it's really fear of nobody being in control.

Bob, much more than Jack, had this drive to the direct approach. Jack was much more resigned to the restraints of institutional life. He was wry about it; that was what was 18th century about him . . . he had such a sense of the limitations of what human life was all about; I'm not sure Bob ever accepted that there were limitations; maybe he did in his last few years, but his notion was that every wrong . . . somehow . . . if you can't right it, you've got to bust in the attempt. It's extraordinary. I've never met anybody like him; I've never met anybody like either of them, but they were quite different.

GENERAL MAXWELL D. TAYLOR, *director, IDA*

One of the impressions that I received early was the rather protective attitude which Bobby had toward his brother; in contrast to what one normally expects of the older brother looking after the younger one, one had the feeling that he was looking after his older brother. In that cause, he showed an energy and a devotion that were really very touching. He seemed to look at every aspect of a given situation, asking himself, "Now, how can this affect Jack? How can it hurt Jack?"

AVERELL HARRIMAN, *diplomat*

I think Bob felt that he was finding expression through his brother in the things that were being done. It's generally fair to say that when things went well, the President took the bows; when things went badly, why, Bobby took the blame. There wasn't any agreement or understanding, but it automatically worked that way.

CHARLES SPALDING, *family friend*

Bobby's feelings were tremendously deep; Jack's were controlled, hidden and easy. It was like a lot of flags on a ship with Jack, gay and bright. Gaiety was the key to his nature. It was what he appreciated and enjoyed the most. He felt he had sufficient seriousness in his life with the sicknesses, and one thing and another. Because he understood this, perhaps Bobby was more appreciative of his brother's greatness than anybody else.

ROBERT McNAMARA, *former Secretary of Defense*

His role with the President went far beyond the limits and responsibilities of the Attorney General. It was a role that really reflected his understanding of what the President needed, and his equal understanding of the lack of organization within the government to handle such an assignment. The departments of the government needed to be coordinated and brought together . . . forced to concentrate on the problem at hand and the alternative ways of handling it . . . so that these could be shown to the President, who could then make a decision. This required an organized approach, and there wasn't anyone organizing it. Bobby realized that and stepped in; and he was a major factor in assuring that the so-called Excom was set up, and that it did function, and that the President's interests—the nation's interests, if you will— were constantly kept in mind, as opposed to the parochial interests of a particular department or a particular individual.

DOUGLAS DILLON, *former Secretary of the Treasury*

In the Eisenhower period when I was in the State Department, the basic big decisions were taken in the National Security Council after full discussion. Those meetings were held once a week. There was a feeling on President Kennedy's part when he came into office that this procedure had been overdone because often these meetings took place on days when there wasn't really anything of importance to discuss. He thought this procedure was too bureaucratic, and that he'd like to work on a more informal basis. So he never really used the National Security Council, though the Excom was a similar organization, which he created and used during the Cuban missile crisis to great effect.

I think President Kennedy made a mistake in changing the Eisenhower method so radically. The loss of the checks and balances inherent in the National Security Council procedure was the chief reason for the Bay of Pigs fiasco. I think it could have been avoided if the previous procedures had been continued until something had been developed to take their place. But instead, the Eisenhower National Security Council procedures were abolished before the new Administration had had time to establish anything effective in their place.

CHARLES SPALDING

The President was really distraught about the Bay of Pigs. He was totally different after Cuba. That really changed him, I think, as a President. The job then became more than ever a hard day-to-day slugging, worrisome, constantly-on-your-guard, always-look-behind-you, never-relax-for-a-minute kind of work. He was a happy man who enjoyed himself in everything he did, but if he ever had any illusions—which I doubt—that the presidency could be something more diverting than breaking your back, the Bay of Pigs dispelled them.

CHESTER BOWLES, *U.S. Ambassador to India*

Bob Kennedy's reaction to the news of the Bay of Pigs fiasco was emotional and belligerent. During a series of National Security Council meetings following the invasion by the Cuban expatriates, he was one of many who felt that we must do something—anything—to somehow regain the ground that we had lost. The Kennedy Administration had suffered acute embarrassment, and neither Jack nor Bob Kennedy was accustomed to setbacks. For years they moved from success to success, and here, for perhaps the first time in their political careers, was evidence of a gross misjudgment.

ARTHUR SCHLESINGER, JR., *historian*

He knew about it because his brother discussed it with him, but he never had any opportunity to hear the briefings or the discussions, hear what the CIA was intending, what the Joint Chiefs of Staff thought about it, or the Secretaries of State and Defense, or why Senator Fulbright and others opposed it. In other words, he did not participate in any of the formal discussions leading up to the Bay of Pigs, but he did know about it. A few days before it happened, there was a party at Bobby's house at which he said, "I understand you don't like the Cuban thing." I said I didn't, and he looked rather unhappy and said, "My brother

130

has decided to go ahead . . . so that even if you disagree with this, don't . . ."

The fact that neither Robert Kennedy nor Ted Sorensen was involved in the discussions made the President thereafter get them both in on every major foreign policy question. His two White House representatives, Mac Bundy and I, both of us failed him by not taking more of an effective position, Mac because he more or less agreed with the idea . . . and I, well, *both* of us because we were new in government, and inexperienced, and felt our job was to be silent rather than engage in arguments with the generals and Secretaries. In the middle of the Bay of Pigs fiasco, President Kennedy talked about the problems of having to take people on their trust. He said Allen Dulles, of the CIA, was a legendary figure. It was very hard to deal with legendary figures, and he said he wished he had Robert to advise him instead.

ROGER HILSMAN, *university professor*

John Kennedy was badly served with the Bay of Pigs. Kennedy was presented with the problem in a way that made it very difficult for him to act otherwise; that is, the Republicans had started something, and if Eisenhower had continued, it would have gone on. The principal people involved were holdovers—Dick Bissell, Allen Dulles, and then General Lemnitzer, of the Joint Chiefs of Staff. Using secrecy as an excuse, they kept a lot of the people who came in with Kennedy from knowing much about it. For example I was director of the Bureau of Intelligence and Research in the State Department and had every right to be involved, but was cut out from it. So was Bob Amory, who was director of the research side of the CIA. So the President was boxed in, at the beginning of his Administration, by people who were emotionally committed to that course of action. He was very badly served by everybody around him, and Bob, I think, was outraged by this and vowed never again to let it happen.

ARTHUR SCHLESINGER, JR.

There's a phrase, I think of T. S. Eliot's, about people having an experiencing nature. Robert Kennedy had to an extraordinary degree an experiencing nature, and I think this was really a result not of childhood experience, but of a certain capacity for vividness of imagination and a sense that you could not understand the world unless you systematically tried to see it from the viewpoint of others. John Kennedy had that sense too, particularly in foreign affairs. During the Cuban missile

131

crisis in mid-October 1962, for example, he constantly tried to put himself in Khrushchev's shoes . . . leaving an exit for an honorable retreat, and not pushing him up against the wall.

AVERELL HARRIMAN

His advisers should be allowed to discuss problems without his presence . . . because it's almost impossible in his presence to step up and call the Secretary of State a stupid so-and-so and utterly disagree with him. There has to be a certain decorum. Besides, if the President indicates a certain line of thinking, not very many people will stand up against him. I had learned this very early from my work with other Presidents. Mac Bundy gave me the nickname of "the crocodile." He said that whenever the President, looking around the room, reached me, I said two or three sentences very sharply and very briskly. He accused me of sort of chomping at people. I knew that you had a split second to decide whether to speak up and say what you wanted to say; you couldn't argue. Kennedy's idea during the Cuban missile crisis was that the advisers should meet separately; this was very important.

McGEORGE BUNDY, *president, the Ford Foundation*

There were three different rooms that were important in the missile crisis. One was the Cabinet Room, where the so-called Excom regularly met. I don't remember where in the room Bob sat. He sometimes wouldn't even sit at the Cabinet table. I can remember times when he would deliberately put himself in one of the smaller chairs against the wall rather than seem to be asserting himself. But it didn't make much difference; because, in a generic way, wherever he sat was one of the most important places in the room, and everybody knew that. Then there was George Ball's conference room on the seventh floor of the Department of State. The third place was the President's own office. In all these rooms, RFK was really the senior person whenever he was there, because though he was careful not to throw his weight around because he was the President's brother—still he *was* the Attorney General, and he *was* the person closest to the President in human terms.

They talked to each other on the phone; neither one of them had any respect for the notion that the telephones were insecure. They talked to each other just as freely on the phone as they would have face-to-face.

LORD HARLECH, *former British Ambassador to the United States*

There was such a *total* intermeshing of minds that there didn't have to be a long exposition. Their sentences were very short and covered an immense amount of ground very quickly. President Kennedy found it very difficult dealing with advisers who talked at great length. He felt that he knew all the nuances of a situation; he didn't mind if people were interrupted in the middle of a sentence, which is, on the whole, rather regarded as bad manners in America . . . though not in England, where everybody's interrupted halfway through a sentence, since once you see the point you start talking. He liked that kind of conversation. And, of course, with Bobby, the President's conversations went very fast.

ROBERT LOVETT, *banker*

I was in the midst of a Carnegie Foundation board meeting. As happens so frequently, the little girl who took the message came in and, instead of typing the message, blurted out at this board meeting that "the White House is calling you urgently." There wasn't anything to do but excuse myself and go out and take it. The President said, "A serious matter's come up. I wish you'd come down as soon as you can." I remember saying, "Well, I've got my car parked outside. If I can get it into some garage quickly, I'll take the next plane down. In any event, I'll be down just as soon as I can."

I was met at the airport by one of the White House cars and taken at once to Mac Bundy's office in the basement, and then into the Map Room—the so-called War Room—down there. I received a note from the President saying, "I want you to receive precisely the information which I was given. Various people will brief you as they did me this morning."

That was when we first picked up definitive evidence of the missiles in Cuba. I spent about three or four hours in the Map Room, going over the information we had. Then I received a message from the President saying that Gromyko was coming in to see him some time that evening, and he wanted to see me immediately afterwards. Would I stay over? Which I, of course, did. I went upstairs right after Gromyko left and saw the President with Secretary of State Rusk and Llewellyn Thompson. It took about an hour and a half to go over all the information. At that point, Bobby came in. We went over the high spots of what we'd discussed to that point. It was during those discussions that I had said, "I think the thing to do is not to get trapped in using a sledgehammer to kill a fly. What we'd better do is see if we can't throw a *cordon sanitaire* around the whole thing." I believe that was the

133

first time that that expression had been brought into the conversation. That meant, of course, a general embargo in and out.

No decision was reached at that time, but it was agreed that we'd come back tomorrow morning and pick it up again. During this, it was obvious that Bob was one of the principal personal consultants of the President. There was a wide diversity of opinion and advice being given by those directly in the government service at that time. That includes McNamara, Rusk, and the others. The reason the President called in outsiders was that some of us had been through rather similar circumstances in the past . . . similar types of emergencies. Certainly I had a feeling of *déjà vu*, in the sense that here's just another crisis that perhaps should have been foreseen, but wasn't. Here are the different points of view being put up by the militant group, on one hand, and by a more careful, more restrained group, on the other. The State Department has no single opinion; it has two or three opinions. And that's very common in government. After all, the big thing is to be able to exercise judgment.

ELIE ABEL, *television correspondent*

The discussion became a kind of war game in which people would throw out various dread possibilities. You know, if we did *this*, what would *they* do? What's the argument for the opposite course from the one now being discussed? It was apparently a kind of formless discussion, by and large, except for certain high points such as the Dean Acheson-Bobby Kennedy debate. The gist of Acheson's arguments was that on the whole we weren't being tough enough and that we had the Russians with, as he put it, "their tail caught in a screen door, and we ought to twist it." There was no need for any special warning. Everybody knew that in the early 19th century, the Monroe Doctrine had proclaimed as American policy that if any European power tried to intervene in our part of the world, by God, we'd come down on them like a ton of bricks. He repeated this in discussion, and at various times it took various forms: essentially, he was in favor of something much tougher than the blockade, namely, the air strike. He didn't feel we had to feel squeamish about using force. The argument went against him, and the day they decided to go to the blockade, Acheson withdrew from the discussions and went home. He went to his country place in Sandy Spring, Maryland. Of course, he was drawn into the thing again, not into the discussion, but as a special ambassador to inform General De Gaulle and then Adenauer of the presidential decision, which he did and did very well. He's a great raconteur, and he acts out the scene with De Gaulle beautifully: De Gaulle, whose eyesight was terrible, squinted at these aerial photographs and not seeing much, and sending for a magnifying glass and then playing this game about, "Can you tell the different MIGs? There are four different kinds of MIGs in that picture." Which, for an old gentleman whose sight was fast fading, must have been an interesting exercise.

GEORGE BALL, U.S. *Ambassador to the United Nations*

The most important meetings were those when the President was not present—the continuous meetings in my own conference room at the State Department, which, with great imagination, they nicknamed the "Think Tank." We met in almost continuous session—the so-called Cocom—the Coordinating Committee: McNamara, Bundy . . . all the usual suspects. Bobby played a very useful role. I myself had been opposed to an air strike because I found it totally abhorrent. I had used a phrase that I thought no country could act in a manner that was completely inconsistent with its own pattern of behavior without doing irrevocable damage to itself. A little later in the meeting, Bobby referred to this and translated it into much more effective terms. He said, "My brother's got to be able to live with himself. If we did this"—the surgical air strike—"I don't think America could, and I don't think my brother could." This had, of course, a major effect. It was one thing for me to say; it was something else for the President's brother to say it.

To be entirely candid, I was very much surprised at his performance in Cocom. I had always had a feeling that Bobby had a much too simplistic and categorical position toward things—either you condemn something utterly or you accept it enthusiastically . . . and there seemed no intermediate positions.

He reflected this rather determined view that you always acted decisively and that you always went in and damned the torpedoes . . . even though it might cause an awful lot of problems elsewhere in the world. But he behaved quite differently during the Cuban missile crisis.

In the Cocom meetings, McNamara was very forceful and articulate. He was originally for the surgical air strike, but then he came around to the idea of the quarantine. Bundy made the complete leap from saying in the first place that probably the thing to do was ignore it . . . to saying that we should go in and take them out with air power. Dillon was always one of the extreme hard-line fellows.

DOUGLAS DILLON

The President asked the people who shared similar points of view to work together and develop a scenario as to how matters should be handled; then the whole group was to discuss these different scenarios and come back to him. That's where the two main courses of action came up. My first inclination was to join with those who believed that we should send airplanes in and knock the missile bases out. The Soviets, I felt, would understand that. They were the kind of people who wouldn't hesitate to take such action themselves in a similar situation. I thought that course would work. The other course, which was the one eventually followed, might or might not work; it seemed risky.

There was considerable argument in the Excom regarding these alternatives. One of the chief arguments against the surgical strike was that the Soviets were dangerous people; if you did this, they would blow up . . . they might do something dangerous and even start a major war. That argument, at that time and under those circumstances, did not particularly impress me. I didn't think that would happen. I thought that the Soviets were sensible people. They were overextended in Cuba, and I did not think they would be pushed into anything rash at a time when they obviously were in a weak position. So that didn't really impress me as a good argument at all. If that was the only argument against a strike, I was more convinced than before that the surgical way of getting it over quickly would be the best.

Then Bob Kennedy came out with a quite different thought. He didn't belong to either of the groups that had prepared scenarios. He was sitting near the end of a long table around which we were gathered. He spoke with an intense but quiet passion. As he spoke, I felt that I was at a real turning point in history. Bob said, "Well, there's another side to this. I've listened to all these arguments. . . . But there's another argument for not doing this, and it's a very strong and compelling one to me. . . . No matter what the excuse is, this would be America perpetrating a Pearl Harbor on Cuba. We've got to look at history over its length. We never want it said that the United States did the very same thing that we so resented when the Japanese did it to us in 1941. And it would be much worse since we are so much larger and stronger than Cuba."

Well, the way Bob Kennedy spoke was totally convincing to me. I knew then that we should not undertake a strike without warning. If we had to use force, it should only be after we had very clearly given an indication that we were going to be forced to use it.

136

With only one or two possible exceptions, all the members of the Excom were convinced by Bob's argument. But it should always be remembered that nobody thought that we had given up the option to use force at some later date if the Soviets just kept on and on. We were still fully determined not to accept the existence of offensive missiles in Cuba.

ROBERT McNAMARA

Various parties didn't really see clearly that the President's actions and decisions were all designed to communicate to Khrushchev the necessity for removing those missiles and avoiding escalation of the conflict between the two nations; it was the President's objective to communicate this thought to Khrushchev in a way that allowed him maximum maneuver room to respond . . . both in terms of time and in terms of form. And hence, a quarantine, or a blockade—was simply a substitute for a letter—a method of communication—and had to be managed in a way that kept it from being considered an act of war. That was the problem in dealing with some individuals in the Defense Department; it was quite understandable that individuals who had been trained that blockades are for military purposes would find it difficult to understand that they can at times be used as a substitute for a letter, and in any event, as a means of communication. The letter to Khrushchev needed to be written precisely. It really wasn't a matter of great concern whether a particular tanker got through the alleged line of quarantine. What was a matter of great concern was that Khrushchev understand that the President felt it absolutely essential that these missiles be removed; and further, that the President wanted to make it as easy as possible for Khrushchev to come to that same conclusion himself *and* to remove them.

Bob contributed importantly in three ways: one, in joining with those who opposed the use of military action to take out the missiles; and two, in supporting a full evaluation of the alternative response, which was the quarantine. Further, after the receipt of Khrushchev's rambling message, which subsequently was followed by a message that obviously had been staff-prepared and which took quite a different line of attack, Bob initiated the suggestion that we reply to the first instead of the second, because the first was much more in our interest.

GEORGE BALL

There was a kind of general instinct: "Well, let's not pay attention to the second message." It was perfectly apparent that certain messages were written by Khrushchev, who had a habit of putting his secretaries on one side of the room, and then sitting with his back to them and engaging in a kind of stream of consciousness, which was put down in the letters; they're extraordinary because they're discursive, full of rather crude anecdotes and figures of speech that reflect his peasant origin. The first communication was an example of this. Then, the second, less conciliatory message came in—patently something produced officially by a committee. The tone, the literary style . . . it was a bureaucrat's letter, and the others were so obviously not. There was a kind of general reaction to that: Well, look, Mr. President. You're dealing with Khrushchev . . . continue to do so with Khrushchev . . . and not officially with the government.

And this is what he did. His answer went back to Khrushchev, not to the government.

ROBERT McNAMARA
Tempers were getting rather short after several days of constant concentration on this problem . . . and particularly with the difference of opinion that existed among us. I remember one individual who said he'd resign if certain courses of action were carried out. Tempers were high, and Bobby did a lot to keep the members of the group from exploding at each other. He also caused them to pause and think about the implications of their actions—both in relation to the potential military repercussions, and in relation to the traditions of our nation.

McGEORGE BUNDY
On Saturday night, as you recall, tension was very high, and we went to bed feeling it was the worst night of the crisis, not knowing what the morning would bring.

Sunday morning did bring news from Khrushchev that he was taking the missiles out. I got that word, as I recall it, sitting at breakfast here. I took the first reports, telephoned them to the President. He asked me to meet him on his way to church a little later, bring him the full message, and I did that. I do remember that it was a very beautiful morning, and that it had suddenly become many times more beautiful.

LUCY JARVIS, *television producer*
I was in Moscow, making a film on the Kremlin, during the Cuban missile crisis. We were filming in the particular area where Khrushchev

and Gromyko and Mikoyan and all the boys had their offices. We were only allowed to work at night. They didn't want to have Khrushchev climbing over the electric cables during the day. We worked from seven o'clock in the evening until 2:00 or 3:00 in the morning. Suddenly, one night the place was alive with people: Khrushchev and Mikoyan coming in side doors, and so on; there we were, dragging our cables around and carrying on. At one point, I was told a member of the council stuck his head out the door, went back into the meeting, and banged his hand on the table, saying, "Is that woman from America still here?"

I didn't know what was going on; I thought it was a wheat crisis in Siberia. Finally, Foy Kohler, who was our Ambassador at that time, invited me for lunch and told me about the missile crisis. I couldn't conceive the importance and horror—particularly being inside the Kremlin; it all seemed ludicrous!

So I fired off a cable to Pierre Salinger at the White House, and I said, "Couldn't the President wait until I was finished?" When I came back to Washington, Pierre said, "The President wants to see you. Bobby's in with him." With much trepidation, I walked into the President's office. There was Bobby looking very solemn. Later, I realized he was trying to keep from laughing. The President stood up and pointed his finger at me and said, "I saw that cable you sent! Didn't you know that you were part of a bargain? I told Khrushchev if he gets the missiles out of Cuba, I'll take you out of the Kremlin!" That's when I saw Bobby break up.

ROBERT LOVETT

He wrote me a *very* touching letter—in that strange, little cramped handwriting he had—about his brother and the gratitude which *he* had felt toward the association that we'd had . . . which was, in my opinion, minimal and really quite normal. He said that I had quoted something to him that made an impression on him. It was a quotation that I had read in a house organ published by a Danish shipping company. It was as follows: "Good judgment is usually the result of experience. And experience is frequently the result of bad judgment."

8

WILLIAM RICHARDS II, *journalist*

I kept a notebook. Here's how it reads about Elizabeth, New Jersey, and the accident there:

An old man carrying a cane (I'm at the platform now) walked by. "Just curiosity. You only see something like this once in a lifetime." Time is about 11:45. There were maybe 300 people lining the westbound platform.

[I wrote that the platform was narrow, maybe 10–12 feet wide.] The sun was shining through blue skies. Some clouds. Men in Bermuda shorts, women in gay print dresses. Some people with movie cameras.

12:32—Crowd somber, quiet, pensive. Not much talking. Maybe 500 to 600 people.

Elizabeth Honor Guard and Mayor Dunn arrive 12:35.

Police constantly moving along, moving people back from edge of walkway.

People at every overpass. Maybe 1,500 at station, lining both sides of the tracks, 5 to 7 deep.

A breeze blew intermittently, helping to cool it off. There were three men atop Goerke's, near the water tower on the roof.

Four more men on the Elizabeth Town Gas Co. building.

A baby kept crying. Seemed like maybe 2,500 people there.

A light appeared. "Here comes something." The people started to lean, their necks craning, looking.

It came on. It was an engine, black, huge. Three cars.

Police cars began radioing the word down the line. "That was the pilot," the radio crackled.

Then another message: "Forty-five miles an hour—that's the best they can do. The remains are in the last car, the observation car."

Another broadcast: "We got a call that some kids are gonna attempt to switch the tracks. All units watch switches and tracks."

Forty minutes late.

At 1:10, another broadcast: "It's in Secaucus Flats."

Up to the north, the tracks are lined with people.

"His major contribution was that he was," a woman said.

1:16—"Train passing through Penn Station, Newark." Police radio.

Another murmur. People guessing how long it will take to get here.

Cops: concentrating on people on tracks; getting people on platform; some dangling legs over edges.

"The feeling of being here is important," a man said as he passed.

"The draw of the man, even in death, is amazing," another guy remarked.

The man with the crew cut, and the Bermudas and glasses, said, "His contribution is that he had the courage to be different."

Broadcast: "Train is moving at a high rate of speed. Keep those people off the tracks."

Seriousness impressive. Quiet, eyes fixed to the north, awaiting appearance.

Good twenty minutes pass . . . nervous, awaiting train. Light appears.

I get goose-pimples. At North Avenue at 1:20.

Bright light. People run across track north of station. A plane in air following route. Two helicopters.

Light and black mass loom larger. Noise. Crowd chattering more now. Copter overhead, roaring—U.S. Army copter.

People stepping on tracks to take pictures.

Slow, very slow. Hats being taken off. Fifteen miles an hour. Large and black. Secret Service men in engine.

Nuns and photographers on board. Sonny Fox of Channel 5.

It slows even more.

Ethel, Jackie. Coffin, a Kennedy child on rear, garlands streaming. Jackie and Ethel together. Ethel wide-eyed. Jackie pointing at something over us.

Panic. Woman been hit. Faces turning away from train.

Rush of crowd.

A cop shouts: "Get them people the hell outa here."

The woman, blonde, blue dress.

Second train came through from other direction on north side. People never saw it coming. Many on north side didn't even see Kennedy car.

Another woman hurt, receiving oxygen. Kennedy train slowing.

A black and white shoe lying on tracks.

One woman

One man

Screams.

Cops trying to clear people on West Grand Street to get emergency vehicles through.

Train No. 50, Chicago to New York. Penn Central. Dragged from station to bridge. Put emergency brake on.

Dr. Henares, intern, looks at woman. It didn't look like a person. More like a bundle that's been pounded.

A penny, a camera case. Down a bit farther, the woman. Then some more, the man's leg on the other side of the outside track. On the bridge is his body.

Another woman got her hand hit by train.

GENEVIEVE MURPHY, *housewife, Elizabeth, New Jersey*

The first few cars had very few people in them, and Michael—poor Mike is retarded, my son, he's fourteen—well, he was looking for Sidney Poitier. He saw him in *To Sir With Love*, and since then he's admired him so. Whenever he sees him on TV, he gets excited. I think because Poitier was a schoolteacher, and the children were giving him a hard time—I think that's why. When the Senator died, and we were watching the TV—constantly, we never left the TV—Mike and I saw Sidney Poitier at the vigil in the Cathedral; he was standing at the coffin. Mike couldn't get over that—that Sidney Poitier could know the Kennedys and feel as bad as everybody else. Then we watched it again Saturday morning, and we knew he was going to be on the train. I wanted to go down anyway; I didn't know about Mike. So I said, "Mike, maybe you'll see Sidney Poitier." He wanted to know if Sidney Poitier would cry . . . this is Michael's way of feeling. So I said I thought he might. If we cried, he would cry too. So we went to the train station. When we saw the first few cars, they had very few people in them, then I saw the more

142

crowded cars coming. I said, "Look, Mike! Look, Mike!" I wanted him to see Sidney Poitier if he could.

I was quite far away from most of the crowd because my husband, who was with us too, was ill and he had to hold onto things to stand. So we were at the very edge of the crowd—I guess closest to the bend of the other train when it came through. I didn't see or hear the train. I did hear a horn, but I thought it was the Kennedy train. Just as I heard the train horn, it was then—you know when I try to recall I get such a headache because this is when it all happened—the train must have *bumped* me, because I feel now as if I had my left hand out—I had my back to the train—and that's all it hit, my left hand. But when it hit my left hand, it threw me back into the crowd so that I knocked people over with the force. I didn't know that I was hurt until my husband picked me up. I saw the contents of my pocketbook all over . . . and especially some letters that I treasured; so I went running after them. Then, as I went to pick up something, I felt a pain in my left hand; I looked down, and that was the first I realized that I had been hit. My hand was covered with grease; it was bleeding; it was swollen. With that, I turned around to my husband: "Look—the train hit me."

FELICIA TEDESCHI, *high school student, Elizabeth, New Jersey*
We still had our pajamas on that morning. We saw the train on television, and when they said it was delayed, Lucy and I decided to go. We just made it there on time, about thirty-five minutes before the train finally came.

We could see the helicopters flying overhead, and we were really getting excited. Lucy and I started sobbing—we were going to be emotional. We saw four cars of the Kennedy train, and there were people waving to people on the platform.

Then we saw the light of the train coming in the opposite direction, and people were standing on the tracks. It was horrible. The best way I can describe it is when you see a movie and someone's about to die— someone's falling over a cliff—and you hear this horrible scream of terror. It was heartbreaking.

That was it. After the accident, I didn't even care to look in the direction of the Kennedy train.

I think the grandmother tripped over the track. In the *Superman* comics or movies, Superman comes and stops the train just before . . . well, that didn't happen, because her legs were right over the track and

143

the train was about two feet from her. I saw a man try to pull her up, and this man—John Curia—died also.

The baby was turning with the wheel; the baby's clothes were caught into the wheel, or maybe it was the friction or the air suction of the train, but she rolled about two or three times. She was completely still. And I was scared to death because I've never seen a dead person in my life. I've never been to a wake, and my mother says I'm afraid of a mosquito, which is true. I didn't really want to pick up the child because I thought she was dead. There were plenty of adults around, and I didn't really think it was my duty to go to her. But no one else moved. I guess people were in shock. Since no one else moved, I went to pick her up. People thought she was my baby. They were just pointing at me and saying, "Look at the lady with the dead baby!" No one would help me.

I thought the baby was dead. I ran out into the street, and I thought everyone knew what had happened; but people were just coming out of the stores. They just saw me screaming. They didn't know what was the matter with me.

There happened to be a detective out there, for security reasons. He didn't know what had happened, but he saw the baby was injured and took me to the hospital.

He was driving, and I was crying—really, I couldn't control myself— and the detective said he was going to sock me. He said, "Control yourself, because you're going to do something to that kid." He thought it was mine. It's funny because before school, I always went for breakfast to a store across the street, and this detective goes there also. I never noticed him, but he happened to notice me. After a while, we began talking, and he realized that I was only in high school and not this baby's mother.

The little girl was unconscious, and the following day the detective told me that at the time he thought she was dead. But finally, she started crying. She had no blood on her. She just had bruises.

My mother wanted me to go and see the child afterwards, but I couldn't bring myself to do it. She was two and a half years old.

MARIAN JAVITS (*Mrs. Jacob Javits*)
All those nervous Congressmen just to do something were serving sandwiches. I guess they felt they had to get out of their seats; or perhaps they did not feel the need to sit down because it had been such a long church service. So they were serving *sandwiches,* and I remember it was about an hour and a half out of New York. I had passed one group of sandwiches by and also an offer to go into the next car. Then another

Congressman came by with a bunch of sandwiches, and I took one. I started to bite into the sandwich as we were pulling in toward a station. We slowed down a little, and I remember seeing the beginnings of a huge crowd of people standing at the edge of a platform. And then, suddenly, the other train came by. I had chewed into the sandwich, and turned to look back—slightly back—and saw the body of a woman thrown up into the air. I remember that she wore a green dress, and her legs went up.

SAUL STEINBERG, *artist*

A ship is isolated by the ocean; a plane flies high up; but a train—the way a train travels is very near reality. Except the American train is air-conditioned; you can't open the windows . . . so that the whole train had this dramatic reality of a giant coffin. It's isolated; it's sealed . . . so that this train was really a coffin on wheels, advancing, and expecting to be buried—the whole train—in Washington.

Part of the primitive system of the political funeral was that this coffin on wheels took along some sacrificial victims. It's part of this dramatic system of marking somebody of political importance; the hero cannot seem to die alone.

ROBERT MORGENTHAU, *U.S. Attorney*

Just the four of us were sitting by the pool eating lunch. It was a sunny day. Bobby had gone for a swim. They were painting the new wing of their house; there were some workmen around. This workman, who had a hand-carried radio, came over and said something. Nobody quite heard what he said. Then, just at that point a maid, or perhaps a houseman, came over and said, "Mr. Hoover's on the White House phone." Then I realized what the workman had said, "They say the President is shot." It didn't sink in. There was a telephone on the other side of the pool. As soon as Bobby took the call, he turned away, and he clapped his hand to his mouth. Ethel realized what had happened . . . or at least had an idea . . . and she ran over to him.

ARTHUR SCHLESINGER, JR., *historian*

Bob Kennedy developed after Dallas a sense of the unpredictability of things, which made long-term planning absolutely impossible for him. I think no one would have been less surprised by the manner of his death than he. He used to read Edith Hamilton and Aeschylus, and he always

145

carried in his briefcase some really terribly dog-eared volumes of Greek tragedies, which he read again and again. I think he got out of this a mixture of Christian stoicism, existentialism, and a sense that you could not escape your destiny. But this did not relieve man of the responsibility of striving in every way that he could—the Greek image of man against fate. Man against fate was very much his sense of life, plus the existentialist view that man defines himself by his choices. He knew the risks that he was running; he saw no choice but to run them. There was a sense of fatality about it all. I was always afraid that he'd fall off a mountain or drown in the ocean.

DAVID BRINKLEY, *television commentator*

It was the first time he'd been out after his brother's death. Teddy brought along a recorded tape—and it was of some New England character, some nice, likable, Irish storyteller in Boston. If it wasn't Dave Powers, it was somebody sort of like him. I don't really remember now. I think it was some sort of old character there they liked and admired. It was this New England raconteur talking about Jack Kennedy. They thought maybe Bobby and Ethel would enjoy hearing it. So they took it and put it on the tape recorder, started playing it, and they listened for just a few minutes. Then both of them soon left; they went home. I've been sorry about that ever since. It took him a long time. It reminded me of something somebody said during the day after John Kennedy's murder. They said, "We may work again, and we may play again, and we may have some fun again . . . but we'll never be young again."

PETER MAAS, *author*

About three weeks after President Kennedy was assassinated, I got a call from Ed Guthman. Bobby wasn't seeing anybody. He was terribly depressed, withdrawn. I'd written him a note about what I thought of him and what I thought he had to do. Ed Guthman said, "I think you ought to come down. This is just the time for people he cares about and who care about him to get him out a little bit." So I flew down. That day he was going out publicly, really for the first time—to a Christmas party for an orphanage in Washington. He had promised long before the assassination that he'd come. I went along. On the way we bought some toys. We walked, I remember, from the Justice Department to this place where the party was. We went up the stairs and walked in. The moment he walked in the room, all these little children—screaming and

146

playing—there was just suddenly silence. Everybody was still . . . all standing there, and the adults too, and I was standing off to one side. Bob stepped into the middle of the room and just then, a little boy—I don't suppose he was more than six or seven years old—suddenly darted forward, and stopped in front of him, and said, "Your brother's dead! Your brother's dead!" Gosh, you know, you could hear a pin drop. The adults, all of us, we just kind of turned away . . . you know, to the wall. The little boy knew he had done something wrong, but he didn't know *what*; so he started to cry. Bobby stepped forward and picked him up, in kind of one motion, and held him very close for a moment, and he said, "That's all right. I have another brother."

DANIEL P. MOYNIHAN, *director, Joint Center for Urban Studies*
It was really as difficult an occasion as you could ever have. He would listen to us, and he would be looking over our shoulders at some place in the middle of the room. Shriver, much of whose strength lies in a certain lack of sensitivity sometimes, *was* sensitive to this. Shriver would talk on and on and then he'd stop. Bob would ask a question—normally about the poor people and the poverty programs—something like that. But then, I remember very vividly, at a certain point, Shriver stopped talking, and Kennedy said *nothing*. He had just forgotten that we were there. We both just got up and left.

ADAM WALINSKY, *legislative aide, speechwriter*
You know, he's the only one of those people—of all the people who were associated with John F. Kennedy—he's the only one who grew or who went on living after he died. The rest of them just stopped. They're relics. They go on functioning; they do things, but nothing's changed in them. Something got cut out and it stopped, as if somebody did a lobotomy on them. He was the only one that started a new process of growth.

DR. LEONARD DUHL, *psychiatrist*
At the point when the President died and Bobby went into his own private grief world, the intriguing thing to me is that he shifted course and, instead of moving in the direction that the President was moving— the McNamara-Bundy approach—he went toward the Hackett-Boone-Walinsky-Edelman view. Suddenly he was in touch, through these guys, with the poor and the black, the kids, the music; and he began to link up with all the people who were beginning to question the society and really wanted to change—Kennedy's Guerrillas. There were oddballs

147

and characters trying to change the world of business; there were similar guys in labor; guys working with Indians who *were* Indians. You really began to see what a floating crap game it was. Bobby essentially began to evolve a form of coalition politics. Now, I don't think he understood all this verbally, and he couldn't put it together. But yet, he was sensing this; so many people on the train could not understand why everybody else was there; they didn't understand this floating crap game in which he was the center and connecting link, and that all the other players were not like themselves.

KAY EVANS, *family friend*

I think the trips to Asia and Europe that first year were the beginning of his coming back to life again after his brother's death. He made a speech at the University of Heidelberg. In that speech, he said suddenly, as he ended it, that he realized how much President Kennedy had meant to this country, and he saw that there was still much to be done and there were new things to do. I think it was the moment in which he took a breath and started again. Until the trip to Germany and Poland he seemed to be in the grip of grief. And then he began to move again.

JOHN SEIGENTHALER, *campaign aide, editor,* Nashville Tennessean

We were in a hall at Nihon University, where there were it seemed like 10,000 kids stacked up in tiers, rising maybe 100 feet in the air. They had distributed his speech in Japanese. It was about six long pages, and each time he got to the bottom of a page and turned to the next, suddenly 10,000 pages turned at once. I mean whoosh—this great whooshing sound —like water running over a cliff. That same afternoon, we went to Waseda University. In a hall of 1,800 students, about 100 zengakuren Communist students were raising hell: "Kennedy go home!" "Free Okinawa!" He had done his homework and knew the answers. But 150 people can disrupt a meeting and stop you from speaking. So he went down and grabbed this kid by the hand, and he pulled him up on the stage. He was a skinny little kid, but he had a great set of lungs. Bob said, "Let's do this in a democratic fashion. If you have something to say, if you have a question to ask, if you have a speech you want to make, you say it I'll share the microphone with you."

Well, this kid began a whole barrage against the United States government—about the bomb, nuclear weapons, Okinawa, imperialism. When Bob got the microphone, they pulled the switch on him. All the light went out. The electric power went off. We had brought along a bull horn. So he finished it off with a very impromptu speech—all the shouting, all the screaming still going on. Every time he'd make a point, the great majority of those kids would give him the same sort of applause he'd gotten from the 10,000 kids earlier at Nihon University who had turned the pages with him. Then the cheerleader for the school got up and led everybody in the school song, the Waseda school song. There's a recording of it, which I've got at home. If you listen to it, you can hear: Mi-ah-kon-oh-say-ho-ku. . . ." And as they pause for breath, you hear one of these zengakuren kids yell, "Kennedy go home!"

We've laughed about it a hundred times. The Friday before the assassination, we were riding along the expressway in San Francisco to the airport. He had been to the Japanese Cultural Center the day before. He said, "You should have gone! We sang the Waseda song." And then driving along, he and I and Ethel—with Dick Harwood sitting there, stunned—we burst into: "Mi-ah-kon-oh-say-ho-ku."

In Indonesia, Sukarno had us just surrounded by police everywhere we went. But this little wraith of a guy steps out, does a full pitcher's wind-up, and hurls this piece of hard-shell fruit, which just bounces off the beak of Bob's nose. Bob never blanched. He looked around at me, and by this time, they had this guy and they jerked him, twisted his arm, and God knows what happened to him. Bob subsequently said to Sukarno that he hoped this man was not mistreated. But his first reaction was a natural, angry reaction—this fellow tried to hurt me. He said, "Did you see that?" It stung. His nose was red. And I think of him in Latin America, walking along that floor in Concepción, and the eggs and the coins and the garbage raining down and having him turn around and say, "If these kids are going to be young revolutionaries, they're going to have to improve their aim."

PETER MAAS

Traveling, anywhere, just out his door, he was always out of cash; he never had any small change; I guess every rich man has this, but he was *particularly* like that. We'd stop by a newsstand, and he'd hit me for a quarter for this or that; or if he wanted *Life* or *Time*, or a candy bar at Schrafft's. He tried to *charge* a sandwich at Schrafft's once. So, over a period of time, this amounted to $100 and $150, and I started needling him, you know, that I was keeping very close track of all the money that he owed me, and one of these days would be the day of reckoning. A couple of times, he got a little uptight about it. But then he had his revenge, and he put me down forever, and it was worth all the money. We were in Korea on a trip around the world after President Kennedy had been assassinated, in January of '64, and we were at Mass in an Army chapel in Korea. The collection plate started coming up the aisle towards us, and I could see him starting to look around. I knew what was going to happen. The basket got closer and closer, and finally it was just one pew away, and he nudged me, and I reached in my pocket and pulled out a dollar and gave it to him. He looked at it, and he turned around to me and nudged me again and whispered, "Don't you think I should give more?"

JOSEPH KRAFT, *columnist*
His wit always was turned on in very nice ways. I remember in the Polish trip, he'd had problems because they weren't giving out his schedule. Nothing appeared in the newspapers. The crowds were very large only when they were able to discover where he was going to be. So he devised a tactic of announcing at his appearances where he was going to be for the rest of the day. One day he announced that he was having dinner at the American Ambassador's house, which was in a suburb. We got out there at about 8:30 or 9:00, and an enormous crowd had gathered outside the residence. Bob got up on his car and began talking to them; they wouldn't let him alone. Finally he said, "Well, I guess I have to go in to dinner now. Maybe I'll ask you all in to have dinner with me." He leaned over and said to Ambassador Cabot, "Ambassador, is it all right?" Then he said to them, "No. The Ambassador says no."

RICHARD GOODWIN, *politician*
I think that had President Kennedy lived, his intention was to move Bobby from the Justice Department and put him in charge of Latin American affairs. I remember almost the last thing that John F. Kennedy did before he was killed . . . I think it was his last day in Washington . . . was to talk to a group of Latin Americans—artists and writers—who were visiting the United States. They said that he ought to put someone like his brother in charge of Latin American affairs. He said, "When you go over to see him, ask him if he wants it." They did, and he sort of mumbled. He had a keen interest in that area.

FRANK MANKIEWICZ, *press secretary*
I was asked to come to the State Department briefing before his South American trip. He was Senator then. As a Peace Corps director, in a sense,

I was sitting in that meeting on the government side, rather than on Robert Kennedy's side. He had Adam Walinsky with him. The briefing was just a shambles. Jack Vaughn, who was then the Assistant Secretary of State for Latin America and later became the Peace Corps Director, was in charge. I've never seen Jack so hostile. Senator Kennedy asked, "What should I say in Latin America about the Dominican Republic?" which was then a rather important issue. Our takeover had only been about four or five months before.

Vaughn said, "Well, in the first place, nobody will ask you about the Dominican Republic because they don't care about that issue. No one asks about that anymore."

Senator Kennedy said, "Well, you and I don't talk to the same Latins because that's all they ever ask me."

They made a bet of ten dollars that it would be one of the first three questions asked him when he got to Latin America. Of course, as soon as he got to Latin America, they asked him that, and he sent a telegram to Jack Vaughn which said, "You lose."

Then Vaughn said, "If they *do* ask you, you can always tell them what your brother said about Cuba." The Senator sort of cooled noticeably and said, "Which statement of President Kennedy's did you have in mind?" Vaughn couldn't remember it exactly. He said, "Well, it was something about Communism in the Western Hemisphere." The Senator said, "I hope you're not using any quotations from President Kennedy to bolster your entry into the Dominican Republic, because you know I opposed that."

The briefing just went downhill from there. Vaughn persisted in referring to President Kennedy as "your brother," which was not very helpful.

Then they talked about the fact that the U.S. had cut off aid to Peru because their government was having a dispute with the Standard Oil Company of New Jersey, which had a subsidiary there—a fight over royalties. The Senator said, "Why should the government get into a contest between the Peruvian government and a private American oil company?" Vaughn said, "If the Peruvians get too much of a royalty, then it will affect other oil companies in other countries." He explained that an eighty per cent royalty was too high.

At this point I intervened and said, "The Senator ought to understand that as far as the Peruvian government is concerned, eighty per cent is too low; and one hundred per cent is the appropriate figure. It isn't a question of royalty. The position of the Peruvian government is that the concession was illegal in the first place." I went on to say that it was not the fault of the American company; they had bought the subsidiary from an English company. I explained all that. I don't think it helped me very much with my colleagues on the government side.

Then we went on and talked about Brazil. The Senator said, "What can I say in Brazil where they've outlawed political parties and closed down the Congress, and are denying people their rights, and so forth?" Vaughn said, "Well, you could say nothing. That's what they say when they come up here." The Senator said, "Well, I can't do that." So then some Brazil desk officer from State read off some marvelous sort of State Department thing where he said, "Why don't you say that we regret that a great power has temporarily seen fit to suspend certain elements." And on and on and on. The Senator cut him off right in the middle of it, and he said, "Well, I don't talk like that."

Finally we got close to the end of it, and the Senator said, "Well, Mr. Vaughn, let me see if I understand what you're saying. You're saying that what the Alliance for Progress has come down to is that if you outlaw political parties and close down the Congress and put people in jail, you can get all the aid you want. But if you mess around with an American oil company, then you don't get anything. Is that about right?" And Vaughn said, "Yeah, that's about right." On that cheerful note, the briefing broke up.

RICHARD GOODWIN

We had arranged a meeting with a group of Peruvian intellectuals—poets and artists and people I knew—in the apartment of the Peruvian artist Fernando de Szyszlo. Earlier, the United States had suspended its aid programs to Peru because there was a disagreement about the royalty division with the International Petroleum Company, really a rather trivial sort of argument. The debate seemed to be one that any mediator could probably settle in a month or two. There was no legal necessity to cut off aid. But Tom Mann did it as a way of putting pressure on the Peruvians. Of course, the sufferers were first of all people who were struggling to build schoolhouses and water-supply complexes; secondly, Peru had a sort of democratic, liberal government, non-Communist, anti-Communist, the first in a long time; it would seem to have been to all our interests to support it. But we were undermining it, which was one of the principal contributions to the fall of that government and its replacement by a military regime.

Well, we went to this meeting and, of course, they wanted to know about American politics; Kennedy kept defending the United States; then the question of the petroleum company came up. He said to them, "Look, why do you always look to the United States?" They said, "Well, the United States won't let us do anything about the International Petroleum Company." He said, "Well, what are you talking about? Why don't you go ahead and do what you want. It's your country. You can't be both cursing the United States and then looking to it for permission to do what you want to do; what you have to do is to act on your own and take the consequences."

Well, they began talking about David Rockefeller, who had been down there and gone around telling them that they couldn't do anything about the International Petroleum Company. Kennedy looked at them, and he said, "Well, you know, we Kennedys, we *eat* Rockefellers for breakfast." They all sort of laughed; but unknown to us, at this off-the-record meeting, there was a magazine writer with a tape recorder. So it all appeared . . . and soon the thing was all over the Peruvian newspapers, spreading through Latin America, and causing quite a furor with the State Department. When we got to Argentina, an Argentine reporter came up and asked, "Tell me, Senator, is it true that you have breakfast with Rockefeller every morning?"

MARTIN ARNOLD, *journalist*

He was always amazed that the embassy people did not know how to sell Lyndon Johnson in South America. He did a good job for President Johnson, really, in the sense that he used to tell these people that Lyndon Johnson had come from the soil and that he would understand their type of problems. He was very good that way, even though the two men obviously hated each other.

It was very hard to explain to South Americans why he wasn't President of the United States. If he wasn't, why didn't he just march on Washington and throw Johnson out and *become* President then, you know?

Every embassy just wanted him to get out of *their* country alive, with a minimum amount of trouble, and into the next poor guy's backyard.

WILLIAM VANDEN HEUVEL, *campaign aide*

We ended one day in Recife. And it was one of the great, colorful, emotional receptions that he must have ever received in his life; well over 100,000 people lined the streets; it was a five-hour journey through the streets of the town. He was very much taken by northeast Brazil.

That's where the human problems of Brazil were centered; the economic depression was there; the poverty; that's where Archbishop Helder Câmara of Recife was active—the great revolutionary churchman whom Bobby admired. Bobby toured the sugar-cane fields, and he talked to the workers and to the owners, and he was appalled that the minimum-wage laws, for example, which only guaranteed sixty cents a day to a sugar-cane cutter, were not even enforced, so that frequently cutters got less than that. And that the operation of the sugar-cane mills was such that the streams were polluted, and the fish were killed; that seven out of ten children in some of the villages died before the age of *one* . . . that's a statistic he always recited years after in speeches.

MARTIN ARNOLD

On one side of the gymnasium in Concepción were the pro people, and on the other side were the radical leftists, who were shouting and screaming, "Go home, Bobby!" It was an odd kind of a mixed thing, because when you first got there even though they were shouting at him and screaming at him, they also wanted to shake his hand. A lot of them were leaning over the rails to shake his hand, and then other kids would grab the ones back who'd shaken his hand and say, "Don't shake the bastard's hand. He's just been sent down here by an imperialistic government." I guess they really accepted him as the most acceptable of Americans, but that really wasn't good enough. So they shouted and screamed and carried on; and they'd spit over the railings and throw things: food, and eggs, and stuff like that. I think Bill vanden Heuvel got whacked with an egg.

RICHARD GOODWIN

We met El Cordobés, the great bullfighter. Afterwards, we went to the home of a very wealthy Peruvian oligarch, who had a huge room full of animal heads . . . the most obscene room I have ever seen in my life, all these dead animals looking out at you everywhere you went. The garden had deer in it. On the way out, in the growing darkness, Bobby and Cordobés began fighting the deer with jackets, pretending to be bullfighters; Bobby challenged El Cordobés to a *mano a mano* . . . bullfighter versus bullfighter. But the deer wouldn't cooperate. They were petrified—this spectacle of grown men waving their jackets at them.

MARTIN ARNOLD

We walked into the Bernbaums' house—the Ambassador in Venezuela. He was not a bad guy. But his wife was unable to cope with the situation.

154

You could hear her in the next room saying, "Where did all these people come from? Who are they? Why are they sleeping here?" And we could hear the Ambassador trying to say, "Calm down. We have to do this." In the other room, the servants were preparing for this huge luncheon, which she was obviously against. Guests began arriving for the big reception. I looked for Bobby, and he was in the swimming pool, which was visible from where they were having the reception. Bobby said, "Come on in." I said, "I haven't got a bathing suit." So he said, "I'm in here without a suit." I figured, "What the hell! If *he* was in there without a suit, there was no reason why I couldn't be in there without a suit." So I peeled down naked and jumped in this swimming pool. By this time, hundreds of people were gathered for the diplomatic reception. As we were swimming around, finally it dawned upon me. . . . I saw Bobby get up out of the pool in a bathing suit. He'd tricked me. Mrs. Bernbaum was yelling and screaming already, and here I was in their pool, in the middle of the day, naked and with all these people arriving. Her husband got very excited about the whole thing.

TOM JOHNSTON, *administrative aide*
Usually, the State Department was worried about their cars being scratched up when he'd stand on top of them. I think they were willing to sacrifice a few Lincolns if they could just get him out of there without any huge amount of trouble.

In South Africa hundreds of thousands of people live all together behind wires, and they come in and out every day with cards to work in Johannesburg. It's really a sort of concentration camp. RFK asked this priest what he should tell them. And the priest said, "Patience. Patience." He went out and he didn't give a terribly "burn-'em-down" speech, but it was not a speech that counseled patience either.

He was initially in a position of being very much the intruder, the man coming over to exploit the South Africa situation for his own short-term political benefit, with a lot of self-righteousness and preaching . . . and yet he came out of it five days later, just terribly close to as popular a person and as widely and warmly acclaimed by all sorts of people in that country as you can imagine. He made people see that a liberal, white, Western foreigner could come and state a position diametrically opposed to the apartheid policy of the government, and yet not polarize the subject . . . but actually give the people the sense that there were some practical, intermediate, specific things that could be done. He did it all with a disarming amount of candor and humor and directness

which they, as a people—even the most conservative of them—appreciated.

The impression was that of that kind of warmth coming out; they
were very eager to hear and understand that there must be some other
way down to the stone fence, which went about two acres, and all of
really, as we moved from Cape Town to Durban, you began to sense
this great change; there were so many more people . . . and instead of
standing there passive, sort of hostile, why, they were like the crowds in
a campaign that begins terribly slowly and then moves to this climax,
all condensed into four and a half days! So that, by the end of it, the
government resistance seemed so ridiculous, and sort of crusty and
empty, that the whole thing looked like it would crumble if he just stayed
two more days.

LUCY JARVIS, *television producer*

In a country where apartheid is the ruling law, and where blacks
simply do not socialize in any way or even visit or concern themselves
with the whites—when the word got out that Ethel and Bobby were at
the Menil household, they started to come from miles—blacks coming up
that road. It's an area that looks like Greenwich, Connecticut—great
houses and great stone fences around—and the blacks were marching up
that road . . . where blacks were not allowed to be. And they were
coming in that driveway and filling that enormous lawn in front of the
house, and the big, wide staircase that comes up to the house, and pushing so that Bobby and Ethel were backed up into the house itself, the
people coming in with them in this great entrance hall until Bob and
Ethel were standing with their backs up against the fireplace. Behind
them was a painting done by a black artist in South Africa; it's of a small,
black shepherd boy with some sheep, and the boy is standing in the front
of the painting, and his mouth is open as though he's calling his flock.
One of the blacks said to Bobby, "He looks like he's singing. I wonder
what he's singing." Bobby said, "He's singing 'We Shall Overcome.' "
And then they all started to sing! Bobby and Ethel and Tom Johnston
standing there with their backs to the fireplace, looking out at this sea of
black faces inside the house and spilling out onto the lawn and all the
way down to the stone fence, which went about two acres, and all of
them singing "We Shall Overcome."

While on the train I was remembering all of this, and I was thinking,
"My God, what kind of an effect can Bobby's death have on people like
this all over the world?"

156

ANN BUCHWALD, *family friend*
She looked just perfect—if it hadn't been black, which Ethel hates. Somebody said, "She's never liked black. She once told me that she wouldn't buy a dress with any black in it." You look at her house, and you see her adoration of pinks and greens and blues, and her bedroom and her pool house. I can't think of anything that has black in it. So that was a shocker. You had never seen her in black! Nobody had. Yes. Then she came through and did all this talking to people.

ROOSEVELT GRIER, *former professional football player*
She wanted to go through and thank all the people. I was sitting up a couple of cars when I saw her coming. I said, "You know, there's twenty cars on this train and it's real hot, but if you want to go, we're going to take you." She said, "We're going to go." And that was it. So we took her the rest of the way, all the way up front. Then we sat down for a little while. A couple of times I got her some water. She just talked to people and she thanked them for coming. I felt so much for her. I remember that any time I would drift off into a really down feeling, she'd say, "Now, Rosey, come on over here." She'd keep pulling me back, you know. Pulling me back.

ADALBERT DE SEGONZAC, *journalist*
The rumor came through that Ethel was coming. There was a man sleeping two or three seats in front of me, and his wife rushed to wake

him up. She shook him and said, "Wake up! Wake up! Mrs. Kennedy's coming. Put on your shoes! You've got to put on your shoes!"

JOSÉ TORRES, *former light heavyweight champion*

The first one who came by was Matthew, the small one, and he says—very proud—that he just took a nap, that he didn't know what was going on. He was very excited seeing all those people in the train. Then I think the second one to come was little Bobby, and then the other kids came by and I said, "Do you remember me?" Kerry, the girl, said, "Yes, I know who you are." And she went like this with her fist. "You are the fighter," she says. And then she walked away, and then Joseph came, and he saw me and he said, "Hi, José," and shook my hand, and he kept walking. Ethel came, and you know I had the crutches because I had this operation on my foot, and it was the first time I saw her since this happened. She says, "José, where have you been?" I couldn't talk, of course, and she says, "Look at that, half a day campaigning for Bobby and look what happened, you have crutches." She was just kidding around. When she got no response from me, then she took both my hands, pressing very hard.

PETE HAMILL, *columnist*

Holy Christ! She had enough problems. Everybody just sort of shrunk back and gasped. They didn't know what the hell to do. She came through trying to cheer us up, but everybody was in tears by the time she got through the car. That was the first time I broke on the train. Of all the people, she was the one that had the right to grieve . . . and yet she was worried about our grief more than anything else. Remarkable! She's really some woman. Jacqueline was wandering around with a tray at one point, and looking sort of icy; it was an interesting contrast. I don't know how she remembered everybody's name. José Torres was with me, and he had a cast on his leg, and all she wanted to know about was the cast; what had happened and was it going to be all right. That wrecked him.

SHIRLEY MacLAINE, *actress*

The two women: Mrs. Ethel Kennedy and Mrs. Jackie Kennedy came through. Jackie first, very regal, as only she can be, with this marvelous sense of sort of anticipatory dignity. She was always able, somehow, to anticipate when the train was going to lurch or when it would bump, and queenlike, take hold of something so that when the bump came, she wasn't disturbed or dislodged. Ethel, standing right beside her, was so unaware, with a complete lack of self-consciousness about herself, that she got bumped every single time. She lurched and fell against a chair or against somebody, always recovering and doing it with humor; but it was so poignant that she allowed herself to be exposed that much.

Ethel stopped and talked with everyone, and remembered things like people's second-removed-generation cousin's names and how did that tennis match turn out.

BURT GLINN, *photographer*

It stopped your heart! In the car where I was sitting, Joe was the first of the family to come out. I was sitting with a guy from the Chicago *Sun-Times*, Dave Murray, who was at Harvard at the same time that I was there. All of a sudden, Dave looked over my shoulder and kind of stiffened, and he said, "My God! It's Bobby when we first knew him!" I turned around. Well, Joe was sixteen, and I guess Bobby was eighteen or nineteen when we first saw him, but a lot of it was there. The strange images that people have who knew him back at Harvard that time, like Dave and myself, Tony Lewis . . . my memory is of a strangely slight young man, standing on the Harvard football field. He looked so out of place there. But the personal gestures and characteristics carried on.

DOLORES HUERTA, *vice president, United Farm Workers Organizing Committee*

And the little Kennedy children were coming by. . . . You know, they kept passing by, going back and forth, and one of the little children said to his sister, "Well, California. . . . Weren't we in California? I remember California," he said to her, as he passed by.

PETE HAMILL

I was doing a two-part piece: one on how his office functions and the other on Bobby at home—the usual, *schlocky* approach to life. So, he invited me out to the house after we talked in the office, and the next thing I knew I was out on the goddamn field playing with a football, which I hadn't done in fifteen years! He and his kids were really running me into the ground; they knew they had a live one. And I ended up pooped out. But it was a great house to be in, a marvelous sense of family . . . which the Kennedys have always had. Bobby really liked his kids; you know, he enjoyed them, and he never had enough time really, I guess, to get to know them all very intimately. Walking in there was like walking into a centipede; there'd be this thing in the middle of the floor coming at you, and it was all the kids together! He dug the kids, and he worried about them . . . especially the older kid, Joe, who was always breaking arms and legs, getting gored by bulls.

LaDONNA HARRIS (*Mrs. Fred Harris*)

If the kids were mad at each other, he would tease them and get them to where they wouldn't be fussing. He'd grab one up and kind of throw him in the air, or hug him real tight and say something like, Oh, you can't be mad. You don't want to be mad. And just talk them all out of it. One thing I remember is the big dog Brumus, the Labrador. All the dogs were something else. The girls were in a horse show: Kathleen and Kerry and Caroline, and Jackie was there. We were all standing there talking, and Brumus—the lumbering ox—went out and sat right in the middle of the show! He just was sitting there! The ringmaster—or whatever his title is—said, "Would somebody kindly get their dog out of here? The dog is disturbing the horses. Would you get the dog. . . ." And he nudged the dog with his foot. The Senator leaned over the rail and said, "Don't kick my dog." The ringmaster . . . well, it kind of took him back. He said, "Senator, I didn't kick . . ." The Senator said, "I saw you! Don't you ever kick my dog again." He went and got Brumus out. Jackie said, "Oh, my gosh, we're going to lose the horse show."

ART BUCHWALD, *columnist*

Brumus was always a big problem at the pet shows at Hickory Hill because he was ready to eat the pets and bite the children. But when Bobby was around, he wouldn't lock Brumus up. So Brumus was there that first year, and sure enough, Brumus went up to these two women sitting having their lunch on the lawn, and he lifted a leg and peed on their backs. Bobby saw this happen, and he ran into the house. I accused him of having a questionable profile in courage.

GEORGE PLIMPTON, *author*

The great thing was that these two women wandered around for a while and then sat down again to watch the children and the carrousels, and so forth, down the hill, and Brumus came ambling out of the house—and did it again . . . to those same two!

KAY EVANS, *family friend*

One time, André Malraux came in, and there were Brumus, the black dog, and Meegan, the white dog, and the children were there in their red pajamas. And then he referred to one dog as a black-tie dog and the other as a white-tie dog, and he said, "This house is 'hellzapopping.'"

For a while at Hickory Hill, they had one of those dwarf ponies, about as big as a dog. Then they had a seal who lived in the swimming pool. He was named Sandy. One day, he got out of the pool and started down the road toward McLean. Now he lives at the zoo. They also had a honey bear—a nocturnal animal that was always climbing around at night, and getting into the icebox. In the daytime, he'd be sleeping in the bookcases, doing heaven knows what damage. The falcon was rather quiet. The coati-mundi . . . a frightening animal, some relation to an anteater . . . actually *bit* Ethel. Two writers Ethel had never met before were waiting in the living room to interview Bobby. She was trying to entertain them until Bobby was ready, filling up the time as best she could. She took them down to the basement to see little Bobby's terrarium. Just as she was showing them the cage with the snakes and the turtles in it, suddenly the coati-mundi leaped up and wrapped himself around her leg. Both writers had to extricate the animal from her. The afternoon Bobby made a speech in the Senate, and Ethel was there, as she always was, but this time her legs were in bandages.

GEORGE PLIMPTON

He must have enjoyed those pet shows enormously—his place full of children, the town pitching in so that the lawn down by the tennis court had children's rides placed around, and there was a fire truck for them to ride, and ponies, and if you were under the age of eight, it would be an occasion you'd remember forever. It was a civic affair, really—to benefit the Northwest Settlement House. The main event was the pet show itself—with an odd assortment of contests for "dogs with the longest tail," "strangest pet," "longest-eared pet," and so forth, and it was a rare pet that didn't get some sort of a ribbon. The judges—who were Art Buchwald and Phil Geyelin the year I dropped in on the proceedings—were very broad-minded. I remember during the judging of the reptile class, a very small girl brought up a glass jar to the judges' stand, which Buchwald looked into and poked around in some grass at the bottom, and finally asked, "Well, what's in here?" "It's a dead snake," the girl said. "It died on the way here in the car." She seemed quite nonplused. "Oh," said Buchwald. He called for a short period of silence over the loudspeaker system, and he awarded the dead snake's owner a consolation ribbon, which, come to think of it, was appropriate enough.

ELIZABETH STEVENS, *family friend*

At Hickory Hill, they were never inhibited by strangers or crowds. Ken McCormick, their dignified editor from Doubleday, came down to get the proofs of Bobby's book [*Thirteen Days*]. Angie Novello, Bobby's secretary, was sitting in the secretary's room trying to decipher the last bits of Bobby's handwriting, and was typing it out and handing it to McCormick, who was collecting it all to take back. He had come down because everything was late as usual. I guess there were about fifteen or twenty people there for dinner. After dinner, we played . . . oh, what's the one where one person hides and then you find them and crawl in with them. You know . . . Sardines. Ethel went and got in the clothes closet next to the secretary's room, where McCormick was working. Byron White found her, and he climbed in with her, and then Bob McNamara; finally there were about fifteen men in there with Ethel. And then Bobby opened the door, and they all tumbled out. Poor Ken McCormick just hadn't a clue to what was going on. Then Bob McNamara, when it was his turn, went and hid behind the curtains in the secretary's room. There was Ken McCormick looking on and trying to get the papers from Angie, with people sneaking around and hiding behind the curtains with the Secretary of Defense. I mean, it must have been the most extraordinary evening, particularly for someone who had never been through it before. I think he was undone by the whole thing.

GEORGE STEVENS, JR., *director, American Film Institute*

I was in charge of finding movies for them to show out there at Hickory Hill. They built a projection room down by the pool; it was a big project. It became a tremendous possibility for relaxation: they could always squeeze in an hour and a half. They'd have dinner and then see a movie. The taste and sophistication levels were kept fairly low. You had to please the audience from four to eighty. Little Kerry or Maxwell sitting there, and you had to find something suitable for them and interesting for us. It was always quite difficult. I helped them get the movies at first, and then finally I stopped. I couldn't stand the responsibility. The movie would come on, and a well-developed girl would walk across the screen, and everybody would look at the children and then they'd look at me and say, "George!" Then the children would all be sent off to bed. Somehow, it was invariably my fault. I was the villain to young and old alike.

JOSEPH KRAFT, *columnist*

The parties were not Camelot—not anything like those his brother had—because John Kennedy, it seemed to me, kept pretty carefully apart from the people that were around him. His parties were layered and structured, and not all mixed up and randomly sorted and put together. I mean it would not have been typical of John Kennedy, I think, to have a dinner for six and invite us, let's say, the McCones, and, oh, the Harlechs. But Bob and Ethel would mix them up—without even thinking—and sometimes the results were disastrous. But he would do that.

THEODORE WHITE, *author*

How sweet the occasions were. First of all, if the party was outside, all the little kids would be in nightgowns, standing around peeping over the hedge, barefooted, in those little nightgowns. Wherever it was, any-time you'd walk in, they'd say, "This party is for *you*." For Harry Belafonte, for Georgei Bolshakov, or for Teddy White. Once, Bobby challenged everybody to do push-ups. I'm pretty good at push-ups; I'm very muscular. So first he licked Kenny O'Donnell at push-ups. He looked around, and he said, "Now you!" Of course, I was glad to accept at that point because he must have been tired out. So I beat Bobby by about push-up thirty-two, something like that. Bobby had been exhausted by Kenny first. When I beat Bobby, I felt so goddamn proud of myself. Then they made me the champion against Bolshakov. I've got a good torso; I'm very strong up here in the arms, and I did some arm wrestling with Bolshakov. As I was getting Bolshakov down, Ethel was screaming, "We're winning! Our side is winning! We're winning!" Bolshakov began to lift his elbow off the table. Ethel yelled, "You're cheating! You're cheating! He's cheating! He's cheating!" Well, it was all great fun! It was great fun. Oh, Christ! How many parties I remember there. I remember Chip Bohlen and Georgei Bolshakov sitting in a cor-ner discussing Soviet-American policy. I remember Eunice Shriver going around, trying to raise funds for retarded children. Everybody was off pushing their own thing—whether it was Russian foreign policy, or re-tarded children, or just girl chasing or American defense. I drifted from conversation to conversation. It was a panorama of life in Washington.

It was absolutely impossible for me to get Nancy home. We were enjoying ourselves.

ALICE ROOSEVELT LONGWORTH (*Mrs. Nicholas Longworth*)

He was not only good with the young, he was awfully good with the old . . . with myself, you see. But I was damned good myself, so there we were! We managed to be extremely good together. At dinners we'd gossip about things. No splendid serious conversations. Nothing like that! Trivia. We spoke to amuse the other and also to amuse oneself. I thought I was a splendid guest! We were a sheer delight—both of us.

GEORGE PLIMPTON

McLean is a network of macadam roads. If you could *find* Hickory Hill, the house stood back from the road up a steep incline, with a steep U-shaped driveway that went up past the front door and was always choked with cars. When they had the big affairs, the cars were parked for a hundred yards along Chain Bridge Road. The guests would walk through the house out onto the back terrace and see the tables set down the hill by the swimming pool. You'd get a drink on the terrace and amble down past the big hickory that had a swing hanging from one of the high boughs, and a tree house in which there was usually a Kennedy child watching you go by, owl-like, with grave, proprietary eyes.

There were always some added features to make the parties memorable. For Averell Harriman's seventy-fifth birthday everyone came dressed in a costume to commemorate some aspect of Harriman's life. A great many people came in railroad engineer's outfits—Harriman, of course, had started in his family's Union Pacific. I wore an Arab gown and headdress. That didn't make any sense. It was the only outfit I had, I guess, and I supposed Harriman had probably put in a tour in the Middle East at some point. The others were more appropriate. Art Buchwald came as the Yale coxswain—Harriman had been an oarsman there—and he did a lot of very funny shouting through a megaphone. Bobby greeted Harriman at the door in a long black overcoat that came down to his shoe tops and the same sort of distinctive hat that Harriman wore when he was the ambassador in Moscow. It gave Harriman quite a shock. He knew something was up. But then the extraordinary thing they did—and it showed what effort and ingenuity they went to—was to cart in from some wax museum a life-size wax replica of the world leaders of the

Yalta Conference—the famous grouping of Churchill, Roosevelt, Stalin seated for a camera portrait—and they set this outside on the porch beyond a curtained bay window. Then at some appropriate moment during the dinner, the curtains were drawn back and there this group was, staring in at the festivities. I remember it was very cold, and they looked forlorn out there, like waifs, and awfully cold, too, because of that spooky wax color. Someone had furled a scarf around Stalin's neck and Roosevelt had a beanie-type hat to make them look a bit more cheerful.

There was always something like that to make the party stick in your mind. One year they had huge muslin screens set about the lawns with motion pictures going on them. At the party for John Glenn, Ethel had a sort of catwalk built over the pool with a table set for two placed out there. Very precarious. Glenn was supposed to sit with her. He was extremely reluctant to venture out. I don't think he ever did. I remember he took a balloon and wrote a message on a paper napkin: "Help! I'm a prisoner at the Kennedys!" He tied the message to the balloon and let the wind take it off across the trees. One had the feeling that evening that *someone* was going to wind up in the pool. And of course Arthur Schlesinger *did*—someone, a girl in a print evening dress, got a good running start so that her shove, getting him just right, really put him far out into the pool. He was very indignant.

ALICE ROOSEVELT LONGWORTH

I shall never forget Arthur Schlesinger shooting over my shoulder that night. It was the funniest thing. Ethel was so naughty for doing it. She had put a chicken walk across the pool with a bridge table on it and a chair, and I thought, Ha-ha! I don't have to be told what *that's* for. And indeed I didn't. Out went Ethel with Colonel John Glenn. Did he play along with his hostess? No. I had to respect him from then on. He kept just as far away from her as he could get. He was not going to be pulled into the water with her, which was very good to see. Then, suddenly, practically over my shoulder, shot Arthur Schlesinger. He claims that he doesn't know whether he was pushed, or whether he jumped, or what happened. He says he doesn't remember, but he gave the impression of being catapulted!

ART BUCHWALD

The social life at Hickory Hill was sort of a combination of people got there to amuse Bobby or whom Bobby would like. He liked anybody who Ethel liked. Bobby would bring in some of his people, but I think Ethel, as far as the social life went, decided on most of them. And you found, which is true of most Kennedys, you did most of the talking and they did most of the listening. It's a trick I noticed the few times I met President Kennedy; he had it and all the girls have it: they were picking your brains, but you were very flattered that they cared what you thought.

LYDIA KATZENBACH (*Mrs. Nicholas deB. Katzenbach*)

The Hickory Hill seminars were started by Bobby. The guest list and the format remained pretty much the same: the meetings were held in different homes; the main speaker talked for forty minutes or so, and then there was open discussion. One of the first seminars was conducted by Dr. Lawrence S. Kubie, the famous psychoanalyst, on the subject, "Urban Problems and Poverty Children." During the discussion period, Dr. Kubie got into a heated argument with Bobby—who just didn't feel that society had time to psychoanalyze the ghetto. The argument got worse, until someone finally asked Dr. Kubie if the psychological problems of the ghetto were any different than those of the well to do. Dr. Kubie went on to describe how he'd spent a summer vacation on the most isolated island he could find. It was near Alaska—and on the first day of his vacation, he went out with a local fisherman, who asked him what he did. Dr. Kubie said he wasn't the sort of doctor they'd know much about, that he was a special doctor who dealt in people's personal problems. Well, it turned out that someone on the island had been to a psychoanalyst, and the fisherman knew all about it. Dr. Kubie spent the rest of the afternoon listening to the fisherman's problems. The next day the word was out, and the fishermen were lined up to take Dr. Kubie out. By the end of his vacation, Dr. Kubie was an expert on the problems, the anxieties, the frustrations, and so forth, of that little village, and he could guarantee that what he heard on the fishing boats was no different from the problems he ran into every day in his office in Baltimore. At this point Ethel piped up, "Dr. Kubie, how would you like to spend your vacation at Hyannis Port this summer?"

ALICE ROOSEVELT LONGWORTH

They sound rather precious, but there was nothing precious about these lectures. It was all sorts of fun, that was all. Fun to watch all the people who were there. And Udall went to sleep—that was at Averell Harriman's. He went to sleep, and they woke him up. He went to sleep again while that shrink Dr. Kubie was talking. Yes. I know Kubie, you see, fairly well because I knew him out in the West on the ranch. Is Kubie still plying his trade? That evening at Averell's, he was talking about education. Udall just went to sleep! Bored, probably. He went to sleep, and he snored a lot. Remember? Then he was waked up. We always laughed about it. He was waked up, yes, and he went back to sleep again.

JOHN KENNETH GALBRAITH, *economist*

An evening at Potter Stewart's house was devoted to a kind of critical discussion of economic policy. Present, among many others, were Bob and Ethel, Walter Heller, Walt Rostow and Elspeth, Arthur Goldberg and his wife. I was making the case—not a novel one for me—that the objectives of the New Frontier were insufficient; that beyond maintaining an adequate level of employment, income, and growth, we needed to be much more concerned than we were with the incipient starvation of the cities, of the arts, and of welfare—all things which could be ameliorated only by very much increased spending of public funds. I said that the Kennedy policies of the New Frontier were basically too conservative in assuming that a large part of the task could be accomplished by simply having prosperity and a high-level output. This was interpreted by Walter Heller as an attack on him, as indeed it was intended to be. So the evening became an amiable, but rather vigorous exchange between Heller and myself. My supporter during the evening was Arthur Goldberg. He and I always see eye to eye on these matters. Walt Rostow also took part; he came into the discussion with a very long and involved effort at reconciliation of the two positions that sort of petered out halfway through. That's the only time that I ever saw Walt run out of steam. Bobby confined his role to interrogation. But he was a very rapt and eager prosecutor of the positions; you had the feeling that if you were shabby on any important point you could pretty well count on Bobby to come in and press you on it. This was matched in some degree by the eagerness of the questioning that Ethel put. It stands in my mind as a bright, lively, and professional evening.

PIERRE SALINGER, *campaign aide*

Look at the kind of guys he liked: the John Glenns, the Jim Whittakers, El Cordobés, José Torres. They were all adventurers, all guys who took their lives in their hands, and they were willing to lay their lives on the line for something they believed in, whether it was flying in space, or climbing a mountain, or facing a bull. There was the element of challenge and danger about them. For example, Bob Kennedy hated to climb mountains, but he did it because it was a discipline for himself. He had to be strong, to overcome obstacles. It was almost a cleansing experience for him.

ED GUTHMAN, *national editor*, Los Angeles Times

President Kennedy thought the Marines weren't tough enough and that, theoretically, they should be able to hike fifty miles in three days. He got everybody doing it. One day, Bob said, "I think I'll take a fifty-mile hike tomorrow!" I said, "Have a great time." He said, "Well, you're going with me, aren't you?" I said, "I wasn't planning on it." He said, "You're not going to let me go alone, are you?" As it turned out, he had said the same thing to Dave Hackett and Lou Oberdorfer and Jimmy Symington. It was in the dead of winter, and we walked up the towpath of the Chesapeake and Ohio Canal. It was so shady that the snow hadn't melted; so we were going along this ice-covered towpath. Bob was the only one who went the whole fifty miles. I was the last one to drop out after about forty miles. We started at five o'clock in the morning and walked until the sun went down and it was cold. My legs just stopped functioning. But he went on. As he left, he said to me: "You're lucky your brother isn't the President of the United States!"

SONNY FOX, *television performer*

He mentioned hiking a few times. I was sitting next to Ethel, and she poked me. She said, "You're missing your cue." I said, "What's that?" She said, "You're supposed to ask him, 'How much is the farthest you ever hiked?'" I said, "Oh, what's the farthest you ever hiked?" He said, "Oh, well, we hiked fifty miles." Ethel said, "You've got to watch those things, Sonny." I said, "Okay, Ethel."

TRUMAN CAPOTE, *author*

I went downstairs from my apartment at United Nations Plaza to walk the dog. It was about seven o'clock on a Sunday morning. There wasn't anybody in the lobby; there wasn't anybody around. But I walked out in the street, and there I saw Bobby standing with two boys—they were about twelve and thirteen years old—and he had them by the arm. He was shaking them and talking. I called to him, "What's going on here?" He said, "Truman, come over here." He said, "You won't believe this." "What is it?" I said. He had the spaniel dog he always had with him. "I came out here to take my dog for a walk, and I walked down the street," he said, "and here come these two kids smoking cigarettes!" He said, "Look at them. Look at these little punks. They're twelve or thirteen years old. They're smoking cigarettes." One of the kids looked up at him and said, "Honestly, honestly, Mr. Kennedy. I swear we'll never do it again." It was as if he was some sort of avenging angel who had fallen out of heaven upon them. They recognized him. They were terrified. I said, "Oh, well, I'm sure they won't do that any more." He said, "Now, you swear and promise me you're never going to smoke another cigarette." And they said, "Oh, honest. Honest to God, we swear we never will." So he let them go, and they turned around and they ran free like a pair of maniacs. They got to the corner, and one turned and came all the way back. He said, "Can I have your autograph, Mr. Kennedy?"

JOSÉ TORRES

He asked me if I wanted to stay in his home. So I said okay. I went to Hyannis Port on a Friday night. We went to bed about three o'clock. The next day he woke me up at 8:00, and I said I had a headache. So he waited; and then about 9:30 he came back and woke me up again. I had breakfast. Then we played tennis; then we went out in the yacht, about five miles out; we were swimming you know. All the kids and Ted Kennedy and everyone was there. We came back to Hyannis. Then we decided to box. The kids were learning boxing. They had an instructor to teach them. They wanted me to box with him. So I was boxing with the guy and I took it easy, and Ethel Kennedy wanted me to hit the guy hard. I figured I should not do that because it would discourage the guy and also discourage the *kids*. Then I decided to box with Bobby Kennedy. His kids were giving me instructions, "Hit him in the head, hit him in the belly," something like that, very loud. One of his sons says, "Let him go eight rounds and *then* knock him out." Then another one said, "No, it's better to hit him in the first round so he won't suffer." Then Bobby asked Ethel to bring the camera. At one point, Bobby said, "Let me knock you out." So I said, "Okay, go ahead." So he hit me, and I fall to the floor, and I'm on the floor, laughing. He says, "Don't laugh," he says, "you'll spoil it." He was kidding. He asked me to stay one more day, and I said that I couldn't stay one more day.

GEORGE PLIMPTON

It was unbearably hot that day, enervating and *dangerous* heat . . . they'd hauled a couple of dead people out of the Grand Canyon the week before. Damn, it was July, and we were walking out with the Senator, and Ethel, of course, from the bottom of the Canyon to the rim, which is a hell of a long climb, and we picked midday to do it with the temperature well over 100. There were some for whom it was easy—the older Kennedy kids, who climbed like lizards, and Jim Whittaker who'd . . . well, *practiced* for this jaunt by climbing Mount Everest. But the rest of us would gather under a shelf of rock, just to rest and get out of the sun, and we knew we couldn't stay there for too long because leg cramps and so forth were a possibility—you *had* to keep going. So the Senator would haul himself out from under the ledge and stand facing us—this motley, dusty group, who wished they hadn't come—and he'd recite the St. Crispin's Day speech from *Henry V.* We'd stare at him, popeyed, and then we'd groan and push ourselves up; and we'd follow him for another brutal half an hour or so. That was the procedure at each rest stop; a peppermint drop, a slug of warm water, and inspirational verse from the Senator. He knew an awful lot of it.

MARTIN ARNOLD, *journalist*
We were in a motel together in Seattle, and he called his mother before he climbed Mount Kennedy. His mother said to him: "Don't slip, Son." It was really nice. "Don't slip, Son."

He didn't like the whole experience; he hated it. He suffered acrophobia—fear of heights, and he told me later if he had known what it involved, he would never have done it. But once he was there, he was very gung-ho to get started. He wanted to get it over with. While he was climbing, what he was doing the whole time was repeating to himself the words of every popular song he knew. It's a terrible thing, climbing a mountain. So he was repeating the words of all the popular songs he knew so he wouldn't be thinking about what the hell he was doing.

JIM WHITTAKER, *mountaineer, family friend*
It was through his skiing that he learned to be comfortable in snow and ice. He was an accomplished skier—with a style that was rugged and challenging, and based more on speed than form. He liked to keep just on the edge of control. Some skiers ski within their ability, and they pride themselves on how few times they fall in a week. If Bobby got by half a day without falling, and that a pretty spectacular one, it would be very unusual. With him you always had to stretch yourself a

little further. It was the same on Mount Kennedy, which is a difficult mountain and hadn't been climbed up to that time, the highest in the Yukon—a shade under 14,000 feet—and Bobby, on snowshoes, which he had never worn before, was just breathing down my neck he was coming after me so fast. He had no training in mountains. He was afraid of heights, and he'd shake. He told me that in preparation he had run up and down the stairs at Hickory Hill and practiced yelling "Help!" And yet on that climb, I had continually to pick up the pace. At the top, as lead man, I stopped and belayed him up to me. The crest was about fifty feet away. We trailed him as he broke through the snow, which was knee deep, to the summit. It was pretty emotional—to reach the top of the mountain honoring his brother. He was very concerned to get there.

FRANK GIFFORD, *sportscaster*

Whenever I was around him, he always wanted to know about the different athletes . . . particularly the good ones. He was always interested about the make-up of the guys who were playing; for instance, we'd be talking about Jimmy Brown, and he was curious about Jimmy Brown as a person. He was always asking about those who had done something rather extraordinary. He was curious about what gave them the drive to become a little bit better than what they were. He probably did like football better than baseball because of the more competitive thing, the more physical thing involved, and the element of danger. That's just speculation on my part. He loved football, I know. They played touch football, but it boiled down to breaking your neck!

GEORGE PLIMPTON

When the touch-football games were played at Hyannis Port—down on the lawns in front of the Ambassador's house—often the Secret Service people were asked to join in. So you had *them*, along with the dogs and the children and the sisters and the house guests . . . quite a mob of people. But the numbers were cut down quite quickly . . . severe attrition—mostly, it always seemed to me, because of the hard-nose play of the Secret Service people. They'd been shut up in sentry houses or lurking about, whatever it is they do, and the touch-football games gave them a chance to *star*, to perform. So they played a fairly brutal and humorless and knowledgeable game. In the huddle they'd talk about running "post patterns," and they'd scrabble plays in the grass. The slightly hysterical and charming play of Jackie, say, which was full of little yells and darting, unpredictable runs in the wrong direction, wasn't quite suitable. So, by and by, people would drift away from the game—ostensibly, to get ready for dinner or tend to the children's supper, or the children would wander down the long pier to meet Uncle Ted coming in from his afternoon yacht race, and there were telephone calls to be made, and so forth—and finally, in the dusk, there'd be four or five adults left, furious and panting, rushing quickly across the lawn and most of them were Secret Service people.

KAY EVANS
I think Bobby spent less time sailing than either of his brothers, but he loved it and considered it a direct challenge. I remember in the summer of 1967 about ten of us went cruising off the coast of Maine on a boat with a German captain. The first day we sailed to North Haven Island. It was a bitter cold afternoon . . . the wind was blowing . . . the very last of August. . . . We had no sooner got out of the harbor and really into the open sea when Bobby said, "Well, I guess I'll go swimming." He didn't really say it for anyone in particular; he just muttered it and peeled off his socks and shoes and his shirt, and dove over the side as we were under full sail. The captain had never seen anything like that before in his life. Those were considered un-swimmable waters. The captain gave a great yell, and he brought the boat into the wind. He lowered a ladder and got Bobby back on board. I don't know what the temperature of the water was—not much over forty—but no one could have survived in it very long.

Bobby dove over the side periodically during that cruise, and by the time we finally got to Campobello, off the coast of Canada, *all* of us were doing it. The water was just paralyzing. You couldn't really swim. You just went in and hung on so that you could pull yourself back out as quickly as possible. But there was some enormous exhilaration in having done it. I've always been a Chicken Little about everything . . . but there was something about Bobby's own brand of physical courage that was contagious, and we suddenly began to do some of the things that he did . . . and found there was a joy in it, oddly . . . in doing difficult, slightly scary things you never thought you could do.

Normally, when you cruise, it's all very tight and taut, and there are just the right number of people for the boat, slim rations, and every-thing is highly controlled. On the Kennedy cruises, it's quite unlike that. There are lots too many people and thousands of suitcases. And then all that food that Ethel brings . . . turkeys and hams and choco-late cakes . . . and sometimes a dog: one year we took Freckles. There

172

were all sorts of funny things that happened. I remember George Stevens on one of those cruises—he'd never really been sailing before at all—went below when things were rather quiet, and he came up dressed in a costume he'd gotten from a costume company, a kind of Napoleonic admiral's costume. Very bizarre, with one of those great big hats, and braid, and it was so funny sitting out in the middle of the Atlantic Ocean with this guy suddenly coming up out of the hatch dressed like that.

Then we saw a boat coming toward us, closer and closer, and it turned out to be Mike Forrestal, right out in the middle of the Atlantic. When he saw all of us and then George Stevens dressed in this incredible costume, he must have been so glad he wasn't on board. He's a great seaman, and I think the way those cruises were operated was not quite the way . . . well not like what Forrestal was *used* to.

MICHAEL FORRESTAL, *attorney*

They were on an immense, pale blue yawl. I recognized them in a rather isolated channel called Muscle Ridge, off Rockland, Maine, where one didn't expect to see anybody one knew. And, as a matter of fact, one had gone quite a long ways away from New York to avoid just this sort of thing. As their vessel approached out of the mists, it seemed as if there were a circus on board. There were not only a great many people on the boat, some in costume, but also a menagerie of animals. We came alongside . . . and it's true . . . I came about rather sharply and found Bobby in the bow, standing outboard of the genoa, really looking as if he wanted to have nothing to do with this turmoil that was going on on the deck behind him. He shouted something like, "I'll bet you rather wish you'd never met us, Forrestal!" And we fell off and turned away. I used to kid him a lot about sailing; he was very teasable on those subjects.

KAY EVANS

Everything on a Kennedy cruise was different. Instead of spending the night on the boat, which most salty people do when they cruise, the Kennedys would all quickly rush ashore for a hot bath and a lobster dinner. Friends along the coast of Maine were more or less alerted that we were coming in. Year after year, the same friends kept putting us up . . . Anne Chamberlin, and the Watsons and the Dillons . . . until I began to feel those people were beginning to figure that it might be easier if they could just go *away* during the month of August, go *abroad*, anywhere to avoid the Kennedy cruise. They never knew how many people were coming. Tom Watson could hardly believe it when he saw us disembark at his pier. It was like the clowns coming out of the tiny car at the circus—all the people, all the luggage, the hat boxes, and the wig boxes, and the turkeys, and the cakes . . . an incredible cargo. But for us it was such a relief to get ashore.

ROWLAND EVANS, *columnist*

Once, going out of Portland at midnight, Bobby told me to take the wheel. "Navigate," he said. I don't know *how* to navigate. It took me a while to get started even *towards* where we were going, and we almost hit a shelf of rocks right in the harbor at Portland, went just within an inch of it. That's when the authorities sent that boat out to follow us, and to lead us out of the harbor. Bobby sent it back; he was furious that the harbormaster had sent a boat out to lead him out of the harbor. Actually, it was a very dangerous business; the water was cold up there, very cold, about forty-eight degrees, fifty degrees; but that was the way Bobby liked to do things . . . unplanned, spur of the moment, and that's what gave it that special element of pleasure and fun for the rest of us.

Once out of the harbor, we got lost. We saw this big boat the next morning, very well-provisioned and well-manned, and several figures in white ducks sprawled on the afterdeck in rather elegant postures, and we looked like, well, we must have looked like Rub-a-dub-dub-Three-men-in-a-tub, or just about. We hailed them, and the voice that answered I identified immediately as Senator Saltonstall's, from Massachusetts. So Bobby began calling over for directions, which was a little bit embarrassing, but we didn't know where we were. Saltonstall's reply was, "Don't you know, Senator, enough about the rules of the road and especially cruising Maine waters, that you can't have . . . well, you have too many *people* aboard that boat, and you're not sailing in safe conditions." It went on and on. . . . He was being funny, and I remember Bobby's reply as being something like, "Well, Senator [in this Massachusetts voice], I'm from New York, you know, not a Massachusetts man."

KAY EVANS

There are rocks all up the coast of Maine, just one long reef. But Rowly charted some kind of crazy course, and then we tried to stay on it. It was all very haphazard because different people kept taking the wheel.

Luckily, it was a very calm night. Just rolls, great rolls of sea. We headed for some number on the compass that Rowly had said was the right heading. Mathematics is not his big course, and he's not a Mr. Fixit in any sense. I never went to sleep that night at all—I felt I was the only one on board who realized that we were in such ghastly peril, and I wanted to be sure to be aware if we were going down. I didn't want to find myself in cold water without a little *notice*. Even in the night you could see great spurts of foam going into the air where the reefs were. It was about 3:00 or 4:00 in the morning when Dean Markham was at the helm—I was sitting beside him with my eyes propped open, waiting for the end to come—when somebody asked, "What's your course, Dean, where are you steering?" He said, "I'm steering just a little bit to the left of the moon," quite unaware that the moon, rising or setting, doesn't stay in the same place. Well, we sailed all that night and when morning came it was just the same glassy sea, with the coast off in the distance but no sign of life, nothing to recognize, and we couldn't get the stove going so there was nothing hot to eat and we couldn't make the radio work. I was supposed to be in charge of the stove. I was given this assignment by Bobby as we sailed out of Portland Harbor . . . but I never did make the kerosene flame do what it was supposed to. All we ate that day were doughnuts and Danish pastry. The ones who weren't scared the way I was were either exhausted, because there weren't enough places to sleep, or hungry, because there was nothing to eat, or furious, because they had agreed to come on the expedition, or seasick. . . . There were only two people who were having a good time . . . one was Bobby, who just loved the whole thing, and the other was Ethel, who was happy because Bobby was. The rest of us were wrecks. When we got to the Watsons' that night it was like getting to heaven after a hideous time in purgatory . . . everything was so beautiful at the Watsons'. We took hot baths and had a wonderful lobster dinner. At that dinner, I said to Bobby, "That was the most terrified I've ever been in my life, last night." And he said, "But doesn't it just make it twice as wonderful that we're here? Aren't you having twice as good a time because you did that last night?" And then I began to see the whole thing. . . .

10

GILLIAN WALKER, *theatrical producer*

I was in the ladies' room. You can't see out those windows. I just heard this noise coming from outside the train, and I couldn't imagine what it was—people singing or what it was.

KATE HADDAD (*Mrs. William Haddad*)

The bands! You couldn't hear anything from where we were—just see the bands playing. All the people along the way just were miles and miles and miles of little strings of people . . . not at the station, where there were crowds, but just all along the way . . . people who had stopped obviously in the middle of doing something else, even girls in bathing suits; but it wasn't disrespectful! All the hair curlers—Americana, you know. It was an American Saturday afternoon, and people were in hair curlers.

GEORGE KRAUSS, *bandmaster, New Brunswick, New Jersey*

Now, the question was raised why we were not in uniform. The main reason: we had collected our uniforms at the conclusion of the Memorial Day parade. We had them in storage. Due to Field Day, it was just an impossibility to get children into uniforms. So we were dressed in regular school clothes. I told them to come dressed presentable in school clothes. The most important thing was not the fact that they did not wear uniforms, but that they contributed their musical contributions in the

176

best traditions of dedication. Our band has done many fine projects for the school, community, and the state. The group has played in the Miss America Pageant; they've been to perform for Vice-President Humphrey and Governor Hughes; we've had a *variety* of experiences around here. The band is highly integrated. Sometimes people say, "How do you do it?" Well, we just *involve* our children in activities. We have had Chinese, Negroes, Japanese this year—all types—we even had a *Redskin* in there—so we've had Indians and *everything*.

Actually, I don't do much directing in front of an orchestra. That's not my job. But this was a special occasion. I was amused that Edwin Newman, the broadcaster—I've learned this from my wife's remarks and other remarks that have come in—said that I conducted in a "Toscanini-like" manner. Quite something. My children have been kidding me about the little bald spot I've got back here, and all the TV coverage it got.

The singers on the platform who joined in and sang along were not organized. They were strictly people singing from the platform and becoming involved. I was very pleased and, to be frank with you, I personally feel, and I think this is the reaction they have from NBC, that the singing was *fitting* . . . and appropriate, that it added dignity and a somber feeling to what could have been bedlam because that station was so overcrowded.

I was in a position in front of the band to see down the track. When I saw the train reach a certain point, I started my "Taps." I was facing away from the train; I purposely stationed myself so that I could see it coming and gear the length of the "Taps" so that the train, which must have been going three or five miles an hour, would reach me just as I had concluded "Taps." Then we'd swing into the "Battle Hymn of the Republic." In every single letter that comes through, people ask who played "Taps." Well, there's a reason why I did it. Under an emotional crisis like that, I've seen professional musicians *crack* on "Taps," and it was a hot day, and I did not want to put any boy in the band under that type of strain; it takes great control. It's not easy to do, because you can choke up. It's a situation whereby experience prepares you. I was in the Navy on the battleship *New York*, leading the band at burial services, and many times I experienced the playing of it, so I know the problems. Besides, I thought it would be wiser if I played it and gave the band a chance to get ready because we wanted to get the "Battle Hymn" in there. It worked out very satisfactorily.

ARTHUR GOLDBERG, *attorney*

I was one of those who urged him to run for Senator from New York when he didn't want to run. I felt he ought to be in public life, and I thought it was a natural for him to do it in New York. The state needed a leader, and he had associations with New York rising from early childhood. I was responsible for the first story, actually. I said to Dorothy McCardle of the Washington *Post*, "Dorothy, let's promote a candidacy. You can write a story that friends of Bobby Kennedy are talking about him as Senator from New York. It'll be an accurate story because *I'm* talking about it." And she did. She wrote the first story. He was not too anxious; he was bruised at that time.

CHARLES EVERS, *civil-rights leader*

The rumor came that he was going to quit the Justice Department. I again took off to Washington, trying to convince him to stay on. He said how much he appreciated my concern. "But Charles," he said, "let me tell you something. The greatest time in the world to quit is when you're wanted most."

JOSEPH KRAFT, *columnist*

The vice-presidency was something that he was, it seemed to me, quite interested in. He had become convinced that there were certain things that he could bring to the Democratic Party and to the Johnson ticket that no one else could. Certainly people were telling him—I know Averell Harriman was one of them—to run for the Senate in New York; the vice-presidency doesn't make any sense. But my impression was that Bob was quite interested in it, certainly through the Polish trip. He kept using that phrase about taking up the torch that had been passed. He cited the torch's passing to the younger generation in his speech in Berlin. It had that kind of significance: that he was getting back into active politics. Now that perspective clearly changed when the Republicans nominated Barry Goldwater. It must have been pretty clear to Bob that the circumstances in which he could be valuable to the ticket weren't about to happen . . . because he was a realistic fellow. On the other hand, he was quite clearly upset when President Johnson called him in and told him that he was taking him out of the running; Bobby came over here—I think it was right after that episode—and spent about an hour or so. He was pretty upset by the general toughness and harshness that he felt he saw in Johnson. He recalled that

178

Johnson had said to him, "You know, none of the people that work for me are any good." Bob was astonished that Johnson would say that to him—Bob Kennedy—about the people that had worked for Johnson for so long.

The President invented this gag about taking all the Cabinet officers out of the running for the vice-presidency. Bob was very contemptuous about what he regarded as a kind of cowardly dodge. He made some kind of comment like, It must be bitter medicine to Dean Rusk to know that he can't become Vice-President. The thrust of it was, If you're taking me out, why not announce it? The day afterward, Lyndon Johnson called in a lot of his cronies in the press—the so-called "old pro gang"—and gave them his version of how Bobby had behaved like a little kid . . . that was the general portrait that he painted.

AVERRELL HARRIMAN, *diplomat*
He did seem to want to be Vice-President. He sort of clung to it for quite a while. I don't think Bobby was at his best moment when Johnson said he didn't want him. It was a very stiff meeting. The two men were like oil and water. They couldn't possibly get on, you know.

CHARLES EVERS
With the vice-presidency out, it was the Senate, and one day he called me up and he said, "I want you to come and help me." I said, "What about Dr. King, and Roy Wilkins and those fellows. They have much more pull and know-how than I have." He said, "No, I want you to come." I went to New York and spoke in behalf of Bobby. I told them what he'd meant to us; what he'd done and how we should support him.

The next day Roy Wilkins heard about it. Boy, they got on the phone and told me I couldn't mix NAACP and politics—that I was a traitor to the rules of the NAACP. I've always been a person who hates anybody to tell me what I couldn't do when I was doing no wrong. I said, "I'm not doing this as the NAACP; I'm doing it as Charles Evers and a friend of Bobby Kennedy's. Nobody's going to tell me who my friends are."

My association with Bobby was causing me a lot of problems with the organization, because they really were behind Kenneth Keating, the incumbent. They felt that Kennedy shouldn't be coming in. I felt different.

Then came the time for the New York State convention of the NAACP at Buffalo, New York. Bobby was not invited, intentionally, and Keating was. So the banquet began, and they brought on the platform all these persons who were telling how great Senator Keating had been and why the Negro should vote for him. Then they brought on Keating; Keating got up there, and he reared and stomped, and he told how Bobby had forsaken the civil-rights movement because he had left the Justice Department, that he was no friend of the Negro. As for himself, he said he'd been in there fighting all these years and, compared to him, Bobby Kennedy was a youngster and a Johnny-come-later.

He was taking advantage of the man. I just couldn't take it. All of my people were there—all the big shots with the NAACP. They were just urging him on. Then Gene Reed, who was a state president of the NAACP at the time, wrote me a note: "Dear Charles—I know Bobby's your man, but not here."

Can you imagine? God, I was so mad. I just bit my tongue.

When Keating finally finished, I got up to speak. I said nothing about civil rights. I said I wanted to make one thing clear. Nobody tells me what to say. "I'm going to say tonight what I think is right, and if I never come back to Buffalo no more it's all right with me."

And then I took off on what Bobby meant to us, and how wrong I thought it was for them to invite one and not the other, and how cruel it was for Senator Keating to try and say that Bobby Kennedy had done nothing. I said, "When we in Mississippi knew nothing about you, Senator, during all the time that the Emmett Tills and all those men were murdered and destroyed and beaten, bub, you never opened your mouth. Bobby Kennedy means more to us in Mississippi than any white man I know, including yourself, Senator."

I said, "All of you sitting here know all the Senator has done is voted right. What else has he done? You got the worst laws in the world in New York. You got the most poverty areas in the world in New York. Up in Bedford-Stuyvesant, there's a bunch of maniacs running around— lack of work, dope, and everything else."

Then I said, "Let me tell you about Bobby Kennedy." I went right down the line. How he got us out of jail; how he began to open up the Attorney General's office; how he had appointed a Negro as United States Marshal—the first one since Reconstruction; and how he had come to Ole Miss. Oh, I told his whole story. And I was mad.

The whole rostrum refused to speak to me when it was over. I really was hurt in one way, but then again I was proud because I knew I'd done what was right. I couldn't sit there and allow Keating, Joe Louis, Gene Reed, Bill Booth, and everybody else talk that way about a man who'd meant so much to us.

180

JACK ENGLISH, *Nassau County Democratic Chairman*

One day I had set up a whole bunch of appointments for him to meet all sorts of leaders in New York. One of the major fellows I wanted him to meet had political ambitions. He had a big ethnic group in Queens behind him. I said, "Pay a lot of attention to this fellow. He's not too bright, but don't let that concern you too much." So he said, "Okay." When he met him, he gave him a little spiel, and about thirty seconds into it, the fellow interrupted. "Listen. You want to be President. What's in it for me?" Bobby looked up and, at first, I don't think he knew what this fellow meant. So he replied, "Well, it would be better for the State of New York because I'm from New York now." This fellow said, "I don't mean that! What I mean is what's in it for *me?*" I interrupted, and I said, "Listen. Why don't we go out around the corner here, and I'll talk to you about this." I started pulling the guy by the arm to get him out, because I could see that Kennedy was *mad as hell.* I didn't want to lose the guy but I knew how mad Kennedy gets. I got him outside the door, and I thought I'd saved the day, when an arm came around behind me and Kennedy was grabbing me from the back; he spun me around, and hell, while I've still got the guy by the other hand, he shouts at me, *"Don't you make any deals with him!"* I really think that's the character of the guy. He would kick away any damn thing if he didn't like it.

JOHN BURNS, *New York State Democratic Chairman*

I don't think he disliked politicians. I think he disliked the system. Of course, there were some politicians who tried to attack him and were unfriendly for a long time; he didn't really mind that, but he never really liked people that had been unfriendly to his brother. He never forgot. President Kennedy once said, "We forgive, but we don't forget."

BARBARA SHALVEY, *campaign worker*

Important points would be given to the candidate on index cards. I remember one time when he was speaking outdoors in New York City, and reference cards were made up for him that said something like "The Bronx is to the north, Queens on your right, Brooklyn below you, and New Jersey on your left." Maybe it was done as a joke—but that was one of his main problems. A great many letters—a lot of criticism— came in from people calling the candidate a carpetbagger. The letters charging this were answered by explaining that the Attorney General had grown up in Bronxville and attended school there, and that he owned a home in Glen Cove, Long Island. The letters answering such charges were sent to "the Machine" at the 42nd Street headquarters for signature. It was a huge, all-enveloping black thing with a hole in the front. You would place the letter in the hole under a fountain pen in mid-air. When you stepped on a foot pedal, the pen would magically move, lower to the page, and sign Robert Kennedy's name.

BILL BARRY, *campaign aide*

The night of the election, it was just a terrible mob scene in the headquarters in the hotel. As only New York political crowds and Democrats can be, it was unruly and nasty and noisy . . . just completely unfeeling for anybody else. The first chance I had to congratulate him, he said, "Well, if my brother was alive, I wouldn't be here. I'd rather have it that way." He didn't feel as though it were a great evening that night. It was so very sad and tearing.

JOSEPH TYDINGS, *Senator from the State of Maryland*

We were elected the same year: he from New York, and I of course from Maryland. We sat next to each other on the new back row—the back row behind the back row in the Senate.

Each Senator will write his name who sits there, so you generally have ten, fifteen, twenty, sometimes thirty or forty names on the older desks. Some of the desks were there before the British burned the Capitol in 1812. It depends where you sit. In the old desks, of course, you could pick the top of the desk up like a briefcase and carry it to your room at night—your hotel room, because in those days they didn't have offices in the Capitol; you worked out of it in the hotel room, and then you carried the top back and put it back down on its supports.

The Women's Press Club always has a banquet for the "new baby Senators," as they call them, and it was there that Bobby offered his quip about his seat being in the back row. He said his mother had better seats to *Hello, Dolly!*

DUN GIFFORD, *campaign aide*

In the Senate committees, on the floor, you always had the feeling that Bobby was about to explode. He had this tremendous energy, and he was never very good at hiding it. There was so much to do, and he never saw any good reason for just not going ahead and doing it. You could always see those explosions coming, and it made us all a little nervous sometimes. His brother Ted was different. Two completely different styles. Ted always wants everyone to know what he's trying to do, to understand that he has studied and thought and talked the whole thing over, which he generally has. It's not caution, really, as much as it is knowing how the Senate really works. I mean, you can go up to some Senator and try to knock him over with a lot of forceful and general arguments, or you can sort of sidle up to him and try to *ease* him onto your side. There was a lot of give and take between the two brothers about all this. Ted had the reputation of being a "Senate man," working hard at a lot of long committee hearings, and Bobby was always being criticized for zooming around the country making speeches. They were always passing notes back and forth, Bobby zinging Ted about being a member of the Senate club, and Ted zinging Bobby about being unable to sit still for five minutes. If Ted was in the middle of a complicated debate on the Senate floor, Bobby would write him a note—or even walk slowly behind his chair and whisper—"Is this how you become a member of the club, Senator?" Or, "How long do you have to go on with this to make them think you're a good Senator?" There were endless variations on this theme, of course, and Ted used to give it right back to Bobby. Bobby would get confused about some complicated amendment Adam Walinsky or Peter Edelman had just put in front of him. They used to sit beside each other at the Labor Committee meetings. Bobby always felt he had to explain the amendment even if he wasn't sure himself exactly what it meant. When he got going on one of these rambles, Ted would whisper or write, "Well, you just lost Lister—stop talking and let's vote, or you'll lose all the others too"; or, "Don't you wish you were in the club so you wouldn't have to do all this?"; or, "Do you want me to bail you out?" And so on.

Well, the deliberative body *is* slow. That's the whole difference between the executive and the legislative, and it was a difference that turned up later in the campaign between Bobby and Eugene McCarthy. McCarthy represented the legislative branch, and he expressed himself from that point of view. Bobby came out of the executive experience—action-oriented, you can change things. You don't have to philosophize about them. I remember that in one of the first campaign staff meetings after he announced for President, he said over and over that he wanted us to stress his *executive* experience. He had been Attorney General, and a *de facto* member of the National Security Council—and just about every other council, for that matter—and Gene McCarthy had not. We used to wonder what the men would have been like had their backgrounds been reversed, if Bobby had been a Senator only, and McCarthy had been Attorney General, associated with the executive, and then Senator. I don't suppose you can draw too much out of it. But surely Bobby was not a philosopher-king—he wanted to lead the troops.

FRED HARRIS, *Senator from the State of Oklahoma*
We used to sit around and giggle a lot. Fritz Mondale and Bob Kennedy and I laughed down there in the Senate—just like school kids. I remember one time during a serious matter, the three of us got giggling on extraneous matters . . . nothing to do with that, but you know, we were in the chamber that day, giggling among ourselves and worrying about what it *looked* like.

JOHN SHERMAN COOPER, *Senator from the State of Kentucky*
When he came he attracted attention. Every place he moved, there would be groups following him: young people, older people . . . that attraction that the Kennedy family had. He never stayed in the Senate chamber for long periods of time. He was rather shy as a member of the Senate. He usually came in from the door nearest the elevators; he walked to the rear of the Senate chamber, some of his staff with him, and he would move quickly to his seat. He did not stop and talk and chat like a great many members do. As a speaker, he had something of the style of John Kennedy. His speeches in the Senate and in debate didn't have the type of humor that John could use, but they at times had greater passion.

If I would try to fix a role he held in the Senate, it was in the cause of . . . to use a very overused word . . . the "disadvantaged." I think he had a definite place—a place of leadership—in those fields while he was in the Senate.

I have been asked if Robert Kennedy was a member of the Senate club. There is a lot of talk, you know, about the Senate being "a club." I've never thought of it that way. It's a very courteous place and we all refer to each other as "the distinguished Senator," "the able Senator." Such niceties have their proper place because they tend to keep debate, I think, on more reasonable grounds. But I do not think the Senate is a place where very strong friendships are formed. Every Senator, with his colleague from his state, represents his state. Everyone feels of himself as being equal in that capacity; everyone's intent on his work. If there is a club, Robert Kennedy was not a member of it. That's true of many of us. We're not members in the sense of being in the small group

184

that runs the organization of the Senate. But that doesn't mean you can't have an effective place, whether you're in that inner circle or not. Sometimes it's much better to be outside that inner circle, to be independent.

SENATOR JOSEPH TYDINGS

It was mainly the older Senators that didn't understand him. The older Senators in both the Democratic Party and the Republican Party. He ruffled their feathers sometimes. Very few of them would say anything to him directly. Bobby was a more influential leader in the Senate when he was there than President Kennedy had been in his Senate years. That was because of his tenure as Attorney General with President Kennedy and his being heir to the mantle of the Kennedy future, so to speak. And then too, he spoke out much more. President Kennedy was very cautious when he was United States Senator. His only speech on foreign policy which went contrary to public sentiment was about Algeria. He was not a trailblazer to the extent Bobby was. On the other hand, he lived in a different era. Bobby's pronouncements were partially acceptable because of the climate that JFK had created and changed. But Bobby was far more outspoken.

He was willing to be candid and truthful even if it hurt him politically. This candor was exemplified time and time again on the Senate floor. He rubbed many Senators the wrong way. In diplomacy or politics, the temptation is to reshape one's phrases or to perfect one's language so as not to offend or upset the persons or large blocs being criticized. Bobby didn't take the trouble to so polish his phraseology very often. To me, it was a plus rather than a minus. To many, it was a minus rather than a plus. Many people—even those of his own party—interpreted it as being blunt and rough and harsh.

DANIEL P. MOYNIHAN, *director, Joint Center for Urban Studies*

I learned what he thought of me not long ago. I was having dinner with Fritz Mondale and Fred Harris. Fred Harris told me that he had once asked Bob Kennedy what Kennedy had thought of me, and Kennedy had said, "He knows all the facts, and he's against all the solutions."

ROWLAND EVANS, *columnist*

If you were one of the powerful, you were afraid of Bobby Kennedy; you reacted adversely to him because he was going to somehow reduce your power. That's why labor didn't like Bobby; George Meany was afraid of him. So much of the Democratic Party—the old politics— they were afraid of Bobby! What was he going to do to their power once he got control of the party?

SHIRLEY MacLAINE, *actress*

I don't think a hero can be a man that many people are afraid of. A lot of people were afraid of Bobby Kennedy. We might as well call it like it is. To many people, he meant what he said a little too strongly. A hero is usually a man who doesn't offend anyone; who doesn't upset their *status quo*; who doesn't force them to look at the cancer in their society.

ALLEN GINSBERG, *poet*

I went around to Senator Kennedy's office to visit Peter Edelman and talk about the dope-fuzz-Mafia problem in 1965. I asked Peter Edelman if Kennedy was around—I was curious to see if he'd meet me. Edelman said he would inquire, and then he said that Kennedy had gone out. I had the impression that he had gone out just to avoid me.

Then I came back in early 1968. I called because there were hearings in various committees to continue narcotics legislation going on then. I went to see my Congressman from New Jersey; I went to see Farbstein from the lower East Side. I wandered up and down the corridors looking for Senators and Representatives. I remember popping in and out of people's offices . . . like Wayne Morse's and bugging his secretary, trying to dictate a little memo. Finally, I called up Peter Edelman to see him, and Edelman suggested that I might see the Senator. Edelman went off, then came back and said that Senator Kennedy would see me.

I went in and sat down in front of his desk. I put my harmonium box down and a little manuscript. Immediately, without waiting for any preliminary conversation, I launched into a long explanation of the whole dope problem. I cited him statistics by Judge Botein of New York showing that the majority of court cases in New York were connected with heroin, or crimes committed in order to get heroin or hard drugs that something like forty per cent of the men and seventy per cent of the women in jail in New York were in for crimes connected with heroin; that the cost of heroin might run to fifty dollars a day for an addict; that some of the narco police—federal, state and local—sold heroin; that being an addict was like being a diabetic who needed daily

186

injections, and that the only way out was to adopt the old English system—that is, to send junkies off to doctors to either cure them or else give them their needed medicines. That was the first basic thing that I laid down, meanwhile diving into my bag and pulling out scraps of newspaper clippings to illustrate what I was saying. He listened, sort of, but I could see that his attention was wandering. I'm sure he thought that I was indulging in inappropriate behavior of some sort or other.

So then I shut up and let him talk. He wanted to know the relationships between the flower-power people or the hip-generation people and the black-power leaders. He wanted to know whether there was any kind of political relationship or any political muscle behind such a coalition. I said that I had turned onto grass a number of times in Nashville with Stokely Carmichael. But it didn't extend to any formal political alliance. The conversation moved on to ecology. I began to describe my conception of the urban ecological crisis. I said that New York City itself was not inhabitable. The junk terror had increased the general anxiety level in the slums. I said that people didn't realize they were in the universe. They couldn't even see the stars any more, so they were getting more and more of a physically narrow, apartment-block perspective. You couldn't see anything clearly for real, or see yourself in perspective; and also you were constantly being attacked by your neighbors and stolen from. On top of that, there was garbage piled all over the streets, and the children in my block, East 10th Street, grew up in an ecology where their big main toys were garbage. It really was a nonhuman environment. Then I repeated to him Timothy Leary's compass thought for the reconstruction of the human universe, which is that "all the metal should be put back underground." The natural place of man was near vegetation, which made him feel better than metal or any inorganic vibrations. Then I said, "Am I making sense to you? Do you understand what I'm saying?" I'd gone through a long-structured, coherent, unified field theory, and I wondered if he understood it. He answered, "Well, I don't fully understand it, but it sounds very poetic."

Then I asked him if he'd ever turned on to pot. He smiled and said no. I said, "Oh, come on! You can tell me. I won't tell anyone." Then he said, "Well, the returns aren't in scientifically." He was smiling when he said it though. So I said, not smiling, "That's a pretty inhuman answer to give. What kind of President do you want to be? On the subject of something as spiritual and sweet as pot, if you're going to sit around giving an IBM-machine answer, that's not going to satisfy the new generations." He laughed. I didn't expect to get an answer out of him.

Then he asked me what LSD was. I said that I thought it was a basically religious experience equivalent to those described in William James's book, *The Varieties of Religious Experience*. I thought it as important historically as the development of the atom bomb, and that it was an interesting coincidence that both had come up the same year—1945, when LSD was discovered in Switzerland by Dr. Hoffman. He just nodded and listened, which was friendly, though shirtsleeved and impersonal. His face was generally quizzical. Friendly enough. He looked me in the eye occasionally.

PETER EDELMAN, *legislative aide*
They got onto talking about Voznesensky and Yevtushenko. Ginsberg said he understood that Kennedy knew both of them; he wanted to mention that he also knew them. One asked the other which of the Russian poets they liked best, and both agreed they liked Voznesensky better. Kennedy said that he thought Voznesensky was more sensitive; but I recall most what Ginsberg said about why *he* liked Voznesensky better. He said it was because when he appeared on a platform with both of them, Yevtushenko had embraced him; but Voznesensky was clearly the more open person because they had kissed deeply and soulfully. Kennedy received that with equanimity.

ALLEN GINSBERG
After I left his office, I remembered something that was most important—to sing him the "Hare Krishna" mantra. He passed through the corridor. I asked, "Can you stay and listen to one thing?" He said, "Yes." I said, "It'll just take one minute. Give me a minute. One minute more." So he said, "Okay." I pulled out a little harmonium and sang through two choruses. He stayed to listen. The "Hare Krishna" mantra was more important than the whole conversation. So he stood there, and I sang for a minute and then quit.

PETER EDELMAN
He finished up, "Om. Hare Krishna. Om. Om. Hare Krishna. Om," and so on, as he does, and Kennedy looked at him and asked, "Now what's supposed to happen?" Ginsberg said, "Magic prayer to preserver god, bringing peace and salvation. You're supposed to feel better and

188

see things clearly." Kennedy said, "Well, I don't need that so much. You probably ought to take that up to the guy at the other end of the street. He needs it more than I do," meaning, of course, the White House.

ALLEN GINSBERG
So I said, "Well, make an appointment for me."

GILLIAN WALKER, *theatrical producer*
I remember taking Kierkegaard to read. I thought I should meditate on death. But Kierkegaard was awfully heavy, and somehow it really didn't fit the levity of the atmosphere.

WILLIAM WALTON, *artist, family friend*
It was very hot. The air conditioner started to work but it didn't work all the way. I had on my respectable dark blue suit. It was not a summer suit. A man who was sitting behind me in St. Patrick's told me later, "You express your emotions through your sweat glands."

ANN BUCHWALD, *family friend*
Ed Morgan standing with his hands on his hips, just looking; and he opened a ginger ale with a nail file.

WILLIAM WALTON
His life, in a way, was all aboard that funeral train; all the phases: the people he had known, from school friends, family friends, college friends, his early political friends and associates; and non-friends, but people who had gotten woven into his life, up through Tom Watson of IBM and Doug Dillon and then lowly campaign workers from the New York office, they were all aboard. We all knew that Bobby would have had such a marvelous time moving from end to end of that train and seeing just about everyone he'd ever known. He would have said, "Wh

190

advanced this train?" because we were so slow and behind schedule. We began to run out of food and drink and everything else. He would have raised holy hell.

It was remarkable the way faces would come down the aisle of the train—someone one had known, perhaps politically, maybe four years, eight years, or ten years before—all of us connected by the one thread of the Kennedys. It took me back to an earlier campaign with him: the West Virginia primary in 1960, and the beginning of being friends. Before that, he had always been "the younger brother." I had watched him grow up from being a sort of nuisance to the older boys. In the West Virginia campaign, I got to know him much better because the Kennedy structure was very small in those days; there weren't many people, and Bobby was our boss and also the inspector general. We weren't surrounded by retainers. He and I would get in my car, and we would drive from village to village and coal mine to coal mine. In those drives between villages and coal-mine shafts, we'd be driving through this glorious spring weather and talking about everything. I remember discussing books with him. He was reading mostly the books on the best-seller lists, and he couldn't understand why I hadn't read all these books. He said, "What *do* you read?" I would name histories and biographies. He thought that I was a kook because I didn't read his sort of books. But four years later, we were on a plane coming back from the Cape, and he was reading Edith Hamilton's *The Greek Way*. Every now and then, he'd read a quotation aloud to me. Then he'd switch to a Greek poet; he had a couple of paperbacks in his pocket. All of this was very genuine. He had made a step in his self-education. It was marvelous to see his development and his expandability.

MARY BAILEY GIMBEL, *family friend*

He always had a book in his pocket. That had been a habit from a long time back. One winter he read a big dog-eared book on all of Western literature. It must have weighed four pounds and he carried it under his arm like a football. Finally he finished it, and we asked him what he'd got out of it. He said, "I liked the poet . . . the delicate Parisian one: Gérard de Nerval. He walked his lobster on a leash. People in the street said, 'What's your lobster doing out here on a leash?' The poet said, 'He doesn't bark and he knows the secrets of the deep.'" What made you feel so tender was that he'd read the book in dead earnest, determined (the way he always was) to be better and know more, and at the same time he felt there was a funniness and irony to such ambitions.

ROBERT LOWELL, *poet*

When I met him, it was arranged by his sister-in-law, by Jackie, and we were supposed to do something for each other; it wasn't exactly a scheme of hers; it was nothing *we* felt. She thought we should walk around the reservoir together. It's very hard to say whether it came off or didn't come off. At Jackie's, someone asked him a very dull question on taxes or something of that kind; he looked at me and said, "If Cal won't interrupt me, I'll try to explain this, unless *he* wants to." Then he gave a rather competent, dull explanation. We never became very good friends. If he'd been the only candidate in 1968, I'd have been completely for him. But I couldn't have traveled with him. I think there'd have been no room for someone like me; no leisure, as there was later with McCarthy; that McCarthy wanted to get away from the hail and brimstone of the campaign, and talk and relax and talk seriously. And I can't imagine doing that with Bobby. You'd go and have a good afternoon with him when he was President, but that's very different.

The first letter I wrote to Bobby, I made this point: that an artist isn't meant to celebrate a politician, but if he understands and knows politicians, he can use them. Dante is the best example in Western literature. He was one of the mayors of Florence. If he hadn't known a lot of politicians, he couldn't have made such characters as Farinata. The whole framework of the *Divine Comedy* is a Ghibelline epic, so that when Dante takes a dead person, like Farinata, he's like some living Florentine politician that Dante knew. You feel that in the poem. I think that's the real role of art in politics, not Robert Frost giving a poem at the Inauguration. I don't think that's serious. But if Frost had been a young man, he'd have put people like Jack Kennedy in some kind of a poem. That would have been the real use. I remember André Malraux once said in Washington that all a Minister of Culture could do for the arts was provide a stage and a museum, and a place to create therein. But I think that interaction of people in politics, people in the arts, is very good for both of them, though both tend to be very provincial in their own ruts.

I took him a book, and I knew he'd like it. It is one of the few good anthologies, *Short Lives*, and it begins with Plutarch, and it goes through Sainte-Beuve and Jeanne d'Arc, and there are several in this century. It was a big book, and almost none were entirely worthless and most of

192

them were very interesting. I marked about ten of them—I mean that sounds too patronizing, but you need it in a big book—and he said, "Oh, there's nothing I'd like to read better!"

WILLIAM VANDEN HEUVEL, *campaign aide*

He and Lowell discussed *The Education of Henry Adams*. Bobby said he found it a boring book and pulled it off a bookshelf. Robert Lowell took it and proceeded to read the part of it that describes the funeral of John Quincy Adams—which is a very moving and eloquent portion of the book. Bobby suddenly got up and excused himself. Lowell followed him, right to the door of the bathroom, still reading. Bobby shut the door and said, "If you don't mind." Lowell said, "If you were Louis XIV, you wouldn't mind."

ROBERT LOWELL

I'd given Jackie a Plutarch, and Bobby used to come and borrow it and read the ones I'd mark; then he'd mark some more for her to read. They had this queer sort of thing. She told me. I didn't know until after his death that he'd borrowed the book. I imagine he did read a good many. I think he took it skiing or something. McCarthy wouldn't want to be a Plutarchian hero, but Bobby would; and he'd know all the dangers, and I say "Plutarchian," though Plutarch has no one kind of hero. Each one is different. But, on the whole, he's very terrified of the man of *hubris:* Caesar and Alexander come off, on the whole, badly, but in a complicated way; particularly Caesar does, in Plutarch; he's sort of like Shakespeare's Caesar, only much more interesting; of course that's where Shakespeare gets this Caesar. Plutarch's hero is Cato, who was against Caesar. Bobby was very conscious of the nobility and danger of pride and fate.

ALICE ROOSEVELT LONGWORTH (*Mrs. Nicholas Longworth*)

I see Jack in older years as the nice little rosy-faced old Irishman with the clay pipe in his mouth, a rather nice broth of a boy. Not Bobby. Bobby could have been a revolutionary priest.

STAUGHTON LYND, *historian*

Perhaps Kennedy was interested in a couple of radicals because the radical view of the world . . . of the war . . . was becoming more persuasive to him. The night Tom Hayden and I talked with him, my son was with me. One of the things that stands out most clearly in my mind is that he—who was then about eight—spilled some Coke on the rug. Kennedy said that was all right—that's what he always put on his rug after the dog had dirtied it. He made my son feel at ease.

He was very slender and tense, simple in his manner . . . and we began right away to talk about the war. Kennedy took the process of conversation seriously; that is, it wasn't the usual kind of cocktail discourse where one thinks of clever ways to say nothing . . . to comment on the last thing that had been said. An attempt was made to follow a thread of argument, and Kennedy would go back to points made several minutes before. On the other hand, I felt that the assumptions from which he proceeded were quite conventional, very Ivy League. He would produce such stunning observations as: "It's impossible to conduct a free election in which Communists participate." Not that there isn't a good deal of historical truth in that statement, but it is just oversimplified—a cliché that he had accepted without thinking about it. And so I had a double kind of feeling. I felt the attractiveness of the man; and yet, at the same time, I felt apprehensive about his whole way of approaching social problems. He was going on to supper with Galbraith and Schlesinger, and so on, and he asked me if I wanted to come. But the talk had said what was on my mind about the war; I respected him for wanting a dialogue; but I just had no desire to become a part of that circle of intellectuals, because I didn't feel I belonged there.

JACK NEWFIELD, *author*

Tom Hayden and Staughton Lynd went to see Kennedy in his apartment in February '67. Kennedy had read their book based on their trip to Hanoi in December of '65. I was there while they spent about an hour with Kennedy talking about Vietnam. But, in the course of the evening, Tom told Kennedy about his project in Newark, where he was trying to organize local Negroes into a community union. Hayden found Kennedy incredibly appealing personally, and couldn't understand why liberals didn't like Kennedy . . . Tom thought he was much superior to McCarthy in terms of both politics and character. But Tom is essentially a revolutionary. He didn't support Kennedy for President . . . although he was really charmed by him. I once asked Kennedy, "If you weren't born a Kennedy, what would you have been?" He said, "Either a juvenile delinquent or a revolutionary." But in effect, he *was* a politician, and therefore he couldn't have been a revolutionary. Being a Kennedy, and the President's brother, and a Senator, and a candidate himself for President knocked him out as a revolutionary but established him as the best liberal politician. Still, he had empathy with people who were revolutionaries, and he admired that role. If Kennedy had a Walter Mitty life, he would have been Che Guevara.

TOM HAYDEN, *a founder of SDS*

It's one thing to admire Che Guevara, but that didn't lead Bobby to support the Cuban revolution, even privately. What he supported privately was the re-examination of American policies towards Cuba. I'm not talking about his public position. Bobby Kennedy was attracted to strong human beings and unorthodox people, and he had a romantic feeling towards guerrillas and people who struggled; but he was a very shrewd politician and careful to repress those romantic instincts. You can admire Che Guevara like you admire anyone, but it's another thing to support an Alliance for Progress—which Che Guevara wanted wiped out. Even with the kind of youth that he would try and appeal to, he would try to foster an NSA rather than an SDS; Mississippi Young Democrats rather than SNCC; CORE instead of the Black Panther Party. Bobby Kennedy met with Floyd McKissick continually and gave him money; but he didn't meet with Rap Brown or Bobby Seale or Eldridge Cleaver, or say a word about Huey Newton when he was in San Francisco. There's an age-old tendency on the part of liberal members of a dictatorial establishment when faced with insurgency to look for the most acceptable wing of the insurgency and have a relationship with it. Not even deliberately, necessarily. But simply because it's easiest to work with those people.

ADAM WALINSKY, *legislative aide, speechwriter*

Robert Kennedy tended to move toward the moderate elements. I mean they're easier to deal with. But one of the great things about Robert Kennedy was that he understood that we all have our own role to play. Robert Kennedy understood that there was a place in the society for people like Tom Hayden, and that you could say, "That's good what he's doing. We need that point of view around, and somebody should be pushing it." And, yet, that's not his position. I mean that's his *thinking*. He wouldn't *be* Tom Hayden, I mean, from his perspective. But he could like him, admire him, and feel he was playing a constructive role.

ROBERT SCHEER, *editor*, Ramparts

There was a certain kind of madness to him—a petty madness, not a grand madness; but a certain kind of madness that occasionally allowed him to be spontaneous and open. Just once in a while he would come away from the hack and either put down the whole scene or put himself down or his advisers or his advance men. Like once I had said, "Come on, you know Castro is five times the man you are, and that the Cuban revolution is great, and you are a fool to go up against it." And he said, "Yeah," you know, a kind of controlled "yeah." It was very clear that Kennedy had an admiration for the revolutionaries around the world, although he lacked the guts and commitment to be one. He'd been raised in a traditional, political bag, and he was fundamentally a hack, but he could be awed by the radicals.

ADAM YARMOLINSKY, *professor of law*

What were the causes of the hostility of intellectuals to Bob Kennedy? I think really it wasn't so much hostility to Bobby as it was early attachment to Eugene McCarthy because McCarthy did declare himself, and then an unwillingness to shift. Also, McCarthy was in many ways a kind of a clean slate on whom liberal-minded people could write almost anything they chose to write. McCarthy was anything they chose to make him. Bobby was emphatically himself and therefore harder for intellectual prima donnas to attach themselves to. Also McCarthy didn't have a circle of friends and admirers that extended very far beyond the intellectual community; therefore, he belonged more wholeheartedly to those people than Bobby could because Bobby belonged to all the people. The liberals, of course, were suspicious of him because he was young and rich, because he had immediately moved to a position of power and influence; there was always the residue—which I had to deal with when I was campaigning—of his service on the Joseph McCarthy committee, which had to be explained and could be explained; but anything that has to be explained is going to present a problem because the explanation never catches up with the charge. Also, there was this notion of ruthlessness and a feeling that he had somehow misused the office of Attorney General; it was awfully hard to bridge the gap between the myth and the reality in that area; although I think eventually we succeeded. The image of Gene McCarthy among the intellectuals, particularly in the Jewish community . . . was that Gene McCarthy was the professor who gave your bright son an A, and Bobby Kennedy was the tough kid on the block who beat up your son on his way to school.

ADAM WALINSKY

There were legions who were very hostile. He was a man of whom it was almost impossible to say that you were not a lesser man. That's a very important thing. After all, look at the pantheon of heroes of that particular group. Adlai Stevenson was obviously not much of a he-man. So, while he might be very intellectual, he was safe. So, even if you said, Gee, I like Stevenson. I love him. And he's terrific, there was still the feeling, Well, I'm better than him at some things, which is very important for people. When Lyndon Johnson won his great electoral victory, it probably helped him that people were able to feel superior to him in intellect. But Robert Kennedy—there was nothing that he didn't do better. He was immensely attractive to women. He had the money, and political success, and power; he was tough; he had brains. And he could put all of these things together. I mean a guy like that is—unless you're a very secure person—a constant threat. Especially if your wife and daughter are googling over him. I think that's one reason why he was always surrounded by people of fairly strong personality or character.

IVANHOE DONALDSON, *fellow, Institute for Policy Studies*

He'd take you out there—to see the whole operation. I guess he was pretty proud of it. One day I was coming down to Washington again, and there he was on the plane. I asked if I could sit down. We chit-chatted about politics. I told him what a bastard I thought Johnson was. So at the National Airport, he was met by his chauffeur—short black fellow, hippy kind of character—and he asked me if I wanted a ride. I said, "Sure I do." You know, why not? So, he took me out to McLean, Virginia, you know, which seemed a little bit out of the way. So, here's his house. So I pedaddled around there for about fifteen, twenty minutes, watching him play with his dogs. I finally got my ride back into Washington. I met a lot of people around his house. I saw the operation. His house looked like a guerrilla front. I was thinking that would be a great place to get a good revolutionary movement going from there. We could *operate* out of there.

JEAN STEIN VANDEN HEUVEL, *journalist*

Bobby asked Yevtushenko what it was in American society that he disliked most. Yevtushenko said, "I must answer in symbols. When I came from Kennedy Airport into New York City on the road leading through Long Island, there is a cemetery that goes on for blocks and blocks. It is a gigantic surrealist sculpture, and the gravestones are one next to another, so that it gives you the appearance of a solid wall of concrete stretching over acres of land. There is no humanity reflected in it; neither the humanity of life nor of death. What really appalls me, what I dislike most about your society, is the fact that there is no grass between the tombstones—the trouble with you Americans is that no grass grows between you."

WILLIAM VANDEN HEUVEL

Yevtushenko told Bobby of the meaning of the President's death in the Soviet Union. He was giving a reading at the time in a hall in Moscow, and a whisper started through the auditorium. He noticed that as each whisper passed from each person to the next, the face of that person took on a tragic expression—as if that person had just lost a mother or a father or a brother. During the whole time that he was telling that story, Bobby's left hand was clenched tightly. Yevtushenko went on to say how he had written this poem like a psalm, and how it had been banned. When they denied him permission to publish it, he went to the censoring officials and asked them why. They relayed word from the top echelons of government, presumably Khrushchev, that this wound was so grievous to the people of the United States and Russia, it would be wrong for them to publish it and make the wound bleed even more. Yevtushenko said that he thought that it was the first time he could understand their reason for censorship.

Ethel Kennedy asked him what he thought of Nureyev, having forgotten that he defected. He said, "Yuk, that ballerina." That's when he launched into his thing about defection—that he didn't believe in it. Bobby asked him how he'd feel about it if he'd been living under the Nazis. He said, "Under certain conditions."

Bobby gave Yevtushenko a Kennedy PT-boat tie-clip, explaining its meaning, and he said that the real test of their friendship would be if when he met President Johnson, he kept it on.

Afterward, we went over with him to Jacqueline Kennedy's. It was fascinating how the mood changed—nuances of the conversation all became very delicate, rather ethereal; there was candlelight in her apartment, rugs on the couches. Caroline and another friend greeted us in black velvet ballet costumes with pink stockings, and everything was very low-keyed—in contrast with the direct conversation that went on with Bobby at his apartment.

TRUMAN CAPOTE, *author*

Tom Wolfe wrote a very interesting article called "Watch 'em Jump." It's about people with power complexes; what power really does to those who have a highly developed sense of it. Meaning, if you move through a room and everything is galvanized on you and you're terribly aware of it, and people make room . . . they move out of their way to make room for you . . . in effect, they "jump." I think Bobby had that power, but he rarely used it. I mean, over a period of six years, I must have gone to thirty-five dinner parties that Bobby was at one way or another, and you could tell exactly what degree of discomfiture he felt being in that room. Often, he was very shy and stuttery and off in a corner on a couch. But, on the other hand, I'd been to his apartment when they were just having . . . oh, I don't know, the people that were working for him and a few friends in for a drink. And it was fascinating to watch, because everyone . . . the moment he would come into the room, they would go on talking to each other, but their eyes weren't there. They were completely, totally concentrated on Bobby being in the room. Although they kept on saying this and that to each other, they weren't even hearing each other. The whole thing had a kind of curious grotesquerie.

I always felt that he was very uneasy with me and that his friendship with me was really based on my friendship with other people that he himself was fond of. It wasn't that he really had any particular feeling about me at all, but he did care about people that he knew who cared about me. And, on that basis, we were friends. But I always felt that he was asking himself, Well, what is this all about? There was something exotic about me that he couldn't entirely accept; I mean, he was trying to accept it like a father doesn't want to accept long hair on a kid, or sideburns, but yet, he's sort of stuck with him. In the back of his mind, there was this ultimate reservation, and he just wasn't going to be able to get rid of it. When he died, I got a telegram from the family inviting me to go on the train, but I had the flu and it was terribly hot that day. It was terrifically hot. I said, "Well, I'll go anyway. I want to go." I drove in from the country, and I got a little briefcase together and a suit, and I got in a taxi to go down there; and it was so hot, and I was coughing and really sick and running a slight temperature, and I said, "Well, this is insane. If I go on this train ride, I'm going to be sick, and I'm going to cause other people a lot of nuisance and trouble . . . best not do it." So, I went to the funeral. Then I watched the train on television. Watching the train moving, I cried. That ride of the century. I don't cry over anything because I've had a pretty long, rough, tough life, emotionally speaking, since I was a child. It takes a great deal to do that, but I did . . . I cried. And I hadn't cried for a long time, and it made me physically sick to cry. And so I cared about him . . . yes. And that was that.

12

WILLIAM J. SHIELDS, *Penn Central supervisor*
I don't think too many people saw the accident in Trenton—it all happened so quickly. But I had the radio on, and Jerry Bruno was with me when the engineer yelled over it, "Holy smoke! Someone just touched the wire right next to me!" It was an 11,000-volt wire over a freight car on a siding.

VINCENT EMANUEL, *electrician*
The boy touched the wire just as we passed by. I didn't see it because it was on the side of the Secret Service man. He seen him when he fell to the ground. He said, "Boy, that fellow just got it! From the overhead wire!" People were doing foolish things . . . on top of boxcars, waving their arms, and that was real foolish. Oh, they were close! We always consider that wire energized . . . even if it's dead, we always consider it energized—alive. Because you never know. You only get one chance with that! That kid is lucky, recovering. See, he was on top of a boxcar, probably standing on the wooden runway on top of the boxcar and just got enough juice to knock him off.

RUSSELL BAKER, *columnist*
I was leaning out the window there, as we were coming into Trenton, and I looked ahead. Maybe several hundred yards down the track I could see a commotion, some guy getting a boy down off the top of a boxcar. And I thought, you know, they've caught a kid on a boxcar, and it's the railway police chasing him down. But he was lying on the

ground and I looked down as we went by, very slowly, and he was lying out there, you know, still smoking!

ARTHUR SCHLESINGER, JR., *historian*
The accident gave a kind of terrible sense—a kind of juggernaut of violence tearing through the country.

JAMES C. THOMSON, JR., *educator*
Vietnam. Yes. The Kennedy instincts plus the enthusiasm of certain types of social scientists—all the way from Roger Hilsman to Walt Rostow, and they are very different types of people, obviously—did a considerable disservice to the foreign policy of President Kennedy, especially in Vietnam. In an effort to get away from the much denounced Dulles doctrine of massive retaliation, the Democrats tried to devise something else that would look as if we were still in there with our muscle, but much more adept—what was called "flexible response." In part, it came from the social scientists sitting up at MIT and other places, racking their brains through the fifties trying to find some "answer" to guerrilla warfare . . . since, obviously, air power and bombing and the like weren't the answer. Now, you add to that the third ingredient, which is sort of the Kennedy family ethic of toughness, touch football, the cult of vigor. Robert Kennedy was sold, to some extent, a bill of goods—the notion of counter-insurgency.

DAVID HALBERSTAM, *author*
The Kennedy people had taken over from the Eisenhower people, who were flabby and soft; the Kennedy people saw themselves as eggheads, but tough. They had good war records, had climbed mountains and won awards, and did not talk about their intellectualism. Someone like Chester Bowles, who was the old kind of egghead, the soft liberal egghead, a little too Stevensonian, was out, and people like Bundy and McNamara were in. Taylor was the favorite general—he had written a book. And Bobby was very important in this thing. There was a way somehow that they were going to do this; it was going to be an American decade of intellectualism harnessed to toughness. Robert Frost had told Jack Kennedy at the time of the inauguration: "Be more Irish than Harvard." There was a bit of an outgrowth of the McCarthy period in this: the fact that the Democratic Party had been accused of being the party of treason, that it would never be accused of being soft again.

One of the things it got us into was counter-insurgency; it became quite a fad in Washington. Everybody went around reading Che Guevara and Lin Piao. It really was a sort of romantic period, with a certain naïveté to it, and the whole notion of counter-insurgency—these brilliant, young, great physical specimens in their green berets, swinging through the trees, you know, arm over arm, and speaking six languages, including Chinese and Russian, and who had Ph.D.'s in history and literature, and ate snake meat at night. It was all very nice, but the Kennedys never understood the difference between guerrillas and commandos. I don't think they really made the connection as to how political it was. The guerrilla was essentially, first and foremost, a political person.

JOSEPH KRAFT, columnist

General Maxwell Taylor, in particular, and to some extent, Roger Hilsman, and Mike Forrestal led Bob down the garden path on what counter-insurgency could do. The inscription Bob wrote on a copy of his last book that he gave to General Taylor said something like, "I told it like it was, or at least the way you told me it was." Bob became a partisan of the low-level Lansdale-type effort in Vietnam. I don't think he really altogether ever kicked the habit. Bob wasn't alone in this; you'll find that the New York *Times* and David Halberstam and John Vann and all those guys thought: If only we could do this thing in terms of counter-insurgency, small-unit things, and be guerrilla warriors, the counter-guerrillas, we could stop this thing. Bob was a partisan of that effort. He was the muscle and the energy in the counter-insurgency group.

GENERAL MAXWELL D. TAYLOR, director, IDA

I never laid eyes on Bobby until I met him in the White House two or three days after the fall of the beachhead at the Bay of Pigs. We came together as complete strangers, men of much different backgrounds and, of course, I was much older than he. But in the course of very intense work together for a month, we got to know each other quite well, and that was really the start of our friendship. From the outset, we developed a quick and easy mutual rapport. I told him I thought he could have qualified for my old airborne division, the 101st Airborne, because I thought he could sack a town or storm a hill with the same enthusiasm as my soldiers did.

He often said that I was his military adviser, that all he knew about military affairs he had got from me, and he knew that it might be a little embarrassing to me in later years if it were bruited about. I responded by offering to give him a field marshal's baton for his aptitude.

ROGER HILSMAN, *university professor*

President Kennedy called me in . . . for a talk. He had read a speech I had written on guerrilla warfare . . . and he asked me to go to Honolulu and talk to General Harkins, who was the next designated commander in Vietnam, and then to go on out to Vietnam and look the situation over and come on back and report to him . . . very quietly. Well, I did. When I got back, I gave the President my report. He asked me to see a number of people and give them the same report. One was Bob. One was Lyndon Johnson. I went over to talk to Lyndon about the report, but he was busy with some petty political crisis in Texas and just never heard a word I said. I'd say two or three words, and he'd say, "Excuse me," and he'd go and make a phone call. Then he'd say, "What were you saying?" Then he'd dictate something. You know, he just couldn't care *less*.

From that point on, the way it went was that on one side were the escalators—the military, the Pentagon, Walt Rostow, and so forth, with Robert McNamara tending to be more with them than with us, although much more cautious. They were extreme hawk, and Rusk was a mild hawk, though much more of a hawk than he ever permitted to be known. Then there was a group of people who were not doves in the 1968 sense, but who were convinced that Vietnam was morally a political struggle and not a war, and that it had to be done by the South Vietnamese and not the Americans, that bombing in the North wouldn't work, the introduction of American troops wouldn't work, and that what you had to do was get the South Vietnamese somehow to protect their people—to win their allegiance through political moves, by civic action, by medical programs, land reform, and all this. It had to be done by the Vietnamese and not the Americans, and it had to be political rather than military. The group that was agreed this was the way it had to be done were lined up this way: the President, Bobby, Averell Harriman, Mike Forrestal, myself, and McGeorge Bundy for a long time, although he eventually became a hawk in the Johnson Administration. Lyndon Johnson was out of it; he was not involved at all.

But as soon as John Kennedy was assassinated, he's in it: Harriman gets shifted out of the lion's job to a roving ambassador . . . put on a shelf. I end up resigning. If I hadn't resigned, I'd have been fired or sent to . . . well, when I resigned, Johnson tried to make me take the ambassadorship to Manila. Rather than go out and be an opponent. That was a clever move, but I didn't buy it. Mike Forrestal quit. Bob Kennedy was put out of it. Nobody was left on that side of the equation except George Ball, and in my day, George was only intermittently involved, sort of like McNamara. Mac Bundy's later role puzzled me. I think Johnson mousetrapped him. Mac got the idea that if he was ever going to be Secretary of State, he was going to have to bite the bullet on Vietnam, and there wasn't much of a bullet to bite except escalation. I think he became an escalator, partly out of these kinds of pressures. I have a lot of admiration for Mac. Very able guy. As for Bobby, you'll remember that he offered to go to Vietnam as an ambassador. I don't know what his motives were: I think he thought he could head off the disaster that seemed to be coming.

MICHAEL FORRESTAL, *attorney*

Bobby's principal interest with Vietnam was brought about by a speech that Khrushchev gave in December of 1960. Khrushchev said, among other things, that there were three kinds of war in the world: first was a nuclear war, which was clearly impossible . . . which had ceased to be a real possibility because of the strength of the two superpowers. The second was a conventional war. Khrushchev said that Korea had pretty well demonstrated that *that* kind of a war was unlikely to happen again, because it involved so many men that at a certain stage the problem was reached of having to use nuclear weapons because of the commitment made by both sides. That left the third kind of war, which was a revolutionary, internal war *within* countries, not between countries. This kind of war was still a viable kind of war, one that might well happen, and in which the Soviet Union, insofar as such wars involved the socialist camp versus the capitalist camp, would continue to give support to the socialist participants. Now this raised in the minds of both Kennedys—and I think maybe more in Bobby's than in his brother's—the thought that what Khrushchev said should be taken seriously—that one might very well foresee in a number of countries internal efforts by Communist or socialist revolutionaries to upset a legitimate government for the purposes of establishing a dictatorial, authoritarian kind of control. Since the Soviet Union had declared its intention to support that kind of an effort, this was a danger, and the United States should be prepared to . . . or be at least capable of . . . counterbalancing Soviet influence in this type of war.

That drove Bobby to consider a technique that I believe he named himself: counter-insurgency. In '62 and '63 that was his main foreign policy concern. He was thinking, I think, largely about Latin America . . . but he would have included Southeast Asia. Vietnam wasn't at that time, as you remember, that important. We had a mess in Laos, but we were getting rid of it then. Bobby was spending a lot of his energy on the Special Group CI (for Counter-Insurgency), which was a committee in the White House that met once a week; Maxwell Taylor was the chairman, then succeeded by Averell Harriman. Roswell Gilpatric was a member of it. The head of the AID agency and the deputy CIA fellow came to all the meetings, and so did Buzz Wheeler, the chief of the Joint Chiefs of Staff. So it was a *very* high-level group. It was Bobby's major touch with foreign affairs. He wanted to be sure that the government was prepared for counter-insurgency efforts. These never involved the thought of American troops. Counter-insurgency, in Bobby's mind, was largely a civilian effort backed up by the right kind of supplies delivered at the right time to the right place. The kind of thing that he was trying to do through this group was to make it possible, for example, for Venezuela to have an election for the first time in some thirty years. Betancourt's term had run out; there was an election that damn near didn't come off because of terrorism in Caracas.

This group, under Bobby's prodding, was able to see that enough police-communication equipment got down to Caracas to permit the police to set up the necessary riot barricades so that the terrorists couldn't prevent the election.

Or the case of Thailand. The northeastern part of Thailand had been continuously neglected. It was an area where there was a kind of latent discontent and disaffection from the Thai government. The reason was there were no communications with the area; most people living there didn't even know who the King of Thailand was. They knew who the King of Laos was, but not the King of Thailand. So Bobby got a couple of things done: he got some locomotives; he got a railroad laid up there, and he pushed our government into helping the Thais build feeder roads so that the villages could (a) communicate with each other, and (b) have access to the more populated part of the country. That's the type of thing that he did.

At that time, he was not directly concerned with Vietnam. He was concerned with this problem of what the United States does in the event there is an effort in a friendly country to overthrow the legitimate government and establish a dictatorship. He was as worried about the dictatorships of the right as he was about dictatorships of the left.

Vietnam became interesting to him for the first time in the summer of 1963 because a serious problem had been forced on his brother, the President. On May 8th of '63, the Buddhists were attacked by government forces in the town of Hue. And between May 8th and November 1st of 1963, the situation in Vietnam went from what we thought was a manageable mess rapidly downhill into an unmanageable mess, because of the difficulties that Diem got himself into, partly because of his own brother, Mr. Nhu.

Some time in the summer of '63 Bobby for the first time said to me that he was beginning to have serious doubts about the whole effort in Vietnam . . . not from a moral point of view, but from a pragmatic point of view. Was the United States capable of achieving even the limited objectives that we then had in Vietnam? Did the United States have the resources, the men and the philosophy and the thinking to have anything useful to contribute or say in a country as politically unstable as South Vietnam was? Was it not possible that we had overestimated our own resources and underestimated the problem in South Vietnam? He mainly raised questions—hard questions—which most of us had assumed had been answered many years before. He began forcing people to take a harder look at what we were doing there, and whether or not we were really capable of doing it.

The death of Diem seriously shook up his brother. Diem's downfall was . . . to be precise . . . possibly speeded by our inaction. It is conceivable—though I myself doubt it—that we might have kept him going for another couple of months . . . but no longer than that. What we, in effect, did was not to try to prop him up any longer. Just before the President died, Bobby, as well as the President—but I think it was principally Bobby—started asking about ways and means of planning for the future: How is the United States going to extricate itself from this area? Because we had seen that the Diem government was very weak, and there was absolutely no assurance that any succeeding government would be any stronger . . . or any more popular, for that matter.

GEORGE BALL, U.S. *Ambassador to the United Nations*
I always thought counter-insurgency was for the birds. The Senator had been sold this . . . by Walt Rostow or Max Taylor or someone.

"Counter-insurgency" sounds slightly Rostovian! The amount of effort and theology with which that whole business was invested was totally incommensurate with anything we ever got out of it. It led us into messing into situations where we would have done much better to have stayed out. There was a time when every Ambassador about to go abroad . . . even if he were to go to the Court of St. James's . . . was supposed to spend three months going to counter-insurgency school—just in case some activity began to develop in Green Park. I never argued on a bilateral basis with the Senator. I used to put my heresies forth in meetings, and when the Senator was present I don't think he agreed with me at all. It was very much of a fashionable thing at that time; counter-insurgency was the wave of the future. I thought it was grossly overdone. Part of my quarrel with it was that it would lead us deeper and deeper into situations where it required *more* than this kind of theorizing to deal with them, and that therefore we ought to commit our power and our effort to places where the terrain was more suited. I don't mean physical terrain. I mean political terrain. I suppose the classic example is Vietnam. We got in deeper and deeper. There was no rational basis for us doing this; we ought to have been quite sure that we were selecting a political and physical terrain that would support the weight of the kind of power that we were putting in; you couldn't make bricks without straw, particularly when the quality of the clay was as poor as it was there.

The impression I had at the time was that counter-insurgency was a bright new toy, and that a lot of people were applying an enormous lot of effort to it, as though this were something that had never existed before. Well, insurgency has been an aspect of life for a thousand years. It had been intellectualized by both the Soviet and Chinese side, and they'd given it a kind of new patina. But I didn't have a feeling that it was wholly new in kind; I thought it was simply an application of some fairly rudimentary principles, which one had learned over a long period of time; and that for us to be treating it as though it were a new church that we had to deal with was a great misapplication of effort, and led to some very serious errors of judgment, in my opinion.

I once sent a memorandum . . . not specifically about Vietnam; it happened to be about the "Chinese takeover" in Zanzibar, which aroused the wrath of Averell Harriman and also got the Senator's back up, as I recall. The memorandum was simply: "God watches every sparrow that may fall, so I don't see why we have to compete in that league."

208

ADAM WALINSKY, *legislative aide, speechwriter*

I was just learning about counter-insurgency, what it was supposed to be; the Senator had been full of it. But I remember going to see Bernard Fall, in July 1965. His death has been such a great loss. He said, "Counter-insurgency is dead. This is the end of it." He said that all of the political maneuvering was over . . . that the Americans were going to come in with their weight and power and armament, and they were just going to blast the country out of existence. The whole theory of the practice of counter-insurgency, which had to do with very pseudo-sophisticated concepts of politics, and winning the hearts and minds, and all of that . . . that was all over; that was finished.

JOSEPH KRAFT

The one virtue there was in the counter-insurgency position was that it stood against doing the big things, and I think that Bob would have always held off from doing the big things. He would, I think, have held off from doing what was irreversible, which was the bombing—which got us into a hell of a lot of trouble. I think he would have avoided that. If you looked at the people who were involved in the shaping of Vietnam policy, there was nobody there intimately involved who was temperamentally equipped to understand. Mac Bundy, Dean Rusk, Max Taylor, and Robert McNamara—the last thing they could understand in the world would be a Buddhist monk. They had, I think, very little feel, indeed almost no feeling for the inner politics of Saigon.

SENATOR JOSEPH TYDINGS

McNamara was used to having facts presented to him and making decisions on the basis of facts. He was a brilliant business leader; he made a great national contribution in reorganizing and restructuring the Pentagon . . . cost factors and budgeting, and possibly he saved the taxpayers billions of dollars. But when he went out to Vietnam, he was exposed to only one side; he was never given the facts or the truth of the situation. I can only assume that the same holds true for Maxwell Taylor and others. He came back, and he made his decision from recommendations based on what he thought were facts. Of course, the facts were all wrong, and he never apparently questioned the source of his information there—at least not to the point where he was willing to publicly stand up to Johnson and tell him that our Vietnam policy was wrong and we had to reverse our direction, which was what Clark Clifford eventually did. Of course, Clifford had certain advantages. He was very close personally to Johnson, who could have no doubts about his loyalty. Johnson relied on him greatly, and always had. McNamara came in from Kennedy; he wasn't a Johnson man.

It's amazing how Maxwell Taylor and Robert McNamara and all of those top persons were deceived in Vietnam each time they would go over. It partly was the holdover atmosphere from the McCarthy era . . . the people in the State Department who *should* have been speaking up were scared to death. No one except George Ball seemed to question and speak out against our policy. They'd seen the power of the China lobby. They remembered the purges of those who had spoken up on the China policy and criticized Chiang Kai-shek. The young, inquisitive, objective voices in the State Department were so scared by what happened . . . and by the purges by Dulles, Congress, and others during and after the McCarthy era . . . that they just didn't speak up. As a result, the Robert McNamaras and the Maxwell Taylors went to Vietnam, and all they were exposed to was the line that the United States' vital national security was involved; we've just *got* to stay there; the war was going to be over in X minutes, so send in two more divisions. How else can you account for the incredible misjudgments, which cost the nation billions of dollars and thousands of dead! We continue to suffer from the McCarthy phobia. In a country . . . no matter how corrupt the existing government, no matter how totalitarian or how vicious it is to the people . . . when there is internal or civil revolt and the government in power shouts "Communist!" we have a tendency to rush out with military aid and foreign aid without question one . . . inevitably a tragedy. I think Bobby recognized this.

ADAM YARMOLINSKY, *professor of law*
The relationship between Bob McNamara and Bobby was a nephew-uncle relationship. McNamara was really terribly fond of him, and admired his dedication and his energy and his unwillingness to accept second choices; his indignation, which appealed to a very deep strain in McNamara. And Bobby, in turn, I think was impressed with McNamara's wisdom and tremendous intellectual power. I don't know of any major decision that he made without consulting McNamara. McNamara, as you know, was deeply concerned about the course of the war, though he was completely loyal to President Johnson.

HUBERT HUMPHREY, *Vice-President of the United States*
I never considered Robert Kennedy, from my personal, subjective

point of view, an irresponsible critic of the war. I think that he recognized that our being there was, from his point of view and our national point of view, necessary . . . painful as it was. What he was most concerned about was the structure of government in South Vietnam and the failure to get reform, knowing that this war was essentially a political struggle. You had to have the support of the people. There had to be some feeling that the people were getting benefits and were going to have reforms made that were vital to their lives. And this is where I think he started to have a renaissance, so to speak, or a change of attitude about our involvement. He felt that we were doing it with far too much power and military, rather than the political adjustments that were required.

TOM HAYDEN, *a founder of SDS*

I think that he had a more rational and realistic understanding of the Vietnam situation than President Johnson. Especially I think he had been influenced by his trip to Europe, where he had some discussions with French officials. He could see that the policy of counter-insurgency that he and his brother had initiated by this point was becoming a disaster; but he didn't look forward to the only other alternative, which would be an unending so-called limit to the war, a policy that would eventually destroy Vietnam. So he was looking for a way out that would satisfy American political reality. That was where I thought the difficulties in his position came about; that in order to maintain his prestige and his possible presidential candidacy, he had to take a position on Vietnam that was supposedly acceptable to the middle range of voters and to the Democratic Party establishment, whose support he had to have. This led to very difficult problems. He would keep referring to a Vietnam that never was, as if Johnson had botched a problem that John F. Kennedy could have solved. He seemed to say that the United States had a legitimate role in Vietnam and that if it were operated correctly, it could have introduced land reform and established a civilian government and brought the people out of their support for Communism. He was perpetuating a myth of the Cold War. He wouldn't break with that. He couldn't embrace the truth because it was politically inadvisable, and because he himself had never had any sympathy for Communism. He couldn't bring himself to believe that there could be a popular Communist revolution that was good for people. It came up in his conversations. He said, "One of the difficulties with Communists is they don't believe in elections, so it will be very difficult to negotiate a solution there." But in his private position, the healthy thing was when we said, "If you want to get out of Vietnam, you have to try to negotiate; but you have to be prepared to risk, from your point of view, a Communist government and a unified Communist Vietnam within ten years." He said, "That's true. That has to be risked." That position I thought was at least frank and courageous, though his public position was not as courageous as it might have been.

PETER EDELMAN, *legislative aide*

There were two major Vietnam crunches in Robert Kennedy's Senate career. In February of 1966, he gave the speech about sharing the power and the responsibility. It was the first time that any major political figure had got up and said, Lookit, Johnson and you guys, if you're talking about negotiations, you'd better start thinking about what's *involved* in negotiations; you'd better start making it clear that you don't just mean by "negotiations" that the other side should come in and surrender, lay down its arms and come in on its knees to the table. You've got to understand that negotiations involve compromise and giving up something. That was the point of the speech. It took a long time for that lesson to sink in on the other end of Pennsylvania Avenue. Then Hubert Humphrey said that to consider participation by the Viet Cong or the NLF in a future government in Saigon was like putting the fox in the chicken coop. The Administration hauled out all of its political and military guns to say that Robert Kennedy was either wrong, or he was promoting his political ambitions. We sat around in the Senator's office—like being in a little fortress—waiting for the next bomb to be dropped on us by the Administration. There was kind of a command-post feeling about it: sitting till all hours of the night trying to decide what to do when you had the government against you and none of the agencies available to which you could turn to speak on your behalf.

It was the same thing in March of '67. That was the "stop the bombing" speech. I was sick in bed with a strep throat for the three days before he gave the speech; they would send me the drafts at home, and I would call up and croak into the phone what I thought ought to be done. Adam Walinsky and I were working it out, and I suppose some others; but Adam and I were always trying to push him to be more critical and more straightforward. There were others who would say, "Well, now, you have got to fudge on that a little." So the morn ing he was going to give the speech, I got myself together and came into the office. I hadn't seen him for about two or three days. He came in, and I was sitting reading over the draft. He said to me, "Well, am I dove enough for you?" And I said, "No." So he said, "That's good."

WILLIAM VANDEN HEUVEL, *campaign aide*

Bobby was not one who ever believed in immediate withdrawal from Vietnam. He never advocated that. He always thought of a negotiated settlement as being possible; he always thought of an eventual withdrawal over a period of time. But he thought it was counter to everybody's interest to just have us cut and run, and he never talked in those terms. He did look upon Vietnam basically as much more of a nationalist civil war than as the forum for the confrontation of the great powers.

I remember him in conversation with a young man, a very skilled and brilliant student in the Pentagon, who had been studying in depth the whole American involvement in Vietnam. This fellow asked him, "What do you think President Kennedy would have done?" Bobby said, "He just never would have gone on with this escalation." And this fellow said, "Well, why was it that you and President Kennedy would have acted so differently?" Bobby replied: "Because we were *there*." Now that, to me, has always been a major factor in the understanding of the difference between the way John Kennedy and Lyndon Johnson looked at the world. John Kennedy was in Indo-China. He saw the costs of that war to France. Bobby accompanied him at that time; I think it was in 1951 or '52. They talked to the young men in the embassy who were then in rebellion against the American diplomatic establishment and against American policy in support of the French position. Out of that came a very real sense that the Viet Minh then and the Viet Cong now were both nationalist forces genuinely fighting for their own national freedom and independence. I just can't imagine that John Kennedy or Robert Kennedy would have permitted our involvement in that way . . . because what we essentially did was succeed to the position of the French . . . which is just exactly what we tried to avoid.

JAMES C. THOMSON, JR.

The Vietnam problem under Kennedy, from roughly May 1963 through Kennedy's death, was dealt with with immense passion and energy and intelligence by a whole series of people in the government who disagreed violently among themselves, and what you had in the autumn of '63 was a government rent by factions, disagreements, different interpretations, different solutions . . . among people like Roger Hilsman, Mike Forrestal, Averell Harriman, Robert McNamara, Walt Rostow, *et al.* A very bad feeling came out of all that; but basically, the right policy emerged, though, unfortunately, once Diem was out of office . . . we had no plan for what to do next. But the net product of that kind of bloodletting within the government was a decision . . . almost a reflex, once Johnson came in, and Hilsman had been kicked out and Harriman shunted to the side . . . that we were not going to have this kind of internal infighting again. We were going to have a team sense, and much more mutual trust and respect. The circle would be much smaller and the decision making much quieter. In effect, a group ethic was developed to try and avoid the kind of factionalism that had occurred. That was compounded by the temperament of Lyndon Johnson, the most secretive of all President types, who wanted to keep everything absolutely in his own hands and quiet. Kennedy wouldn't have permitted it to happen because his temperament was to force things out into the open, into major meeting-type confrontations.

JOSEPH A. CALIFANO, JR., *special assistant to President Lyndon B. Johnson*

On the war, I think that obviously both LBJ and RFK wanted peace; there's no disagreement about that. But there's a really big disagreement on the way of getting peace: it went beyond the question of whether or not there should be a pause on bombing, beyond the question of the problem of corruption of the South Vietnamese government, or lack of will there. I always suspected that they really disagreed about the basic issue of whether or not Southeast Asia was really worth fighting for— which is really a great part of the split in the country today. There are people who don't believe it's worth losing thousands and thousands of American soldiers in a war so far away. But also I feel that a difference of opinion about the war would not have existed for almost any of the candidates for President had they been running the war for the past two or three years.

DAVID HALBERSTAM

Jack Kennedy sent advisers, and he sent Special Forces; he deliberately kept the cut-off point below the combat-troops level. So you can't blam him for the bombing or the combat-troop thing. On the other hand, the Kennedy era did set up the Vietnam rhetoric, did deepen the commitment, and did establish a position that made it a little bit harder for his successor to get out. At the time of the assassination, I think the Kennedys were probably a little cynical about the "We will stand in Vietnam" rhetoric. But Lyndon Johnson, who had not gone through Jack Kennedy's experiences in the three years, which would have made him wary of generals' predictions and the use of force, went in there. You could make a case that both Lyndon Johnson and Jack Kennedy had a Bay of Pigs. One lasted about four days, and the other lasted about four years.

ELIE ABEL, *television correspondent*

We made a strange date to meet at Winston Churchill's grave at Bladon, which is in a little churchyard on the edge of Blenheim, the Duke of Marlborough's estate. He said he'd like to talk to me before he addressed the Oxford Union. He showed up late, as always, and it was raining like hell. We walked up to the tomb, and he deposited the wreath. It was a very short ride to Oxford. He said, "What do they expect me to say?" I said, "My guess is that they expect you to say the bombing in Vietnam is a terrible thing." He said, "Well, I'm not sure I can go that far." He was still groping. He was a little wary of being mousetrapped—he was being criticized for having turned soft. As the car raced down the wet motorway, we talked about a number of things. He was very upset about the stink about the William Manchester book on his brother. He was telling me about how upset Jackie was. He kept saying, "The poor little thing, the poor little thing." But he kept getting back to this: "What can I say at the Union?" I said, "Look. Don't get so uptight about it. They will respond to you as a youthful and glamorous figure; they'll be happy to listen to anything you have to say, but if you're going to say anything about Vietnam, you had better express, to a degree, your disenchantment, your unhappiness with the present course of American policy; that's what they all feel, and that's what they expect of you."

In the High Street there were about 500 people waiting for us, as if we were running for public office. He said, "Well, here we go again," and the first thing I knew, he was standing on top of the car shaking hands. There were a fair number of students among them, and a number of workers from the big automobile plant and their wives. Obviously, he was a much loved figure to them. They responded to him. So we went through this weird campaign scene. Inside the Union he spoke quite effectively. He didn't come right out and denounce the Administration for its actions in Vietnam, but he made it very clear that he did not feel comfortable with what we were doing. Then, the next day, he went on to Paris. This was early in 1967.

WILLIAM VANDEN HEUVEL

When the Senator and I were in France, we went to see Etienne Manac'h, who was the Deputy Foreign Minister in France for the Far East. He's the most knowledgeable man about the Far East. He said to Bobby, "This thing has to be settled in pieces. First of all, you have to stop the bombing. Then you have to permit this kind of coalition negotiation to go on. Don't worry about the merger of North Vietnam and South Vietnam. It may or may not come about, but it's not a crucial factor; a coalition government *is* possible in the South."

On the basis of those reports and other things he told us, a cable was sent back to the State Department. *Newsweek* picked it up as a peace feeler.

Bobby was always rather startled at the publicity that visit got. He thought it was an important conversation; he thought that Manac'h spoke very sensibly about it; but he didn't think it was anything so dramatically new that he would have bothered to communicate it to the President, who thought he was acting on his own, behind his back. He just considered the steps were a logical sequence of events that Manac'h, from his own encounters with the Viet Cong, knew were possible! They were relayed to the State Department *in that sense* . . . not as a dramatic new proposal to bring the end to the war.

Then came that famous confrontation between Bobby and President Johnson.

FRANK MANKIEWICZ, *press secretary*

When he returned from Paris, *Newsweek* had a story saying he'd got ten a peace feeler. He didn't know anything about any peace feeler He'd had a conversation with some guy in Paris, but he didn't pay much attention to it; the cable describing the conversation had gone to the State Department. That's all he knew about it. He said to the President "The leak came from your State Department." The President said t him, "It's *your* State Department." What did that mean, "It's *you*

State Department"? What he probably meant was that he thought there were a lot of Kennedy Easterners in the State Department whom he could not control, which is of course dead wrong, and paranoid, and rather typical of Johnson's style. The leak certainly had not come from Robert Kennedy, because he didn't even know about it. He'd gotten home the night before, and I called him and told him about the *Newsweek* story. He didn't know what I was talking about. But the President got very sore at him and said that they were going to win the war by the summer—this was '67—and that within six months "all you doves" will be dead. He meant politically. And he got very mad. Bobby had a number of suggestions. He suggested stopping the bombing, and expanding the International Control Commission. And the President said, "Well, I want you to know that I'm not going to adopt any single one of those suggestions because we're going to win the war, and you doves will all be dead in six months." Bobby told him, "I don't have to listen to that," and he got up and left.

RICHARD GOODWIN, *politician*

When Johnson was Vice-President, he was treated very deferentially by Bobby, and maybe, in his view, rather rudely. He never liked Bobby Kennedy. But I don't think it was a totally rational thing. Bobby symbolized everything Johnson hated; he became *the* symbol of all the things Johnson wasn't. It really wasn't fair to Bobby, but he was a sort of surrogate for his brother—with these characteristics of wealth and power and ease and Eastern elegance, et cetera; with Johnson always looking upon himself as a guy from Texas whom they probably looked upon as being *illiterate*, a sort of rude, crude guy. They didn't like his style and his language, and they laughed at him behind his back. I think he felt all of that.

CHARLES SPALDING, *family friend*

Practically no President ever really liked his Vice-President. Maybe his current duo is an exception; they deserve each other. But certainly Eisenhower and Nixon never got along. There was nothing malevolent about the President's feelings. He just knew that Johnson was an overwhelmingly ambitious guy stuck in this dismal job. He knew it was just bugging him. Johnson was very gracious about that. One of the few things he said that I recall with fondness is that when somebody asked him about the job under President Kennedy, he said, "Well, he's done much better by me than I would have by him under the same circumstances." That's rather nice.

CHARLES BARTLETT, *journalist*
I remember once I was over in the White House with Jack Valenti. This was quite late in the game—about '67—and I got into a pitch there about how I thought this whole antagonism was overdone, and that it was something being built up by subordinates. The President just was stonily silent; he made no response at all to what I said. So I gathered at that point that the relationship was hopeless. But up to that time, I'd done what I could to try and keep the lines straight, and to urge Bobby not to let these little people aggravate this thing. It was a great misfortune.

BILL MOYERS, *publisher,* Newsday
There was a kind of inevitable escalation of tension between the two men. Each misunderstood the other's particular constituencies, so that as the months wore on, reconciliation was impossible. Every speech Kennedy made was seen by the White House as a political maneuver against Johnson. Kennedy may well have thought that he was trying to be useful and constructive, but it was hard for the President and his advisers to look at that objectively in 1968. Then Kennedy's advisers, and perhaps Kennedy himself, felt that every position the White House took toward peace talks, or cessation of the bombings, or other strategies in South Vietnam, was devised by Johnson for political purposes, particularly to offset Kennedy. I think this is one of the reasons why Johnson finally withdrew . . . he realized that every move he made toward peace in Vietnam, or toward a stepping down of the tensions and the fighting, was being interpreted in the American press, and by Kennedy's friends and associates, and probably by Kennedy himself—and indeed in Hanoi—as singularly a political ploy without any substance or sincerity behind it.

BURKE MARSHALL, *attorney*
Bob did discuss with Clark Clifford this business of finding some way of dealing with Vietnam; in a way, he was trying to find a way where the President could gracefully do what ought to be done, which was to turn around and de-escalate. He committed himself to have a conversation with Clark Clifford about this notion, which, as I say, I didn't think was a very good idea—to form a separate body to reassess the situation—

but he'd committed himself to it. His mind was not firm at that point. But if something had come out of that, and the President had made some gesture so that there was some commitment about re-examination of Vietnam, then maybe Bob wouldn't have run. I don't think he made up his mind until that door was closed.

CHARLOTTE CURTIS, *journalist*

More of my notes: "Then the Little Leaguers waving their caps; the nuns in sunglasses." I'd never seen a nun in sunglasses before, I guess. "And the baseball games had stopped on the diamonds. And on the embankments: daisies, lavender, clover, wild raspberrry bushes, and white blossoms." Do you remember? It was June, and it was beautiful. "And the yellow mustard blossoms and ferns all through the fields. And the children standing near a pond." In fact, I remember this. There were rushes, kind of, and then there was a pond in the background. Four little boys in T-shirts and short pants stood with their black caps held over their hearts.

GEORGE McGOVERN, *Senator from the State of South Dakota*

I didn't even want to be interrupted. I just sat there looking out the window all the time. My wife was the same way; she was looking out one side, and I was looking out the other. I resented it when people came along and started talking politics.

JOHN KENNETH GALBRAITH, *economist*

I kept an open seat beside me. I omitted the obeisances because it seems to me the political process *does* go on. As the train moved along, people did drop down beside me. And, frankly, I don't see any need for apology. Life does go on. So I omitted the effort to give an immature imitation of a bad undertaker, and instead I engaged in political conversations during the course of the trip. We discussed who would represent the poor and what the effect would be on the sort of people along the tracks who no longer felt they had a champion like Bob Kennedy; and how people with such concerns could continue to be engaged politically; how much their belief in the political process would be shaken by the assassination of not only Bob Kennedy, but John F. Kennedy and Martin Luther King; we talked about the meaning of this on the more immediate political future; and about the effect it would have on the convention.

One of the people who came along and sat down at the beginning of the long ride was Stewart Udall. He told me that he was doing a book on poetry and politics. Or poets as politicians. I told him the last—almost the last—time I had seen Bob in his office in Washington, he had come in with a copy, I think, of Aeschylus and read me a verse or two, and had commented on its appropriateness to some current situation. All of which I'd forgotten. We talked a little bit about Bob Kennedy's reading and the fact that he did have a sense of words, a sense of the music of words.

Earlier a man came by with a tape recorder and said he was making an oral history of the journey for the Kennedy family, and could I tape my impressions; since we were just a few hundred yards out of Newark, I told him I hadn't formed any. He gave me the impression that I was very much in default; that certainly, having gone through the Pennsylvania tunnel and having gone across the Jersey flats, I should have some pretty strong impressions. So he went away and never came back. Then, a little while later, a man from CBS came along and said, "Professor Galbraith, could we interview you on your impressions of the train?" And, I said—I felt so badly, having disappointed the earlier man—I said, "Yes." So he said, "That's fine. I'll be back." And then he disappeared, and I never saw him again either.

ROGER HILSMAN, *university professor*
We talked about Bob mainly . . . the things we remembered. But it always turned to the question, What the hell are we going to do now? . . . phrased that way . . . What the hell are we going to do now? . . . we, meaning the nation, not so much the individuals . . . What the hell was the nation going to do now?

SENATOR GEORGE McGOVERN
I had started talking to Bobby about running for the presidency by the

fall of '65—shortly after he came to the Senate. I was convinced that Johnson was going to go for a military decision in Vietnam, and that we weren't going to pull out. I predicted disaster for that course. I talked to him about this in '66 and '67; all the way along I thought that he should challenge Johnson and that he might defeat him. The only point at which I wavered was when Ted Sorensen came to me one day—acting apparently under Bob's instructions—and said, "Now, look. You and other people are urging Bob to go. You really ought to know what you're talking about before you do that. Is there support for him? If there is, you should try to establish that fact. You should call some of the people you know."

So I called a number of Governors and Senators in my area, and I couldn't find one person who thought he ought to go! Acting within the criteria of whether there was support, I reported back that I couldn't find any. Still, I urged him to defer any judgment, not to say that he *wouldn't* go. This was early in 1966. My instinct was that the country would not tolerate the Johnson policy on Vietnam once it was understood, and that an articulate, forceful figure who could attract nationwide press like Bobby could explode the policy . . . if he challenged the President directly. This was the course that I urged. But I began to think that maybe I was a dreamer—especially when Ted Sorensen laid down the guidelines of not urging him to run unless there was significant support for him. There wasn't! So I reported that, and I think it had something to do with his decision to defer running. I couldn't, at that point, take it on myself to say, "Well, all these other people are wrong, and you should go."

Ted Kennedy stopped me down in the Senate gym one afternoon, maybe two weeks before the New Hampshire primary, and just in a friendly sort of way, he said, "Now, you know, let's really think this thing through. Because I think if just one or two people push him, he'll go." What he was saying, in effect, was, Now, be careful! Because if you push him, he's going to go. It won't take very much. Just one guy, really I think that's true. I now think that if I had been relentless on this . . . let us say through the fall and on into the winter of '67 . . . I think Bobby could've been pressed to the point where he might have gone. But there weren't other members of the Senate urging him. They thought he'd get hurt. That he'd split the party and wreck himself. And that even if he got the nomination, it would have been worthless. Of course New Hampshire demonstrated that was not true, that the party was already split.

ADAM WALINSKY, *legislative aide, speechwriter*

The day after the 1966 elections, I had done a memorandum. It was clear that people were much more disturbed about Vietnam than the polls had said. The position for outright withdrawal had never gotten over eight per cent on a poll. But in a couple of places, the proposal had been put on a secret ballot, and it went immediately to forty per cent. That was in Dearborn, Michigan. It was the first real clue that people were obviously much more disturbed than the polls had ever indicated. Secondly, people were terribly disturbed about the race question. The only way for something decent to be done about blacks was by someone who would be trusted personally; what had gone sour with Johnson was that people just didn't believe him and didn't trust him, and they felt that the whole thing was a swindle. I said all of this in the memorandum . . . and I said it flatly . . . that Lyndon Johnson was a lame duck: he *had* to lose in 1968 . . . no question. He was finished. The only question was who was going to replace him. I said I thought the Senator could beat him in a primary; if he didn't try, I thought that one of the young Republicans would jump up and take the lead; he'd pull the academic community around him, and the youth, and some of the disenchanted people, and just go right on through; he would have enormous publicity value in the press; all of the opinion makers would be with him. He would be the next hero of the country. The one thing I didn't figure was Eugene McCarthy . . . that it would be a Democrat.

The Senator was very concerned about the whole problem. Several times he said if he could only be sure that he wouldn't go through all that just to end up with Richard Nixon as President of the United States. That was the outcome that he thought would really be undesirable. At one point, I remember, he asked me what I would do in a Johnson versus Nixon election. "Well, I'll tell you," I said. "The measure of my desperation is that last year I said I'd vote for *anybody* over Lyndon Johnson, with the possible exception of Richard Nixon. This year I'd vote for anybody against Lyndon Johnson." And he said, "You'd *do* that? You'd vote for Richard Nixon?" I said, "Against Lyndon Johnson, I'd vote for the devil." He went, "Tsk, tsk, tsk."

ALLARD LOWENSTEIN, *congressional candidate*

He said he would not run except under some unforeseen circumstance. So I marched in and said, "I'm an unforeseen circumstance." He recited all that business he used to recite in that period about why so-and-so said it couldn't be done. But you could see he wanted to do it. It made

223

me very sad, but angry, too. I kept saying that if things were to be judged by traditional political standards, and by traditional politicians, by traditional judgments of what was possible, then of course nothing could be done. But that was the whole point! Nothing was the way it had been before, and if he didn't know that, he wasn't anywhere near as smart as I thought he was; and furthermore, if he didn't try, with things going the way they were, it was hard to believe he cared as much as millions of people thought he did.

He said, I think the phrase was, "It can't be put together." Then the concluding note of this rather sticky conversation was when I just glared at him, and I said, "You understand, of course, that there are those of us that think the honor and direction of the country are at stake. I don't give a damn whether you think it can be put together or not." I said, "So now, we're going to do it without you, and that's too bad because you could have been President of the United States."

I turned, like any sort of fly landing on an elephant, and flew out. He came soaring out after me and in that familiar gesture, he turned me around with his hand on my shoulder. We both were standing there blowing our noses in this thick sense of emotion. It really was very unexpected. I didn't think it would happen, but he just said, "Well, I hope you understand I want to do it, and that I know what you're doing *should* be done; but I just can't do it."

RICHARD GOODWIN, *politician*

Everybody in the country said that he had absolutely no chance; that it was absolute suicide; you couldn't unseat an incumbent President; it was just a foolish, quixotic gesture—and more than that, he would divide the party and might very well drag down guys like Frank Church and George McGovern and damage a lot of good people. But his instinct was to do it. I remember at the time he said, "Whether you believe it or not, why don't you give me the best case for my running." Which I did. Then he asked me to get together with Teddy. Teddy and I had dinner down at the Charles Restaurant for three hours. Teddy was always against it, but he thought maybe he was wrong; he knew Bob's instincts were to go. But around the country, politicians were almost unanimous that it was an absolutely fruitless, quixotic thing. I would never have been for him doing it as a quixotic gesture. I said to Bob, "I don't ask you to do it as a 'profile in courage.' I think that's foolish. I think you've got too much to offer the country to throw it away on a gesture, but I think you've got a very good chance of winning."

224

JOHN KENNETH GALBRAITH

Lowenstein had come to me. But the question of my running was never very serious. It had first come up several months earlier in California, when I was approached by a group of the CDCs—California Democratic Council—saying they were desperate for somebody who would go on the California ticket, and whose name had some slight recognition value. This was before McCarthy, before Bobby or McGovern were on the scene at all. I dismissed it immediately, not because I wouldn't like to have done it—I *would* have—but because I am Canadian-born of Canadian parents. The Constitution is fairly explicit on that subject: one must be a native-born American. But on the way home the next day . . . this shows you what a terrible poison this is and how it goes through the system . . . I began speculating on the whole possibility, and thinking how enormously amusing it would have been to do it, and how useful it would have been to do it; for the first time in my life, I found myself with a sense of discrimination—a grievance against the Constitution! I had dismissed the whole question from my mind until one day Arthur Schlesinger called up and said, "You must consider this. You must consider it very seriously because somebody must oppose the President on the issue of the Vietnam war." So, I did. We had a legal study made; my son is a lawyer, and he made a study which agreed strongly with the opinion that the Constitution was explicit. There were some rather more amiable lawyers who had some theory that the Fourteenth Amendment overruled the constitutional bar by proclaiming all people equal. But I was most influenced by my son, who argued first that if I did this and ran seriously, it would quickly become a constitutional argument rather than an argument over Vietnam; also my case was so palpably bogus that I would lose such reputation for honesty as I had tried to cultivate, however meritoriously, over the years. So, coupled with the fact that there wasn't any grass-root enthusiasm, I dismissed the thing.

Some time in October—late October or early November—I had lunch with Bobby, and we canvassed all the possibilities. Bobby said that he thought he could get the nomination; and he thought, having got the nomination, that he could defeat whomever the Republicans put up. But he also thought the bitterness that would rise with taking on Johnson would be extreme, and that the issues would be raised that he was running in pique because the death of JFK had robbed him of his association with the presidency, and that furthermore he was reacting because of personal dislike of Johnson. He said that he just couldn't face the barrage of argument that would be made along those lines.

Then we talked about possibilities. He said Gene McCarthy was the only possibility; George McGovern would not do it. We talked about the strategy of the New Hampshire campaign. He knew I had an appointment later in the afternoon with Gene, and he said, "You must tell Gene to do it."

Some of the advice that he gave me was quite bad. He told me to tell Gene not to get the Dartmouth kids or the college kids involved, not to make it a children's crusade, but to go up there and run against the war, against the Governor and the Senator, neither of whom was popular, against the *local* Democratic organizations, which, as elsewhere in New England, are always *un*popular; and that out of those components, he could put together a coalition of people who would come very close to winning for him. But he said, "Don't get the kids involved—that will frighten people off."

I repeated this advice to Gene, and Gene was initially rather impressed. When he came to Cambridge a few days later and we arranged to speak to the Young Democrats up there at a "spontaneous demonstration," he was quite definite on the point. He said, "If I go into this, it will not be to lead a children's crusade."

WILLIAM VANDEN HEUVEL, *campaign aide*
The tragedy of the McCarthy victory in New Hampshire—the so-called victory, the forty-two per cent vote that he had—was that the results suddenly made him a credible candidate. He took himself seriously. I don't think Bobby ever blamed McCarthy for moving ahead. Eugene McCarthy said when he announced his candidacy that he expected Robert Kennedy to carry the flag to Chicago. Along the way, he decided to try it himself.

JOHN KENNETH GALBRAITH
Bobby took McCarthy seriously as a focus of opposition to the war; he didn't take him seriously as a candidate. Bobby didn't see that once McCarthy became a serious candidate, *his* position became intolerable. A Senator from New York, given his depth of feeling about the war, couldn't be for Johnson; he couldn't be neutral; therefore, if McCarthy became a serious possibility . . . a possibility that would demand a choice . . . he had to support him! So the minute McCarthy became a

serious possibility, Bobby had the choice of either going in the race himself or supporting Gene.

MICHAEL NOVAK, *educator*

I remember a sentence that Paul Goodman once wrote in an article about Bobby. He said Bobby's zeal and his resentment against certain evil was like that of an adolescent Catholic boy who'd been struggling against masturbation. A sort of moral severity. There was that streak in Bobby's character. What some people would call the puritan streak in him.

My own feeling in watching Bobby from a distance was that this particular characteristic was softened by his brother's death; that is, stated mythically, Bobby had then determined that the forces of good obviously don't win. Life is not a morality play, and you've simply got to tangle with complexity and uncertainty. That dissipated the puritan streak. But I think he also missed it. John Seigenthaler told me that Bobby really felt guilty for not declaring himself a candidate earlier than he did. Idealism is such a double-edged sword. I mean it brought us Prohibition; and even our anti-Communism comes out of a puritan streak. On the other hand, when you try to fight it or get rid of it, you sometimes find yourself, against your nature and your inclination, saying, "Okay, I'll be pragmatic, and I won't be puritan; I won't be too pure." And then you don't do something you later wish you had done. I always felt sad for Bobby on that account.

Robert Kennedy's very commitment to the pragmatic and the concrete was in conflict with his need to give witness. If you remember T. S. Eliot's play *Murder in the Cathedral*, one of the temptations is to give witness, to be the martyr. One of the tempters tells Becket something like: "You desire martyrdom. You really want us to kill you, don't you? You're just dying to be a martyr, aren't you? You're not doing this for God's sake. You're doing this out of a love for martyrdom."

It really is a traditional problem. This love, this quest for martyrdom . . . the quest for witness . . . is the purest and most delicious temptation of all. This is the last hurdle your conscience has to judge: Am I doing this, not to be a martyr, but because it needs to be done?

TOM WICKER, *columnist*

My own feeling was that Robert Kennedy felt somehow that he basically hadn't been true to himself. I don't say that in an accusing way, because I was among those reporters who wrote in late 1967 that it was madness for Bobby Kennedy to run for President at that point. I believed that. I was still in the grip of the old politics, and I had not understood—as indeed he had not, apparently—all the changes that had come about. McCarthy grasped that much more quickly than Robert Kennedy did. But after that became clear, I thought this was a very poignant thing about Robert Kennedy: here was a man who really hadn't met quite the standard he set for himself, and who spent the rest of his life—which was not very long from that point—really trying to regain that position; I think to regain it in his own mind, as well as in the public's . . . but probably more so in his own mind, because the public didn't feel that strongly about it.

JACK ENGLISH, *Nassau County Democratic Chairman*
There were so many pressures on him that you really couldn't have a serious conversation. We were over in the Watergate, and we'd have a party; everybody would come and stay until 4:00 or 5:00 in the morning and never leave. We used to go to the bathroom to talk. Everybody's always going to the bathroom in politics. Carmine DeSapio is famous for that; won't talk to anybody *but* in the bathroom.

ARTHUR SCHLESINGER, JR., *historian*
I always felt that Robert Kennedy's own disposition was to go during this whole time. He once said to me: "The only people who are in favor of my going are you and Ethel and Jesse Unruh." He said, "Unruh's doing it because he thinks it will help him in California."

SENATOR GEORGE McGOVERN
Bobby was on the verge of going in even before the results were announced in New Hampshire. If he had jumped in with the polls showing Gene coming up fast in New Hampshire, there would have then been a heavy write-in vote, which would have diluted the McCarthy victory and looked like a spoiling operation. So I urged him not to do that. So did Dick Goodwin. I frankly still think to this day his timing was terrible in announcing the day after the New Hampshire primary. He sat in my office for three hours at lunch that day and just agonized over the thing. Ted Sorensen was with him. We were a group that occasionally got together—we used to serve in the House together: Gene McCarthy, Lee Metcalf, and myself in the Senate; and then Frank Thompson from the House, and Stewart Udall. We were going to have

lunch that day with McCarthy . . . and he didn't show up! Because, I suppose, of all the phone calls coming in from his great victory in New Hampshire. We called Bob and asked him if he'd like to come by. A few minutes later, he appeared. He stayed probably for two or two and a half hours . . . just agonizing. At one point, I realized that he wasn't even communicating with us, that he was with his own thoughts. He was speaking mechanically about his concern about the United States, you know, using phrases that you don't use in an informal exchange with other Senators. You don't say, "I am deeply concerned about the United States and the future—the 1970s. . . ." This is a *speech*. He was just mechanically going through the phrases he would use if he were at a press conference. He was very tired. I'm just sure he was punishing himself inwardly for not having made the decision six months earlier. I think he died a thousand deaths over that New Hampshire thing. In fact, I've *always* thought that the moment Bobby knew that Gene was going to announce—when he came over there to the Senate floor and said to two or three of us that he was going to get in the race later on—I think Bobby's heart sank right to the soles of his feet. I think he no sooner realized that when one Senator was going to go, then *he* should have gone. He never really got over that. That was his principal problem from that time on . . . the fact that he looked like he was coming in after Gene had paved the way. I think that bothered him more than anything else. We urged him not to make any statement at all right away, but if he did make any statement, to announce that he was going to campaign for Gene in Wisconsin and do what he could to help in the primaries, and that he would defer any judgment about his own situation; we suggested that he acknowledge that Senator McCarthy had demonstrated great strength, and that he'd made a great race in New Hampshire and was entitled to the support of those who were against the war, and that he was going to do what he could to help him. We were horrified when he just jumped into the race that night!

JACK ENGLISH

The day before he announced, he was scheduled for a Fall Guy luncheon in which he was supposed to be the Fall Guy. The comedian —Joey Adams—was making fun of him. They finally brought in some show girls, very scantily clad, dancing right up in front of him. He had his head down in his plate and he wouldn't look! It was the weirdest scene! He was making believe he was writing something.

SENATOR FRED HARRIS

He and Ethel had a dinner for upstate New York publishers. He asked us to come by the house. He had some people over, like Rene Carpenter; Jack Newfield was there; LaDonna and I; Jim Whittaker. We didn't talk about whether he was going to run for President. He made some very clever remarks that night. The presidential flag—his brother's flag—was behind him when he got up to make the toast, and he kept saying, "This has no special significance. I hope you understand that," and so forth. It was a very clever evening. Ethel was kidding me; she said something to Jim Whittaker about my being for Lyndon Johnson. I had long since been committed to Johnson-Humphrey. I was chairman of an outfit called Town & Country for Johnson & Humphrey. I said, "The difference between me and Bob is that I made my announcement about the time he did, but I felt I had to stick by it." We laughed about that. Then I said to Bob, "You know that I can't help you with your decision, but I'll just say, 'Do what your heart tells you and that'll be the right thing.'"

SYLVIA WRIGHT, *reporter*

That day, Ted Sorensen was making one last check with the White House to get a final answer on the proposal that President Johnson appoint a commission of twelve, with or without Senator Kennedy's participation, to study the war and make recommendations for a future course in Vietnam. That Lyndon Johnson would turn over that much of his power was unlikely, but Bobby was apparently determined to test every alternative to challenging the President before making his final decision. Bobby and Ethel had to act very calm, as though they had nothing better to do than entertain those twenty upstate publishers; but what they were really doing was waiting for President Johnson's answer. Clark Clifford was to phone that night. We had cocktails, and then we sat down to dinner at four or five separate tables. I was seated at Bobby's table with two newspaper publishers and their wives. The butler came and leaned over Senator Kennedy and said, "There's a phone call for you." He got up and went off to the phone, then came back and sat down. When we were starting the second course, the butler came and said again, "There's a phone call for you." Senator Kennedy grinned and said, "Excuse me again." Pretty soon he came back and sat down. Then a third time the butler came and said, "Senator Kennedy, I'm sorry. There's a phone call for you." They had just served the main course. Bobby stood up and said, as though he were just being funny,

"If you people will excuse me just once more. This time it's the President. . . ." When he returned to the table, he paused at my chair, tapped on my shoulder, and said, "You know, it really *was* the President." Then he ate two desserts. It had been Clark Clifford calling to say that President Johnson's answer was no; that he would not have the presidency weakened by twelve other people.

We all started to leave. Jack Newfield and I were standing out on the front porch with Bobby—it was about 1:00 A.M. and terribly cold—and he had his hands in his pockets and was all hunched up against the wind saying, "What should I do? Why will it look so awful? Why does everybody think it's awful if *I* do it, but it's *not* awful if Gene McCarthy or somebody *else* challenges the President?" And that's when he kept saying, "I don't see why the *more* people that are in it, and the *more* choices offered to the people . . . why it isn't *that* much better for the people and for the country!" We all felt then that he was still debating. The next day he had a series of speaking engagements in New York. About 3:30 A.M. in my room the phone rang, and it was Frank Mankiewicz saying, "The Senator doesn't want to go on the 8:30 American flight because there's too much press following him; they're trying to find out what 'reassess' means, and they will look for him there. So he says meet him at the eight o'clock shuttle." When we got there, Frank was there with his little bag, ready to go. Frank *still* didn't know. Bobby said, "Frank, you'd better stay behind." Frank said, "What do you mean?" He said, "Well, I want to have a press conference tomorrow, and you'd better stay and arrange it. I want it in the Senate Caucus Room, in the same room that my brother announced in." And that's how we knew; that's *when* we knew.

FRED DUTTON, *campaign aide*
He came back to Hickory Hill that night. They had *another* party going. The door between the two rooms was open with loud music booming in. One of the minor, more entertaining aspects of the scene was three generations of speechwriters: Schlesinger from the 1950s, Sorensen from the early '60s, and Walinsky from the latter '60s—all trying to combine on one statement of a thousand words or so.

BURT DRUCKER, *campaign worker*
He'd come back to New York for the Fifth Avenue St. Patrick's Day parade. They had it on the 16th that year. It was a day of tremendous pressure, and I remember Carter Burden saying, "Now, Burt, the minute

231

he leaves Charley O's, make sure you pin a green carnation on him. Make sure he's wearing it while he's in the parade." As he came out, I pinned a green carnation on him, and I was actually eyeball to eyeball with him, and there was not the least bit of recognition! I thought, "Oh, my God, I've done something wrong. He isn't going to say hello." We walked up toward Fifth Avenue; we hadn't gone more than twenty yards and someone came and ripped the carnation right off him. So I turned to someone and took another one. And again, I pinned it on him. And again we were eyeball to eyeball, and still like he wasn't there . . . like he was beyond me; he was thinking. It worried me; it really worried me for a whole week until the next Saturday, when he was going out to California and I was at the airport, and he saw me as he was near the gate to go in. He turned around and walked clear across the huge waiting room, and he put his hand out and said, "Oh, Burt. So nice of you to come and see me off." I just couldn't believe it. There were times when he just wasn't conscious of what was going on around him. That St. Patrick's Day was one of them.

SYLVIA WRIGHT
Bobby asked me, "Do you think I'm crazy, running? My brother thinks I'm crazy. But my brother . . . you know, Teddy and I are such different people. We don't hear the same music. Everyone's got to march to his own music."

The next day, St. Patrick's Day, Bobby and Teddy marched together in Boston. I was in the car with Bobby going back to the airport. I said, "It looks to me, Senator, that you were marching to the same music." Bobby looked at me mischievously and said, "My brother learns fast."

JIM STEVENSON, *journalist*
I went up to his apartment on the East River a day or so after he announced and I sat in the bedroom there by myself. I was sort of aghast at taking his time. I didn't think it was right. And yet, suddenly, he came into the room in his shirtsleeves with a drink in his hand, and he made me feel that this was what he wanted to do . . . to sit down in a big chair and talk.

I had nothing interesting to tell him. It was just his generosity and his doing things the way he felt like doing them, instead of what the rule book would say, or the politically significant or smart thing to do would be. So I had a marvelous time, and I went away kind of changed by him; this is the sort of thing you could never explain to people, and

I never tried to write about it. How do you convey to other people the truth of someone . . . especially if they're in the public eye and viewed with suspicion all the time? He had talked about what a relief it was for him to have made the decision. I remember that very well because he seemed like someone who for just a brief moment was riding on the exuberance of having decided what to do and doing it. Having wanted to do it . . . finally, he *was* doing it. So he was kind of celebrating. He was sort of relieved and joyful, I guess . . . though wary.

THE REVEREND ANDREW J. YOUNG, *civil-rights leader*
I guess I was afraid of the train ride. I didn't know whether I could take a long, mournful train ride—and yet I was afraid if people got too casual, I'd get mad.

STEWART ALSOP, *columnist*
The trip had a slightly phantasmagoric, unreal quality to it. A little like that play, *Outward Bound.* All those gay creatures going off into a kind of nothingness. The train went on and on, and you saw those enormous crowds . . . particularly near the big cities and particularly the blacks. You got a curious feeling of disembodiment, as if the experience were wholly unreal . . . especially after those people were killed by the train . . . and as the train got later and later.

There was a good deal of liquor on board, and some people had a good deal; and there was a kind of macabre party spirit to it, too, which I'm not sure was entirely inappropriate, because Bobby liked politics, and he liked people having a good time.

BURT GLINN, *photographer*
Lots of conversations were, What are you going to do now? I think it was on the train that Adam Walinsky said to somebody, "Well, who knows? I'm very narrowly programmed. I can do research and write speeches for a candidate named Robert Kennedy. What can I do now?"

JEFF GREENFIELD, *campaign aide*

A lot of the conversation was the way it can be with Jimmy Breslin and with Pete Hamill: very despairing; very intensely despairing. The notion keeps coming up that there was simply no place to turn. Jack Newfield said, using the myth of Sisyphus that Camus used so much— and it was a book that Kennedy was quite fond of—that "the stone was at the bottom of the hill again." And my wife or somebody else's wife said that the point really wasn't to drop out; the point was to start pushing it back up again.

IVANHOE DONALDSON, *fellow, Institute for Policy Studies*

When Kennedy declared, I thought it was tragic in a way. I thought it would have been better if he had supported Gene McCarthy's campaign. But it's complex. I think I understood why he declared; and I agreed that probably only *he* could have gotten that nomination. Bob was a very good politician. The difference between Bob and McCarthy would have been that Bob Kennedy really *wanted* to be President. I'm still not sure to this day that McCarthy wanted to. McCarthy would have woke up one morning, if he had gotten the nomination, and said, "Oh, my God. What did I do? What can I do to go back to the monastery?"

MICHAEL NOVAK, *educator*

There was a lot of that in McCarthy's campaign. People thought he didn't want to be President. But there's another streak in him that says, Whether or not I'm President, this is worth doing. If I'm not President, it doesn't really matter, because what really matters is the kind of witness I give in politics.

With Robert Kennedy, it was the same. He didn't really know if he could win the thing. He just knew that he, Robert Kennedy, had to do it now . . . if it killed him. And I think he meant that both literally and emotionally. It just had to be done. When Eugene said something about being a good loser, Robert Kennedy was full of disgust. He said something like, "A Kennedy learns not to be a loser at the age of two."

Well, that's misleading. It is true that Robert Kennedy had a much more bitter sense of competition and being a winner; but it was also true that if he was going to be a loser, there are some things worth losing for. And that was pretty close to Eugene McCarthy. They do it with a different style, as I say, and the different styles have class repercussions. It's a mixture of lower-class-Catholicism-become-wealthy against middle-class Midwestern Catholicism, which is rather comfortable and easygoing. They don't understand one another too much.

BLAIR CLARK, *campaign manager for Senator Eugene McCarthy*
He hated it when Bobby came in after New Hampshire . . . he hated it. He'd made the point, and along comes Bobby and wants to pick up the pieces.

ALICE ROOSEVELT LONGWORTH (*Mrs. Nicholas Longworth*)
I don't blame Eugene McCarthy for being put out. Because after all, he broke the ground . . . the old ballad, " 'Twas *I* that beat the bush that the bird to others flew." He was in that position, but he couldn't take it with laughter, apparently.

JOHN KENNETH GALBRAITH, *economist*
I think that Bobby felt very little antagonism toward Gene, but I think that the antagonism Gene felt toward Jack Kennedy and toward Bobby had elements of competitiveness about it. Gene felt that they were both of the same age, they were both Catholics, they were both Irish; the Kennedys were accustomed to power, accustomed to being in. Gene felt that he was intellectually in many ways better qualified than the Kennedys. He had worked harder, studied harder, was a better economist and knew more about philosophy, poetry, and theology—the elements of an educated man—than did either Bobby or the President. I think that competitiveness translated itself into personal dislike.

BLAIR CLARK
His attitude toward Bobby was so incredibly complicated. I think that he did not like the Kennedys as a political phenomenon. I mean just *that*. He had a sort of partly old-fashioned populist view that you just shouldn't make it through money and power . . . mixed with some envy, I would think. The phenomenon of the rich, highly motivated kids who were going to make it in politics 'cause that's what Daddy wanted them to do, was half comic and half repellent to McCarthy.

TOM WICKER, *columnist*
I think Senator McCarthy saw more clearly than Senator Kennedy did—*in 1968*—that something new was really abroad in the land in

236

politics; he was much more willing to stake his fortunes on the new thing: on the young people, on educated people—those two classes in particular—and to see that they were a rising force in American politics; to see that many of the shibboleths—not only of politics, but of government, foreign policy, and domestic policy—had to be cast aside. I've always thought of 1968 as the year to judge the candidates—Republicans as well as Democrats—in terms of who was willing to start anew. Think of it this way: on January 20th, 1969, a President would be inaugurated; he would take the oath at noon, and he'd spend the rest of the day watching the parade, and that night going to the balls; on January 21st, he'd report for duty in the Oval office, and he would sit down behind the desk; and at precisely 8:30 A.M., I imagine, the door would open and the federal bureaucracy would walk in. I always think of the bureaucracy as looking rather like Bill Bundy . . . or maybe Mac Bundy . . . whichever, the federal bureaucracy will walk through the door, and it will lay the papers on the President's desk that will define the problems and suggest the solutions. And the papers that it will lay on the President's desk on January 21st are *precisely,* without one iota of change, exactly the papers that were laid on the old President's desk on January 19th. I thought the measure of candidates in 1968 was which one would be most willing to reach out and sweep all those papers off on the floor and say flatly, "We are starting over. We are not necessarily changing, but we are re-examining from the start. We are starting over. We are not operating on the old assumptions any more."

Senator McCarthy's attraction and his advantage in the campaign was in the sense that he was new; he was unaffiliated; he had broken loose from the past. Senator Kennedy's advantage, on the other hand, and *his* attraction was that—quite aside from spurious and cynical slogans—he was literally able to bring us together and to unite factions that otherwise had nothing in common. He still retained a great many elements of older faiths and older attitudes. For instance, I never doubted that if he could have gotten the nomination, Robert Kennedy would have wished for the support of all the more traditional—even reactionary—elements in the Democratic Party. At one and the same time, he wanted to have Mayor Daley's support and the support of the college students. The two are incompatible in the long run. I'm not trying to say that you could not, by force of personality and personal example—as Robert Kennedy did—have uneasily allied them for a time. I'm trying to say that in the long run, it isn't a feasible alliance, and it isn't an alliance that's going to hold political power.

TOM HAYDEN, *a founder of SDS*

In one corner of his very complicated mind, he believed that he could use the structure and then destroy it. Use Mayor Daley to become President and, at the same time, encourage the ghetto to rise up against Mayor Daley; use Latin American dictators to get agreement on questions, while encouraging Latin American people to rise up and throw them over. He had a theory of modernization that is an alternative to both socialist revolution on the one hand, and reactionary corrupt dictatorships on the other. I think it's a pragmatic position that's not pragmatic. It doesn't work. It leads back into embracing the Mayor Daleys and right-wingers because they ultimately become the people you must depend on to remain the leader of their power structure.

ADAM WALINSKY, *legislative aide, speechwriter*

Do you remember back in the forties and fifties, Arthur Murray used to illustrate his dancing lessons, and there were always those steps, you know, that were laid out with the arrows and the footprints on the ground? Well, I mean, you watch somebody dance that way, you know he's not dancing. Somebody has told him that this is where the steps are, and he does it. The relationship of that to dancing . . . it's not in the same world. Then you watch some guy get out there and *dance* who really knows what he's doing, and it's all different. Well, that's what I mean. I mean Hubert Humphrey and Richard Nixon go through these motions because their intellect tells them, "Now people are bothered about law and order. Therefore, I will make a speech about law and order, and it will say . . ."

Robert Kennedy was the instinctive dancer. I think probably, from the accounts of him, that Franklin Roosevelt might very well have been one of those guys that instinctively understood what people were looking for. Eisenhower . . . or some of Eisenhower's appeal was based on an instinctive feeling about what people wanted. The remarkable thing about Robert Kennedy was that not only did he have that understanding and empathy, but he could *use* it, rather than conform himself to it; that somehow he could get across his own conviction, his own emotional urgency, and use it to bring people along with him. And that was something.

FRED DUTTON, *campaign aide*

When he announced, Bob asked me to travel with him. To be quite frank, I thought I was going to travel with him for a few days. I had no idea I wasn't going to be back to my law office for more than three hours in the next two and a half months. But then, that is indicative of Bob's sort of relaxed way of going about these things. There was no big production, no big scene.

It was very much a campaign that had to be put together on the run due to the lateness and suddenness with which Bob made his decision to get in. It jelled as we went along. At one early stage, there came a question—I don't know how it got raised—of who would have titles; we'd already begun to have functional roles: speechwriting, research, schedule making, and so forth. Bob decided there shouldn't be any titles. He didn't say it, but it was my impression there were too many prima donnas, too many personalities out of diverse backgrounds—either from the Senate staff or from the '60 campaign, and so forth—and the best thing was to let it all shake down. There were all kinds of complex personalities that he had to bridge and reconcile. And the age differences between the Walinsky crowd and the others. It was, I think, a talented and totally dedicated group for the most part, but it was about as heterogeneous as you could pull together. The closest to a real campaign manager was Steve Smith. Bob's closest adviser was Teddy, personally.

PETE HAMILL, *columnist*

So many of them were different from the guys who usually get around a candidate. They didn't want jobs. They go nuts sitting in an office. They wanted to get the guy elected, and he understood that. There are very few candidates who end up with guys who don't want to become deputy under-secretaries of state.

FRANK MANKIEWICZ, *press secretary*

I was getting ready to leave Washington and go back to California, probably. I was thinking about going to one of the state colleges where there was some possibility of becoming president. Then I got a call from the Senator one morning. He said, "Won't you come over and talk to us about joining the staff?" I thought the offer was pretty good. It was becoming clear that Senator Kennedy's office was one of the few places in Washington where anything interesting was going on. There had been one incident before that that sold me. In April of that year, Robert Thompson, who was one of the leaders of the American Communist Party, had served some time in prison under the Smith Act and died. His wife wanted to bury him at Arlington Cemetery.

She had every right to bury him at Arlington Cemetery: he was a World War II hero; he had earned, in fact, the Distinguished Service Cross in the Pacific for charging a machine-gun nest across a creek. It was an authentic medal, unlike some that you see around Washington. Here was this guy—a hero, a holder of the Distinguished Service Cross—and the Pentagon made up some regulation on the spot that said that if you'd served so many years of time under a law like the Smith Act you couldn't be buried at Arlington. It was a patent fraud. I called Adam Walinsky and said, "Don't you think this is the kind of issue that Senator Kennedy ought to speak out on?" He said, "Yeah. I sure do!" I pointed out an editorial to him in one of the papers that I thought had been pretty good. He said he would talk to him. And then I saw the next day that . . . I think almost alone among the Senators . . . he had made a speech on the subject, and he had put that editorial into the Congressional Record. I thought at the time that there were damn few United States Senators who felt it was very helpful to them to take up the cause of a Communist, particularly a dead one!

So when the Senator called about joining the staff, I went over, and it turned out he wanted me to be press secretary. I thought, Well, I don't know anything about that. I had never been involved in journalism at all. But if he was willing to gamble on that, why wasn't I? So I said, "Fine." And that was that.

DICK TUCK, *campaign aide*

I think the first time I worked for him was when he called me in September 1967, and asked me if I would go to Gary, Indiana, to help a man by the name of Dick Hatcher, who was running for Mayor. I was sitting in San Francisco in a very pleasant house. Friends of mine were in Europe, and I was house-sitting, and I said, "What do I want to go to Gary, Indiana, for?" He said this Negro candidate was going to get a raw deal, and so he said he'd appreciate it if I went. And so I did. I went to Gary. He was right. We had to go into federal court, and we had to stop a vote fraud; people have gone to jail or been indicted since over this. And we squeaked through. Hatcher won by 1,300 votes, and I got a call from the Senator a day or so after. He said, "Look. Would you come to Hickory Hill for a party tonight?" And I said, "Well, I should clean up things here in Gary." He said again, "I wish you'd come." So I came, and I landed at the airport in Washington.

He sent some people out with signs that said, WELCOME LANDSLIDE TUCK!

JOSEPH KRAFT, *columnist*

There were the President's people; there were Bob's Justice Department people; there were Bob's Senate people; and there were Ted's people; so there were four generations of people. Not, I thought, a well-run campaign. There were too many people. There were many too many stars. There were more chiefs than Indians. It was very hard to fit all these people in together. And yet, you know, it did all right. I think it was done hastily; done off the cuff; and it was not altogether well ordered. All campaigns are messy. This one lacked Bob himself to manage it.

HELEN KEYES, *administrator, John F. Kennedy Library*

It was the first time that all these factions were together, and I can remember sitting there thinking, How are these people all going to work out—I mean, how on earth are we ever going to get them to work together? A fresh young monkey like Jeff Greenfield with an old sobersides like Ted Sorensen, a wild-eyed activist like Peter Edelman with a former wild-eyed activist like Kenny O'Donnell, who, through experience, had become a lot more moderate. Then Teddy's kids who were thrown headlong into this thing, really wanted *their* guy to be the candidate, and had had no experience. I can remember sitting there thinking, Oh, this is going to be a beaut. And it was, I tell you, it was *something*. As a matter of fact, Dave Burke said to me one day, "When are we ever going to get together?" I said, "After the first win. Once we win *something*, everyone will be able to work together."

FRED DUTTON

The campaign started out, of course, emphasizing the Vietnam war, the need for a different kind of leadership than this country had been getting from President Johnson, the need to do something about the racial problems and the problems of the cities—these were the primary themes. There were other problems, but those were the main ones. Within ten days after Bob had announced, Johnson withdrew. In an immediate sense, that removed the anti-Johnson theme and lessened the Vietnam issue. We were in the air while Johnson was speaking, and landed at La Guardia several minutes after LBJ finished. As soon as we landed, John Burns, the state chairman in New York, rushed aboard the plane. We were sitting in the front seat. Burns was absolutely ashen-faced; you'd thought that he'd just seen a ghost. He said, "He's withdrawn. He's withdrawn." Other than that, he was just about unintelligible. Bob sank back in his seat and was very quiet. I believe he was smoking a cigar. I was sitting by him; there were a couple of others: Dick Dougherty, of the New York bureau of the Los Angeles *Times*, was right in back of him. Bob said, "What do you think?" Both Dougherty's and my comments were that, "You didn't hear what the President said. You don't know exactly what it is, so why say anything until you've had a chance to look at it yourself?" He listened to everybody for a minute or two and said, "I won't say anything now." He turned to me and said, "You tell the press that."

BURT DRUCKER, *campaign worker*

The night when Johnson took himself out of the race, I went in the kitchen with Ethel, and she said, "Are you going to be my bartender?" I said, "Glad to." She had a feeling of jubilation that night. She said, "Let's open some champagne." With that, Fred Dutton came in and said to her, "Oh, Ethel. The Senator doesn't really think it's a night for celebrating—not champagne." She turned and looked at me and looked at him, and with a twinkle she said, "Scotch?"

RICHARD GOODWIN, *politician*

I do think that ultimately Johnson got out because Kennedy was in the race. Of course, it never would have happened if it hadn't been for McCarthy, because it's clear that if McCarthy hadn't done what he did in New Hampshire, Kennedy never would have entered the race. So that precipitated it. But Johnson was confronted with a dual thing: maybe he could beat McCarthy, but what he never could stand would be the idea of Kennedy being nominated. Humphrey was his weapon against Kennedy and that's why he lost interest in Humphrey after Kennedy died. Frankly, I think if Johnson had his choice he would have declared the office vacant after he left. He's the Samson of American politics, with his hands around the pillars of the temple as he goes out.

JACK NEWFIELD, *author*

That line Saul Bellow uses about Augie March . . . that he touched both extremes at once. And I guess that's what Kennedy did. That was also carried through on the train, where I could walk through and see people like John McCone and McGeorge Bundy, whom I consider to be war criminals . . . who were equally as grieved as I was. Certainly someone like Robert McNamara was.

RUSSELL BAKER, *columnist*

There were a couple of people who had left Kennedy during the campaign and sided with McCarthy—which is the normal kind of thing you get in a campaign. But they were people who had known Kennedy a really long time, and they were especially broken up—as if somehow, the fact they'd made a political decision to oppose him meant somehow that they'd been responsible for his death. It was the worst kind of guilt.

RICHARD GOODWIN, *politician*

Fred Harris sat there—glum and isolated. He was a good friend, at one point, of Senator Kennedy; but then he was co-chairman of the Humphrey campaign.

SENATOR FRED HARRIS

I had already endorsed Johnson and Humphrey. I think both Humphrey and Kennedy understood the problems of the country and would have done something about them. But I chose Humphley because I felt that he had the better chance to put together the majority in the House and Senate that could actually get some of these programs enacted into law. So, on balance at that time, that's the way I saw it.

Ethel sent me a funny telegram. "Say it isn't so," was the way it wound up. I fooled around with it, trying to think of one to send back to her. I thought of one or two, you know, like saying, "Does this mean that we can't be friends with Brumus any more?" That was the crazy dog they had that used to come around and turn everybody's garbage over. Two or three funny things like that to send back, but they sounded wrong. It was really too serious to be funny about; and any kind of serious attempt wasn't any good either. So I just finally didn't do anything at all.

MICHAEL HARRINGTON, *author*

I think perhaps one of the saddest political aspects of the funeral train was that an awful lot of people felt there was nowhere to go. The Kennedy camp was a very broad camp, politically speaking, and it ranged from relatively conservative machine Democrats who favored Robert Kennedy out of loyalty—or past connections, or the idealization of John Kennedy—to the New Left, and some middle-aged old left radicals like me, and Norman Mailer, who calls himself a left conservative. I thoroughly expected that the traditional machine Democrats would go to the traditional machine candidate, now that the exception was no longer a possibility. I think what surprised me is that more of the intellectual, ideologically motivated people had not moved to McCarthy. I had personally hoped that everybody of that stripe would have moved *en bloc* into the McCarthy camp. But it was clear, from conversations on the train, that quite a few people did not agree. Pat Moynihan did not agree. Arthur Schlesinger did not agree. A lot of those people could not bring themselves to go to McCarthy.

They certainly could not go to Humphrey, whom they had been fighting by supporting Robert Kennedy. And so they were nowhere, faced with the probable election of Richard Nixon.

I still believed that the long shot of Eugene McCarthy had to be played to the end with all the vigor possible. But I remember, most of all, Pat Moynihan's remarks. He said what we have to understand, above all, is that we've lost. We may bury our dead very well, but that's really the only thing right now that we do well. We have lost.

JOE DOLAN, *campaign aide*

The first primary was in Indiana, and we didn't have much time. Jerry Bruno and I thought of the idea for the Wabash Cannonball. The problem was that Robert needed time to confer with people. If you have a train, why you can do a hell of a lot of business on a train. In your compartment you can meet the local pols. You can shave; you can take a nap. It's a self-contained life, you see.

So, I was looking for a train to give him a rest; do some campaigning; get to some places that were hard to get into. So we looked at the Monon Railroad. The Monon didn't look too great; so we looked at one other railroad that went across the northern part of the state; and then we looked at this route around Indianapolis, across the north of Indianapolis on the Wabash. I picked out about eight or nine cities and towns, and then I went to the railroad and got a time schedule from them.

The train got to be one of the most successful campaign devices because it was fresh and different, and an awful lot of people came out. Bobby liked it. He really liked it. After that, all he did was complain and ask, "Can't you think of something new? Why don't you think of something like the Wabash Cannonball?"

JIM STEVENSON, *journalist*

He would get off and he would speak and then Mrs. Kennedy, who was pregnant at that time, would stand and shake hands with 3,000 people, and they'd have to shake every hand and look at every face and say something. Exhausting, after a long day of campaigning outside of factories, speeches, and going through plants, rallies, motorcades. . . . The demands on him were just endless . . . endless, aside from the planning, but just the physical grabbing of that many hands and reacting, as he was apt to do, to people as human beings. If he were a different kind of politician, he might not react at all; but I know that he was always looking around and seeing things . . . and that's wearing. And so about 12:30 at night, you'd be driving through the country, everybody exhausted, and maybe they would be having drinks by then; and he would be there, and the reporters and photographers would come up to tell him stories and try to get his attention or to entertain him; or some guy would play a tape that he thought was funny and that the Senator should hear because it would amuse him. But it was

12:30 at night, and his face was exhausted. But he would smile and try to respond and be nice. Then he would turn and look out the dark window, out at the night, and he would be miles and miles away.

DAVID BRINKLEY, *television commentator*

We took some pictures of him on the train. One that impressed me showed him sitting in his Pullman car in the back, alone—and maybe I'm seeing it now with the knowledge of what has happened since—but, anyway, it was a terribly poignant picture. And it wasn't anything special. It was just a picture of Bobby, looking sort of lonesome, kind of small—you know, he's not a very large man physically—slightly lonesome, back there in the middle of a big political entourage, but sitting all by himself.

We did a long story about the Wabash Cannonball and his campaign on it. I remember at one stop one of those little towns that calls itself the Petunia Capital of the World, somebody gave him a little wooden strawberry basket full of dirt, wrapped in Reynolds Wrap, with some petunias in it—handed it up to the back platform; of course, he took it and didn't then quite know what to do with it; so he handed it to somebody and made a little remark about petunias.

BURT GLINN, *photographer*

It was great to hear Bobby when he got sparked by something. The medical-school group in Indianapolis sparked him to the most passionate moments of his campaign. They did this by asking what he felt were unfeeling questions. One of the medical students asked him, "Well, this program sounds very fine, Senator, but who's going to pay for it?" And he looked out over this upper-middle-class group—who were going to graduate into the medical profession and all obviously make a lot of money or a very comfortable living—and he said, "*You're* going to pay for it," and he went on from there, really dishing it out to them. He deplored that kind of attitude from people who he felt should certainly know better and should certainly *feel* deeper; and if they didn't feel this, that got him started. He wasn't eloquent except when he got moved.

TOM WICKER, *columnist*

We saw in Indiana, in particular, where in very rough steel-mill towns he could talk reassuringly to low-income ethnic groups who had no love for blacks, that he could, at the same time, attract the black folk in places like Gary and elsewhere. He straddled that issue very clearly. I'm not using "straddled" there in a derogatory sense. He was able to create a sense of confidence in both of these groups. I think that would have been a great leg up.

CHARLES QUINN, *television correspondent*
I talked to a dozen or so of them after the Gary rally—I guess they were Poles or Lithuanians.

"Well, what do you think of Kennedy?"

"We like Kennedy very much."

"Why do you like him?"

"He's a good man. We like him for what his brother did. Besides, he makes sense. We like what he says."

"You know how he feels about Negroes?"

"Yeah."

"But I understand you're not terribly crazy about Negroes."

"Naw, don't like Negroes. Nobody around here likes Negroes."

"Here's a man who stands for helping the Negro, and you say you don't like them. How can you vote for him?"

"I don't know. Just like him."

I found this over and over in the campaign. Not only did I find *that* . . . which is a contradiction . . . but three or four days after Kennedy was buried, I was in Memphis, Tennessee, at a Wallace rally; I stood outside this big amphitheater in Memphis, and I talked to three or four men out there—white rednecks, ardent, fierce George Wallace supporters. I said, "What do you think would have happened if Kennedy had won?"

"Aw, he would have carried Tennessee."

"Why?"

"Everybody liked Kennedy."

"What about you?"

"Sure, I liked Kennedy . . . very much."

"Do you know how Kennedy felt about Negroes?"

"Yeah."

"Well, why did you like him?"

"I just liked him. I thought he would have made a good President."

The second guy said to me, "You know, of all the people running, it emed to me Kennedy could best draw all the country together again . bring us all together again." I talked to a girl in Hawaii who was

247

for Wallace, and I said, "Really?" "Yeah, but my real candidate is dead."

You know what I think it was? All these whites, all these blue-collar people and ethnic people who supported Kennedy . . . as they did in Indiana, and in Nebraska (they did *not* in Oregon—but that's a curious state) and as they did to a lesser degree in California . . . all of these people felt that Kennedy would really do what he thought was right for the black people but, at the same time, would not tolerate lawlessness and violence. The Kennedy toughness came through on that. They were willing to gamble . . . because they knew in their hearts that the country was not right . . . they were willing to gamble on this man, maybe, who would try to keep things within reasonable order; and at the same time, do some of the things that they knew really should be done.

DAVID BRINKLEY

But he kept discovering in Indiana, as in other places, that there were lots of people who were very outspoken in their dislike: they booed and hollered at him, and so on. He kept telling me, with real fervor in his voice, "They *hate* me in Kokomo!" As I recall, they went to Kokomo, and it wasn't all that bad. But he was very conscious of the fact that a lot of people disliked him.

Late one night after they'd been out traveling in the Indiana primary, he and about ten of us had dinner in Indianapolis. He was talking about his appearance and style on television, and asked me what I thought of it. I told him. He said his *own* opinion was that he was too strident, meaning, I guess, that his voice was somewhat high-pitched and assertive. He thought it didn't go over too well on television, and he was trying to work on it; trying to slow it down, tone it down, soften it a little bit. I never thought it was all that important. People liked him for what he was, and what he had been, and what they hoped he would be, and for *what* he said. Not so much in the *way* he said it. We don't elect orators in this country so much. If we did, we'd probably have had Everett Dirksen as President. Slick, theatrical oratory is not all that important. The quality people in this country admire most is what they call "sincerity." I never have known exactly what that meant in this context; but if you ask them, they say, "Yes, he seems sincere." Or, "He does not seem sincere." Maybe they mean "phony" or "not phony." I don't quite know. But anyway, that's the word you hear all the time.

Anyway, we talked about that a little bit. It worried him—that he wasn't liked.

SENATOR GEORGE McGOVERN

The farmers voted for him, which was an interesting thing . . . a guy from Boston and New York! He always laughed at his own farm record; he used that line out there: he said, "New York is first in the production of sour cherries!" Somebody yelled from the back of the room, "I can't hear you!" And he said, "You just missed my farm program!"

CHARLES QUINN

We went to a little private airport, and he addressed a couple of hundred farmers who had gathered out there; he talked to them about farming. He didn't know anything about farming, or agriculture. He admitted as much.

Back on the plane I was telling a couple of Kennedy's aides, Dutton and Dick Drayne, or maybe Frank Mankiewicz, about this lady who had attended this rally, and she went away kind of scornful and contemptuous and she said, "Hrmph." And about the time I said that, I looked over, and there was Kennedy hunched over our chair. "What did she say, Chuck? What did she say?"

There was this awkward silence. I said, "I can't tell you what she said, Senator. It's kind of embarrassing."

He said, "Tell me what she said."

So I said, "All right. I'll tell you what she said. She said, 'Hrmph. The only reason I came down here is to find out if he looked like Bugs Bunny, and he does.' "

So Kennedy laughed and laughed, and finally he threw himself down in his seat, exhausted, and he said, "You know what? I *feel* like Bugs Bunny too!"

16

THE REVEREND WILLIAM GLENN, *Baptist minister, Philadelphia*

The pilot train came first, slowly. This brought the people up on
their feet. They had been dangling their feet over the platform. The
crowd seemed to be hushed—a mourning tone. A woman in back of
me said in a Southern drawl, "This engine looks like death itself."

NAIDA COHN, *tourist, Philadelphia*

There were thousands of people at North Philadelphia Station . . .
absolutely thousands. We were right on the platform in the front line
We must have been there about three hours. Originally no one was to be
allowed on the platform, but then they finally had to . . . it was very
warm. As the train began to approach, maybe three or four hundred
police disgorged from I don't know how many paddy wagons. They
didn't go on the station platform; they marched down and lined th
tracks.

JOHN McHUGH, *patrolman, Philadelphia*

It was just a human herd of policemen standing on the tracks belo:
the platform. We usually face the crowd. We would love to have salute
the train, but we were facing the wrong way.

NAIDA COHN

Then, as the train passed by, Ted Kennedy was standing on the ba
platform . . . which was the real shock! He wasn't really waving; he w

nodding. The crowd reacted frightfully; they were just in complete shock. No one expected him. There were two smaller Kennedy children standing with him; and you could see the flag. You could see Ted sort of standing there with his hand slightly raised . . . and nodding. It was just very shocking and kind of frightening. The crowd gasped. He wasn't really waving; he was more acknowledging. Then the singing began again. After the train went through, people stood there transfixed for maybe five or six minutes. It was difficult to leave . . . so people mainly stood there.

MILLIE WILLIAMS, *staff secretary*
I tried to get drunk, but I couldn't. Jay Cooper, who was organizing black students and young people for Kennedy said, "Millie, here's a beer, and if you go two cars down, there's a bar. Remember, this isn't an Irish wake. It's a Negro wake."

SHIRLEY MacLAINE, *actress*
I was the one who was feeling violent. I was the one on the train who for *eight* hours agreed with Stokely Carmichael. I really was far more violent than they were. But they're used to that kind of tragedy. They're used to their leaders being slain, and a bullet is more of a reality to them than it is to me. They were literally calming my violence down. Those Negroes. I was feeling more like a disillusioned black person than I was a white person who could go back to my swimming pool.

MILLIE WILLIAMS
To tell you the truth, I was surprised that there were only five black women I could count on the train, not including Coretta King and her group. But we were well represented on the outside. I was looking outside for my people, and I knew they'd be there. In Manhattan, there were gobs of them. And then when we hit Philly, it was solid black. All along there, both sides of the track were just completely lined. That's where all my people were. I'm sure everyone in the crowd appreciated seeing the train. But how many were really for the Senator? How many would have voted for him, or talked to their friends about him? My feeling is, Don't send me flowers when I can't smell them any more. Why is it that after somebody's death, you suddenly realize how great he is. It's like waiting till after a famous painter dies to realize his works are great. You know, "After I'm dead, I can't hear your praise."

THE REVEREND ANDREW J. YOUNG, *civil-rights leader*

When we made the decision to go to Birmingham, I remember Dr. King saying, "Now, we can go join Jesus." He was saying it jokingly; he said, "You can *believe* that some of us are going to go see Jesus. We may not all make it back." We laughed about it. Then somebody said, "You know, you are going through Selma." Well, right outside Selma there was a place in Lowndes County where Jonathan Daniels was killed, and Viola Liuzzo. So I guess maybe we were a little nervous that day. Martin remembered when we passed Montgomery, which is right next to Lowndes County, that somebody went and pulled a man out of his house and beat him to death while his wife and children watched, and threatened to kill them if they cried. That county is just full of such horror stories. We would recall these and laugh, figuring that there wasn't anything you can do about it. When we first went to Selma, the ministers were all standing around him to get their pictures taken. This guy walked right in the middle of the crowd and said, "Are you Martin Luther King?" "Yes," he said. The guy hauled off and hit him. The television cameras were there, and they just pushed us out of the way, the way when folks start fighting, the camera joins in to record it. He hit Dr. King across the jaw. He was expecting to get beat up by us; we just held him and took him out and turned him over to the police. We never hit. . . . It was just something you got used to living with.

With Dr. King, we lived for the first few years just taking it for granted that one or all of us would be killed some kind of way. I mean in the time when there were regular bombings and shootings in the South. Each place, we'd say, "Well, we probably won't make . . . all of us are not going to make it out of here." And then we'd get through that. You know, starting back in Selma, and the Freedom Rides in Albany, and then Birmingham. St. Augustine, Florida, was probably the only place where we just refused to let him participate in demonstrations —not to keep *him* from getting killed, interestingly enough—but because the mobs were so fanatic every day and night that they would probably have killed a whole lot of other people too. He never curtailed his activities. We would get threats almost every time he went someplace. So much so that we didn't pay attention to them. The only time we'd pay attention was when the reports came directly from the FBI or the Justice Department. When it got to the point where none of those panned out, we sort of figured we had it made. In fact, I remember having a conversation with him not long before his death, saying tha originally, as long as we figured none of us were going to live to forty anyway, it was all right if we didn't care about sleep, about eating regular; we'd stay up every night till about four or five o'clock, till 7:00, and go right on again. He could do this all the time. I mean he could go for weeks and months on two or three hours sleep a night. It was wearing me out. So I was trying to convince him that it looked like we were going to be around for awhile; so there was no need, you know, to be knocking off at forty-five with a heart attack.

He had been stabbed in 1957 in New York. He was autographing copies . . . this was right after the Montgomery bus boycott . . . and this black woman in Harlem came up and stabbed him with a letter opener, right next to the aorta of his heart. He used to preach about that every now and then. The doctor said if he had *sneezed* even, the letter opener would probably have cut his aorta. And he certainly would have died.

Every now and then, when he was thinking about death, you could tell, because that story would creep into his preaching; he told it the night before he was killed. That was where he said that "I've been to the mountaintop and . . ." Well, he told the story about this, and about receiving a letter from a little girl saying, "I'm glad you didn't sneeze." He said that he was glad he didn't sneeze, but he didn't care now because he'd seen so much. That was when he talked about the Biblical analogy of having been to the mountaintop and seeing the promised land.

I was almost strangely relieved when Martin died. This was the only way he could know peace. He was so tormented by the violence in this country. He could not understand it. At our last staff meeting, the day he was killed, we were all sitting around joking. He said that he had no fear about dying. He had come so close to it years earlier that he had made his peace with death. It was our problem, not his, if we had any fears.

THE REVEREND RALPH ABERNATHY, *civil-rights leader*

There were odd premonitions, thinking back on it. When we flew to Memphis, there was a long wait before the plane took off, and then the pilot came out and said: "Ladies and gentlemen, I want to apologize, but we have Dr. Martin Luther King on board and there have been some *threats*. We have had to take this time to search every piece of luggage."

Well, naturally we were a little nervous. Afterwards, it was clear that Dr. King had some sort of premonition, a tornado warning, because that evening in Memphis, he asked me to stand in for him at a mass meeting. That surprised me because King loved crowds. So I went over to the church, and when I got there, I found such an enthusiastic group that I called him on the telephone. He said if you say come, I'll come. That night (and that was strange), I decided to give him a very full introduction. I took twenty-five minutes. I went through his career. I said that so often we take the leader for granted that sometimes we ought to pause and give a man his proper introduction. Of course, I was giving him his last introduction. Then he got up and spoke for about an hour and a half. The next day, when they were teasing me, I said, "Well, I introduced him for twenty-five minutes, and as long as he speaks an hour and a half, that doesn't look too bad."

So we laughed about it, and he called his mother and talked to her. I fell asleep, and then he called me on the phone and told me where he was. He was down in his brother's room. I went down there, and he said, "Oh, I just called Mother and talked with her for an hour." He said, "You know, she's so happy whenever A.D. is with me." That's his brother.

Then we decided to go back to our room and dress for dinner and get shaved. Just as we were setting out I said, "Oh, wait just a minute, I'm putting on some after-shave lotion." He said, "Okay, I'll be waiting on the balcony."

I heard something like a firecracker and I jumped, naturally, and then I looked and I saw nothing but his feet; I thought somebody was shooting up the place, and I wondered if I should take cover. I thought *he* had taken cover, and then I heard the people in the courtyard say, "Oh, Lord. Lord." They began to groan, and I knew then what had happened and I rushed to his side and picked his head up and patted his cheek and said, "Martin, this is Ralph." He was looking frightened. I said, "This is Ralph. This is Ralph." He looked at me and attempted to say something, but no words came out because the windpipe and the spine had been severed. But he gave me a firm, solid look. I knew he was conscious . . . and he began to communicate with his eyes and I got the impression he was saying, "Well, Ralph, this has happened now, and for God sake don't let me down."

JOHN J. LINDSAY, *correspondent*

We had been in Muncie, Indiana, at Ball State University, and the place was jammed to overflowing in the gymnasium. Near the end of the

254

program, a young Negro stood up and said that he wasn't being at all truculent about it . . . he was just asking a question. He said, "You seem to believe in the good faith of the white people toward the minorities in this country. Do you think that faith is justified?" And Bob replied, "Yes," and this kid seemed totally satisfied with that and said, "Thank you, sir," and sat down. We walked out five minutes later, and we got the first news.

FRED DUTTON, *campaign aide*

As we got on the plane to go from Terre Haute to Indianapolis, somebody rushed up and said, "Martin Luther King's been shot in Memphis." I didn't say anything to Bob. I thought I'd wait until we got to Indianapolis and find out what the full story was, and tell him then. That might have been overly protective on my part. Staff people tend to get that way. In any event, some of the newspaper guys had learned about the story and they told him on the plane as we flew back. It was the end of the day. We had one more campaign appearance. By coincidence, it was in the Negro area of Indianapolis. By the time the plane landed, Ethel also knew about the report. She thought that we should all go back to the hotel, that there was bound to be trouble. Bob said, "No," he was going to go to this meeting. He did, however, send Ethel to the hotel after we learned from the airport police that King was dead. He and I immediately got in a car with a driver and headed for the rally, with the press buses coming along behind. He had no prepared speech. He had planned a fairly standard stump talk. But he sat alone in the back seat, thinking to himself and gazing out the window in the dark. We had a twenty- to twenty-five-minute ride from the airport to the black section of Indianapolis. At one point, he asked, "What do you think I should say?" I made a couple of inadequate responses. He made no notes of his own thoughts. When we got to the outdoor rally, the audience was about eighty per cent black. He was to speak from a flat-bed truck, which already had ten times too many people on it. Bob climbed up on the truck, was briefly introduced, and began to speak. The crowd was in a festive mood. There were signs KENNEDY FOR PRESIDENT all over the place. He opened by saying, "I have some terrible news for you. Martin Luther King's been shot."

There was an audible gasp through the crowd. Then Bob gave the most moving talk I ever heard. It was the first time he had ever publicly referred to his brother being shot. He spoke only seven or eight minutes.

It was pure Robert Kennedy. It came from a heart that hurt and knew the meaning of what had happened that night as only a handful of people could really feel it.

CHARLES QUINN, *television correspondent*

This huge gasp went out from the people. Some of the women got hysterical. Then Kennedy made this great, moving speech, asking the people to be calm, telling them that things looked dark for America, but that there was always hope; telling them that his own brother had been killed by a white man; that he could understand the emotions that they were undergoing at that time. It was a cold night, and he was up there, hunched in his black overcoat, his face gaunt and distressed and full of anguish for the country. He spoke out very forcefully and firmly to those people; on the fringes of the crowd there was some hostility; a couple of kids yelled, "Black power!" But for the most part, the people then just broke up and went home. That's what he asked them to do, and that's what they did.

FRED DUTTON

Bob completed his remarks, came down and went right to the hotel. He was overwhelmed. Much by King's assassination. Much by the tragedy for America that he alluded to. When he got to the hotel, he said he wanted to place a call to Mrs. King. "I want to talk to her." He got on the phone with her. He asked, "Is there anything I can do for you?" That was when she asked him to help arrange transportation for her from Memphis to Atlanta. He had me call Burke Marshall; then he talked with Burke and asked him to follow through. But it always amazed me that nobody at the White House at the same time had gotten on the phone and called up and said, We'll send Air Force One down. Or even after Bob had volunteered it, if the President had said, You can have a larger plane, and so forth. But Bob ended up taking care of it— and being criticized too. It was one of those both tragic and grotesque evenings, really, in so many ways.

CORETTA SCOTT KING (*Mrs. Martin Luther King, Jr.*)

I spoke with him on the phone about 2:00 A.M. the night of the assassination; he offered his services and furnished a plane for us to bring my husband's body back from Memphis. There was some concern within the organization as to whether or not this was quite the proper thing to do. I said that "I don't really see anything wrong, period; one friend to another friend."

He said, "You probably need more phones in your house." It was something I hadn't thought about. I think he offered three at the time, and we already had two. He said, "I'll get that done tonight." I said, "How fantastic! Tonight!" I'd never heard of such a thing. But, of course, the telephone men came in that same evening and put the phones in, and they stayed in for several weeks. I graciously accepted his offer because I felt that he was a friend.

They were political figures; but, aside from that, they were human beings first, and that humanness in them reached out to the needs of other people. I felt that on that evening when Bobby Kennedy called. He came down, and he brought his wife, Ethel, whom I had never met either; we had a visit in my bedroom. When we met, although I hadn't met her previously, we embraced each other! It was a natural reaction from her to me, and I had that kind of a warm feeling about her as a woman who reached out to me. Jackie had sent her sympathy and really wanted to come. Bobby said, "This would be very hard for her because of her own experiences; but if it meant anything to you perhaps she would try to come." I said, "Oh, yes. It would mean a great deal to me if she did come." He went out, and we heard later that she was coming . . . for the funeral.

She came to my house just a few minutes before I was to go to the ceremony; she came back to the bedroom, and we met for the first time. We exchanged greetings, and I thanked her for coming and also for what her family and her husband had meant to us. . . . I told her that I felt very close to her family for this reason . . . and I said, "for our people." She was very gracious. She said something about how strong I was and how much she admired me. I said the same thing back to her because I did feel that way. Then she said to me, "And you're such a good speaker. You speak so well." That's what she said. I guess she had heard me speak in Memphis on that Monday; that must have been what she was referring to. I introduced her to some of the family people around.

BLAIR CLARK, *campaign manager for Senator Eugene McCarthy*
Eugene McCarthy's first reaction was that he knew there'd be a great big vulgar public spectacle at the funeral. And there was. There were a lot of people unquestionably—I'm not talking about Kennedy in this at

all—who went there for bad reasons. So, he knew that. His first reaction was very strong that he would go to some black community and go to a church privately, wherever he was . . . whether it was in San Francisco Los Angeles or Washington or Chicago, or wherever, and just go and pray with some blacks on the day when the funeral happened. I felt that such symbolic kinds of behavior were not understandable to wide spec trums of the community. In other words, he *had* to go to the Atlanta funeral. I'm sure I was just one of the people who told him that he had to go.

ALLARD LOWENSTEIN, *congressional candidate*
McCarthy and Kennedy were sitting in pews one behind the other Burke Marshall, Coretta, so many of my heroes gathered with all these poor Southern blacks—it seemed like everything I cared about was here in this great crush of grief. Then we were singing, "Earnestly, Tenderly Jesus Is Calling," which ends up: "Come home, come home. Ye who ar weary, come home, come home." Everything after that was, well, *less* than that. What a hymn to sing with Robert Kennedy and all thes people who had endured so much, and right after Martin Luther King' death: "Ye who are weary, come home."

DR. VINCENT HARDING, *educator*
Bobby walked . . . yeah . . . in the procession. Our house in Atlant is right at the point where they make the turn to go onto the Morehous campus. For a whole lot of reasons that I won't go into, I didn't go to th funeral. I simply stayed in the house and watched the passing crowd . . and I saw Bobby then . . . gathered into the midst of the crowd and hustled and tussled around. I remember somebody saying on the porch "Wow! He looks much smaller than I thought he was."

JOHN MAGUIRE, *educator*
He was very conspicuous . . . even in 100,000 people walking alon in the seven-mile march . . . that typical thing with his jacket off and over his shoulders—terribly hot—and his shirtsleeves rolled up. It struc me that of *all* the celebrities there, the only two people that were con *stantly* cheered wherever they walked . . . the spontaneous applaus of the people lining the streets . . . were Sammy Davis, junior, and Robert Kennedy. I've always tried to figure out what that told us about ou culture and about black people! But there was *everybody!* I mean Gen McCarthy, Richard Nixon . . . walking along with Wilt Chamberlai

. . . trying to identify with black people . . . or give that illusion! The *only* people who just constantly . . . wherever they went . . . there was this spontaneous applause . . . were Robert Kennedy and Sammy Davis, junior! He walked the whole way that day.

ROGER WILKINS, *director of the Community Relations Service, Department of Justice*

The white politicians started to come. And they came. And they came. And they came. And they came. And a lot of people—both black and white came to see the show—like to a carnival. And that made me resent the politicians—and the President, who didn't come—even more. And Richard Nixon was there. And we know what Richard Nixon's civil-rights posture had been . . . and we know what Richard Nixon's civil-rights posture is now. And Gene McCarthy came, and he had been so busy talking about peace that he had no time even to recognize black pain. But he had time to come and have his picture taken at that funeral. And Lyndon Johnson sent a whole planeload of people down to sit in that church when we didn't even have seats for some of the poor blacks who gave meaning to Martin's life and to his death. There were just many black people outside that church who couldn't get in that day who cared deeply for Martin King. All those white politicians were sitting in that church. I was furious. Bob Kennedy had become a different kind of man. I think by then he really cared about Martin King and about our cause and he was there because of that. But he also wanted to be President. We saw *that* too. Bob had a political meeting with some leaders . . . black leaders who happened to be at the funeral while he was there. I thought that was very bad.

THE REVEREND ANDREW J. YOUNG

It was in his suite at the Regency hotel. I guess our staff didn't quite riot, but there was a whole lot of undirected hostility present, you know, in our group. People were just angry and bitter and grieving. But they decided to take it out on him, which was very uncalled for. James Bevel opened the discussion, saying, "We just buried our leader. He had a program for helping to bridge the economy, you know, between the haves and the have-nots; and somebody has got to find a way to feed hungry people. Now, whoever is the next President of the United States has got to have an economic program to bring poor people into the economy and into the society, and I just want to know . . . Do you have a program, or do you know anybody that does?"

It was filled with profanity and when preachers get to cuss, they cuss good. It's kind of poetic. There were others, two or three people, who really jumped all over him. On one hand, I was embarrassed, and yet, I wouldn't cut it off. I was impressed with the way he was reacting. He listened while we blew off steam. But I mean, he wasn't upset. He just handled himself very well. He refused to say he had a program. He said, "Well, maybe we can get together and talk about that some time." He said, "I do have one or two ideas. But really, I didn't come here to discuss politics. That would be in the worst taste." He said, "I just came to pay a tribute to a man that I had a lot of respect for." Some people who heard of the meeting but not of Bobby's refusal to talk politics, were understandably critical, and even angered.

JULIAN BOND, *member, Georgia House of Representatives*

We were in this very plush hotel in Atlanta. I had been invited to a meeting with him, but had been given directions to the wrong hotel. I was supposed to have met him in a discussion with other Negro legislators. But I missed that meeting and came instead to a meeting with a lot of entertainers. Very strange. Eartha Kitt was there; Bill Cosby was there; and Peter Lawford, and some guy who occasionally takes over the Johnny Carson show—an entertainer-comedian—Alan King. John Lewis and Dr. Benjamin Mays were there. Kennedy directed the conversation toward the problem of what will happen now that King is dead. Strangely, it became a matter of each of these entertainers saying, in what I thought was a *very* egotistical way, how much they were doing for the movement. Cosby finally said, "This is a lot of shit! I'm going to leave." And he left. John Conyers, Congressman from Detroit, said something to the same effect. And he also left. But the entertainers kept at it, on and on. Each one said something like: "The problem is . . ." I remember Eartha Kitt saying, "The problem is juvenile delinquency," and telling how much she had done with juvenile delinquents. And I'm sure she *had* done a great deal, but that wasn't quite what the problem was. Kennedy, during all this, listened and didn't say much. Sammy Davis was there. . . . He listened and didn't say very much either; he smoked and he had a drink, and once in awhile he walked over and looked out of the window. I remember his shirt . . . he had a coat on, but his shirt was hanging out underneath the coat. I thought it looked kind of funny. Then the meeting sort of broke up. The last thing Kennedy said to me was, "Julian, I bet you've been to a lot of meetings like this before, haven't you?" I said, "Yes." And he said, "I bet you don't want to go to any more, do you?" And I said, "No."

ROGER WILKINS

During the day, the reaction set in across the country. Blacks started burning cities across the country; one of them was Washington, and we began to get these reports about Washington burning. So we flew back and got there about eight o'clock at night and circled the city, and just saw the smoke and the fires.

THE REVEREND WALTER FAUNTROY, Vice Chairman, City Council, Washington, D.C.

The stench of burning wood and broken glass were all over the place. We walked the streets. The troops were on duty. A crowd gathered behind us, following Bobby Kennedy. The troops saw us coming at a distance, and they put on their gas masks and got the guns at ready, waiting for this horde of blacks coming up the street. When they saw it was Bobby Kennedy, they took off their masks and let us through. They looked awfully relieved.

HOSEA WILLIAMS, aide to Dr. Martin Luther King, Jr.

We felt as long as Dr. King lived, he would lead us to higher grounds. I used to say that God had enabled Dr. King to put together a better staff than Jesus Christ, considering none of us would have sold him for thirty pieces of silver or even thirty million dollars. But after he was killed, it left us hopeless, very desperate, dangerous men. I was so despondent and frustrated at Dr. King's death, I had to seriously ask myself . . . Can this country be saved? I guess the thing that kept us going was that maybe Bobby Kennedy would come up with some answers for this country. We kept telling ourselves that God has someone who's come along to lead us out of the land of Egypt, so to speak. After Dr. King was killed, there was just about nobody else left but Bobby Kennedy. I remember telling him he had a chance to be a prophet. But prophets get shot.

17

MARGARET BADDERS, *housewife, Delaware*

My father used to run the Congressional Limited from New York to Washington. I said to my husband, "This is going to be a beautiful train." I was so surprised when it *did* come. Why, I couldn't believe my *eyes* that the Pennsylvania Railroad would put out such a disgraceful train. There were no two coaches that *matched*, and right in the dead middle there were two that were a very dull gray as though—it's a heck of a comparison—they were burying someone in a very cheap casket covered with gray velvet! Well, I said to my husband, "I can't believe it—of all trains for the Kennedy funeral! That every coach would look different!" One was red and silver; one was silver and green. I rode with my father once on the Congressional Limited back in 1950, and every coach blended. And the observation car! Perhaps they preferred the old-fashioned observation car, but this was a *very* old one. It all looked so careless and sloppy! I don't know who selected it. It wouldn't have been my choice if I had had the say-so. As I say, the Congressional Limited was a beauty; and the Silver Meteor, *that* was a beauty—just like a great big long silver bullet, greenish blue glass windows. They still have trains that match. I've seen them go through here. There's your Orange Blossom Special; your Super Chief. The Kennedy train looked to me like one of these locals that take a lot of businessmen to work in the morning. Here was a man who was almost the President of the United States! He died—not meaning to sound on a box—for a *cause*, for the American people, and I think that he deserved the best that the railroad could offer. The Lincoln funeral train had big wooden cars, and each one matched. And

262

on the last car were the Union soldiers by the flag-draped casket. That was one more thing I mentioned to my husband: "There's somebody in *white* standing by that casket!" I knew it was the casket because I saw the flag. He said, "Maybe it was the chef!" I said, "Oh, heavens, the chef wouldn't be back there!" I said, "Maybe it was a nurse." I didn't know. It *could* have been a chef or a nurse the way they were running things. I had thought, This is going to be *the* train. I thought of so many thousands of Americans looking at this thing, and the Pennsylvania Railroad —I mean there is such a controversy now over planes, and the railroads merging—they'd be sure to come up with something especially good.

My father rode what they called a "GG-1"—that's a super-special engine with many dials on the dashboard, and the throttle is to the right. Your engineer never takes his hand off it; the only thing that brakes your engine is a heart attack; that's how they can tell when an engineer has a heart attack—his hand will leave the throttle and the train automatically comes to a stop. Well, when the Kennedy train came through, it was a Diesel engine, and I saw that the man did have his hand right on the throttle. But I wondered who he was; because he was dressed in a black suit, white shirt, dark tie, and these two men in gray were standing talking to him. I thought: "Well, they must be Secret Service men." *This fellow was turning his head*. He didn't have his eye on the track. I said to my husband, "You know, my father had two detached retinas from the strain of looking at that track." The retina is the muscle in back of the eye. My father'd say, "Your eyes just don't leave the track. You look straight ahead." The eye lacks exercise by looking ahead all the time. So that's what happened to him. My father always wore dark trousers, a dark coat and any color shirt and cap. More or less regulation. There was a "Book of Rules." No, this man didn't have a cap on. No hat at *all*.

Still, I am glad I went.

The police were very good—going up and down blowing their whistles and keeping everyone a good distance away. I had heard about the Elizabeth accident up in New Jersey. I used to ride a lot—I used to have a pass before I was married, my father being an employee, and I know he used to tell me when I'd go to Philly to shop, "Don't stand close to where the track is. Stand back. There's a suction from the breeze." The wind will pull a dress, and I always automatically backed up when I saw a train coming. They must have been too close to the tracks. I said to my husband, "That can happen from what my father told me. You can't brake an engine that's going too fast." My father once had a suicide on his tracks. He was going eighty-five miles per hour, southbound to Washington, and he saw the man come out about three blocks away, out onto the tracks and he took off his black derby hat, and Papa said, "Well, something's going to happen here." He threw on his brakes; then he pulled the cord to notify the conductor to come up immediately. There wasn't anything he could do. You can't brake it that fast.

While I waited for the train, I was just sitting there talking to my husband, smoking a cigarette. It was hot, and a little humid. But there was a little bit of breeze going . . . I note that I usually perspire freely and I wasn't. Then I picked up this piece of paper, and I decided to write what was popping into my mind. I brought along a pad and a paper. It's standard equipment in my purse. I write letters to the editor once in a while in the *News-Journal*. I thought, Maybe this sounds childish and maybe it doesn't. Here's what I wrote:

> As I stood on the embankment through the long, long wait,
> I certainly hoped that Bobby's train wouldn't be so late.
> As I glanced at the faces about me, I thought, everyone here appeared so overwrought.
> And I thought of Bobby's words, "I dare to dream and ask why not."
> And I thought of Lincoln, King, Brother John and the lot
> And I silently prayed that these men died not in vain.
> I returned to my home, went about my chores like a busy old bee
> And I suddenly thought, "Wake up America, we know not for whom the bell tolls.
> It could toll for thee."

I wrote it and stuck it back into my purse and then, just like many people do, I just looked around and watched people's faces. I like to study people. Their faces were ghastly and sad and shocked. Some ladies were in shorts and blouses. Some were in linen dresses. I had on a culotte dress. Slacks. Just casual Saturday afternoon—you'd wear out on your patio. We talked about the train. I said: "Wait until you see this! This will really be something for the Kennedys." And we talked about Kennedy himself. I thought that he was a very good-living family man, a broad-minded man. He didn't care if you were rich, if you were poor; or if you were a movie actor who took LSD. He would shake hands with you and give you the benefit of the doubt. To me, he's a Christian. And an influence to sort of wake people up a little bit and not let their days go by and think, Oh, dah, dah, dah. He had personality. You can sit in a room full of people, but there's always going to be one person there who has that answer . . . who has that smile . . . who has that vivid

264

personality . . . who makes you want to ignore everybody else. Have you ever been in a room full of company like that? I have. His personality was par excellence.

But that's more than I can say about that train that came through. My father would have been very upset. The trains were his whole life. He met people. He met Margaret Truman. He had her on his train, had his picture taken with her. He used to love to come home with those things. He had President Truman. One Congressman wrote the railroad a letter and told them his wife was pregnant. He notified my father when they were coming northbound to New York on the Congressional Limited. Papa came through very nicely, with no rough braking of the engine, and a week after the trip, the Congressman wrote Papa a letter and thanked him for the smooth ride, and he sent him a box of cigars. Papa crowed about that for the longest time.

My father loved it. And I did too. I've often told my husband I bet I could get on that engine right now and read the signals, and know when to stop and when not to stop, and when to slow up and when to switch over, because I used to sit there night after night, and he'd say, "You want to hear my questions?" I'd say, "Pass me the questions and hear my answers."

RICHARD DRAYNE, *campaign aide*

Nebraska, with Indiana behind us, was Nixon territory. We were hours late, coming through some town in Nebraska in a motorcade, people watching from along the side. It must have been ten o'clock at night, and it was dark. It was a residential section. At one point, there were these kids—three of them—little kids sleeping. It was springtime. They were sleeping on top of a car; their parents had allowed them to wait outside for the Senator, but they had to be in their pajamas. We saw this, and everybody was very touched. I called out to Dick Tuck, very loudly so everybody on the bus could hear. I said: "When are we going to see those kids again, Tuck?" He said, "We're shipping them out to Oregon after tonight." It was like the standing joke every time we saw a group of nuns. Somebody would say: "Where'd you get the nuns? Aren't those the same nuns we saw in Indianapolis?" Dick Tuck would say, "Well, of *course* they are."

DICK TUCK, *campaign aide*

His great campaigner was that dog, Freckles. He was with us from the beginning. He came and raced up the steps and got aboard the plane. Brumus, the big Labrador, of course had to be chained back. So the Senator looked at me and said, "Can we bring him?" I said, "I guess we can bring him." So Freckles became an institution. The dog loved the Senator. There was no question about that. In moments for relaxation, we would stop our car caravans in the middle of Nebraska, and the Senator and the dog would walk off into the woods; it was good for both of them. The dog was pretty smart; he could ride in the back of convertibles; if it was a small crowd, the dog would go to sleep, and the Senator would get Jerry Bruno or the other advance men and say, "The dog's pretty upset with this crowd. You didn't do much of a job getting this crowd together." I pointed out that sometimes the dog would sleep during *his* speeches. He'd sneak up to the rostrum and sleep at his feet.

Once, we were coming down the elevator in Fresno, California—Freckles, Fred Dutton, the Senator, and I—late for a breakfast where he was to make a speech. The Senator looked at Fred and he looked at me, and he said, "Do you suppose that somebody could walk the dog?" I said, "Ambassadorship to Rome?" He said, "All right." And so I took the dog out.

Then one day the dog disappeared. I went chasing after him. Somebody said, "You know, it's just a dog." I said, "To you it's a dog. To me it's an ambassadorship."

We used to joke about that. Once I was getting off the plane someplace, and I was talking to somebody who was saying how smart Freckles was. I said, "Well, he's *pretty* smart. If there are three cars in the caravan, he will run and jump in the middle car, which is clever because that's the Senator's car. But if there are *four* cars," I said, "you know, he's confused, and he doesn't quite know what to do. He's really kind of a dumb dog." The Senator happened to be walking right behind me, and he overheard. He said, "What did you say? Well, that's too bad. Yesterday it was Rome. Tomorrow it's Luxembourg." I said, "I wasn't talking about the dog. I was talking about you. You don't know which car to get in. I said the dog was very smart." He said, "It's still Luxembourg."

CHARLES QUINN, *television correspondent*

He developed a little code to let the press know when his speech was at a close so we could run for the train or the buses. He used to say, "As George Bernard Shaw once said, 'Most men look at things as they are and wonder why. I dream of things that never were and ask why not?'" One time in Oregon, he didn't use it, and I almost missed a train. I berated him for not saying it. Bill Barry said he *had* said it, but I hadn't been listening. I was talking to some sheriff out there, and I missed it.

He was getting punchy at the end of the Nebraska campaign, and we were standing out in the rain in Omaha the last day. He was talking to a lot of people—maybe 800 or 900 people; and we're all standing underneath these store awnings so we wouldn't get wet. He was saying, "Anybody who would stand out here in the rain, listening to a politician, is nuts." Then he got through, and we were all pretty thoroughly drenched; he said, "Well, as George Bernard Shaw once said, 'Run for the bus!' " And all the people stood there. They didn't know what he was talking about. The press were all laughing. In Oregon, we used to tell him, "Every time you say that now, you know, that Bernard Shaw phrase, even Freckles runs for the bus!"

JOHN J. LINDSAY, *correspondent*
I remember one night we were flying somewhere over Nebraska at about 30,000 feet. We ran into turbulence, and we were bouncing all over the place. Somebody said, "Who in hell is flying this airplane?" Bob said, "Freckles." And he added, "And he's very ruthless."

JOSEPH KRAFT, *columnist*
On the heels of the Indiana primary victory, I think he was pessimistic about Oregon. He referred to it as a suburb and said there weren't any problems; there wasn't anything for him to get a hold on. I asked him what he would do after this in California. He said he would chase Hubert Humphrey all over the country, forcing him to come to grips with the big issues. He knew all along that I had recommended against his going into the campaign. He knew that. I asked him during the Oregon primary whether he had any regrets about this. He said, "No. Because I've done what I could." He looked terrible; I'd never seen him look so bad, so tired; his blue eyes were standing out really like a death's head from his skull. But he was very brown from the sun.

MARIAN SCHLESINGER, *family friend*
Oregon is a pioneer state; as a result it's a matriarchal society; very strong women have kept the whole thing together. My theory was that the men, because they live in a matriarchal society, are passive, sort of hag-ridden, and they identified with McCarthy. Bobby Kennedy repre-

sented a masculine threat to them. They adhered very closely to Mc-Carthy because he seemed by comparison passive, and a product of female domination.

JOHN STEWART, *campaign aide*

I mentioned to the Senator that it was very hip for the young people to be for McCarthy. He said, yeah, he knew that. He said, "Don't they realize that they're choosing the President of the United States, not the president of a frat club?" In the campaign one morning, I staggered down at about eight o'clock, and he was sitting with about fifteen students. He'd had breakfast, and been up since about 6:30 or so. At this restaurant, there were some McCarthy people sitting at the table right across from us, and they were speaking very loudly and obviously so he could hear—and one guy just looked over, staring at the Senator. Kennedy stared him down with that great animal stare. There was a great deal of friction there.

ANDREAS TEUBER, *campaign aide to Senator Eugene McCarthy*

He walked out along the beach and then decided to strip to his waist, and dove into the waters. The Oregonians, I think, reacted to that like, That's silly! Why do you do *that?* It represented some kind of invigorating response. This was in May. There was something about the tide, and you don't do that. There wasn't somebody there to help him, and there was a very strong undertow. You don't just jump into the water like that without taking more precautions.

ROBERT LOWELL, *poet*

I gave two speeches on Bobby in Oregon. One for him and one against him. They're very short.

Here's the one I gave on May 19th: "It is rare now that a politician in the running remains himself and is not devalued into a machine or medium for catching votes. I must not be abusive. All men are more than liable to corrupt and go dry; and even the most oxided candidates once had feelings and faces; faces turning to rubber, so used they were to stretching for advantage this way, then that way till they were rubber." I was thinking of Humphrey.

"What we want and seldom get is the President with an eye for the unexpected. One bold and generous in his mind, but also still not paralyzed by his ambitions and self-consideration. One with the serenity of casualness. Many think this is a dark hour for Senator McCarthy, and

268

we who are for him are aware that it is our dark hour. It is a time when we can look forward to the chance and, perhaps, likelihood that we will see a race between . . . I'll use an adjective much favored by the convention orator . . . we will see a race between two great Vice-Presidents . . . ex-Vice-President Nixon and active Vice-President Humphrey. We must stick by Senator McCarthy and stick as fiercely as we can to the end, to the turn of the tide; so that he, or if not he, alas another, may defeat Humphrey at Chicago, and Nixon in November."

Well, the "other" has to be Bobby.

The other speech is quite mean. But I think it has certain truth to it. This was given in Portland on May 26th. McCarthy spoke. Then, after he left, I spoke.

"Senator Kennedy's wardrobe has taken a beating during the primaries; particularly his cuff links. First, they were diamonds. Then they were merely sterling silver. Now they have gone down to Lyndon Johnson copper-filled dimes. But he has just bought a hundred charisma suits. A charisma suit is made of cloth and cardboard; at the touch of a feather, at the touch of the weakest admirer, it pulls apart. But under the charisma suit is an anti-charisma Bobby-suit. It is made of cloth and steel wool. It doesn't tear at all and leaves metal threads in the rash admirer for months."

This is an attack, you see. Second paragraph: "Now, I must supply some local color. Yesterday night, when we were dining on the roof of the Portland Hilton . . . we seem to live in Hiltons . . . the headwaiter told us with great joy that a tire-repairing factory was on fire. It was a four-alarm fire, he said. And before we had finished our first course, the headwaiter, at last almost manic with satisfaction, and feeling that his hotel had lived up to its reputation, said the fire was now a six-alarm fire. Do you know how it started? You've all heard of Senator Kennedy's sudden rash dip in the Pacific? Now, this northern Portland ocean is cold, as I knew from summers spent near Portland, Maine. It was headlong and lacking in foresight for the Senator to plunge in this way. When he came out, he had chills and fevers. Trying to warm himself, he lit a fire by the tire factory. Now nothing smells worse and has a blacker smoke than burning rubber."

I just can hear his disgust if he heard me read this.

"I must be serious. I would be dishonorable if I didn't confess that I pesronally like and admire Senator Kennedy. He is not in the same class as Senator McCarthy's other Democratic and Republican opponents. I've too little sympathy with Vice-President Humphrey, old Vice-President Nixon, and Governor Rockefeller or Governor Reagan to lift a finger against them. Isn't it self-evident that these strong and formidable vote-getters are in no way morally serious contenders? Besides, they're not running against McCarthy in Oregon."

Then I have my little last paragraph, which is very bitter about Bobby.

"Still I wish to end up with invective; it's hard for one to forgive Kennedy his shy, calculating delay in declaring himself, or forgive the shaggy rudeness of his final entrance. And who can look forward to the return of the old 'new frontiersmen'? They don't look as good as they once did, after eight years. These men, tarnished with former power and thirsting to return to that power. We cannot forgive Senator Kennedy for trying to bury us under a pile of gold."

That's tough. It's all in the game. I think I thought it was fighting enough, not that this had any effect. It was given to an audience who was all going to vote for McCarthy anyway, and probably didn't hear the speech very well.

JOHN STEWART

He said, "I can't understand why people hate me. In some towns I go to, there's no need for a psychiatrist because they get their hatred out on me. I just got word that some college students went out on a canvassing campaign, and they couldn't find *one* person who liked me." He said, "I just can't get a foothold here in Oregon. There's just no problems. Everyone is too comfortable here."

He'd said, "If I lose Oregon, it's all over with me. I *have* to prove that I can win in every state to get the nomination." You could tell this was the eleventh hour because all the big guns, Arthur Schlesinger and everyone, were on board. I've never seen him like that. He was pacing like a tiger in this back car. At each stop, he would be lashing out with these great speeches.

BONNIE LEFKOWITZ, *campaign worker*

We knew there was something wrong from the day we got there. We had been told it was okay because Edith Green had a strong organization in Oregon. So we expected a functioning campaign. All we saw was this little tearoom off the street where little old ladies with shopping bags came in and ate cookies. Upstairs there was a *huge* empty room with one telephone line and two desks. They told us we couldn't put any more desks up there because the floor was weak.

Later on we found out Mrs. Green wanted the headquarters that way —a "mushroom" effect, I think they called it. In Oregon, it's not considered nice to show that you are working hard on a political campaign. So they have a little homey office on the first floor and the workers hidden away upstairs.

There were four of us, besides Bill vanden Heuvel, at first, and three or four Oregon people. That was it! We were the underdogs. The McCarthy people had all their best people in Oregon, and all the best students. They actually had them believing that McCarthy would do more for blacks than Kennedy—that he cared more. And I think McCarthy himself was nastier there than anyplace else. We heard him tell a student rally two days before the primary, "There are a number of reasons why Kennedy's moral character is inferior to mine, but I'm not going to tell you what they are today." For that moment, I could have sworn it was the other McCarthy speaking.

All the while, the Kennedy people were relying on a last-minute blitz. They were worried about Indiana, and then about California, and they said, "Well, Edith Green will take care of Oregon for us." But it didn't work there. The McCarthy people had done too much groundwork; there was too much prejudice against Kennedy as a late-comer; and there were none of the problems that would make people realize how much they needed him.

The Senator knew it, too. He was talking to a group of us one night at dinner—he always liked to talk to campaign workers; he was great that way—and he looked very depressed. He said, "These are just not my kind of people. My people have problems." And one of the people with us said, "Well, Senator, I think we can turn it around." I didn't think he should have said that. It wasn't true, and we all knew it.

ANDREAS TEUBER

In the Rose Gardens at the zoo in Portland, Oregon, McCarthy and Kennedy met! They were constantly avoiding each other. Kennedy's party was a little late in leaving and McCarthy's party was early. McCarthy was coming up over the hill just as Kennedy was arriving to climb into the cavalcade and drive off. When Kennedy looked over his shoulder and when he saw McCarthy, he got into his car. McCarthy arrived and climbed onto Kennedy's press bus! He chatted with Bobby's press. The television cameras caught it all. It was a fantastic moment on the news because the cameras actually panned directly from Mc-Carthy coming over by the hill, a quick pan to Kennedy exiting from the scene, and McCarthy climbing onto Kennedy's press bus. I think that was just another reason that the Kennedy people finally decided, Yes, we're going to have to debate. We can't afford such disasters.

FRED DUTTON, *campaign aide*

Bob had decided that he wasn't going to debate in Oregon. But Bill vanden Heuvel, Pierre Salinger, Adam Walinsky, and a couple of others hit him with it again. "You've got to debate." Bob listened to them. He asked me, and I said, "At some stage or other, you've just got to bring this to an end. You can't rehash and keep rehashing the whole thing." So he went and took a nap. After his nap, they came back to urge that he debate again. He got pretty annoyed. He kicked everybody out of the suite. They stood out in the hallway, laughing and joking. Finally Bob came stomping out in his white shorts. Poor Walinsky and Jeff Greenfield were there, and he said, "My speechwriters should have something better to do than stand around and laugh in hotel corridors. I think they should be ringing doorbells and making phone calls. They don't know anything about politics." Adam had been carrying a guitar around for folk songs and Bob said, "Besides that, I don't see why my speechwriters have to carry around guitars."

LAWRENCE F. O'BRIEN, *campaign director*

It became apparent to us at least a couple of days prior to the primary that it would be nothing short of miraculous if we were able to get by Oregon. We had a feeling that I had never experienced with the Kennedys: your sixth sense told you you hadn't overcome, and you didn't seem to have any specific views on how to overcome.

It brought us to Bob Kennedy's suite that night. We walked into the hotel to see a defeated candidate. It was the first defeat experienced by a Kennedy in public life—in some twenty-plus contests of one sort or another. And I thought that he showed again the stature. He showed immediate concern for the workers who were gathered in the hall in the hotel. He walked in and embraced Edith Green, our chairman out there, and said, "I guess we just didn't have enough votes. It's as simple as that."

272

RICHARD HARWOOD, *national editor,* The Washington Post

There was no bewailing the fact that he was the first Kennedy to ever lose an election. There was some talk about other people fouling up Oregon, and he said, "Well, that's a lot of malarky. If I had won it, it would have been my victory; and I've lost it, and it's my defeat." He said, "McCarthy wasn't running against anybody but Bobby Kennedy. I got beat." He took it beautifully and without a word of self-pity . . . and I think that's the night we did a lot of singing on the plane going back, and he was having a hell of a time.

SENATOR GEORGE McGOVERN

He came to South Dakota in late May—just after the Oregon primary. He really had given a disproportionate amount of time to South Dakota. He wanted to win there very badly. He thought he might be in trouble because it was the one place where Humphrey made a bid—with advertisements that identified a slate of candidates as the Humphrey-Johnson slate. It was frankly a test of Administration strength versus his. Also Gene McCarthy was there. So Bobby was running against a native South Dakotan, Humphrey, whose relatives still lived in South Dakota, and against McCarthy who lives next door in Minnesota. On the last day Bob was there, I introduced him in my home town of Mitchell, South Dakota, where he spoke at the Corn Palace. He was *so* tired after the Oregon primary. He didn't do well. But, in the excitement of the campaign, people are more interested in *seeing* the candidate and having him come, and I think the general impression then was good. The crowd was enthusiastic, even though the candidate was fatigued. He told the George Bernard Shaw story three times that night without realizing he was repeating himself!

When I introduced him, I cited a couple of phrases from *Man of La Mancha*—"The Impossible Dream"—because I'd heard that he liked that very much. After the meeting was over, he turned to me and said, "Why did you use that?" I said, "Well, I just thought it was appropriate." He said very seriously, "Do you really think it is impossible?" And I said, "No. I don't think it's impossible. I just think you're willing to try something that's awfully hard, and I wanted the audience to understand that it's worth making the effort—whether you win or lose." And he said, "Well, that's what I think."

He went to bed at the Lawler Hotel in Mitchell, and then we had breakfast together the next morning. He came in after taking his dog for a run nearby, and he looked rested and relaxed. I left Bob at the airport at Mitchell. He walked toward this small airplane to fly to Brookings, South Dakota. I remember that morning being seized with a feeling of sadness. For some reason, he looked so small. Bob, at various times, appeared different sizes to me. Sometimes he seemed like a large man . . . I mean physically. At other times, he seemed very slight, small. It depended, I guess, on the angle of vision. But, as he walked away, he looked like such a frail and small person. I just had such a feeling of sadness as he got on the plane that day.

SHERRYE HENRY, *family friend*

As we went along on the level of the factory tops, you saw the silent men up there on the roofs holding up large, homemade signs made of brown wrapping paper, you know, that they'd stretched out—crackling in the wind, you could *see* as we went by; and they said, OUR CONDO-LENCES, SENATOR KENNEDY. I remember a sign in a small station that really got me, SHALOM, RFK. I loved that! And I remember seeing out in the *real* countryside . . . and wondering how they got that far . . . a group of nuns—maybe four or five—standing by the roadside in the weeds, all together, very proud, with their hands at their sides . . . just standing there. One woman in the middle of them *had* to be the Mother Superior because nobody ever looked so much like one, with a beautiful cherubic face—you know, big fat face—and she stood there with a beatific smile on her face and put her hands up in the air just as the train went by. That got me. And then the group of girls in bridesmaids' dresses. They must have been teenagers—three or four of them in pinks and yellows and greens—with a little cluster of flowers held in their hands, and a little coronet of flowers around their heads. Either straight out of a May Day celebration, or somebody had got married the day before, and they'd dressed back up and came!

JAY PATTON (*nine years old*), *Delaware*

I went down to see Mrs. Jackie Kennedy and the coffin. I saw her on the caboose. She was standing there waving to the people. Three younger boys were with her. I don't know their names. I also saw the coffin; there

275

was some ivy around the rails of the caboose—it wasn't growing there—it was probably plastic.

We had flowers. We got them from Mrs. Lind's backyard to throw on the track just as a little gift like. We threw them after the train left, but then another dummy train came along and went over them. We meant to throw them at the train, but we forgot until after.

I thought he was a nice man. I liked the way he talked and the way he looked. He looked funny, because he's from another state. His hair, the way it was combed, I guess, and his mouth was different from people from Delaware. His hair came in a swirl up at the top. And his mouth. It just didn't look like anybody else's. I liked him. Yes, if I were old enough, I would have voted for him.

ANN BUCHWALD, *family friend*
Ethel asked Andy Williams to go see Rose Kennedy. So Andy did . . . in the car where Bobby lay, and where his sisters and Teddy were. She was waving from the window. She looked at Andy and she told Andy to wave too. She said, "After all, the people came to see. I think they'd like us to wave." Andy was amazed because he was almost afraid to go sit beside her. He thought she would be so silent and uncommunicative and depressed. He sat down beside her, and she was just like a mother. "Start to wave," she said. "Wave."

LORD HARLECH, *former British Ambassador to the United States*
Then all the young children . . . they tended to get restless on such a long journey. I played heads or tails with them with coins, very lengthy games with young Matthew, for something to do. Children as young as that react much more to immediate situations. They understood and were sad when they thought about it, but more immediately, somebody had bumped into them, and therefore up with their fists, and they were rolling about on the floor. A young child is not capable of thinking for long periods about the consequences and the effects because he hasn't got the experience to understand. You feel very sad one moment; the next moment, you're playing a game, and it's just like any other day.

ARTHUR SCHLESINGER, JR., *historian*
One had the sense about John Kennedy that he was the most brilliant and attractive man of the generation. He was always in control of situation, and one never felt protective about him, because he was much

276

stronger and abler and more competent to deal with problems. It may have been because Robert Kennedy was younger than I was; but I had a different feeling about him. Whereas John Kennedy was invulnerable, Robert Kennedy seemed to me deeply vulnerable, very poignant, complicated by the fact that he was so widely and systematically misunderstood. The public impression of him was certainly wrong. Robert Kennedy had an intensity of identification with the powerless, who were the victims and casualties of our society. It was unique in my political experience; I mean it's different from the kind of concern that Franklin Roosevelt had, or that John Kennedy had, or Adlai Stevenson had. I mean any of those three men were naturally appalled by poverty; if they saw it, they saw it as an irrational, unjust, terrible thing, but they were *external* to it; whereas, when Robert Kennedy went to an Indian reservation or saw poor white families in Appalachia, those children became his children. The food they were eating was the food he might be eating; the hovel in which they were living was his. I think he had a completeness of identification that is extremely rare, and that's why he communicated so proudly to the poor and the excluded groups in general —they felt the intensity of his identification.

ADAM WALINSKY, *legislative aide, speechwriter*

Do you know who A. J. Muste was? In 1963, A. J. Muste and a few of his people were engaged in something called the Quebec-Washington-Guantanamo Peace March. They were walking that whole way. Obviously they couldn't walk across the water, so they were going to take a boat from Florida to Cuba. They made it to Florida after six months of walking. Muste was about eighty-four years old, and he walked all that way. The State Department got very, very excited about this—that this fellow was going to defy the travel ban and actually go to Cuba! And who would suggest that Cuban-U.S. relations be improved! So the State Department wanted to enjoin the boat. They would put a court order on the boat that would keep it from leaving, and A. J. Muste's people—if they tried to go out of the harbor, then the Coast Guard would take their boat. But they didn't really have statutory authority; and if they did, it was probably unconstitutional. In any case, they wanted to go ahead with it. And so, one Friday night, the papers were sent to us for review. This fresh-faced attorney—you know, one of those Fordham kids that are always in the Internal Security Division—came up with a whole set of papers. There's an old dictum that when a U.S. attorney brings an injunctive action under the name of the United

States in a case not specifically authorized by statute, he has to have a letter of authorization from the Attorney General. So, we drew up such a letter in the name of the Attorney General, authorizing them to enjoin Muste and his people. And on this Friday night, with the plane waiting and the attorney from the Internal Security Division set to take the papers down, with the White House approving, and the State Department wanting it, everybody wanting it, Norb Schlei, who was Assistant Attorney General in charge of the Office of Legal Counsel, took the piece of paper in for the Attorney General to sign. This was the first he'd heard of it, and so he asked for an explanation. He said, "What am I signing here?" Norb told him. And then Bob said, "Let me get this straight. You mean you want me to sign that piece of paper to tell an eighty-four-year-old man that he can't walk 800 miles?" And he said, "I don't think the security of the United States is going to be endangered by an eighty-four-year-old man. I'm not going to sign that piece of paper." He didn't. His successor later did. That was after John Kennedy had gone from the White House. Bob wasn't the Assistant President any more.

PETER EDELMAN, *legislative aide*

It was such an irony about Robert Kennedy that this fellow whom people thought was brusque, and indeed could be in situations, had this enormous personal quality. I remember his exchange with Bob Coles during the Ribicoff hearings; they hadn't ever met each other, or if they had met, they'd just sort of exchanged hellos. Coles came on talking about children. He and Kennedy had a beautiful exchange about how slum children had a certain vitality and beauty in their faces that well-fixed middle-class children being pushed around in their baby carriages on Fifth Avenue did not have; and how beautiful that was, and how tragic when those faces would change at the age of eight or ten or twelve, as the black children began to sense the oppressiveness in the world around them. Both of them were speaking back and forth, back and forth, both talking about it—a conversation where a kind of a glow came over it, where he transcended himself, and it was a real—in the current vernacular—"happening."

DR. ROBERT COLES, *child psychiatrist*

There was a tentative quality about his body, about the way he moved and the way he talked, which bespeaks a man who has a lot to say but isn't quite sure how to say it; who has a lot stirring in him but

278

doesn't know how to put it into words; who has a lot of emotional things happening to him but isn't one of these glib, articulate, well-psychoanalyzed, well-intellectualized people who always know what to say, who always know where and how to get it across through either the printed or spoken word.

It was a struggle that one felt must have gone on for a long time before his brother was elected President . . . a kind of groping quality that I think was always with him . . . this activated urgent tension within him, a seeking for expression and then finding it in the plight of other tense people . . . namely, poor tense people with whom, I would add, he shares poverties—because they also don't know how to speak. They are struggling for expression, struggling for things that they feel; they don't know how to implement; and they also are strong on emotional things . . . this quality of the heart; this quality of emotion that sometimes is literally ineffable—that defies language, that defies formulation.

CHARLES EVERS, civil-rights leader

He always talked about poverty. He said, "Charles, is poverty really that bad in Mississippi?" I said, "Bobby, words can't express it." He said, "I'm coming down." Just like that.

He and the committee came down in the spring of 1967, and we sat there at night, at the Heidelberg hotel in Jackson, Mississippi, and we talked, and he listened. The next day, he said, "I want to go see it." He went into one of the worst places I've ever seen. There was no ceiling hardly; the floor had holes in it. There was a little stove over in the corner, and a bed that looked like the color of my arm—black as my arm—and it was propped up with some kind of bricks to keep it from falling. The odor was so bad you could hardly keep the nausea down.

Bobby went in with a little child and looked in the kitchen. This lady came out with hardly any clothes on, and we spoke to her, and he told her who he was. She just put her arms out and said, "Thank God."

This little child, must have been about three or four years old, came toddling out of the back room. His tummy was sticking way out just like he was pregnant. Bobby looked down at the child, and then he picked him up and sat down on that dirty bed. He was rubbing the child's stomach. He said, "My God, I didn't know this kind of thing existed. How can a country like this allow it? Maybe they just don't know."

Roaches and rats were all over the floor. We stayed there ten or fifteen minutes, just sat there talking, and then he said, "I'm going back to Washington to do something about this."

The man cared. You could see it in his eyes, and in the expression on his face. When he got really concerned, his hand would quiver. Or, if he was riding in a car, he'd just slump down and sit there and stare.

He called me once from California, and he wanted me to come out there. I said, "You don't need me, Bobby. You got all those other play people."

He said, "What do you mean, the other people?"

"You know, your people."

And then he said, "You're my people."

MICHAEL HARRINGTON, *author*

Cesar Chavez said it when I campaigned with him in California: Robert Kennedy was the only politician who went to Delano in early 1966 during the grape strike. The grape growers in California are an extremely powerful group of people, and traditionally, many of the growers have been conservative Democrats rather than Republicans. Politically speaking, in California at that time, it was probably a stupid thing to do.

PETER EDELMAN

Jack Conway, the labor leader, called me and said, "Walter Reuther and I think it would be a very good idea if your Senator would go out to Delano with the Senate Migratory Labor Subcommittee, which is going to hold hearings out there." Senator Williams of New Jersey was the chairman of the committee—a very nice man, but not particularly well known. Reuther and Conway correctly figured that if they could get Bob Kennedy to go, the hearings would get more attention and maybe a few fireworks would be sparked.

So I went to the Senator and I said, "These fellows want you to go." He said, "Well, would it be a good thing?" I knew almost nothing about the grape strike; I'd read Andy Kopkind's article in *The New Republic*—that's all I knew. So I said, "Well, I think so. I understand it's a tough business." We went back and forth, as we would do on these things, for a couple of days. I would ask him, and then he wouldn't quite answer. Finally, after about three days, he said, "Well, okay. If Walter Reuther and Jack Conway want me to do it, I suppose I'll do it."

We went out to the hearings. I did some research and discovered statistically how bad off the farm workers were. On the plane on the way out, he said, "What am I going out there for? Why am I going?" He always had a way of sort of testing you. So I gave him all the figures on the grape strike, and he didn't say anything. We got to the hearings. We found a tremendous auditorium full of farm workers and growers, and obvious tension, and the story began to unfold. Witnesses would come on and say, Now, working conditions are such and such, and social conditions are such and such. . . . Life is terrible. . . . Here's what the growers have done to us, and here's what the local law-enforcement people have done to us.

The Senator just, well, because that was his temperament . . . he got *turned on* to it. By the second day of the hearings, he was exasperated with the way the local establishment was treating the farm workers. The sheriff from one of the counties testified that he had been making "preventive arrests." The Senator said, "What's that?" He said, "Well, you know, we've gone out and we've seen these people picketing, and we've seen them threatening people from our town. So we arrested them." The Senator said, "Well, they were peaceful. Why did you do anything?" The guy said, "We were afraid there would be a riot." The Senator said, "But they didn't violate any law. How could you do that?" "Well," the sheriff said, "we were just protecting them." "*Protecting* them?" The Senator went back and forth like that. Finally—this was just before the lunch break—the Senator said, "I suggest that during lunchtime, Sheriff, you read the Constitution of the United States." It was an exchange that has become a great legend in the history of the farm workers.

After that, he was clear in his mind; he had seen for himself. Always after that, we helped Cesar Chavez in whatever way we could.

DOLORES HUERTA, *vice president, United Farm Workers Organizing Committee*
Cesar went on the fast early in 1968 because he was afraid that people would turn to violence. That was a very great fear with him.

CESAR CHAVEZ, *president, United Farm Workers Organizing Committee*
Finally, I was convinced that we could end the fast, that it had gone on long enough to put across our ideas on nonviolence. Besides, there was the concern expressed by many, but very strongly by my family.

My father was getting very old and worried. He started worrying after the twentieth day. He went on a fast once for twenty days for health reasons. So he knew that twenty days could be done because he had done it. But after twenty days, he began to worry. He couldn't sleep at night. I guess I couldn't go much longer. I didn't feel like eating, and I felt very weak. My body was weak; let's put it that way. But my spirit was . . . I know I had full control of my senses and everything. So we ended it. The Senator came out.

DOLORES HUERTA

It was absolute bedlam! When we got out of the car, all of the photographers closed in on us, interviewing the Senator. Then he started walking, and I have never experienced a scene like that in my life. People just kept pushing in. He would start shaking hands. Well, he really didn't know who to avoid. I'm sure he walked through three mud puddles, at least. People were coming up to him, and they would grab him and hug him and kiss him on the mouth! And, you know, "*Un gran hombre*"—great man, Kennedy—"*Un gran hombre!*" People would grab him, and his hands were all scratched up. When he sat down in front of me, his hands were all bloodied where people had pulled him.

Well, when we got up to the front to the little circle that had been cleared, we were finally safe. Then the Senator spoke. . . . There was a man standing at the edge of the circle, and he had on blue jeans and a blue-jeans jacket. He had gray hair and gray eyes. He looked like a Caucasian, but he might have been a very light-skinned, you know, Mexican-American. The Senator said, "Who is that man?" I looked at him and I said, "I don't know." So I walked up and addressed him in Spanish and said, "Are you a member of the union?" He turned around and looked at me, and I could tell he didn't understand what I was saying.

After he got through speaking, I was trying to prevent this crush again. So I started singing. I thought I was going to hold back the crowd. I was singing, "We Shall Overcome," in my cracked voice. Just anything to keep people looking at me so they wouldn't converge on the Senator again. But the people on the flank, nevertheless, went in and started crushing him again. Mack Lyons said that when he was escorting the Senator back to the car . . . and again they went through the whole thing of people, you know, trying to get at him and everything . . . the Senator looked at him and he said, "That man is trying to kill me!" I asked Mack, I said, "What did the man look like?" Mack said, "The

282

guy had on a blue jacket and blue pants and gray hair." It must have been the same guy that the Senator saw in the circle.

CESAR CHAVEZ

I was getting the minute-by-minute details . . . he was on his way: he had gotten in at the airport. So, the pressure, the anticipation, was growing. Finally he arrived where I was staying. It was kind of difficult. He was shy in a way. So he shook hands and asked how I was, and I didn't know what to say; so I asked him how *he* was. And then, about that time, there was a moment of silence, because I didn't know what to say and I don't think *he* knew what to say either.

His hands were scratched where people were trying to touch him. Women mostly, I guess, and so his hands were all scratched so you could see the blood. The bread was passed around and they gave him a piece; and he gave me a piece of his. I looked over to my left side, and I saw everybody taking pictures except ABC. They had the ABC-TV crew trapped. Finally ABC broke away and got set up, and a fellow comes to him and says, "Senator, this is perhaps the most ridiculous remark I've ever made in all my life. Would you mind giving Cesar another piece of bread so we can get a picture." The Senator said, "No. In fact, he should have a lot of bread now." So he gave me another piece of bread.

DOLORES HUERTA

Jim Drake had pinned a little *Huelga* eagle button on his lapel, you know. He said, "Here, Senator, you want one of these. Here." He was going over his speech and asking us to look it over; he was practicing his Bostonian Spanish on us. When he actually started giving the speech, he departed from it completely, and it was very difficult to translate. I really didn't do a very good job of translation, I'm afraid. To begin with, he started speaking in Spanish and I, for one—there were about 10,000 people there that day—didn't know what he was saying, really.

CESAR CHAVEZ

I wasn't that weak. I knew what was going on. He started to speak, and he brought the house down . . . well, you can imagine Spanish with a Boston accent! He knew, and so he looked down where I was sitting, and he says, "Am I murdering the language?" I said, "No. Go ahead." It was a great day.

DOLORES HUERTA

He was such an unreal person to me. He just didn't seem like a human person. Let me show you how this is. I think other people kind of thought this way. When Cesar and Kennedy were in the Mass, you know, we had cold drinking water for Cesar. Nobody brought any water to the Senator. Who would think that he'd get thirsty? It's almost like this thing about him having to go to the bathroom. One time, the first time he came out, he had to go to the bathroom. And nobody . . . It hadn't occurred to any of us that this man would *have* to go to the bathroom. We couldn't find a key to the bathroom. We looked all over: the bathroom in the gas station was locked; and we ran over to the clinic and the bathroom in the clinic was locked. So what do we do with the Senator? He had to go to the bathroom. So we took him over to Jim Drake's house so he could go to the bathroom at Jim Drake's. Jim Drake has a big sign in his bathroom, ROBERT KENNEDY WENT TO THE BATHROOM HERE.

We must have puzzled him at times. Once we came to New York City to picket, but some of our people were arrested. The Senator was over at the Puerto Rican Commonwealth building. We went over there to see him. I said, "Senator, some of our people are in jail." He said, "Every time I see you, you have people in jail! They're either in jail in California, they're in San Francisco or Texas." I said, "Well, now they're in jail in New York."

MICHAEL NOVAK, *educator*

The overwhelming feeling I had about Robert Kennedy was that he was a very fragile, vulnerable person who was absolutely certain that he was going to die. I just couldn't escape the feeling in his eyes. I began all my talks in Oregon and California with that. I said, "You people just won't understand Robert Kennedy unless you understand that he doesn't know if he's going to live tomorrow. And therefore, he's got to do it today. If you think he's ruthless, you're crazy! He's a man who feels anything but ruthless. He feels positively trapped, and he's just got to act because he can't care about the consequences." I would tell them, "Unless you understand that, you won't understand the rest. If you do understand it, you'll see how bad the image of him in the press is, and how it fails to explain things, such as his going out to Cesar Chavez when there weren't enough Mexican-American votes to counter those on the other side. Or going to the Indians. To be elected by the American Indians? It doesn't make sense. And the reason the man has to do

284

that is he just doesn't have too much time, and he just wants to do what he can do."

SENATOR GEORGE McGOVERN

He went to a hearing on the Pine Ridge Indian Reservation and just drew an enormous crowd! I've never seen so many Indian voters assembled in one place as he drew. In the course of that hearing . . . although we were due at Rapid City for a very large street rally that evening . . . I mentioned to him that perhaps the most meaningful monument to the Indians of the Great Plains was a monument at Wounded Knee, which marked the massacre out there in retaliation for what happened to Custer. The U.S. Seventh Cavalry really got even with the Indians at Wounded Knee and killed a large number of Indians—mostly women and children. It's far and away the most meaningful symbol or monument that the Indians of the Great Plains have.

I just happened to mention that to him, and he said, "Well, I'd like to go out there." I said, "Gosh, Bob, we can't do that. We're due at Rapid City." He said, "Let's cut the hearing short." So we brought the hearing to an end, and he jumped in the car and drove thirty miles out to this site and walked around, looked at it, and then left for Rapid City. We were an hour late to catch a crowd of 5,000 people standing out in the rain in Rapid City! But he felt very good about seeing the monument, and I'm sure that the Indians caught the significance of it and the sensitivity that he demonstrated. We just went out by ourselves. It's a very simple, concrete slab with a small obelisk on it, and a little church out on the plains. It's a very desolate area. It's a mass grave, you know, maybe fifty feet long with a list of the names of the people who died—over a hundred.

The Indians had a special response to him that I never detected with any other politician. They're afraid of people who talk too fast. Hubert Humphrey asked me one time if I knew why the Indians didn't like him; and I *did* know. In the first place, they're suspicious of white people . . . and especially people who talk fast. I told him, "You're so eloquent and so articulate that they're afraid that you're going to say something that they don't properly evaluate or don't have a chance to counter. You talk faster than they're willing to think." I think that was his problem; whereas Bobby talked to them very quietly, and he was not the most fluent person in the world. His sentences were frequently broken and punctuated by "ands" and "ahs," and I think that they responded to that; they felt that he was really trying to communicate and not just make a speech. Also he had the kind of lean, lined face that you frequently see with Indians; and he was always heavily tanned, so he looked something like an Indian.

LaDONNA HARRIS (*Mrs. Fred Harris*)
Ethel invited me for lunch one day and told the children that I was an Indian; I remember Kerry—she was about eight then—sitting there goggle-eyed all through luncheon and then afterwards she said, "Mrs. Harris, what's it like living in a tepee?" I said, "Oh, Kerry, we don't live in tepees in Oklahoma." Ethel said, "Don't disillusion her." I said, "But I don't want her to grow up in ignorance." So I went into this lengthy detail about how progressive we were, how we lived in houses like everyone else. I thought I'd done really a great job. Afterwards, down at the pool, Kerry came by and she said, "Mrs. Harris, can you shoot a bow and arrow?" So I don't think I really did very well about educating them.

FRED DUTTON, *campaign aide*
We went to Indian reservations. In Arizona, in late March, we flew in two little planes one black night to a remote landing strip with almost no airstrip lights. We saw Indians all over the country—some in fancy headdresses, but all of them in terrible poverty. In Indian schools and in their huts. In their tribal centers and once, in South Dakota, in a cemetery one terribly cold afternoon after the sun had gone down.

He told city crowds that on some reservations the unemployment was up to eighty per cent and ninety per cent. Many young Indians are taken away from their parents and shipped a thousand miles to an Indian boarding school, where it's sometimes almost like an inmate arrangement. He would remind people in Portland and New York and elsewhere that the highest cause of death among Indian teenagers on reservations is suicide because of all the hopelessness. Bob was always very serious about this problem—so serious that once his close friend, columnist Jimmy Breslin, said, "Well, the only reason, I guess, that Jim Thorpe ever lived to become a great athlete is that the rope broke." Bob just looked at him in that distant, cold-blue way he had sometimes.

At one point I told him I thought he was spending much too much time on Indians, that they had no votes; I agreed it was an important problem, but he could do more after he was elected. Right now—I told him—we're in a campaign, and he should knock off the Injuns. He wrote me back a note, which I kept. It's in longhand on yellow paper

We were using legal tablets. He wrote, "Those of you who think you're running my campaign don't love Indians the way I do. You're a bunch of bastards."

DICK TUCK, *campaign aide*

When Bobby met the guy who was running this Dakota school, he said, "Do you have any books here that say anything about the Indian culture, anything in your library?" The schoolmaster said, "Oh, yes, we have that." Bobby said, "Well, where are they? Could I see them?" He said, "Well . . ." Finally, Bobby forced the guy down to the library, and they pulled out a book, which was the history of the Cherokees. The first chapter had them scalping the whites. So he asked the director of the Indian school, "Do you have anything about the Indian *history?*" He said, "They haven't any history." Bobby said, "Do you have anything about the Indian culture?" He said, "They have no culture." And Bob was incensed—well, not incensed; he was upset—well, not even upset; he was *mad.*

LUCY JARVIS, *television producer*

These are the kinds of things that go through your mind when you're sitting on that train and wondering, Am I really sitting on this train? Is this man dead? This man, whom I shared so many laughs with and so many problems and situations? This man, who used to badger me— "Why don't you do a television program on the American Indians? It's all very glamorous to go to Russia and do a program on the history of the Kremlin, but what we really need to know more about is our own history. Why don't you do something about the American Indian?"

You bet, I'm going to. If I don't do anything else in my lifetime . . . these are the promises I made Bobby.

STEVE RITNER, *college student, Delaware*

To the crowd where I was on the far end, the train seemed like a magnet pulling people toward it. You sort of walked after it in a daze, and you were pulled toward the train like you wanted to follow it all the way to Washington. A lot of people did this, including myself. We started to walk on the tracks. It was just something pulling; I don't know what it was.

JOHN KENNETH GALBRAITH, *economist*

I was struck by the way in which in the last ten years, as a result of the airplane, one has been divorced from the American city. The train going to Washington goes through the oldest and most decrepit and most dilapidated parts of Newark and New Brunswick and Baltimore, and particularly the area just south of Philadelphia—Chester and Wilmington. But one saw the squalor. I remember seeing at one point when we slowed down, a primary school—I think it was in Chester—and wondering if any kids could actually go to this ancient, decrepit, squalid building with its asphalt playing ground, very small, and nothing really very much in it except two half-drunken basketball posts with hoops.

MARK GOLDFUS, *college student, Delaware*

Right behind me as we waited for the train was a young group of Negroes. They were talking about the Olympic Track Team and who's the fastest. That's generally how the conversation went. It wasn't a big

288

memorial to Kennedy. Delaware was graduating the next day; kids were talking about grades and such. I saw the train. There was a little murmur of excitement, and everybody shut up. It looked like any other train. They were in the dining car, and they were drinking sodas or whatever; walking around; looking at us; and there was a porter in one of the dining cars hanging out, waving at everybody. Everybody was waving back to him. Until you got to the last car, you didn't realize what kind of train it was. I think that's why there was some of the shock—because of the contrast.

DR. LEONARD DUHL, *psychiatrist*
Everybody was uncomfortable with everybody else's way of grief. The train was speeding up and then slowing down—"Speeding up to get there on time," as somebody said. But then somebody else said, "On time for what? Let the people feel it. Where the hell are you going?" These were some of the discussions I heard between Mankiewicz and some of the advance men. They were arguing as to whether the train should speed up or slow down. And Frank kept saying, "God damn it. Slow it!" Somebody else would say, efficiently, "Get it there on time. There are buses waiting!"

IVANHOE DONALDSON, *fellow, Institute for Policy Studies*
We just went back, you know, and we stood around the coffin for a while. I felt better there. You know, I wasn't putting on any airs for anybody. Ethel Kennedy was sitting beside the coffin. Her eyes were closed. She didn't open them the whole time we were in there. She had one hand on the coffin. I thought her face was very strained. You know, the Kennedys have this image of being so strong. Well, they *are* in a way, I guess, for the public's benefit. They're good people in their own way. But it was like she was drawing strength, you know—the last strength she could draw. There was some kind of mysticism between her and her husband at that point.

Well, anyway, we were there for a little while. It was maybe an hour and a half out of Washington then. The train was quietly clanking along at about fifteen miles an hour. When we came out, here was this little guy, hanging out from a train window speaking over a walkie-talkie. "Say, there. Can we pick it up five more miles an hour? What's our speed?" He was hanging out of the last coach of the train, looking way up towards the front. Someone told me it was Jerry Bruno. He was the advance man. I said, "What's wrong?" He said, "Bad scene."

Obviously, Jerry couldn't do a damn thing about that train, but he was going to advance it anyway. The engineer kept telling him he couldn't move any faster, there were people all over the tracks. Bruno would tell him to slow down; then he would tell him to pick it up. The train went the same pace whatever he said . . . but there he was. Maybe that's the way he held himself together. He was doing his job. He was advancing his boss to the end, all the way home. . . .

RONNIE ELDRIDGE, *political adviser*

On the train Milly Jeffries introduced me to Walter Reuther. When I was a child, he was a very dashing, youngish labor guy, and I remember so well when he was shot. I remember the pictures of the brick house and everything. We sat down and talked, and I asked him how long ago it was that he was shot. He said it was twenty years . . . practically the same season; and he then went through the problems and, of course, the shock that it was to be shot, although he had sort of expected it. He talked about how his people had tried to eliminate such possibilities in the future, and the heavy security that was placed around him: when they came to get him out of the hospital, they came in a very heavily armored car, a grotesque-looking car, which he just had fits about; he rode in it for about three days, and then that was the end of that. But he said that every time he went to the window to pull the shades down or stand in the window, he just couldn't do it normally; he learned to live within the house in a different kind of way.

KATE HADDAD (*Mrs. William Haddad*)

We had come home from school and Mommy said that my grandfather FDR had died. I remember fleeing to my room and crying—probably more because I thought that was what you were supposed to do. But the big thing I remember was that it meant no Secret Service! It meant they were out of our lives. And you know, within a half an hour, all the Secret Service were gone! They had *lived* with us. We could never go and spend a weekend with another child, never take a walk, without them. They took us to school. People said, "Is that your father?" We *died* of embarrassment to think that anybody thought a Secret Service man was our father! They were with us every moment of our days and nights from the time he was President. And, within a half an hour, they were cleared out and gone. That's the big thing it meant to me—his dying. Isn't that pathetic? Well, I was too young—

only eight at the time—and I didn't really have any kind of personal relationship with him.

ALICE ROOSEVELT LONGWORTH (Mrs. Nicholas Longworth)

The Secret Service always were around, but they were not an enormous protection for anyone. T.R. always had one; when he took what he called "scrambles" in the park . . . it had to be a fairly vigorous Secret Service man to keep up. My father carried a derringer, I think. We never paid much attention to it. There were guns around, but we were taught to be careful . . . never to point a gun . . . not even to point a *toy* gun. We had a healthy respect for guns.

My father was running for the presidency when he was shot. He wouldn't have had Secret Service anyway. He always felt that he could get the man with his derringer if he had to. But he didn't have a chance that time. He just said, "Don't." He carried the bullet in him to the end.

WILLIAM WALTON, *artist, family friend*

It never really came up, but there was no question that Bobby thought of it. We all thought of it when Jack was alive. One evening as we stood in front of the White House, Jackie said, "What targets we are." Jack had said it once when we were in an airfield, and we were isolated, and there were throngs way out around us. He looked around and said, "Boy! Aren't we targets!" Every leading American politician has to think about it. Unfortunately, it isn't new. Assassination is as old a technique as anything, and it is a thread through American history. Both Roosevelts were shot at: Teddy was hit, FDR was just barely missed.

FRED DUTTON, *campaign aide*

We had reports several times of people with guns. Once, in Lansing, Michigan, there was a report somebody was on a rooftop with a gun across the street. The local police went into action promptly. I went in the bedroom where Bob was, and I didn't say anything to him because we always tried to be as low-key as we could. I pulled the blinds shut, but Bob knew immediately what was going on. He said, "I don't want that. Don't do that. I'm not going to start ducking or run." He was changing his shirt to go down to a meeting.

Bill Barry, his bodyguard, had Bob's car put in the basement so we could get out through a garage exit and minimize his exposure to the crowds. After the meeting, Barry and I went down with him in the elevator to the basement, where the chief of police and all the local dignitaries were. Normally we would have gotten off in the lobby and walked through the crowd and gotten in the car. When Bob saw what was going on, he was furious. He said that he was not going to be sealed off; he wasn't going to have any damn foolishness like this. Barry took it, and I sort of shrunk. The chief of police didn't know what to make of it. We got in the car and went tearing up the exit. But when we got out in front of the hotel, Bob said, "Stop the car." And he got out and shook hands. He was not going to be isolated. This was important to him. Barry did a tremendously conscientious and thorough job. I thought Bob used reasonable prudence. And the truth of the matter is, when it finally happened, it was in a narrow back corridor. Had he gone through the crowd that night, as we almost always did, you could argue that it would never have happened. The one time when he was taken away from people, the tragedy occurred.

COURTNEY EVANS, *former assistant director of the FBI*
He used to have a lot of protection at times, but he didn't know about it. Plainclothesmen any place where I thought there might be an incident. Of course he got sharper after a while, and he began to recognize some of these people. He'd joke about it, and he would try to identify our automobiles, our people. He said, "Oh, I can always tell FBI agents because they wear hats." He'd see them walking into the Justice Building, and most of them had hats on, so he thought they always wore hats.

JOHN J. LINDSAY, *correspondent*
Bill Barry, the person responsible for Bob's security, was one of the hardest-working persons on that campaign. He was the one I felt sorriest for when this thing was all over—because it was an impossible duty. All he could do was protect him from personal injury, like rock throwing, but it was not possible to protect him from what ultimately happened. There wasn't a single person in the outfit that didn't know that . . . even Bill knew it. They had a birthday party on board the flight for him, and they put up balloons all over the place, and Ethel took charge of the whole thing; and somebody in the party, one of the television guys, inadvertently burst one of the balloons, and Bob

jumped instinctively. He knew . . . he knew . . . that this kind of thing could happen. It's a dreadful thing to live with, but the Kennedys have always lived with it . . . this is the thing that's always fascinating. This kind of fear would shatter me. I'd become paranoid about it. But these people don't do that.

I guess it was Jimmy Breslin who asked the question, "Do you think this guy has the stuff to go all the way?" And I said, "Yes, of course, he has the stuff to go all the way, but he's not going to go all the way. The reason is that somebody is going to shoot him. I know it and you know it, just as sure as we are sitting here—somebody is going to shoot him. He's out there now waiting for him."

There was a sort of stunned silence around the table, and then, one by one, each of us agreed. This was not only what each of us was thinking, but also what Bob was thinking, and we saw evidence of it as time went on during the campaign . . . not fear, but some reaction, you know, to situations that might have produced that very thing that finally happened. It's just that we all felt that it was in the cards. Bob sensed it all the way through and . . . this is one of the reasons why he always fought upstream, so to speak, rather than floating with the tide . . . get it done, because you only have a short time to do as much as you can while you have the chance.

SENATOR GEORGE McGOVERN

He did talk so much, you know, in a kind of a fatalistic way in the closing months of his life. I felt that he was preoccupied at various times with the divisiveness in our society and with the hatred, and he was using those phrases . . . there was one phrase he used: "To tame the savageness of man and make gentle the life of the world." It seemed to me that that quality of his speeches in the last year or so of his life was a kind of a forecast of the way violence could turn, even on some of the brightest and most attractive of our citizens.

PIERRE SALINGER, *campaign aide*

I'd had lunch with Romain Gary about two weeks earlier at Paul Ziffren's house, and he had said to me, "Your candidate's going to get killed." I said that certainly he was in danger, but that it was impossible to run for President and not be surrounded by people all the time. If you are going to be an effective candidate for President, you have to take some hazard in life. Apparently, he repeated that to Bob that day, that somebody was going to try to kill him. I don't think he said, You're going to be killed. He said, "Somebody is going to try to kill you." Romain Gary felt that Kennedy was a man who was a symbol of change. Anybody who wants to change society or life has always got to be a target. People are afraid of change. I remember during the Indiana primary, I went to a cocktail party being given by the Editors Association. All the local weekly editors from the state of Indiana were there. One of them, a woman, cornered me and said, "I'm really against your candidate." I asked why. She said, "He keeps talking about a new America, and I like the one we've got."

ARTHUR SCHLESINGER, JR., *historian*
Early in the winter I was having dinner with Jackie, and I told her how important I thought it was for Bobby to run. She listened very quietly. Then she said, "I hope Bobby never becomes President of the United States." I said, "Why?" She said, "If he becomes President, they'll do to him what they did to Jack."

JOHN STEWART, *campaign aide*
"Man was not made for safe havens," he said. "If it's going to happen, it's going to happen." The feeling of the possibility of catastrophe was always there, but it was always laughed at. He would ride in the back of a convertible at break-neck speed in thirty-two-degree weather—which happened in South Dakota. My God, we went from Omaha, where it was sunny and warm, and we got to an outdoor rally, and it was just above freezing. A freak cold snap. He just would leap in the middle of crowds. Walk right in the middle of these rednecks, almost laughing in their faces—not, you know, jeering at them, but *feeding* off this danger.

CHARLES QUINN, *television correspondent*
One night on the plane—it was a long flight, I think from Omaha to Washington—Joe Mohbat and I were talking to him alone with Freckles. We were talking about everything that particular night. One of the things Joe Mohbat asked him was, "Have you ever considered the possibility of getting assassinated?" It had been on our minds because he was such a controversial figure; he engendered almost as much hatred as he did love. He said, yes, he thought about it. But he wasn't going to change his campaign; he was going to continue to go out and meet people and let them touch him and pummel him and push him around, and he wanted to get as close to them as possible because that was his style. He felt that there was something about it that was a little

294

different than . . . political gimmickry or pragmatism. The touching of Kennedy and the pulling and the pushing and the screaming and all that frenzy and turmoil and turbulence that used to surround him . . . had a great symbolic meaning. He was not only there, saying, "I'm here because I want to help you." But he was also there to let them touch him so that there was a reaching out . . . so that they really could feel physically—not only just emotionally—that here was a guy who was interested in them. He knew that that was *part* of it, and he knew that he got a lot of publicity and attention by having all this wild hysteria swirling around him to the point of physical danger—not only to himself— but to people who were there! A lot of people were crushed and fainted and got hurt; and we had some close calls in the motorcade when little kids fell under cars. It was hairy. And, of course, he got pulled out of a car and chipped a tooth; and he had shoes stolen from him, cuff links. I have a vivid figure of a lady grabbing him by the tie and pulling him down by the neck; his little head bobbing up and down.

Anyway, getting back to this conversation, he said he had thought about the danger a lot. But then his eyes got that faraway look—kind of glassy, way off in the distance—and he said, "You know, if I'm ever elected President, I'm never going to ride in one of those bubble-top cars." Then suddenly he heaved himself up, hitched his pants up by the belt, and went up front to his seat.

WILLIAM WALTON, *artist, family friend*

When the train left Penn Station, we only knew where the burial service was going to be and what the music would be; but no other decision had been made about what priests would participate and in what order, or what would be said. So when I got on the train, the first people I went looking for were anyone in the church—high in the church. I was overjoyed to find Archbishop Hannan, of New Orleans, because he was an old friend, and a Kennedy friend as well—a man of great calm, wisdom, and highly articulate. He preached a beautiful eulogy at the President's funeral. So I immediately sat down with the Archbishop, and we realized that our first problem was Cardinal Cushing. He was inclined to run on like a babbling brook, given the opportunity, forever. The Archbishop said he thought the easiest way would be for Cardinal Cushing to have the very first part of the service. He couldn't go on forever with his colleagues waiting to pray and read and so forth. And we agreed that he would be first; then we suddenly realized that instead of one Cardinal, which we had at the President's funeral, this time we had two. We had Cardinal O'Boyle, who had been appointed a Cardinal in Washington, and, of course, Cushing. Then it actually turned out that Arlington was the turf of a *third* man because it was in Virginia. Anyway, we discussed all this at great length and finally decided that we were going to leave it entirely in Archbishop Hannan's hands: he would get the two Cardinals together on the train, and they would decide what to do about the third Cardinal, and the lot of them between them would put together a small service.

DUN GIFFORD, *campaign aide*

I went to the very back of the train and stood by the casket for a while. And, you know, I just got caught up in it again. Adam Walinsky said to me: "You know, I think we're going to get there after dark." I said, "Yeah. I think we are too." He said, "You know, we ought to have candles." I said, "I think you're absolutely right!" Absolutely right! So, I went and I found McNamara. I said, "We've got to have candles." He said, "You're absolutely right." So, we called from the train, and somehow, on a Saturday afternoon, found millions of candles! You just got caught up in it.

WILLIAM WALTON

Reverend Abernathy was having trouble with his followers in Resurrection City. One of his problems was trying to talk to his principal lieutenant, Hosea Williams, in Washington. We were going under high-power lines, and it would interfere with the phone connection terribly. For about fifteen minutes, Nick Katzenbach and the Reverend Abernathy were together in a tiny unventilated phone booth talking to Hosea Williams; you could hear the entire conversation outside because he was talking at the top of his lungs, saying: "Hosea! Hosea! I tell you they are *not* going to join the procession. We will bus a group of them across the river." He kept shouting, "I'm calling you from the train!" He couldn't understand the word "train." He said, "I'm calling you from the T-R-A-I-N." Hosea apparently didn't get the idea that it was possible to telephone from a train. This conversation took at least fifteen minutes. Nick Katzenbach emerged *absolutely limp* and bathed in sweat from being in there with Abernathy.

ALFRED FITT, *Assistant Secretary of Defense*

Mrs. Mellon arrived with her husband about 4:00 with her staff of gardeners to arrange the flowers on the hillside. She announced about half an hour later that her husband needed a drink, so she was taking him home. I must have looked desperate at the time because when they returned about 5:00, they had a picnic basket for me—with a choice of gin and bourbon, and so on. I sat in their car and had a drink, which came in very much handy at the time. And which was very thoughtful. Then at 5:20, a call came from the funeral train that the family would like torches at the gravesite. I thought how in the devil are we going to get torches at 5:20 on a Saturday afternoon in June here in Washington.

Well, we never *did* find torches, though people were dispatched all over the place to try to get them. Then, at about 7:00, somebody called from the train. Now the family wanted *candles* for everybody. I think Tom Powers took the call at what we call the guard shack. He's a lawyer here in Washington who used to be with Katzenbach in the Justice Department. So we started a search for candles. I remembered there had been candlelight ceremonies at some point during the year at the Custis Lee mansion. So we had them ransack the mansion, and they turned up thirty-two candles, which were sixteen inches long. I was not very optimistic on this candle business, so I had them cut the thirty-two candles in two. That immediately doubled the supply of candles. I just wasn't sure what we were going to be able to do in the way of candles. The people in the Pentagon turned up about 400 candles at the post exchange at Fort Myer. That still wasn't enough. By this time, it was about 8:00. I told them, "Well, Catholic churches around here must have candles—see what you can do with them." I don't know how many they called. I think the first place they called is where we wound up getting the most candles—it was St. Matthew's, in the District. They had 1,100 candles, which they turned over to us. Bob Jordan, who's the general counsel of the Army, made a wild dash across town, which involved getting through the cordon, which by that time prevented any easy movement from this side of the river to St. Matthew's. He got the candles and came tearing back to the cemetery. We had the candles about 9:00. I had them distributed among the people, and saved about 200 or so for the people in the funeral cavalcade. By then, there really wasn't anything more to do except wait until the train arrived.

JESSE UNRUH, *Speaker of the California Assembly*

He was a much better campaigner the week after the Oregon primary than before. He seemed to be surer of himself; he seemed to have more tolerance and understanding. We felt reasonably sure that he would take the New York primary without any great difficulty. The California win coupled with the South Dakota win, which was outstanding, all this would promulgate a push that would attract the Mayor Daleys and the other big-city delegation leaders who were sitting relatively uncommitted up to that point. I also felt that with the deterioration of the Vice-President in the polls, the dragging on of the peace talks . . . I think we would have had a near stampede going by the time we got to Chicago.

DICK TUCK, *campaign aide*

The campaign began to get rough. Eugene McCarthy even attacked *me* in California. "Can you imagine an Administration," he said, "that has Jesse Unruh as the Appointments Secretary of the White House and Dick Tuck dancing on the White House lawn?" I saw Gene and I said, "I thought we were friends. I've always spoken well of you." He said, "Dick, how about bribing the cocktail waitresses?" It turned out that there was a story out of Oregon that Pierre Salinger and I had bribed the cocktail waitresses at the Benson Hotel to listen in on the conversations of newspapermen, and so forth. I can't think of more worthless reports than you would get from cocktail waitresses overhearing conversations in a bar frequented by campaign workers and newspapermen. I don't know where he got the story, but he apparently believed it. He said, "That's like breaking the seal of the confessional." I didn't know what he was talking about. I said, "Well, you know more about breaking the seal of the confessional than I would."

JOHN J. LINDSAY, *correspondent*

Kennedy got on the plane. They had taken his tie off, his cuff links were gone, and his shirt . . . it adhered to his chest; and he was limping. As he went by my seat, he put his foot up on the chair, on the arm of the chair, and there was no shoe on it. They had stolen his shoe. He said, "Don't tell me people in this country don't love me." And then in that way of deprecating himself, he said, "On the other hand, perhaps all they wanted was a shoe."

JOHN STEWART, *campaign aide*

There was a little boy riding alongside the train on a bicycle, and Bobby yelled out, "Don't ever run for President!" But the word "President" was just a stammer.

Aside from the people who didn't like him, I think the great dangers were from the people who liked him too *much*. The Mexican-American section, my God! There was just a swarm of people, you know, all over the car and all over the press bus. This little Mexican kid hung on the side and poked his head in the press-bus window and shouted to him, "Remember my name, Ernesto Juarez!" and then he jumped off. It was something like out of *Viva Zapata*.

FRED DUTTON, *campaign aide*

In Los Angeles, Bob had *both* shoes taken. The L.A. *Times* found out who the boy was. He was a fifteen- or sixteen-year-old Mexican-American. He said that he was running after the car. The crowd kept trying to shake Bob's hand, and he tried too, and he couldn't quite get to him. After he'd chased the car about three blocks, he looked and there was Senator Kennedy's foot up in the air. He thought, "I'll just take his shoe, like that woman." Then he said, "I took one shoe. So why not two?" The next day, he wore the shoes to his high school, and he said in the newspaper interview, "I'm going to wear them to the senior prom this year, and then I'm going to have them bronzed."

JOHN STEWART

We would be out on the back platform to sing a song as the train pulled into the stations along the San Joaquin Valley . . . because there we were on the back of the train, and there would be no people at all, the tracks stretching back. Then all of a sudden, the train would pull into the station. The people were there—two thousand people surrounding the back of the train, yelling and screaming. We would be standing there with him; then the train would pull away. The people would recede in the distance, and then there'd just be the sound of the wheels on the track; and he would stay out there, looking back.

DANIEL P. MOYNIHAN, *director, Joint Center for Urban Studies*

By this time a lot of people had gone out to California to help. I went out in early May and went through a series of endless cocktail parties in Los Angeles, endless rides along the freeway to endless cocktail parties at either end. Then I went up to San Francisco and spoke up in that part of the world generally. I spoke on the steps of Sproul Hall, the famous plaza there at Berkeley, which is an experience you wouldn't want to have more than once. The students were bitterly anti-Kennedy—nobody was for him, everyone was against him. I came off all right, mostly by the process of being fairly open with the kids, being smart . . . I'm as smart as they are, and I *know* more, so you can come off moderately well. I mean, they would ask me, "Would Kennedy be in this race had McCarthy not won in New Hampshire?" And, while your instinct would be to say, Well, McCarthy didn't win in New Hampshire, my sense at the time said to me to look the man in the eye and say, "No."

Well, they understood that, they accepted that much better than the bullshit.

GEORGE PLIMPTON, *author*

They pulled out every stop in the California campaign—I mean everyone knew it had to be pulled off or the Senator was finished. They had a number of teams criss-crossing the state talking at neighborhood coffee klatches. One evening Larry Rivers, the artist, and I talked to an artistic gathering in a Los Angeles gallery. Larry was in a weird mood. He would take issue with anyone who spoke from the floor—many of whom were Kennedy supporters. I mean someone would get up and say, "I think we ought to work for Kennedy because he'll straighten out the *divisive* [which was the big word in the campaign] aspects in the society," something like that, and Larry Rivers would interrupt, "Hell, no!" and he'd begin arguing. Everyone was awfully puzzled.

But I particularly remember the team I was on with Roger Hilsman, Michael Forrestal, and Peter Duchin. What Peter and I contributed was suspect, for sure, but with Hilsman, who had been a high official with the Kennedys, and Forrestal, one of the architects of JFK's Vietnam policy, it was a fairly heavy-powered group. We would descend on a household in, say, Orange County, where we would be met by a nervous housewife who would immediately apologize for not having had much success getting the neighborhood stirred up. "We expect some people to turn up, but I don't know," she'd say, and we'd troop into her living room, where some fold-up chairs were lined up. I think the Kennedy headquarters supplied the chairs. They also supplied a recipe for a fruit punch that was invariably waiting for us in a big bowl. We would sip the punch for a while, and then the hostess, usually in a bright print dress, would wring her hands and say, "Well, I don't know."

So the program would begin. Very often our crowd outnumbered the neighborhood people sitting in the fold-up chairs. Peter and I would mumble something, four or five minutes apiece, but what was really high-powered and marvelous stuff to listen to was what Forrestal and Hilsman had to offer—which they did with all the intensity of addressing an auditorium of political science majors. Michael talked about the cities, Roger about foreign policy. They were both grand—persuasive, wonderfully informed—and of course all of this was for the benefit of five or six people sitting uncomfortably in these fold-up chairs with an empty fruit-punch glass on their knees. The program lasted about an hour. Then we would move on to the next coffee klatch. Just as we'd go out the door, a Kennedy man who was a movie projectionist would arrive to show a half-hour campaign film on the Senator. He was a very tall young man with a glazed look—I mean he'd probably seen that film a hundred times or so. When Hilsman would answer the last question from our little audience, he'd be there in the door with his equipment—looking to where to plug it in. He was always a half-hour behind us.

So these people got an hour and a half of a barrage that seemed awfully potent to me. But it was all so futile. It seemed such a waste of time and energy. We did so many of these, driving endlessly from dawn to dusk across California. We used to talk about it going from one place to another. We could only hope that the same sort of nonsense was going on in the other camp.

ANDREAS TEUBER, *campaign aide to Senator Eugene McCarthy*
At that time Eugene McCarthy was not using any of the speeches that were written for him. The only hope was really to slip him maybe a paragraph that he *might* use; then he used to put a paragraph *before* that paragraph and a paragraph *after* that paragraph, which usually completely nullified what you had done.

After the speech, there would be a question-and-answer period, and he'd say something in it that was so controversial that *that* got reported in all the newspapers, and the whole speech that had been prepared was just pushed into the background. For example, that happened in Corvallis, Oregon, at the University. In the question-and-answer period, it was going so well and people were responding to him beautifully. He was full of the whole experience. Students were there, basically intellectuals, and he said to them: "You know, I want you to bear in mind when you go to the polls on Tuesday that the opinion polls have shown that the more intelligent people have been voting for me and the less intelligent for Bobby. Anyway, I want you to bear that in mind." Of course, that very night Salinger and other Kennedy people met in a special rump session to decide: Do we run this as an ad, or not? The decision was made, yes, run it as an ad. It quoted this, and then at the bottom it said: "Do you consider this an insult? We do." This ran the last three days right up to the day of the primary. There was nothing we could do. McCarthy *had* said it! We didn't know how to change that.

Robert Lowell and a group of other people were around McCarthy a lot, a group we nicknamed "the astrologers." We saw them as a little ring that somebody had to penetrate in order to get through to McCarthy.

They were Shana Alexander, Mary McGrory, Robert Lowell, and two media people from Minnesota that McCarthy had brought with him: Bill and Mrs. Nee, who we had nicknamed Ma and Pa Kettle. Ma Kettle —Mrs. Nee—always made up McCarthy for his TV appearances . . . and she would talk to him *incessantly* while she made him up. Her big thing was naturalness. And this, of course, became a running feud in the campaign later, particularly between Dick Goodwin, when he was working for Gene before his shift to Kennedy, and the Minnesota people, who liked the idea of the rather natural, sort of homespun McCarthy image. Goodwin tended to go for something with content.

We decided it would be good to run some television specials for half an hour on Friday nights. I remember Dick Goodwin was going to put them together himself. We thought we'd put together twenty minutes from a selection of tapes that had been taken of his speeches around the country. The last ten minutes would be McCarthy addressing the nation. The taping was on a Wednesday morning right after we were in Pittsburgh, delegate hunting. Jeremy Larner, one of the speechwriters, flew in from New York and had actually typed out something for McCarthy to do in those ten minutes. McCarthy read it, it was only four pages, and he liked it. This was very rare for McCarthy. Actually, he liked something! He said, "Put it on the Teleprompter." There wasn't much time, and he was late, and he only had time to do two takes. The Teleprompter guy was turning the cards much too fast; McCarthy himself knew it, and he thought it was rather funny how fast the cards were going. His head was going back and forth as if he were watching a ping-pong match or something. He thought it was rather humorous, but he didn't say anything. Goodwin was still pretty much in awe of McCarthy at that time, and didn't say, "Look. We've got to do that again. That was dreadful!" He couldn't say that.

For the second tape we decided to do it just off the cuff. So he did some extemporaneous sort of speech. Well, then the argument came later in the week: Which do you use? Bill Nee and Art Michaelson argued, "Well, we'll use the second one. He *looks* better." And it was true: he looked great. "But in the first one," Goodwin argued, "he's *saying* something." The argument got to the point where there was no obvious compromise. So Goodwin just *grabbed* the tape and went to New York where it was going to be shown. Just took it up and said, "We're doing the first one!" The feud didn't end. Goodwin, for some reason, was going down in the elevator at the St. Regis at 4:00 in the morning. He met Art Michaelson in the lobby. He asked Art how every-

303

thing was. Art said, "Everything's fine. There's no need to go over there to the TV studio or anything." But he said it in such a way that suggested to Goodwin that maybe he'd better go over to the TV studio and check. He did, and he found the *whole* segment was missing. So Goodwin re-dubbed it and, in fact, even put a bodyguard in the studio to protect the tape. There were some frantic calls to Washington. I remember I was in Washington at that time, and we put a "stop" on all flights to New York that afternoon to keep any alternative tapes from getting to New York. But somehow one person got in the CBS studio half an hour before the tape was to go on. He said, "Put *this* on instead of *that*." He was from the Nee-Michaelson forces. I remember a lot of us felt that we wouldn't see any tape at all. At 9:30 we'd just see Bill Nee wrestling with Dick Goodwin, and no McCarthy!

ROBERT LOWELL, *poet*

Bobby did very alarming things to himself to reach the people. In some of those last television shots in California he sort of swayed back and forth and said, "You elected Reagan?" And the audience said, "No." He said, "Yes, you did." Almost feminine, and it was quite peculiar and unlike him. It had a sort of litany of "yes" and "no," and it was very hypnotic and moving. I don't know that you can do all that without wrecking your whole nervous system. But, anyway, I think he sprained it during the campaign. It might have all recovered if he'd been elected. Well, now McCarthy changed very little . . . *too* little with the campaign. He was perfectly willing to be dull and give dull speeches, but he was not willing to change his personality. His brilliance came out mostly in jokes. They were incredibly brilliant. But the last thing he wanted to do was to be charismatic. His was a mixture of proud contempt and modest distaste, and feeling that he wasn't worth this and might as well at least hold onto what he did believe in. I don't mean that he wasn't stirred by being introduced as the next President, and the crowds of young people in front of him, and so forth. But he never went very far; usually the cheers were greater when he came in than when he finished speaking.

TOM WICKER, *columnist*

Robert Kennedy and his people had the theory that crowds simply didn't want to stand any more and be harangued and lectured to; crowds want to be a part of the thing. Kennedy was always trying to draw the crowd in, so that you had, in a sense, an event that touched everyone.

304

He was very successful at that. He had little exchanges back and forth with the crowds. Some of it, I must confess, seemed to me to be a little juvenile, but I think it worked very well . . . particularly in the ghetto areas, where he would have almost a dialogue going back and forth with the crowd: "What do you think about this?" and "Let me have a show of hands," and so on. He would go through a kind of satirical little thing: "You mean Hubert Humphrey hasn't been here? You mean Gene McCarthy hasn't been here? You mean Dick Nixon hasn't been here? You mean I'm the only presidential candidate who's been here? Well, if that's the case . . ."

This kind of thing . . . bring them back and forth; and he had this big football player, gigantic sort of fellow, *terrible* singer . . . who would get out and sing songs; they would sing together, and Robert Kennedy was even a *worse* singer than he was. I frankly thought this was kind of silly myself. But, on the other hand, what he was trying to do was to give the crowd a sense that they were all one . . . a kind of participatory thing . . . that he was one of them and not some distant figure coming in.

JOHN SEIGENTHALER, *campaign aide, editor,* Nashville Tennessean

When Fred Dutton and I talked to Bob about going to the black caucus in Oakland, he said, "It's going to be a rather disorganized meeting. Do you think any good's going to come out of it?" I said, "I think it will be all right." He said, "No. It's going to be a very disordered meeting . . . and there's going to be some anger."

He was quite right. It was a rough, gut-cutting meeting in which a handful of people stood up and blistered white society and him as a symbol of white society. He sat there and listened and took it, and answered their questions directly and bluntly. He didn't pull any punches with them.

There were three or four people at that meeting who stood up and just raised hell. At one point he was talking about Bedford-Stuyvesant, and some fellow in the back in a red sweater, who was drunk, started saying in a very loud voice, "Talk, talk, talk, talk, talk, talk, talk, talk, talk; go ahead, baby. Talk, talk, talk, talk, talk." Then he suddenly leaped to his feet and said, "Look! I know I'm going to get throwed out of here. But before I get throwed out, I'm going to tell you what I think." He exploded with vituperative attacks on Robert Kennedy and the Kennedy family. He said, "You're just another politician. I've heard all this before." Then another fellow got up, garbed in African dress. The Black Jesus.

CURTIS LEE BAKER, *"Black Jesus," organizer*
Some people call me "Bulletproof." Some call me "King Solomon." Some of them call me "Moses." But most of the people call me "Black Jesus."

I've been running what you call a "black protector" organization since 1948 in California. Before anybody endorses anything they come to me. "What do Jesus say about it? If Jesus okay it, it's mellow with me." I had food stations, clothing, medicine, fine lawyers for getting people out of jail. I've been to hell and back four or five times, seen *every* no-good white, honky dog, and every black Uncle Tom and Aunt Jenny at least one time going and coming. So there was nothing, as far as I was concerned, strange to me about that white man sitting up there. I shocked him. He stood there, amazed, you know. He's looking at this black cat, who was talking, but was talking nitty-gritty talk. I said, "We're not going to pussyfoot around with you." I said, "You bastards haven't did nothing for us. We want to know what are you going to do for us?" I said, "You want this vote? *Prove* you want this vote! If you want this vote, put something *up* for this vote." Understand? "Put up! Put a bank up and let us borrow this money."

He couldn't say anything, really, because it's the first time he had been questioned by a sharp, ghetto attorney Nigger. And that's what I am. I never went to no law school, but I am the people's attorney. I fight for my people. He was being questioned by what I'm concerned is the sharpest black cat in the world. He was questioned by the cat that been to hell and back. He was questioned by the cat that know what hunger is. He was questioned by the cat that know what suffering is; to know what it is to go to jail for nothing. If Kennedy couldn't give my people something better than they had give me, then I don't need him for President.

THE REVEREND HÉCTOR LÓPEZ, *community adviser*
He's very colorful; he's usually zooming around with a beret—a black beret—and a black and gold cape, with a big cane. He's a very tall guy; he's about six foot five, very imposing. He works all the time. He's around . . . God, I guess about thirty-six, thirty-seven. He's a contemporary of Bill Russell; played basketball with him in McClymonds

306

High School in West Oakland. A lady that he helped—a black lady—called him "Black Jesus" when he came to her rescue.

FRED DUTTON
We thought this Black Jesus was going to be out working as hard as he could against Bob. We thought he was one hundred per cent against us. But the next day we went to another rally in Oakland in a city park. The crowd was almost all black, and there was the Black Jesus. Only, instead of being in his flowing red robes, he was in black tight pants, black turtleneck sweater, African hat, and had a big long walking stick. He helped clear the way for us, and he was telling everyone who would listen what a great man Kennedy was. He turned out to be one of the best friends Bob had in the area.

CURTIS LEE BAKER, *"Black Jesus"*
That day they came to me and they said: "Baker, would you please let Kennedy come into the area again?"

So I give the okay. I put a leaflet out that Kennedy was coming back in the area, and that I wanted him to be treated with the utmost respect, that I wanted him to be given a chance; and that we was going to see what he would do for our needs. When he came to the park, they had a few campus signs down there; I didn't ask them to move the signs. But when I came up to the platform where he was to speak, the signs just seemed to disappear. The young cats walked up to me and said, "Baby, what you want us to do, Jesus?" I said, "I want it to be real peaceful, quiet; we want to keep it real sweet. We don't want anybody to have no trouble today." And this is what they did. The meeting went on. At the end I said, "I want you to give him a great ovation and everything."

RAFER JOHNSON, *decathlon champion*
I saw him down in the crowd. I was up on the platform with two little girls and a little boy. I saw him in the crowd and I said to the youngest girl, "Who's that fellow down there?" She said, "Oh, he's the Black Jesus." I said, "How do you know?" She said, "Oh, I know." And the other girl . . . the older girl . . . budged in and she said, "Because my *mother* tolds me he's the Black Jesus." I asked, "Well, do you *believe* he's the black Jesus?" They said, "Yeah. My mother says he is." But then there was an older boy, and he said, "Naw, he isn't. People

say he is, but he's not!" I said, "Who is he?" "Oh, he's just a guy who just lives on the street. He's not Jesus." I said, "Do a lot of people in this community do what he says?" They said, "Oh yeah. A lot of them. He comes around all the time, talking. And a lot of them do what he say." I said, "Do you?" The little boy said, "No." And the girls said, "Oh, we do. He's really the Black Jesus." So I said, "Oh, I don't know if *I* think he is. I don't think you ought to believe everything he says. But today he's a real nice man." The one girl said, "Oh, yeah. He's not always that way, but he *is* nice today." And they all giggled.

THE REVEREND HÉCTOR LÓPEZ

He really looked tired—Bobby did. He really looked tired. They finally got him to the car, and it was really funny because I didn't think Rosey Grier and Rafer Johnson ever worked so hard in their lives. They literally had to hold Bobby by his legs and hips to keep him from toppling into the crowd! Kids, old women, old men, young men . . . everybody just wanted to touch him!

Digression: I wanted to touch him too, but I didn't. You know what I mean? They got in the car . . . but he couldn't go anywhere! How can you go anywhere when you're surrounded by 7,000 people trying to touch this one, crazy, rich, son-of-a-bitching white man? Right? Right! The hanger-on-ers were running around, "Hey! C'mon! Get out of the way! Get outta the way! Get outta the way! What! Move! C'mon, get outta the way! C'mon, Bobby's got a schedule!" Everybody's got a schedule, you know, even those poor fucking people there, *they* had a schedule! But then a fascinating thing took place: the Black Panthers were there to disrupt, and they started disrupting when Bobby started speaking, chanting very loudly, "Free Huey! Free Huey!" That lasted for about four or five minutes, and then pressure from people around them telling them to shut up, and just their own *interest* shut them up. You didn't hear from them until the end of the talk. Then Bobby wanted to get out of there . . . continue in his car caravan. All of a sudden some Panthers got out in front of the car and started shoving the people aside so the car could carry on. That's how Bobby got into West Oakland. The first truly community event I've seen in about eight years in Oakland was at that particular event: Bobby Kennedy coming into West Oakland! No one who has run for office, other than a city councilman of Oakland, has ever come into West Oakland *or* East Oakland to talk to the people. And, you know, politicians don't understand this. I guess they never will.

ROBERT LOWELL

For some reason, the two groups, McCarthy and Kennedy, were put in one hotel. I kept seeing all the Kennedy people—Arthur Schlesinger and so forth—in the lobby. I thought I ought to call on him. I really felt they should harmonize somehow. I really had no plan, and I had no authorization to call on him. But, I was very keen really, that if McCarthy lost, that his people support Kennedy, and vice versa. It had to be worked out, but it had to be done by their coming to some sort of human understanding rather than any sort of political bargain. It wasn't a political bargain that could be made very easily. I wrote a little note, and I think I said, "Dear Bobby, I think things are very gloomy. Could I call on you for a few minutes? It might be of some use to you, or it might not be of some use to you, God knows." And then signed it.

The next day I got a note from him, and I called and went up. The hotel's in two parts; he didn't know what number his room was, and the number he did give turned out to be in our section of the hotel—a tiny room behind the servants' elevator. I had to go down and go up the other part of the hotel into something very different. It was rather grand and high and called "The Presidential Suite." He was there with his dog. It was the day of the debate with McCarthy. Well, when I went in the room with its swell view of San Francisco, I felt anything I said would be slightly ironic. I said it was quite an outlook. But I didn't really mean it to be ironic. It was only something you'd say because it was better than ours over in McCarthy's quarters. Then he gave me a brief lecture, made up entirely of debater's points, that McCarthy couldn't be a serious candidate after losing Indiana and Nebraska. He ought to have withdrawn. I said, "These are just debater's arguments." I said that I'd been with this man for several months, and I could have produced an equivalent sort of argument in his behalf that also wouldn't be very deep. I said, "You mustn't talk to me this way." Well, he more or less said, "Well, I guess we have nothing more to say." But he wasn't rude to me. I sort of said, "I wish I could think up some joke that would cheer you, but it won't do any good." And that was the end.

But still, I think it was worth going. I mean I would have been sorry if I hadn't made the effort, though it was worthless. Bobby really felt he had an inheritance, and it was in his blood and his position. He was born an important person after he was about thirty. I mean he wasn't *literally* born an important person, but by the time he'd held office, his brother had been President; he was an important person and he shouldn't be compared with a mere Senator. Then I'm sure he felt he had much greater ability and energy and youth and realism. That almost explains why McCarthy didn't like him . . . you don't like to be pushed and treated this way by a young man. It hardly matters which provoked it first. Maybe McCarthy did. But it meant much more to Bobby at that point than it did to McCarthy. I've read somewhere that McCarthy didn't think that the Kennedys were very serious Catholics, but essentially none of them are very serious Catholics.

BLAIR CLARK, *campaign manager for Senator Eugene McCarthy*
After seeing Bobby, Lowell said to McCarthy, "I felt like Rudolph Hess parachuting into Scotland."

FRED DUTTON
There had been a long discussion in Oregon on whether or not Bob should debate. The idea then was that McCarthy was not well enough known. The polls didn't indicate that the failure to debate was a serious minus.

After the loss in the Oregon primary, however, we decided to come back fighting, and Bob said he would debate. The decision was made the night of the Oregon primary results. The announcement was made quickly. All the networks offered a possibility—CBS, NBC, ABC. Finally the decision to use ABC was made pretty much because they had more outlets in California than NBC or CBS. Ted Sorensen said he would fly out and participate in the discussions, to provide a brief analytical approach. The research people, Jeff Greenfield, Adam Walinsky, Milt Gwirtzman, Peter Edelman, immediately started preparing background papers. Beyond these moves within our campaign structure, we were inundated by people who wanted to help and rushed to the scene of battle: Burke Marshall, Adam Yarmolinsky, Pat Moynihan, *et al*. There was almost no discussion of what Bobby should say on particular issues. He had his own approach pretty well in mind. The offers of help were more informational than, let's say, strategic or tactical.

As we got towards the end of the week before the California election . . . the debate was to be that Saturday night in San Francisco . . . it became less a question of how much help we needed; we almost were getting too many volunteers. The need was to cut down the number of people involved.

We wanted to make sure that he got a good night's sleep Friday. We had a brief discussion in his hotel room. But it was nothing terribl organized. He took to bed about two pounds of paper prepared by various individuals, but I suspect he went right to sleep. Freckles probably got more out of it than Bob did.

On Saturday he slept much later than usual. We started out with a discussion about 9:30 in the morning. The meeting included about a dozen people. His room looked out on the Golden Gate Bay, and it was a beautiful sunny day. The distraction was almost too much. Bob, in his typical way, curled up on a big long couch at one end of the room; and everyone sort of grouped themselves around. Sorensen started to lead off, making points he thought were relevant as to what were the issues; what questions might come up; what were the hookers that might be raised by the panel. But the conversation, as at most meetings with Bob, was pretty unstructured, and everybody chimed in whenever he wanted to.

DICK TUCK

I'll never forget John Frankenheimer, the director, telling how Bobby should do the TV thing. "What you've got to do," he said, "is be yourself. Be yourself." He said this fifteen times. The Senator said, "Well, who am I going to be if not myself?" Great advice.

ANDREAS TEUBER

McCarthy seemed . . . especially at that debate . . . like Henry V at Agincourt wondering about his crown. He sort of leaned back, sort of Shakespearean, distant . . . politics was not something that you really wanted to get too much involved in because it's not a *human* thing . . or moral. There were certain people within the campaign who seemed to represent that point of view as well. We always thought of Robert Lowell like that. We tried to keep Robert Lowell from McCarthy at very crucial times because we thought he always took the edge off. Every time Lowell and McCarthy would get together, Lowell, or so we thought, would convince McCarthy that really, he was above all this. In fact, Tom Finney, who was managing the campaign, had hidden McCarthy right before the debate in a San Francisco Hilton room, which was not registered. It was mainly to hide him, not from the press, but from people within the campaign itself . . . like Robert Lowell. But Robert Lowell has a very good nose, and he found the room just before the debate.

Finney was trying to brief him à la Kennedy, with little cards that let him know things that were important and would come up, and how he felt McCarthy should respond. And McCarthy was very good. He was going through all this and taking pieces of paper from Finney, looking at them, and dropping those on the floor that he'd studied carefully; he *seemed to be* sorting them out. You're never sure about McCarthy. It *looked* like he was attentive and interested. But then, of course, Lowell got to him fifteen minutes beforehand, and they started to drink—the two of them—and went downstairs. There were two limousines downstairs—identical—to take McCarthy to the TV studio. Somebody thought this was a Dick Tuck joke; he was always doing those sorts of things, and probably had sent the other limousine. Nobody was sure. McCarthy and Lowell got into the same limousine. On the way to the studio, McCarthy wanted to see Alcatraz. And so they took a detour, and McCarthy looked at the prison. He and Lowell composed I think a 20th century version of "Ode to St. Cecilia's Day" in the back seat. So, by the time he got to the studio, yes, he was then like Henry the fifth at Agincourt.

At the studio Tom Morgan remembered there was a set of instructions—something about no top-lighting on McCarthy because it looks like he has a halo. Suddenly he sighted a pillow in one of the chairs, and came running out saying, "Bobby's got a *pillow* on his chair!" But it turned out not to be for Bobby at all; it was for Bill Lawrence, who had a bad back.

They *both* didn't seem to want to debate; they both were backpedaling furiously: Bobby, I think, trying not to be ruthless, and McCarthy trying not to be there.

TOM WICKER

A kind of McCarthy mystique had built up. McCarthy was regarded as being such a savage wit, you know, and an intellectual paragon in many ways; he was known as a pretty tough man with language. My own view is that most people in the audience that night—the press and staff people—really expected McCarthy to win the debate more clearly than, in fact, he did . . . because they felt that it was just more nearly his kind of a scene than it was Robert Kennedy's. I don't think he did. It's typical that McCarthy didn't make any great preparation for the debate. I didn't think he fought his own battle as well as he should have. The same is true of Robert Kennedy. I thought that Kennedy on that night, scored some fairly cheap debating points, which I suppose came across to the TV audience, though of course debating points are debating points in the long run: these were on the question of coalition government in Vietnam, and, Are you going to put black people in Orange County, California? These were kind of quick debater's points.

ANDREAS TEUBER

McCarthy felt such attacks, particularly on his voting record, were unjustified. Often with McCarthy, something that is unjustified is so *totally* unjustified . . . something that's not worth his attention or time or energy to even refute it. It took him quite some time before he even decided to say anything at all to defend his voting record. When we started in Nebraska, he started talking about the voting record and answering some of these charges by the Kennedy people. He was asked by a member of the audience why he even bothered to answer these charges if he thought they were so trivial. McCarthy's response was, "Well, if you're going to litter the court with old tennis shoes and dirty socks and sneakers, you've got to clear it all away before you play basketball." So he did answer the charges. But it took him a while.

The Kennedy attack on McCarthy's voting record was being mailed out from Marin County somewhere, and we had given McCarthy a copy, which he had in his right coat pocket for the debate. We were having some trouble too, because there was an ad that we had run, which had made the charge that Bobby Kennedy had been involved in the Dominican Republic fiasco. It was run in the San Francisco paper and the L.A. *Times*—a big full-page ad. Of course, Bobby wasn't even in the Cabinet at that time. There were a number of courses of action to take: one was to say, "Well, okay. This is a charge that we realize we *shouldn't* have made, and we're withdrawing the ad immediately." That was what McCarthy wanted to do and what was done. Bobby did bring it up in the debate. McCarthy's reaction was: 'Well, I had it withdrawn immediately." Then he said, ". . . which s not what I can say about you and my voting record. When you heard that the charges that you were making about *my* voting record were false you *still* continued to mail it out." Then he put his hand n his right coat pocket. All of us sitting around the television set were convinced that he was going to take out this piece of paper and lunk it on the table. Bobby said, "I don't know what you're talking bout." So it seemed like an obvious time for him to reach into his ocket for this piece of paper. But he *didn't*. It was just a characteristic esture of his; sometimes he reaches into his pocket and leans back.

313

But it's not McCarthy's style to plunk something on the table like that and say, Well, what is this? He didn't do it. In fact, we lost somebody on the campaign then, who stood up as we were watching, just furious that he hadn't pulled that piece of paper out of his pocket.

TOM WICKER

McCarthy was a very low-keyed performer on television, a very good performer on television, I thought. McLuhan—if McLuhan is a prophet —says that anybody who looks like he wants to get elected shouldn't go on television. McCarthy certainly never looked as if he wanted to get elected!

FRED DUTTON

Bob's almost immediate reaction when we got in the car to go back to the hotel was that McCarthy hadn't prepared himself adequately. I think Bob's expression was, "He didn't do his homework." The subsequent newspaper stories, to the extent that you could interpret anything from them, suggested the same thing: that McCarthy thought that it wasn't necessary, or that he was too cool or too aloof . . . or too something to bother with preparation.

BLAIR CLARK

McCarthy got sort of bored by that debate, it's strange to say. Too bad, because he had a chance to show his class. I mean, I think a couple of Bobby's criticisms in that were very bad . . . remarks that were just awful, and opened him up. McCarthy, instead of explaining himself in a dignified way, just sort of folded. He may have thought it was so vulgar, there was no way to deal with it. But you know, he was famous for not preparing much. Well, he *wouldn't*, you know. It would have been better to stand at the side of the pool shaking loose his muscles rather than boning up on tax questions the way the Kennedys would. It wasn't laziness; it was just his characteristic way of behaving, I think.

DUN GIFFORD, *campaign aide*

Kenny O'Donnell was with some old friends from Boston or somewhere, and Teddy came by. They suddenly put their arms around each other and didn't say a word. You know, it really hurt. You could see it in both faces. They couldn't say anything; neither one could say anything to the other; and they didn't try. Kenny has been so close to Bobby for so many years; and it's obvious about Teddy. You know, it really shocked me. It hurt me very badly. You know. Just to see the two grown men so close, unable to speak to one another.

ART BUCHWALD, *columnist*

Every once in a while, when there was a fairly good-sized crowd, Teddy came out on the platform, and he waved to them. It was interesting to see the reaction of the people because, since the last car had the coffin on it, that's what they had come to see; there was, you know, a tremendous reaction once they saw the car—pointing and crying, and there were a couple of scenes that couldn't have been staged by a Hollywood writer. Going through Maryland, I saw a girl with long hair sitting bareback on a horse with high grass and nothing else around. She was all by herself.

FRANK MANKIEWICZ, *press secretary*

It was beginning to get dark after Baltimore. There was one sign that I will always remember. They were standing on a hill by them-

315

selves as the train came around a turn. I think before we got to Baltimore—maybe it was after. They had a big sign that they were all holding—there were four or five of them—and the sign said, THE GEB-HARTS ARE SAD. Somehow, that, more than anything else, just kind of did me in.

CHARLES QUINN, *television correspondent*

In the beginning, he was very shy; he was very *press* shy. I noticed it. But he was trying to get along; he was trying to understand us. Of course, he'd had a lot of experience in running for the Senate in New York. But he still looked upon us with some suspicion, some mistrust; with each week, though, he got successively warmer, friendlier. At the end . . . Kennedy sat in the middle of the plane and was accessible to all reporters. But he never got used to the public. When he spoke from a lectern (and he spoke thousands of times in his public career), he was terribly nervous and his hands shook as though he had palsy; he used to hold his hands down below the lectern so you couldn't see them. He stood up there, and he looked very serene and cool as he spoke. But his hands were just shaking like leaves in a fall wind. I even noticed on the plane . . . I can remember having conversations with him early in the campaign, sitting down and saying, "Hello, Senator. How are things going?" And when he replied, even on the plane, his hands shook—just when he was talking to me! Well, that changed later. But he never got used to it in public. His hands always shook in public.

STEWART ALSOP, *columnist*

I found Bobby in a professional sense *very* difficult to interview. You would go and see him in his office, and you'd ask him a question, and he'd respond either with that enormous grin and no words at all, or he'd just laugh. Sometimes you'd have a carefully prepared question, and all he would say was, "Yes," or, "No," or, "That's what *you* think," or something like that.

There was something hidden and mysterious about him—part of it his curious inability to answer the kind of questions that from an ordinary politician would elicit an ocean of autobiographical material, heavily interlarded with self-congratulation. Bobby was absolutely incapable of doing that.

316

JOHN J. LINDSAY, *correspondent*

I recall the first day that Edward Kennedy came back from his airplane crash . . . the first day of Congress. It was the first day that Senator Robert Kennedy entered Congress. I had to do a double profile. The contrast between the two men at that time was just beyond belief. I went in to see Robert, prepared for fifteen minutes of questions and possibly fifteen minutes of answers. At the end of ten minutes, I was out of the ballgame. I asked rather lengthy questions, and he would say, "No." Or he would say, "Yes." Or he would say, "Well, I don't think it's wise to go into that right now." So I came out without a *line*, really, and I was mopping my brow when I came out. There was one incident in there . . . some potentate in Indonesia had given him a giant stuffed tiger, and it was sitting in the middle of the floor. Halfway through my interview a large group of youngsters from New York came in, twenty or so children, and one of them cringed at the sight of the tiger. Bob pressed the button on his desk and Angie, his secretary, came in, and he said, "Angie, get this tiger out of here. It's scaring my constituents." That's the only thing I got out of the interview.

Then I went down to Ted's office, and there was a real old Irish gathering going on down there, including all the Kennedy sisters, and they were having sandwiches and a few drinks, coffee, tea . . . this kind of thing. The place was totally jammed with well-wishers, mostly from Boston, and the contrast between the two . . . well, Ted at that time being such a terribly outgoing and easy person, with a very wry sense of humor. He gave me a very interesting and lovely interview, mostly anecdotes of his days as a boy with Honey Fitzgerald in Boston. I got a great deal.

ART BUCHWALD

The columns I did on him he never really enjoyed too much. He didn't get mad. But one, I remember, was an imaginary account of how he settled the New York subway strike. I really cut him up pretty badly. So about a week later, I was at a party at Hickory Hill dancing or something, and Bobby yelled, "I didn't invite you. Ethel invited you."

JIM STEVENSON, *journalist*

He kept asking questions. His first question was, "What kind of a

story are you going to do about me?" Then he added, "or, *to* me?"
He always rode in the front seat—he'd turn around and . . . not
exactly glare at you, but he would sort of zap you with this look and
say, What do you think of so-and-so? Then you'd answer, and he
wouldn't respond; he wouldn't react. Then he'd go on, What do you
think of so-and-so? You'd work through Frank O'Connor and John
Lindsay, and all these people I really knew nothing about, and he
knew everything about, and I'd have to give these asinine opinions.
When he got bored or tired, he would turn away, and something else
would get his attention. But this was a habit of his: to ask questions,
which is quite unusual in political figures. Most of them have a kind
of opaque glaze over them and not much is coming in from the outside.

ROBERT LOWELL, *poet*
It relaxed him if you slightly insulted him, and he slightly insulted
you, and so forth. He was very courteous, at least to me. He treated me
better than most people do, I guess. I treated him more humanly than
most people do. Once I hadn't seen him for about a year, and I said,
"You haven't done very well. You haven't done much. You look creased
and wrinkled, and if you go on the way you are, you'll be Dean of Harvard." But he was very decent about that. He said, "Things have been
going very badly with me, and if they go on this way, I *will* be Dean of
Harvard." That wasn't said ironically.

HARRISON SALISBURY, *assistant managing editor*, The New York
    Times
He was always very wry. He was good at these lunches at the New
York *Times*. Almost always, Johnny Oakes had just written something
outrageous about him. Johnny never liked him, and didn't trust him
and was forever publishing editorials that got under Bobby's skin. Bobby
was very cute about that; he would start out by making some clever
remark thanking John for his "guidance" and "insight" into the various
problems. He'd certainly appreciated the *interest* that the *Times* took in
him. Things of that kind, which Johnny really didn't like at all, but the
rest of us enjoyed a great deal!

JEFF GREENFIELD, *campaign aide*
At first, the reporters were almost to a man, unbelieving. They were
the smart guys. They were the pros. The vast majority of political

318

porters have no perception about new political currents. They never understood how unpopular the war was, or how unpopular Johnson was; and they didn't understand the kind of challenge that could be mounted to Johnson. When we landed in San Francisco and walked through one of those kind of immense tubes, you know, that connect the boarding area with planes, we were hit with a flash of people and sounds and screaming and pushing and yelling like I had never seen before. A couple of thousand people had packed into one of these places where people sit and wait for planes. Somehow they got Robert Kennedy up to a platform, where he delivered a three-minute talk that was, you know, unheard. I had somehow fought my way through. The reporters all seemed . . . they were stunned. They had seen something that they'd never seen before. One of them said: "You know, for the first time, I think this guy could make it."

TOM WICKER, *columnist*
Quite frankly, Bobby Kennedy was an easy man to fall in love with . . . if you were a reporter, and too many people did. I wouldn't want to cite names. But it's a fact. I used to say, as a bureau chief, and I still say, that the right way for a reporter to pursue his work is to be neither "in" nor "out," and there isn't any way for anybody to judge where that is except the reporter himself. But there's not any question in my mind, after many years in this work, that if you're really "in" with somebody, then you're not going to do a good job. On the other hand, if you're totally "out," where they won't even take your phone calls, why, obviously, you're in bad shape. You're in no better shape than if you're totally "in." It's all a very difficult adjustment.

I know that the Kennedy organization apparently felt that the *Times* was opposed to them and that they didn't get a fair shake. But, you know, I really discount this because I think all politicians feel that way. The only politician I've ever met who seemed really not to care what the press said about him was Everett Dirksen . . . and every now and then, even *he* would get upset. As bureau chief in Washington . . . I was assigning people to cover various presidential candidates in the early part of 1968, because we do most of the national political writing in the Washington bureau. The one man I thought most carefully about was Robert Kennedy, and I'll be frank as to why it was. Having had considerable experience myself as a White House reporter when John F. Kennedy was there, I felt that the Kennedys were, first, such attractive men; secondly, they stood for such attractive propositions in American

319

life; and third, they understood so thoroughly the extent to which the press could be used . . . that covering any of them on a full-time basis was a very dangerous business. To be frank about it, I have seen reporters —to use our professional jargon—I've seen reporters eaten alive by the Kennedys. This is not to say that they were evil people and tried to manipulate the press; it was that in their own political interests, which one could easily say was in the interests of the best things that one would wish for the country, they attempted to *use* the press. I think they did, and I don't think anyone connected with them would seriously deny that.

So I thought about this very seriously in 1968. When Robert Kennedy became a presidential candidate, I assigned for full-time coverage a very distinguished reporter in our Washington bureau, named John Herbers. Herb had been for years before he came to the *Times*, UPI's lone correspondent in Mississippi, where he came under all imaginable sorts of pressure, including physical threats. He withstood it all to do a magnificent and honest job. He was a liberal Southerner—a backslid Southerner is a very liberal sort of fellow. I thought this was a good assignment, and I felt justified by it as the year went along because, although I know that John Herbers came to be personally extremely fond of and impressed by Robert Kennedy, his coverage throughout the year remained very dispassionate and objective . . . which is what we wanted. I don't think that entirely pleased the Robert Kennedy camp, and I can understand that. They didn't want dispassionate coverage; they wanted favorable coverage. That's their business. Our business was something else entirely. Too many reporters in his press entourage were disciples. I don't think that did him any good.

ROBERT SCHEER, *editor*, Ramparts

Adam Walinsky and Peter Edelman said to me, "Well, why don't *you* write the Vietnam part of the speech?" That's pretty heady. I sat down and I wrote it. Bobby got about half of it into his speech. For a minute I thought: God, I could have influenced history. I can sit here behind the scenes with old Adam Walinsky and Peter Edelman, writing these Kennedy speeches. Why, we're just going to change the world!

Then you realize that Kennedy left the ballsy half of the speech out— the radical half out. This ain't the way to change history, because you change history by building a base for change and getting mass support for change and having a radical program, not by kissing ass behind the scenes with speechwriters of politicians. I could see where it's heady stuff for some people. Newfield was consulted a lot, guys like him.

Of course, it was very clear that Bobby preferred to talk to a guy like Jack Newfield over the guy from *Time* magazine. There was no doubt about it. Every other politician would have gone to the guy from the Washington *Post* or *Time* or AP. Once the plane takes off, that's the ritual. The politician you're covering goes back to the bathroom; and as he passes down, the whole question is, Who is he going to stop and talk to? Well, with Humphrey, or even McCarthy, they'd stop and talk to the more traditional guys—the AP guy or the *Time* magazine guy. But Bobby would do freaky things, you know: he'd stop and talk to some cat like Newfield. Or, if I was on the plane, he'd talk to me. Then all of the other reporters would come rushing up to you, and they'd say: "Jeez! You've got a lot of pull in this campaign. You're important. He talks to *you*."

We used to have arguments all the time and friendly jostling, and I never felt tense. I remember one time I was up in the apartment. I never held back on saying anything; I always laid it out: "Look. When we're threatening American power and the ruling class and the people who run this country, you're going to put me in jail as readily as Hubert Humphrey would." He said, "I'd be doing my duty." Then I said something like, "If you were elected President, are you going to let all the draft resisters out? Are you going to free all the political prisoners? Are you going to do this?" He said, "I don't make any campaign commitments." I said, "Just between me and you, would you really do that?" He said, "No." So, all right, you know. "That's where you are," I said. "You're just another Hubert Humphrey. You're a charming, sexy, little bit mad Hubert Humphrey. Okay?" To me, the thing about him was that he would take that kind of talk every once in a while, and come back and try to debate with you, and argue with you. I think that's what hooked a guy like Newfield. I'm sure Newfield told Bobby a lot of rough things when they were in private; I'm sure he was very critical. I remember one time Bobby said, "Does *Ramparts* support me?" I said, "No." He said, "Why not?" I said, "You ain't done anything." He bounced back. To me, that was flippy because any other politician would say, "I want Scheer off the plane. What's a *Ramparts* guy doing on the plane, to begin with? He's going to shoot me."

SYLVIA WRIGHT, *reporter*

The Kennedy press was just like we were all one family. Oh, much closer than your own family, because your own family you see in the morning, and you come home to them in the evening, and you see them on weekends. So this was really abnormal, and maybe even unhealthy; we got too close to each other . . . too dependent . . . because it wasn't just 9:00 to 5:00. We were with each other twenty-four hours a day; and then not just five days a week—but Saturday and Sunday. And that's abnormal exposure! We were each others' working companions, husbands, fathers, sisters, brothers. If you were sick or grumpy, you were sick with those people. It's a very intimate thing.

Journalists who were on this campaign who had been on others said there was never that feeling on any other campaign; that it was a totally complete world—a complete society; we were so close . . . all these grown men being willing to inconvenience themselves for each other . . . giving up a phone if they know they don't have as fast a deadline as the next guy . . . they'll give him their phone . . . one journalist to another?! Letting somebody use their tape recorder. It was all so family and so close.

I think Bobby had a great deal to do with that. How else do you explain it? Why hadn't this happened to these people when they were on Goldwater's campaign, or Bill Miller's campaign, or Nixon's earlier campaign . . . or even Jack Kennedy's campaign?

Bobby had felt about us like we were not the press. He would say to us, "When we land here, I'm not going to be ready; keep the press away from me." What he meant by "the press" was strangers from the local press that he didn't know. We were friends that he was interested in. I mean it was the very unique thing about the campaign. The press he traveled with were his buddies. He went out to eat dinner with Jimmy Breslin and his wife and Fat Thomas because his attitude was, Look. I'm a Senator. I've got a stuffy job up there in the Senate. It's boring. Tell me, Roger, about the athletes you did the special on. Tell me, Chuck, about the Selma march. Tell me, John, about the time you were in Watts. He thought of the press as individuals, not an entity.

FRED DUTTON, *campaign aide*

One of his favorite press people was Walter Dombrow, the crack CBS cameraman. Once, while campaigning in Watts just before the California election with a thousand or so people crowding around, and Dombrow running alongside (all 220 pounds on a short figure) the car to help fend people off, Bob called to Walt to catch him, and he jumped into Dombrow's startled arms—just for the hell of it.

One night Bob had a rally in Oakland, California with 5,000 people in attendance. Rosemary Clooney was there to help entertain. At the end of his speech, Bob said, "Just a minute. John Glenn, Rosemary Clooney, and I want to sing 'Happy Birthday' to Walter Dombrow." The audience clearly had never heard of Dombrow. They all looked at each other. "Walter who?" At that moment, Walt was not even there. He was outside, lying down on the sidewalk taking pictures for CBS of people walking by. Flat on his back, he suddenly heard Glenn, Kennedy, and Rosemary Clooney singing, "Happy Birthday, dear Walter," back there in the rally in front of 5,000 people.

SYLVIA WRIGHT
One day it was Bill Barry's birthday. Bill Barry, the bodyguard. And we had an enormous party on the plane. Everyone bought gifts. He had about sixty gifts to open. And a huge cake we had made with Bobby's picture painted in frosting and Bill's picture painted in frosting. We had champagne, with champagne glasses for everyone and ribbons tied around all of them, and the whole plane decorated symmetrically—really well done—in red, white, and blue crepe paper, and silver and red balloons all over. We partied *all* the way to L.A.

The Los Angeles rally didn't get over until midnight. When it was over, Bobby had to go to a taping in a TV studio. He wouldn't finish taping till 2:30 in the morning. And we still had to fly from Los Angeles to Portland, Oregon . . . which takes three hours. So on the plane, waiting for him, we started to sing. John Hart is a Baptist preacher's son, and I think I know the words to every song in the Methodist hymnal. John and I knew all the religious songs, and so did Dick Harwood . . . whose father, I think, is a minister! So we started singing Baptist hymns. And we sang *every* hymn we knew. Ethel sang "Onward Christian Soldiers" with us. Then she went up and lay down to listen to us. And we sang: "I Come to the Garden Alone While the Dew Is Still on the Roses" and "Just as I Am Without One Plea." And then we sang "Softly and Tenderly Jesus Is Calling." All these journalists with their sleeves rolled up and drinking, singing ". . . softly and tenderly Jesus is calling . . . ," and we sang it in harmony and with the different parts . . . "Come home," then "Come home," the response. I'm not sure we did justice to those hymns! And then we would sing all the patriotic songs: "It's a Grand Old Flag, It's the Red, White and Blue . . . ," and "I'm a Yankee Doodle Dandy." But mostly we sang hymns. We finally had quit singing because we had sung *every* hymn we knew; and then we had started on folk songs, and we had sung: "Where Have All the Flowers Gone?" and "Yellow Rose" and "Lemon Tree." Well,

Bobby came on the plane about 2:30; and by that time, we had sung every hymn we had ever known: "Faith of Our Fathers," and "Dear Lord and Father of Mankind," and "The Church's One Foundation." That's a great rousing song when sung with gusto! And "What a Friend We Have in Jesus." Sometimes we would sing, "What a Friend We Have in Bobby." We were terrible!

Then he came on the plane, and Ethel said, "Oh, Bobby! You don't know what you missed. I've been lying here for three hours, and the kids have been singing." She said, "You must hear them sing 'Battle Hymn of the Republic' and 'Onward Christian Soldiers.' You must *hear* them!"

Bobby took off his tuxedo and put on slacks and a sweater and got a drink. We started to sing "Battle Hymn" for him the way we knew it, and we really knew how to sing it. He started to sing along. When we got to the verse that goes "In the beauty of the lilies, Christ was born across the sea," we sang it like choirs all do, where you slow way, way down and sing it very much slower than the other verses. But Bobby, singing with us, charged right ahead: "In the beauty of the lilies, Christ . . ." And we all kept trying to sing it *our* way, and he just charged right ahead. When we got through, Dick Harwood said, "All right now, Kennedy. We're going to sing that verse again for you to show how it *should* be done, and you keep quiet! And we'll do it right."

So then we sang it again for him; and he was very sad. It was very pretty. And so then we sang the whole song again so he could do it right too. Because we told him if he would do it right, he could sing. And then we did the whole evening over. We sang for him: "I Come to the Garden Alone" and "Softly and Tenderly" and "Just as I Am Without One Plea." And we went through all the hymns; and then we went through all the folk songs again because, of course, he wanted us to sing "Where Have All the Flowers Gone?" and then we had to sing that again and again.

In the meanwhile, we had taken off. We sang all the way to Portland. Bobby was sitting down, and some of us were sitting on the floor around him, and we were all kind of huddled together. And then pretty soon, it sort of vaguely started to get light out, and it was about a quarter to five; and we all just fell asleep together, huddled up there in the front of the plane. All these great big guys! All the seats were empty in the back of the plane. We all fell asleep lying across each other and huddled up together. Then Bobby got up and snapped the lights off over his shoulder, and went off to sleep with the dog up in the front. I was awake and I couldn't get up to move because Dick Harwood had fallen asleep across me, and Bill Barry was leaning against me, and somebody else was leaning against him. But I was awake and I watched him; and he just got up and snapped the seat lights off, and stood there and looked at us a minute; and then he went off to the front to go to sleep.

JOSEPH MOHBAT, *journalist*

I really was always with him. I almost made a thing out of it. People think I'm a Secret Service man because I got my picture in two St. Patrick's Day parades. I stayed real close to him because the guy was so active and so impulsive that if you turned your back once, you might miss something: a good piece of color, or something he would say.

He used to joke with me. One of them had to do with the fact I was so close all the time. The last event of the Oregon campaign was a big reception at one of the Portland hotels. He was supposed to shake a lot of hands, with no speech planned. About halfway through the reception, at eight o'clock at night, Dick Drayne said, "Look. All he's going to do is shake hands. Let's us all get on a bus and go out to the plane and have some dinner and a drink, and get ready to go to L.A." I didn't want to . . . it was against my principles, but I said okay because I had some writing to do. We got to the plane. I was sitting next to Gail Sheehy, of *New York* magazine, having dinner. Finally, we heard this commotion outside the plane. The rest of them had arrived. The first person to climb aboard was Walt Dombrow, who said, "Jesus, Joe Mohbat. Where were you?" His hair was all disarrayed, and he was panting. I said, "What do you mean, where was I?" My heart was beginning to get into my mouth.

He said, "Oh, my God! What happened was that on the way back from that reception, we stopped in a Chinese restaurant. There were 6,000 Chinese outside that restaurant. Kennedy got on the back of the car. They pulled him off the car. They tore his coat off; he lost both shoes. It was the wildest scene of this whole campaign. We were scared stiff!"

"Oh, my God!" I said. "How did I miss that?"

Then Bob Kennedy got on; he walked by and started talking to the reporter in the seat in front of me. I heard him say: "Oh, my God! I don't know why I ever got into this in the first place! We stopped in this Chinese restaurant on the way back from the reception. I haven't had Chinese food for a long time. There were 6,000 Chinese outside! They practically tore my clothes off me; they got my shoes. They pulled me down to the ground."

I kept trying to ask him, "Had you planned to stop there?" He was talking to this guy, and he wouldn't look at me. I was going out of my mind. Then, at that moment, in the back, the plane door closed so I couldn't go phone the story. Gail was holding my hand, saying, "Come on. You can't win 'em all."

Ethel came past and said, "Oh, Joe! We just had the wildest scene at a Chinese restaurant! There were 6,000 Chinese there. You weren't even there. It's all right though; the UP was there, so we had national coverage." All this time I had a hunk of lamb chop on my fork which was getting stone cold. I figured, "What a bush-league reporter to miss something like this. God! What could have happened?" I felt really down about it. The plane got up in the air and Bob still hadn't looked at me or talked to me. About five minutes later, Bob finally came by and said, "Joe! Don't look so awful. I guess I'd better tell you. I was putting you on."

Driving to the airport, he had looked at the car behind him where I usually was and said, "Where's Joe Mohbat?" "Joe Mohbad," he pronounced it. Walt said, "I guess he went in that group that went on ahead." Bob said, "Hey! Hey! Let's do this! There's this Chinese restaurant and 6,000 . . ."

DICK TUCK, *campaign aide*

During the Nebraska campaign, Ethel heard that Julesburg, Colorado, was Fred Dutton's home town. He's the son of the railroad company doctor. So the day before we went through, she got hold of me and said, "We have got to do something for Fred." She said, "Get some signs and some placards." So we worked back in the last compartment making signs, and Dutton buttons, and so forth. The train wasn't supposed to stop at Julesburg. That took some doing. I talked to the Union Pacific people. Originally, it was going to be Dutton for President and Bobby for Vice-President. But, politics being what it is, I had to make a deal; it was Dutton for President and Ave Harriman for Vice-President. The Harrimans were originally railroad people in the West, and we substituted him to get the Union Pacific to stop the train. They finally agreed.

DAVID BREASTED, *journalist*

At 8:30 in the morning, Ethel commissioned me to do a funny song for Fred's birthday. I got together a bunch of people, and we sat down

326

and parceled out verses. In the Kennedy camp, you were expected at any hour of the day and night to be at your most brilliant; if you weren't, no excuses were acceptable. Our song just wasn't very good. I told Ethel, "I'm quite prepared to make a horse's ass of myself at 2:00 A.M., when everybody's had enough of a taste of booze so they're inclined to laugh; but I really cannot bring myself to make a horse's ass of myself early in the morning in Julesburg, Colorado. I just don't think it'll go over well." So the Dutton-for-President rally went on without benefit of music that morning.

DICK TUCK

The signs were all made. Then we began to pull into Julesburg; we had to divert Fred so the news people could pile off the back with their signs without his knowing. So Dick Harwood of the Washington *Post* and Hays Gorey of *Time* magazine started diverting Fred. In the meantime, all the press guys were running around picking up their placards. I ran into Fred at about the third car, and he was in a state of panic. He said, "The damn press is all moving into the Senator's car. What's going on? You've got to go up and get 'em out." I said, "All right, don't worry. I'll get 'em out."

CHARLES QUINN

At Julesburg, it's raining very slightly. There are about three people standing by the station; there's nothing there: maybe five houses. Three guys slouched there; it's a Saturday, as I remember. Suddenly, they see this train stop. We all come pouring off this train, with our signs, saying, "We want Freddy! We want Freddy!" Ethel and Bobby are right in the forefront. "Come out, Freddy! Come out! Make a speech!"

FRED DUTTON

I thought, "Oh, my God. Something's up." The car was sort of empty. Bill Barry said, "Let's go to the end and see what there is." Well, we went to the back car, and by then the train had stopped, and I knew damn well something was on. Barry took me out to the back platform where Bob usually stood, and I saw all these damn people there. Of course, I'm self-conscious enough anywhere. And here was Bob with his signs, and Ethel and all these reporters who I knew well. They were sort of hooting and howling.

DICK TUCK

Bobby had a sign that said, SOCK IT TO 'EM, FREDDY, and Ethel at one point had a sign that said, MAKE FRED, NOT WAR. They had to switch signs quickly for the photographers. I had a sign that said, FRED DUTTON'S BROTHER FOR ATTORNEY GENERAL. There were three or four, or maybe a half-dozen people that happened to be in the Julesburg station, and they couldn't understand what was going on.

CHARLES QUINN
By this time, the townspeople had heard about this wild thing that was happening down at their station; they began crawling out of the wood-work, coming down, scratching their heads, and looking at us as if we were all nuts . . . which we were!

DICK TUCK
Fred finally came to the rear platform, and he said, "No wonder this train is running late. If you'd stop these darn-fool pranks . . ." We cheered and we shouted, and we said that we had to have the breakaway line the Senator always used, the George Bernard Shaw line that was the signal that he was at the end of his speech. The Senator screamed at Fred, and said, "Give the George Bernard Shaw line or we won't leave." So Dutton made this short speech, a Kennedy-like speech about, "This is not acceptable. We can do better. We can do better. As George Bernard Shaw once said, 'Run for the train.'" We all ran to get on.

FRED DUTTON
Fortunately, the train got out of town fast. My God, I still have all kinds of relatives there.

DICK TUCK
The campaign wouldn't have worked without the whistles. Early in the campaign, a wagonmaster presented me with a pair. It's amazing that nothing else moves people—sirens, horns, shouts. We're all trained to react to a whistle, a gym-instructor's whistle—you know, "Out of the pool!" and so forth. If we were due to leave at 2:00, and everybody in the press was having a drink at the bar, if I came in and said, "All right, gentlemen, we're leaving," half the group would stay there. But if I came in and blew the whistle . . . well, that worked. So, I always had that whistle. During that hysterical thing in the Ambassador kitchen, at one point, trying to get people back, I took the whistle out of my pocket and blew it . . . and it worked, for the last time.

328

SYLVIA WRIGHT

He loved that campaign and he loved all the fun. When we would have a party while he had to be at a TV studio, he would say, "The least you could have done was wait!"

On the night before the election in California we were having a party in Dick Drayne's room, which was on the Senator's floor. The hotel detective came and told us we had to be quiet because Senator Kennedy . . . this was his floor. Fred Dutton got very cross with the detective and said, "We rented this whole floor just so we wouldn't be disturbing other people; and we *are* with Senator Kennedy; we *are* his party." He said, "Come on, kids." And he reached in his pocket and he took out a key, and he walked us all down to Senator Kennedy's suite because the Kennedys were at Malibu; and he opened the door. We all paraded in and closed the door in the detective's face. And what could he do? He couldn't invade the Kennedys' suite. And then we had this fantastic party.

The next day, Fred Dutton went out to Malibu to get Bobby. Bobby said, "What did you do last night?" Fred said, "Oh, I had a party with the kids . . . with the press." And Bobby said, "What do you mean you had a party with the press?" He said, "Well, as a matter of fact, we had the party in your room." He told how we sang; then he said, "Then we started to march, and we marched through all the furniture and over the furniture, and around the tables."

Well! Bobby was fit to be tied! He said, "Fred! Why? Why wasn't I there? Why did I miss it? Tell me again." And he made him tell him every song we sang. Then he said, "Well, now . . . tell me again who was there." Well, finally, he just said: "It's just like missing Christmas! Fred, would you get those same kids together tonight and just have them do it again, 'cause I want to march, and I want . . ." You know, he was *sick* that he wasn't there!

And that was our last . . . that was our last night.

GILLIAN WALKER, *theatrical producer*

Inside the train earlier, everyone had worked themselves up to a kind of an emotional state—despair, anger, grief—aided by the huge crowd singing the "Battle Hymn of the Republic" in the Baltimore station. It was all very moving and satisfying. The train crawled down the platform. Finally, after the throngs of blacks standing stiffly like a welcoming delegation, at the very end of the platform under the bridge, there was this lady—this one lady, wearing a black bathing suit, with her hand on her hip; she was like an exclamation point by Steinberg, marking the end. We saw a few scattered people after that in fields along the track, but it was darkening, and that lady really did mark the end.

MICHAEL HARRINGTON, *author*

It seemed to me that in most of the crowds lining the tracks there was a sort of emotional confusion as to what to do. I assume that some of the people who came to watch the train did so simply for reasons of curiosity and expectancy. But, even taking that into account, many people remained who didn't know quite what to do. There were some people who responded by holding a hand over the heart; there were some who responded by waving; there were those—particularly policemen, soldiers, and, I assume, some veterans—who stood at attention.

But then it seemed to me, at Baltimore, and from Baltimore all the way to Washington, the journey took on a much more solemn note. To someone inside looking out, it seemed that the people outside had learned what to do. There appeared to be some kind of agreed response—not a conscious agreement, but a mood that they all conformed to. It was solemn; very little waving; very restrained. Baltimore was the first place where, inside the train, the conversation and the chattering and all the aspects of an Irish wake stopped. The silence—now really the wake of all those people *outside*—was so powerful that now one had to confront it. The train was on a raised embankment, and you could see the cars stopped and the people watching in the distance. The train slowed down, and the pace became a funeral pace.

JACKIE COOPER, *actor, producer*
They had run out of water, out of air conditioning, out of water for the toilets to flush; they ran out of ice; they ran out of food; they ran out of booze. Everybody *got on* the train neatly, quietly, conservatively dressed . . . but by the time we began to get to Washington, they looked like they'd been through some terrible experience for a couple of days; men's ties were down; women could only undress to a certain extent; people's shirts were open. The mood . . . and the condition of everybody, by the time we got there, in the dark, was terrible.

ANN BUCHWALD, *family friend*
When we knew we were literally almost home, it went back to the old sorrow in the car. It had started sad, and then it got sort of gay; and people changing cars and visiting, and you saw people from Europe or people you hadn't seen from another part of the country, and they were talking politics and showing baby pictures; and we all had a sandwich and coffee, and finally some of us had a drink. And then, all of a sudden, it went down the other way. The light started to fail as it got dark. Everybody was awfully tired. The air conditioning failed. All of a sudden, the very people who had been keeping up conversations just were lumps. Nobody moved. One woman looked across at me. She'd been staring at me for half an hour. I can't remember who she was. She said, "You look just so sad." Well, why wouldn't I? I got mad at her. I thought, Why should she criticize me for looking sad? As though I were a party poop, you know? And from then on, I didn't say a word to anybody.

PETER SMITH, *campaign worker*
There are various descriptions of the Ambassador Hotel. One, that

331

it was a haunted-house type place. But it was this sprawling old hotel, which couldn't have been more suited to us . . . to our purposes. He really enjoyed himself there. It was like an estate. He could take Freckles out. I remember we'd be late, and Ethel would still be upstairs getting ready. But then, instead of going to the bottom level, where all the cars were and all the people were waiting, and so forth, we'd walk out to the backyard with Freckles, and he used to ask me about the campaign. Very nuts-and-bolts questions.

RICHARD GOODWIN, *politician*
On Primary day, I was out at Malibu with him at John Frankenheimer's house. We were talking about politics mostly; Bobby slept a little bit—he was sleeping beside the pool. There were the four of us: Bobby and me and Fred Dutton and Teddy White, and I guess Ethel was there and the children.

Then, about the middle of the afternoon, we got the early projections from CBS. CBS polls people as they come out of the polling places: it was forty-nine per cent to forty-one per cent for Kennedy, and that looked very, very good, better than it turned out to be, of course. We began talking about what we ought to say in the victory statement. Finally, about five o'clock, Bobby went in to take a nap; and I went back to my hotel room to try to write a draft of a possible statement. Then I drove to the Ambassador and met him at his suite, where we spent the evening. A lot of people were there; in fact, we had to go and sit in the bathroom; it was the only room where we could talk privately, sitting on the sink discussing what we could do next. He felt good about what seemed to be a great victory but, as you know, we knew we had serious difficulties coming up—especially in Ohio, New Jersey, Pennsylvania—we were probably going to lose delegates there next week.

DUN GIFFORD, *campaign aide*
He wanted to make a number of telephone calls that night after the returns were in—to various political leaders and friends, and others around the country. But we were missing, for some reason, the phone book with the telephone numbers of, for example, Mayor Daley, Governor Hughes, Ambassador Mahoney, Walter Reuther, John Glenn, and so forth. It was an oversight. I did get a couple. I got George McGovern's. The Senator called him after the South Dakota primary results were in, and he had a nice talk with him. This was just before he went downstairs for his victory statement. He called Kenny O'Don-

nell. Those were the only two calls, really, that he made before he went downstairs. He was going to make a lot more afterwards.

I was sitting there on the bed, on the phone trying to get the numbers. He came over, and he said, "You look very unhappy. What's the matter?" I said, "You know, I'm just trying to get these damn telephone numbers so that you can get these people on the phone." You know the way he looks; he looks down under his eyebrows at you. He was standing in his shirtsleeves with his arms crossed like that. He said, "Do you want to know something?" He said, "We had this exact tableau in 1960, when we were trying to get phone numbers for John Kennedy. I was blistering mad that somebody didn't have those phone numbers!" He said, "Maybe there should be somebody like me who's blistering mad that we don't have those phone numbers." Then he laughed and, you know, he drifted away and looked at the television again.

PETE HAMILL, *columnist*

I guess the last conversation he had on God's earth was with Breslin and me, sitting in the corner on the floor in the room out there in the Ambassador. By then he knew he had won, but it was not really the victory he needed; it wasn't a knockout . . . a decision really. Matter of fact, if he had lived, I suppose they would have said McCarthy won a kind of moral victory. He knew the New York primary was going to be a bloodbath. He couldn't quite understand what it was all about in a way . . . that there was so much anti-Bobby hatred.

New York is really filled with haters . . . unbelievable amount of hate. We were trying to figure out ways to get out of it. Breslin was saying, "It's the goddamn Jews! Ya gotta get to the Jews!" And Bobby was laughing at him, you know. He said, "I'd like to get to the New York *Times* first!" Then we finished. Drysdale had just pitched his sixth straight shutout, and he made a note of that. He was looking for Cesar Chavez; they couldn't find him.

WALTER SHERIDAN, *campaign aide*

All Cesar wanted for his men was to bring them to the victory party. They asked me, and I said, "Of course you can." The night before the election, he had gotten a marimba band. He asked the farm workers if they'd like the marimba band to go with them to the victory party the next night, and they all voted yes. It's just amazing! Everything is democratic; he puts everything to a vote. Steve Smith and Jerry Cummings had told me things were getting too expensive and we couldn't have the marimba band. So I told Cesar, and he said, "That's too bad. I shouldn't have done it, but I put it to a vote. So we've got to have it. So, we just won't come." I said, "Bring your band."

That night, it was beautiful . . . the mob in that hotel. I waited out in front for Cesar and his people. All of a sudden, there they came: the marimba band and 200 Mexican-Americans! We marched through the lower lobby of that hotel. The marimba-band musicians couldn't speak English, but Cesar told them, "Follow *him*," meaning me, "no matter what." They followed me everywhere! I couldn't move without that marimba band!

DOLORES HUERTA, *vice president, United Farm Workers Organizing Committee*

Cesar had been there, but he was uncomfortable without Helen, his wife, and so he went back to East Los Angeles to get her. Then Walter Sheridan came down looking for Cesar, because the Senator wanted Cesar to escort him downstairs. So, Walter said to me, "Dolores, would you like to escort the Senator down?" I said, "Why, I'd be thrilled to death." We went up to the Senator's suite. He came out of the suite and we started downstairs. I told the Senator that we were all so glad that the campaign was over and that he had won. He said, "I'm very grateful for all of the work that you've done for me. To Cesar and all of you. . . ."

That's when I told him that a hundred per cent of the eligible voters came out to vote in four precincts! He said, "Is it . . . really?" I said, "Yeah." He just reached over and gave me this great big hug, you know. So I reached over and gave *him* a hug. It looked silly. Ethel standing there; she probably thought, What is this woman doing? We kept on walking down and we got into the elevator. He was going to walk through the lobby, and somebody said, "No, Senator. You should come through the kitchen to avoid the crowds." I asked the Senator, "How would you like us to go to New York . . . for all the farm workers to go to New York and work on your campaign in New York?"

We were just kind of joshing around. We got down to the kitchen and . . . golly! All of the kitchen help was out there. He went over and shook hands with everyone. Then . . . we went back up to the podium overlooking the ballroom. I kept getting knocked back because

I'm small; people kept pushing me off. But then one of the guys would come and put me up in front again.

FRANK MANKIEWICZ, *press secretary*

We had talked about what he would say. He wanted to be sure that he included every group that participated in the campaign. I told him that Don Drysdale had just pitched his sixth straight shutout for the Los Angeles Dodgers that night, and that might be a good way to begin his speech. He thought that was right. So he wrote that down; and then, of course, the question of the black vote, which had been very decisive, and Cesar Chavez and Dolores Huerta; and he wanted to say something nice about Jesse Unruh, who had done a good job. He put all that down, and then he took that paper with him. Then we talked for a little while about the campaign and about what was going to happen next. Then we walked out and went down to the platform.

PETE HAMILL

The platform, I guess, had two or three steps. While Bob was talking, some kid tried to come in through the drapes in the back. I don't remember what he looked like. I don't know whether it was Sirhan Sirhan or not. Bill Barry said, "Hey! Beat it!" Barry was standing right at the foot of the stairs. The kid disappeared. I couldn't tell you whether it was him or not. I didn't see Sirhan till he started to fire the shots. I was walking backwards, watching Bobby, and this man was right directly to my right. And he fired. He obviously knew how to handle a pistol. He was standing there with his arms straight out: bam! bam! bam! . . . like that, which is the way a pistol shooter, a guy who learns how to shoot a pistol on range, lines a gun.

GEORGE PLIMPTON, *author*

The guy must have run over my heels on his way to the Senator. One wonders so often . . . if only something had happened to hold me up . . . perhaps I would have seen him. But then someone told me he had the gun hidden in a newspaper. So often in one's mind one resets the stage and places the key figures in slightly different positions so that what did happen is avoided. The guy is subdued before he takes a step. It's a pretty sad game. So the shots went off. They didn't sound like balloon pops to me. No. There was nothing frivolous about those sounds, which came in a fearsome succession;

335

a sort of shuddering cry began; the mood in the room changed so abruptly that the difference was palpable . . . like a violent drop in temperature.

JACK GALLIVAN, *campaign aide*

I was pretty close to the doors when I heard the shots. I spun. I remember seeing Bill Barry leaping out of the crowd towards the center of this mayhem. I got there just as Bill had pinned the guy down to disarm him. Bill had Sirhan pinned against a sort of industrial-kitchen steel shelf. When Bill took the gun away from Sirhan, he placed it on that shelf. I told Bill to take care of the Senator and I would take care of Sirhan. Bill let go of the guy before I grabbed him . . . and Sirhan grabbed the gun *back* . . . which had been laid on the counter. Sirhan just grabbed the gun again. So I was stuck with the same problem Bill had. I grabbed the guy's hand and managed to immobilize it with the gun in it, but I had hold of it in such a way that I had no leverage. I couldn't get it away from him.

I did it the wrong way. I cut myself very badly doing it. I stuck the meaty part of my hand between the hammer of the gun and whatever the hammer hits on a gun . . . and kept it there. I cut a big gouge . . . big hole in my hand. An FBI agent who was interviewing me later said, "Well, you did it all wrong! You could have just grabbed the cylinder. If the cylinder can't rotate, then . . ." I felt, Gee! You know, the next time the opportunity comes up, I'll do it!

CHARLES QUINN, *television correspondent*

We were just winding up. Kennedy had just finished his speech, and my instructions from my director were to "wrap it up and throw it back to McGee," who was going to throw it back to Huntley and Brinkley, and we were going to sign off. So I did that. I was taking my gear off. I heard some shrieking. So I said to my floorman, "I think something's happened; I'll come right back."

I walked four or five steps. Then somebody came by shouting "Kennedy's been shot! I think Kennedy's been shot!" So I went charging into this room and, by that time, all pandemonium had broken loose. Girls were yelling, and there was all kinds of hysteria. I got to the entrance to the corridor. There were people blocking the door, yelling for a doctor; I got behind a guy who was a doctor. I just stayed on his back, and we forced our way through a couple of lines. People were streaming out; there was all kinds of confusion and cursing and yelling. I got inside and I really bowled my way through another line. I just *insisted* on getting through. People were going berserk in there; it was an unbelievable scene. Kennedy was lying on the floor, bleeding.

I saw Jimmy Breslin standing up on one of these aluminum kitchen serving tables. I crawled up there because I knew they were going to throw everybody out and I wanted to stay as long as I could. Everybody left, and I was just up there alone. All the press had been pushed out; police were all over the place and, of course, the Kennedy people . . . Ethel was leaning over Bob. Bob's shirt was open. He was still alive, because I could see him fingering some rosary beads that were lying across his belt.

Then there was a big surge of people and police came running in, and there were all kinds of arguments. Policemen were arguing with Bill Barry and Fred Dutton and Frank Mankiewicz. I had a talk with Mankiewicz in there; Mankiewicz was very cool. I asked him a lot of questions: Who did it? How many shots were fired? Where is the assailant? What had happened? and so forth. Mankiewicz, even at that critical moment, answered a lot of my questions. Nobody pushed me out. I stayed up there kind of as inconspicuous as possible. At one point, Kennedy said . . . I think it was Kennedy who said, "Would you please ask them to stand back so I can have some room." So everybody moved back again. At this point, there were not very many people in the room. Ethel looked up at me at one point and said . . . I can see her now . . . she said, "Oh, Chuck, please go away." But I couldn't leave. The serving table was about ten feet long; and so I turned around, and I walked away from her along to the end of the table. I was crouched because the ceiling was low. By the time I turned around again, she had gone back to Bob. Then some other people came in, and they brought a stretcher in, and they lifted Kennedy up on the stretcher. And the last thing I heard him say . . . "No, no, no, no, no," like that, in the voice of a rabbit at the end of his life. At that point, Ethel got excited. Up to then, Ethel had been very calm. At that point, she got terribly excited. Then they all kind of surged out in one big movement of people, out of the room. That's the last time I saw Kennedy.

EARL GRAVES, *campaign aide*
When I saw him lying on the floor . . . the first thing that came to me in just looking at him was the fact that he would shake it off.

He was such a strong individual that I just didn't think he could die like that.

GEORGE PLIMPTON

I saw Gallivan struggling with the gunman and rushed to help. He still had the gun. We pulled him back across the steam table. The guy was strong. The gun kept waving around. Rosey Grier and Rafer Johnson arrived. The gunman had his fingers in the trigger guard, and we kept the gun pointed at the kitchen wall behind the steam tables in case it went off again. The gun was as shiny and black as a beetle. We were all staring at it, wide-eyed and shouting. It was hard to get away from him, perhaps because so many hands and fingers were grappling with it. We did finally, and Rosey Grier dropped the thing into his pocket.

One or two people outside the ring around the guy began throwing punches—arching them like rockets over the people who had him down. None of them landed. Someone outside the ring saw his leg sticking out and twisted it. The guy said: "You're hurting me." The word "hurt" unleashed a storm of abuse, as if under the circumstances it was such an indignity that he *consider* using such a word. I was not very cogent . . . or cool. I remember positioning myself, holding the guy so that my back was to where the Senator was. I did not dare look back there.

JACK GALLIVAN

People there tried awfully hard to hurt Sirhan. I remember one guy leaning over and grabbing *me*, thinking *I* had done it! I was *shocked* at the thought! The guy grabbed me by the hair. Fortunately, I have rather insensitive hair and I just sort of let him yank, screaming all the time that I wasn't the guy. But that was the kind of melee we were in . . . right in the midst of it. Plimpton was three inches from the guy's face just *staring* into it . . . into Sirhan's face. I'll never forget. . . . I have a better recall of Plimpton's face than I do of Sirhan's from that. George was *mesmerized*. Well, we all were dumfounded. As soon as the guy pulling at my hair discovered his mistake, he went on to grab Sirhan.

RICHARD HARWOOD, *national editor*, The Washington Post

Jim Wilson, a CBS cameraman who had been with Bob all through the campaign, was so shocked that he smashed his camera against the wall. He tried to keep other photographers away so that Bobby could have air.

HARRY BENSON, *photographer*

The ambulance people came. Someone got him by the legs and by the shoulders . . . and lifted him onto the stretcher. I couldn't photograph him because it was so dark in there.

They put a rope of sorts up in the kitchen . . . made of sheets it looked like. This girl wearing a straw hat ducked under it, and she took her hat off and put it on top of the bloodstains.

Someone told me they saw roses on the floor the next day.

I never saw them. I only saw the hat—a straw hat with pictures of Kennedy on it.

SAUL STEINBERG, *artist*

Nobody had really the appetite to kill a Johnson. Or people like Coolidge or Hoover. But people like Jack Kennedy, like Bobby . . . represent the hero, handsome, courageous. They look for drama; and it attracts the counterpart. Just the way the hero is in search of a dragon, the dragon is always in search of a hero.

ROBERT SCHEER, *editor,* Ramparts

Sirhan was so much a creature of the American dream . . . much, *much* more than he ever was a creature of the Arab-Israel war or Arab society or Muslim culture. This kid spent his whole life watching television in Los Angeles. He was a little guy. He never could make it with women. He never had any excitement in his life. What we learned in talking to his brothers was that this kid did nothing but watch TV! The only reason he had wanted to be a jockey was he'd get on TV; the only reason Kennedy entered his life was because Kennedy was always on TV. It's like the American dream gone crazy! This kid watching TV . . . which is where America lives; it doesn't live anywhere else. And he's watching it, and Kennedy is somehow important, while he's unimportant, miserable, alienated . . . which must be true of a hundred ninety million other Americans. All of a sudden this kid's got a slant somewhere deep down in his brain that, "Hey, I'm an Arab. This guy's wearing a yarmulke. I'm going to off him, and I'm going to enter history on TV." His model was Oswald. That was the whole bizarre thing about Kennedy's death—the guy that killed him came out of the nightmare of the American dream. Kennedy got killed by his alter ego. It was all a fabrica-

339

tion of television. Before he got off the plane, Kennedy would be fixing himself, and patting his cheeks, and checking how he looked in the mirror, mussing his hair. All for TV. "How'd I do on TV?" That's what's important. "How'd it go over on TV?" And then this poor mother who kills him lives just glued to TV. None of it had anything to do with serious politics. Americans don't live unless they get on TV. Sirhan, this nothing, bland, colorless character had come alive because he'd entered television. All of a sudden he was a person; up until then, he'd been a nonperson. That's the whole syndrome he comes out of. It had to do with that peculiar American dream and ambition to be recognized by television . . . you want to make it within the American system, and for that poor little kid, that was the only way to make it.

RICHARD GOODWIN
McCarthy visited the hospital that morning with Ted Kennedy; he came over, and he said he had heard the name "Sirhan Sirhan" on the radio—the same first name and the same last name, like in Camus' *The Stranger*. A man comes out of nowhere and kills. The same first name and last name was so unreal and mysterious.

DAVID HACKETT, *family friend*
The first clue you really had was when they took him into this operating room. No one said anything to anybody. There was a tough lieutenant standing there who wouldn't get out of the room because he said there was the possibility of someone coming in and shooting up the place. I mean the security was overdone. I asked him to go. Finally, Bill Barry asked him to go. He said, "No. My duty is here 'cause they're going to shoot at us from across in this other room." I said, "No, they're not!" Anyway, we never got rid of him. But then, when they had a conversation about operating, I think that was sort of the first clue that there was really no hope at all. Finally, Steve Smith said to me, "You'd better . . . in case . . . prepare for . . ." So that's when I called McNamara. And I called John Nolan. I called Tom Powers. Then I called Katzenbach. Those guys were to make arrangements. We had someone take a look at Boston, take a look at New York, and someone take a look at Arlington. So those preparations were going on.

ROBERT LOWELL, *poet*
I mean one of his possibilities was that he was always doomed. When it happened . . . it's very strange when you sort of anticipate some

340

thing; then, when it happens, you're almost *more* astonished than if you hadn't anticipated it. He felt he was doomed, and you knew that he felt that. The course he took, it was black, and that gave a kind of tragedy to it all. It wasn't his energy that doomed him. The ambition was a burden . . . that he had to run for President, that he was doomed with that possibility and duty, and it's rather an awful thing. He knew that, and he had no middle course possible to him.

Bobby seemed so much younger than he actually was. His death seemed like the death of one's own adolescence. It's partly his character and something athletic about him, which is typical of schoolboys; he's very much sort of Massachusetts Eastern shore, he's almost *the* Eastern seaboard boy. It's so awful to think of this person, much older than he seemed, much older in some ways than his maturity, and then wise beyond his years in other ways, that this life should be cut off. Visually, any instinct I had was that he would live long after I would in the distant course of years. Bob would outlive me; he was not only younger, but he took better care of himself. Except that I thought he was in some way doomed. How good to live a life where you're not shot at!

THE REVEREND ANDREW J. YOUNG, *civil-rights leader*

You mourn for the loss of Robert Kennedy; you tended to mourn more for the country. I'm really scared to death about where we are now. I don't know whether I'm just tired and haven't gotten a grip on my own thinking process; but there are so many parallels to the period right after the assassination of Lincoln, where a Johnson took office, had trouble; where lots of leadership was taken from the scene—mostly by death: Massachusetts abolitionist Senators died off; Frederick Douglass went out to Haiti. Power was restored to the slavocracy. You ended up with an election for the first time in history giving the presidency to the man with forty-seven per cent of the popular vote and defeating the candidate with fifty-one per cent. The minority Republican victors then formed a coalition with the South, canceling out most of the gains for which the Civil War had been fought. One of the reasons why the Thirteenth, Fourteenth and Fifteenth Amendments were never enforced was because of agreements between the South and the Republicans, with Rutherford Hayes in office. The deal took the federal troops out of the South and appointed conservative judges to the Supreme Court, where several pieces of legislation were declared unconstitutional. Blacks caught hell from the segregationists. From 1865 to 1875, things had been going very well. Liberated blacks wrote some of the most progressive and enlightened legislation in the history of the republic, such as free public education for black and white. Most of the South under slavery had no public schools for either. With the return of the slave oligarchy, we went back to a Ku Klux Klan society. Racism regained its grip on our throat. A country can't afford to lose, you know, three men like Robert Kennedy and John F. Kennedy and Martin King. It takes too long to build people like that.

23

DAVE POWERS, *curator, John F. Kennedy Museum*

I said, "Let's keep it going so that the day will never end." It would mean that you were always with him. You had that feeling while we were riding from New York to Washington: we'll keep it going and then head somewhere else and just keep going . . . on and on, right off into the Pacific Ocean.

ELIE ABEL, *television correspondent*

I had a peculiar sense on that train that it was a little like a time capsule, and that everybody on it had been part of an era of a particular group of people at a particular time in American history, but it was ending that day, and they all knew it. They sat there sipping whisky out of paper cups, talking about everything under the sun—everything they had ever been involved in—and yet with a kind of final sadness that when the train got to Washington and we went on to Arlington, that was it; that was the end. And it was the end not in terms of personal associations, because obviously some of those people were going to see each other again under other circumstances. It was the end of a particular excitement, a particular adventure.

SHIRLEY MacLAINE, *actress*

It's too bad that at times like that you need a common denominator of tragedy to make you realize it, and then this awful feeling of, "My God, we'll get there; we'll get off. We'll go into the buses, and we'll walk on some green grass. There'll be a procession and women in black

343

dresses, and it'll be over! Everything that Bobby ever meant will be gone!" That's what had been going through my mind most of the afternoon as we crept along.

ANN BUCHWALD, *family friend*
Do you remember the noise as we got out of the train? That was the band that met us . . . the Navy band. And it was like the end of the world. I'll always remember that heavy beat, which was part of any funeral; but it echoed so! And it was louder than life! President Johnson's face was so red, and so was the Vice-President's. I couldn't figure it out, until I realized it was a red carpet, and the lights were beaming and making everybody look as if they were going to explode. And then that thump from the band. It was like a huge heart beating.

DAVID HACKETT, *family friend*
They had the U.S. Navy guys waiting there. They wanted to carry him. They had the carpet down and the soldiers lined up all the way down. So it became very serious again, very quickly. We said no.

Lord Harlech had figured out a better way to carry him, and we tried that. It took the weight off; all of us had to get in step because we were clumping on each other. So we carried him down into the hearse.

ANN BUCHWALD
I dreaded the removal of the coffin from the train. I knew that later on that night at the Arlington Cemetery they wouldn't put the casket in the ground because they never do any more; it's too awful. They leave it. You walk away, and after you've left they put it in the ground. So, I knew I didn't have to worry about seeing that. But for some reason, I didn't want to see the coffin taken from the train.

There was this big thumping noise from the Navy band, and we watched. Teddy and everybody lined up, and they pulled the casket off the rear end of the car. The hearse was open and it was all white inside. Everything was out of proportion to me. The noise was too loud. And that hearse looked gaping. It looked like the opening of a mine. I think maybe by then we were all just too sad, or I was. I was almost delirious. It was strange to see the President and Vice-President standing there, looking just as helpless as the rest of us. Nobody had anything to do except the pallbearers.

344

LAUREN BACALL, *actress*

Ann and Art Buchwald and I waited to see them put the coffin in the hearse. You had to see it to believe it; and even so, I looked at that box several times, and I didn't think anyone was in there.

WILLIAM WALTON, *artist, family friend*

We had decided that the ceremony in Washington should emphasize the main parts of his career: the procession should go past the Department of Justice. Then we tried to think how, symbolically, his feeling for the poor and the dispossessed could be expressed; so we thought of passing what was then Resurrection City, past the followers of the Southern Christian Leadership Conference camped opposite the Lincoln Memorial. We also decided that the Lincoln Memorial would be the other symbolic thing. I had been involved in the President's funeral and choosing his gravesite. We were all in agreement that Bobby's must look and feel different; we were all in agreement that it should be non-military. Though the distinguished person's funeral in Washington is ordinarily military, we got a message from Teddy that he felt strongly it shouldn't be military. That set a great deal of the pattern right away. RFK hadn't been a military man, and it just wouldn't have been right. We skipped the Capitol, though he was a Senator, because the President had lain in state there. This would have been possible for Bobby too, but we didn't want it . . . not following in his brother's footsteps quite this much. We wanted to emphasize that he had an individual career, beyond being the brother of the President, and we wanted that implicit in the ceremony.

When we had the procession pause by the Senate Building, by the Justice Department, and by the Lincoln Memorial, we felt that we had symbolically touched the three great phases of his own personal career.

HERB SCHMERTZ, *campaign aide*

There was a press bus in the cortege. The campaign press—the reporters who had been following us around since the beginning of the campaign—petitioned us to have a last press bus in the cortege. I should say they *insisted* on it.

RICHARD DRAYNE, *campaign aide*

So we asked two reporters—Dick Harwood of the Washington *Post* and Hays Gorey of *Time*—who had been along throughout the campaign—to put together a list of the people they thought should be on this last bus. The list was put together not on the basis of loyalty to the Senator but of who had been with him most—the people who had covered the campaign and were part of the traveling press. For instance, the UPI came up and were absolutely furious because one of their guys was not going to be included. They shouted, "What do you mean— there's an AP guy on there—the Washington *Post's* on there—L.A. *Times's* on there . . . all these people are on there. You've *got* to put UPI on there. It's the other wire service." Pierre said, "Well, you didn't cover the campaign. You covered it with your local people at each stop. So you're not on the bus." They fumed and ranted, but they never did get on the bus.

My job was this: I called one of the advance men in Washington, and I said I want you to understand that this bus is there for *sentimental* reasons, and we want it to be right up near the front of the cavalcade, up near the family and not in the back. He said, "Oh, yeah. I under- stand. I understand. Of course, it's terrifically difficult, if not impossible, to get a bus into a funeral motorcade. It just isn't *done.*"

So I knew we were going to have trouble when we got down to the Union Station and saw all those limousines and black Cadillacs lined up. I talked to an advance man. I said, "Where's the special press bus?" "Well," he said, "it's over there," and I said fine. I asked where it was going to be in the procession. He looked at his list and said it's going to be twenty-third. So, counting the hearse, we were twenty-four cars back. So I said okay. There was nothing I could do about it at the time.

Then I went up to Dick Tuck. He was checking the people who were getting on the bus. Lauren Bacall came up and tried to get on the bus, and Tuck said, No, not this one, nobody can get on this one unless he's on my list. Then Arthur Schlesinger came up and *he* was turned down. I said to Tuck: "Tuck, I don't know why this bus ought to be twenty- four cars back—do you?" And he said, "I certainly don't." So we went to Frank Mankiewicz and said, "Frank, this bus is twenty-four cars back. Do you think . . . ?" He said, "No, it shouldn't be that far back."

So when the bus was loaded, we got the bus driver to pull over as close as he could to where the motorcade would be going by. Then Frank peered in each limousine as it went by, to determine if members of the family were sitting in them. We felt that after the members of the family had all gone past—well, *we'd* get into line. We saw about six cars go by without family, and finally we decided rather arbitrarily that it was *our* place. So somebody just stood out there . . . which we had done many times in the campaign, standing out there gesturing an

346

arguing . . . and we stopped the line of limousines so we could pull the bus into the procession. Then off we went. We got up to Capitol Hill, past the corner of Delaware and Constitution, where we turned and then went down the hill and a few blocks up on the other side, and we were still about sixth in line.

Then we realized that there were cars on either side trying to get by us. The Cadillacs were inching up. You could tell the people in those cars were asking themselves what they were doing behind a *bus*. Finally the car in front of us stopped. The whole procession stopped. A guy got out with a radio. We thought he was a Secret Service guy, but we were never sure. He came back and he got on the bus. Unfortunately, the driver let him on. The driver did not have quite the zeal that we had.

Once he was on the bus he said, Okay, you're not supposed to be in line here . . . acting like, you know, we had just blundered into it . . . as if we didn't know what we were doing. Everybody sat up and said, "Get the hell off here," and they *kicked him off*. The guy was flabbergasted; he was pushed right out the door and into the street, the door closed after him, and we said, "Okay, let's go."

We went another mile or so, and then the whole thing started again. The guy was smart this time. He stood in front of the bus . . . he shouted, "You're not going anywhere!" They started moving cars up. Frank and Dick Tuck started arguing with the guy. I got out about thirty feet in front of the bus so that the limousines trying to get by would have had to run me over. Well, they were *going* to run me over, it was quite apparent, so I had to step aside. We let about six or eight cars in before we were finally able to stop the procession again and get ourselves back in.

Later we learned that the cars we let go by were the President of the United States, and six Secret Service cars, and then the Vice-President. They had been breathing the exhaust of the press bus almost the entire way to the cemetery!

ROGER WILKINS, *director of the Community Relations Service, Department of Justice*

We sat in the small room behind the Attorney General's office, and on television we watched the progress of that train down the Eastern seaboard. We knew that when the train got to Washington, the funeral procession would come down Constitution Avenue and would pause briefly in front of the Department of Justice . . . and then move on. Ramsey Clark, who really never gave orders, asked clearly and strongly that the people who were leaders of the Department be there on the sidewalk in front of the Department when that procession went by. We lined up on the curb and stood there in the night. We saw the stream of lights coming down the Hill from the direction of the Capitol toward the Department. And we were all there: Immigration, Anti-Trust, Civil Rights, Deputy Attorney General, Attorney General, Community Relations Service, Civil Division, Criminal Division . . . everybody was there but the FBI. I had been made aware of the arrest of James Earl Ray earlier. The clearest recollection I have is that Attorney General Ramsey Clark had shown me that press release issued by the FBI. It had not been cleared by the Attorney General prior to its release. In my judgment, it was issued on that day to make the FBI look awfully good and let them share in the headlines the next day. It's one of those things in life that makes you awfully sad. A good man had died, and they did not honor him that day. They tried to dilute the national mourning.

We stood and we thought. I remember thinking that we had lost one of the few men in the country who had the capacity to gather the dreams of an awful lot of Americans . . . dreamers, hopers, yearners were drawn to him, and they saw embodied in his spirit and his energy, his fierce drive and compassion, the embodiment of what they hoped for and yearned for . . . for the country and for themselves. And the procession came. It slowed. It stopped. In the front seat of the hearse you could see the pale, white face of Senator Edward Kennedy. And then it moved on. . . .

THE REVEREND FREDERICK D. KIRKPATRICK, *recreation director at Resurrection City*
When the cortege passed Resurrection City, a lot of people raised their hands. A soul brother. Soul force. So that when they raised their hands with the fist clenched, it meant that they were in cahoots. They took him as a soul brother! Right. Blue-eyed soul brother, we used to call him. Right.

SYLVIA WRIGHT, *reporter*
It was so dark at Resurrection City. But then there were those thousands of candles, and people holding matches and lighting pieces of newspaper, tightly rolled so that they could control the flame . . . and to hear all the people singing the "Battle Hymn of the Republic." It was jerky because people at one point we passed in the cortege would be at a different part of the song than the next people. And we

348

could see, as we got near Arlington . . . we could see across the lawn and up to the hill, all the candles.

JACKIE COOPER, *actor, producer*
Evidently, the funeral director had not been up to check on the hill where the plot was. When the pallbearers got to the hearse at Arlington, he told them: "Now, you go up *this* way. I'll be standing there with the Bishop and several priests. Right under a magnolia tree, you'll see all these flowers. That's where the plot is. You just bring the casket right in front of us and set it down." What the funeral director didn't know was that there were so many flowers, many of them had been moved over to another hill underneath *another* magnolia tree! That's where the pallbearers headed for. They took the casket right by the six priests standing there where they were supposed to be, slowly watching, turning and craning their necks around as the casket went by! They didn't know what to say; nobody wanted to say, Where are you going?

RUTH BERLE, *family friend*
John Seigenthaler told me that they were to walk up a hill, and then bear left, and then stop. So, they started up the hill. They kept on walking, and suddenly John said to Steve Smith, "I have a feeling we've walked too far." Steve said, "So do I." John said, "What are we going to do?" Steve said, "Let's stop, and go over and ask the man where we should be." John said, "No, *you* go. You're the campaign manager." So Steve went over and said to the man, "Are we in the right place? Are we going right?" The man said, "You've been doing fine! But you've just gone a little too far!" Just hysterical. John said, "I could hear Bobby laughing so . . . saying, 'You've *really* screwed it up again!' "

ANN BUCHWALD
I didn't see a thing because I was on the hillside looking up through people's waistlines. We were caught in with the crowds. I saw all the people with rolled-up pieces of newspaper, who didn't have candles. Did you see that? Rolled up cones of paper, and they were burning them.

MICHAEL HARRINGTON, *author*
At the graveside, the only words spoken were words from the liturgy. And the traditional words of the Catholic liturgy strike me as superior

349

to what most orators would say under the circumstances. That liturgy, and then "America the Beautiful" being played by a band—the whole quality of the night was simple. After the train ride, it had to be; anything more profound and it would have tipped the whole day over.

CORETTA SCOTT KING (*Mrs. Martin Luther King, Jr.*)
It's just a belief that I have—a strong feeling—that there *has* to be a force in the universe working for good. Bobby Kennedy was doing a lot of good in this world for a lot of people . . . like my husband . . . and perhaps the greater good goes on after him. Because he died in the cause, you know, and many people have been inspired by his work . . . perhaps more than had he died a natural death. You keep thinking about how the death can be redemptive. As my husband said, "Unearned suffering is redemptive."

ALFRED FITT, *Assistant Secretary of Defense*
I saved one candle for myself and stood there feeling quite broken up emotionally at the end of all this. We were all sort of hanging onto these last few moments on earth of Robert Kennedy. And it was utterly hopeless. The service didn't last long. The President and Mrs. Johnson left—I think they were the first ones back to their car. The Secret Service were just terribly nervous. They hustled him out of there. Then the family. Then it was just sort of a disorganized, uncertain milling around as people tried to find their way back to buses and cars.

KATE HADDAD (*Mrs. William Haddad*)
And all the light! And I don't know who it was—which one of the kids—but one of them began calling. It sounded like, "Daddy. Daddy." And one just hoped that it wasn't.

BONNIE LEFKOWITZ, *campaign worker*
What I remember most about the burial was not the ceremony, which was short and simple, but afterwards. The family and close friends practically ran away—they left quickly, as if it were all over anyhow and there was nothing but death there at the grave. Then the crowds from the hillside began to converge on the coffin—in waves, sort of, kneeling and sobbing. There were no guards; no one stopped them. The people behind the ropes strung along the road came up the hill and converged on the coffin, touching it or praying. It went on for

quite a while—no need for security any more; all the important people had left, and the man was dead.

ANTHONY M. BOYSA, *fireman*

We stayed by the engine at Union Station. We stood off to one side because the motors were too hot. It was real hot. We were supposed to put the locomotives in Ivy City Engine House—that's the yard outside Washington—but we never did. We waited for about three and a half hours, and then they told us to deadhead home; that means we rode back as passengers, not working back. We took half the cars that were on the Kennedy train—it was a deadhead train—to New York. No passengers. Just us and a couple of conductors deadheading home.

Biographies

ELIE ABEL—dean, Graduate School of Journalism, Columbia University. Washington and foreign correspondent, the New York *Times* (1949–1959); NBC correspondent (1961–1969). Author of *The Missile Crisis*.

THE REVEREND RALPH ABERNATHY—president, Southern Christian Leadership Conference.

JOSEPH ALSOP — syndicated columnist. Author (with Stewart Alsop): *We Accuse* and *Reporter's Trade; From the Silent Earth*.

STEWART ALSOP—columnist. Author: *Nixon and Rockefeller; The Center*.

MARTIN ARNOLD—journalist, the New New York *Times*.

LAUREN BACALL—actress. Stage: *Applause, Cactus Flower*. Motion pictures: *Key Largo; To Have and Have Not*.

MARGARET BADDERS—housewife, Wilmington, Delaware.

CURTIS LEE BAKER (known as "Black Jesus")—refers to himself as "a fighter for his people." The West End Help Center, West Oakland, California.

RUSSELL BAKER—columnist, the New York *Times*.

JAMES BALDWIN—author: *Go Tell It on the Mountain; The Fire Next Time; Another Country; Giovanni's Room*.

GEORGE BALL—attorney, investment banker. Senior partner, Lehman Brothers. Under Secretary of State (1961–1966).

BILL BARRY—president, Smith & Wesson Security. Personal bodyguard to Robert F. Kennedy, presidential campaign (1968).

CHARLES BARTLETT—columnist, the Chicago *Sun Times*.

JOSEPH BELLINGER—supervisor of services, Penn Central Railroad. Resident of Teaneck, New Jersey.

HARRY BENSON—photographer, American and British publications.

RUTH BERLE (Mrs. Milton Berle).

LEONARD BERNSTEIN—laureate conductor, the New York Philharmonic. Composer: *Age of Anxiety; Jeremiah Symphony; West Side Story*. Author: *The Joy of Music; The Infinite Variety of Music*.

ALEXANDER M. BICKEL—professor of

353

law, Yale Law School. Author: *The Supreme Court and the Idea of Progress; The New Age of Political Reform; Politics and The Warren Court; The Least Dangerous Branch.*

K. LE MOYNE BILLINGS—real-estate investor. Vice president, Lennen & Newell (1958–1968); advertising coordinator, Robert F. Kennedy senatorial campaign (1964).

WILLIAM BLAIR, JR.—attorney. General director, John F. Kennedy Center for the Performing Arts. United States Ambassador to Denmark (1961–1964); United States Ambassador to the Philippines (1964–1967).

AL BLUMENTHAL—New York Assemblyman (64th A.D.); attorney. Staff assistant, Robert F. Kennedy presidential campaign (1968).

JULIAN BOND—member, Georgia House of Representatives. A founder, Student Nonviolent Coordinating Committee; a vice-presidential nominee, 1968 Democratic Convention.

CHESTER BOWLES—government official. Under Secretary of State (1961); Ambassador to India (1951–1953) and (1963–1969). Author: *The Coming Political Breakthrough; The Conscience of a Liberal; The Makings of a Just Society.*

ANTHONY M. BOYSA—fireman, Penn Central Railroad.

DAVID BREASTED—correspondent, Washington bureau, the New York *Daily News.*

DAVID BRINKLEY—television news commentator.

GERALDINE BROOKS (Mrs. Budd Schulberg)—actress. Motion pictures: *Possessed; Cry Wolf; Embraceable You.* Stage: *Follow the Girls; A Winter's Tale; Time of the Cuckoo.*

ANN BUCHWALD (Mrs. Art Buchwald).

ART BUCHWALD—syndicated columnist; humorist. Author: *How Much Is That in Dollars?; The Establishment is Alive and Well in Washington; Sheep on the Runway* (play).

MC GEORGE BUNDY—president, the Ford Foundation. Special assistant to the President for National Security (1961–1966). Author of *The Strength of Government.*

CARTER BURDEN—New York City Councilman. Legislative assistant for New York City and State affairs, Robert F. Kennedy Senate staff (1966–1968); state coordinator, New York Citizens for Kennedy, presidential primary (1968).

JOHN BURNS—New York State Democratic Chairman. Mayor of Binghamton, New York (1958–1965).

JOSEPH A. CALIFANO, JR.—attorney. Special assistant on domestic affairs to the President (1965–1969).

TRUMAN CAPOTE—author: *Other Voices, Other Rooms; Breakfast at Tiffany's; In Cold Blood.*

CESAR CHAVEZ—president, United Farm Workers Organizing Committee.

BLAIR CLARK—journalist, newspaper publisher. Foreign correspondent, CBS News (1953–1956); general manager, vice-president, CBS News (1961–1964).

DR. KENNETH CLARK—educator, psychologist. President, Metropolitan Applied Research Center, Inc.; president-elect, American Psychological Association; professor of psychology, City College, New York. Author of *Dark Ghetto*.

RAMSEY CLARK—attorney. Assistant Attorney General, U.S. Justice Department (1961–1965); Attorney General of the United States (1967–1969).

NAIDA COHN—housewife, Boston, Massachusetts.

DR. ROBERT COLES—research psychiatrist, Harvard University Health Service. Author: *Children of Crisis; Hunger and the Dimness of Anguish; Uprooted Children*.

LOUIS COLLINS—fireboat captain, *The John F. Kennedy*, Passaic, New Jersey.

THE REVEREND THOMAS J. CONNELLAN—Paulist priest, Office of the University Apostolate, New York City.

JACK CONWAY—labor official. President, Center for Community Change, Washington, D.C.

JACKIE COOPER—producer-actor. Former vice president, Screen Gems.

JOHN SHERMAN COOPER—senior Senator from the State of Kentucky.

CHARLOTTE CURTIS—women's news editor, the New York *Times*.

DOUGLAS DILLON—chairman, U.S. and Foreign Securities Corporation and U.S. and International Securities Corporation; president, Metropolitan Museum of Art. Secretary of the Treasury (1960–1965).

JOHN DOAR—attorney. President, the Bedford-Stuyvesant D & S Corporation. Assistant Attorney General, Civil Rights Division, U. S. Justice Department (1965–1967).

JOE DOLAN—attorney. Director, administrative planning section, Great Western United Corporation; president, Shakey's Inc. As-

sistant Deputy Attorney General, U.S. Justice Department (1961–1965); administrative assistant to Robert F. Kennedy (1965–1968).

IVANHOE DONALDSON—resident fellow, Institute for Policy Studies. Former executive committee member, Student Nonviolent Coordinating Committee.

RICHARD DRAYNE—press secretary to Senator Edward M. Kennedy.

BURT DRUCKER—staff assistant to Councilman Carter Burden; Democratic State Committeeman (New York).

DR. LEONARD DUHL—psychiatrist. Professor, urban social policy and public health, College of Environmental Design and School of Public Health, University of California, Berkeley. Author of *Urban Conditions*.

ANGIER BIDDLE DUKE—chairman, Newirth Investment Fund, London. Chief of Protocol, White House and U.S. State Department (1960–1965; 1968); United States Ambassador to Spain (1965–1968); United States Ambassador to Denmark (1968–1969).

FRED DUTTON—attorney. Executive director, Robert F. Kennedy Memorial Foundation. Special assistant to President John F. Kennedy (1961); executive director, Democratic National Convention platform committee (1964); personal aide to Robert F. Kennedy, presidential campaign (1968).

MARIAN WRIGHT EDELMAN—attorney. Partner, Washington Research Project (a public-interest law firm).

PETER EDELMAN—attorney. Campaign aide, Arthur Goldberg New York gubernatorial campaign (1970); associate director, Robert F. Kennedy Memorial Foundation. Legislative assistant to Robert F. Kennedy (1965–1968).

RONNIE ELDRIDGE—special assistant to Mayor John V. Lindsay (New York). Former district leader, West Side reform movement (New York).

JOHN ELLIS—scheduling and advance aide, Robert F. Kennedy presidential campaign (1968); intern on Robert F. Kennedy's Senate staff (1967).

VINCENT EMANUEL—electrician, Penn Central Railroad. Resident of Yonkers, New York.

JACK ENGLISH—New York Democratic National Committeeman. Nassau County (New York) Democratic Chairman (1959–1969).

COURTNEY EVANS—attorney. Assistant director, Federal Bureau of Investigation (1940–1964); director, office of Law Enforcement Assistance, U.S. Justice Department (1965–1969).

KAY EVANS (Mrs. Rowland Evans)—alumnae trustee, Vassar College.

ROWLAND EVANS—syndicated columnist. Author (with Robert Novak) of *Lyndon B. Johnson: The Exercise of Power.*

CHARLES EVERS—Mayor, Fayette, Mississippi; civil-rights leader.

THE REVEREND WALTER FAUNTROY—director, Washington Bureau, Southern Christian Leadership Conference. Former vice chairman, City Council, Washington, D.C.

CHARLES FERRIS—general counsel, U.S. Senate Democratic Policy Committee. Attorney, U.S. Justice Department (1961–1963).

ALFRED FITT—attorney. Special adviser to the president, Yale University. General counsel, Department of the Army (1964–1967); Assistant Secretary of Defense for Manpower (1967–1969).

MICHAEL FORRESTAL—attorney. Executive secretary, Advisory Committee, Institute of Politics, John Fitzgerald Kennedy School of Government, Harvard University. Senior member, White House national security staff (1962–1965).

RON FOX—attorney. Campaign aide, Adam Walinsky for Attorney General of New York campaign (1970). Member, Robert F. Kennedy Senate staff (1966–1968); organizer, New York State Students for Kennedy, Robert F. Kennedy presidential campaign (1968).

SONNY FOX—television producer-performer. Chairman, National Academy of Arts and Sciences.

CLAYTON FRITCHEY—syndicated columnist. Assistant to Secretary of Defense and director, Office of Public Information, U.S. Defense Department (1950–1952); assistant to President Harry S. Truman (1952); special assistant to U.S. Ambassador to the United Nations (1961–1965).

JOHN KENNETH GALBRAITH—economist. Paul M. Warburg professor of economics, Harvard University. Former chairman, Americans for Democratic Action. United States Ambassador to India (1961–1963). Author: *The Affluent Society; The Liberal Hour; The Triumph; Ambassador's Journal.*

JACK GALLIVAN—production assistant, ABC-Sports. Advance man, Robert F. Kennedy presidential campaign (1968).

DUN GIFFORD—real-estate developer.

Campaign aide, Robert F. Kennedy presidential campaign (1968); legislative assistant to Senator Edward M. Kennedy (1967–1970).

FRANK GIFFORD—television sportscaster. Former professional football player, New York Giants (1952–1964).

MARY BAILEY GIMBEL—schoolmate of Robert F. Kennedy at Milton Academy.

ALLEN GINSBERG—poet; lecturer. Author: *Howl and Other Poems; Kaddish and other Poems.*

THE REVEREND WILLIAM GLENN—associate minister, Zion Baptist Church, Philadelphia.

BURT GLINN—photographer, Magnum Photos, Inc.

ARTHUR GOLDBERG—attorney. Democratic candidate for Governor of New York (1970). Secretary of Labor (1961); associate jurist, U.S. Supreme Court (1962–1965); United States Ambassador to the United Nations (1965–1968).

MARK GOLDFUS—Vista volunteer, St. Louis Inner City. Student, University of Delaware (1968).

RICHARD GOODWIN—attorney; politician. Assistant special counsel to President John F. Kennedy (1961); special assistant to President Lyndon B. Johnson (1963–1965). Author: *The Sower's Seed; Triumph or Tragedy: Reflections on Vietnam.*

EARL GRAVES—publisher, *Black Enterprise* magazine; president, Earl Graves Associates, Inc. Legislative assistant to Robert F. Kennedy (1965–1968).

JEFF GREENFIELD—author. Speechwriter to Robert F. Kennedy, presidential campaign (1968); speech-

writer to Mayor John V. Lindsay (1968–1970).

ROOSEVELT GRIER—television host-singer. Former professional football player, Los Angeles Rams.

ED GUTHMAN—national news editor, Los Angeles *Times*. Director, public information, U.S. Justice Department (1961–1964); press secretary to Robert F. Kennedy, senatorial campaign (1964) and 1965.

MILTON GWIRTZMAN—attorney. Campaign aide to John F. Kennedy, Robert F. Kennedy, and Edward M. Kennedy. Author (with William vanden Heuvel) of *On His Own: RFK, 1964–1968.*

DAVID HACKETT—president, David L. Hackett Associates. Special assistant to the Attorney General, U.S. Justice Department (1961–1963); executive director of the President's Committee on Juvenile Delinquency (1961–1963); executive director, the President's Task Force on the Domestic Service Corps (1963).

KATE HADDAD (Mrs. William Haddad)—member, board of trustees, Bank Street School of Education.

DAVID HALBERSTAM—author: *One Very Hot Day; The Unfinished Odyssey of Robert Kennedy; The Making of a Quagmire.* Contributing editor, *Harper's* magazine.

PETE HAMILL—syndicated columnist. Author of *A Killing for Christ.*

CHARLES HARBUTT—photographer, Magnum Photos, Inc.

DR. VINCENT HARDING—chairman, History and Social Sciences, Spelman College, Atlanta; director, Martin Luther King, Jr., Library-Documentation Project. Author of *Must Walls Divide?*

ELIZABETH HARDWICK (Mrs. Robert

Lowell)—author of *A View of My Own*; editor of *The Selected Letters of William James*. Advisory editor, the *New York Review of Books*.

LORD HARLECH (David Ormsby-Gore)—chairman, Harlech Television Company; president, British Board of Film Censors. British Ambassador to the United States (1961–1965); Deputy-Leader of the Opposition, House of Lords (1966–1967). Author of *Must the West Decline?*; co-author of *Change Is Our Ally*.

AVERELL HARRIMAN—limited partner, Brown Brothers Harriman & Co. Governor of the State of New York (1955–1958); Ambassador-at-Large (1961, 1965–1968); Assistant Secretary of State, Far Eastern Affairs (1961–1963); Under Secretary of State, Political Affairs (1963–1965); personal representative of the President to the Paris peace talks (1968–1969).

MICHAEL HARRINGTON—author: *The Other America; Toward a Democratic Left*. Member, national executive committee, Socialist Party.

FRED HARRIS—senior Senator from the State of Oklahoma.

LA DONNA HARRIS (Mrs. Fred Harris)—founder and president, Americans for Indian Opportunity. Chairman, Women's National Advisory Council on Poverty (1967).

RICHARD HARWOOD—national editor, the Washington *Post*.

TOM HAYDEN—New Left leader. Co-founder, Students for a Democratic Society; author: *Rebellion in Newark*; (with Staughton Lynd) *The Other Side*.

SHERRYE HENRY—television reporter, "Newsfront."

ROGER HILSMAN—professor of government, Columbia University. Assistant Secretary of State, Far Eastern Affairs (1963–1964). Author of *To Move a Nation*.

DOLORES HUERTA—vice president, United Farm Workers Organizing Committee.

HUBERT HUMPHREY—Democratic candidate for Senator from the State of Minnesota. Lecturer, Macalester College, St. Paul. Senator from the State of Minnesota (1948–1964); Vice-President of the United States (1965–1968).

LUCY JARVIS — NBC television producer, news and public affairs.

MARIAN JAVITS (Mrs. Jacob K. Javits)—trustee, Experiments in Art and Technology, and New York City Council on the Arts; board member, National Institute of Mental Health, and New York School of Psychiatry.

RAFER JOHNSON—actor, television personality. Olympic decathlon champion, Rome (1960).

TOM JOHNSTON—associate, J. H. Whitney & Company. Administrative aide to Robert F. Kennedy (1965–1968).

LYDIA KATZENBACH (Mrs. Nicholas deB. Katzenbach).

NICHOLAS DE B. KATZENBACH—vice president, general counsel, IBM Corporation. Attorney General of the United States (1965–1966); Under Secretary of State (1966–1968).

MURRAY KEMPTON—journalist. Author: *Part of Our Time; America Comes of Middle Age*.

HELEN KEYES—administrator, John Fitzgerald Kennedy Library. Aide, John F. Kennedy presidential campaign (1960) and Robert F. Kennedy senatorial campaign (1964), presidential campaign (1968).

CORETTA SCOTT KING—civil-rights leader. Author of *My Life with Martin Luther King.*

THE REVEREND FREDERICK D. KIRKPATRICK—folk singer; organizer, Many Cultures Foundation. Recreation director, Resurrection City (1968).

JOSEPH KRAFT—syndicated columnist. Author: *The Struggle for Algeria; The Grand Design; Profiles in Power.*

GEORGE KRAUSS—music supervisor, Board of Education, New Brunswick, New Jersey.

BONNIE LEFKOWITZ—author; district assistant to New York Assemblyman Al Blumenthal (64th A.D.). Campaign worker, Robert F. Kennedy senatorial campaign (1964) and presidential campaign (1968).

STANLEY LEVISON—attorney. Permanent board member, Martin Luther King Memorial Center; board of directors, Southern Christian Leadership Conference.

ANTHONY LEWIS—chief, London bureau, the New York *Times*. Author: *Gideon's Trumpet; Portrait of a Decade: The Second American Revolution.*

JOHN J. LINDSAY—correspondent, Washington bureau, *Newsweek.*

ALICE ROOSEVELT LONGWORTH (Mrs. Nicholas Longworth)—daughter of President Theodore Roosevelt.

THE REVEREND HÉCTOR LÓPEZ—counselor, Center for Urban-Black Studies, Berkeley, California.

ROBERT LOVETT—general partner, Brown Brothers Harriman & Co., Under Secretary of State (1947–1949); Secretary of Defense (1951–1953).

ROBERT LOWELL—poet. Books: *Notebook 1967–68; Lord Weary's Castle; Imitations; For the Union Dead; The Old Glory.*

ALLARD LOWENSTEIN—U.S. Representative, New York. Author of *Brutal Mandate.*

STAUGHTON LYND—historian, educator. Author (with Tom Hayden) of *The Other Side.*

PETER MAAS—journalist. Author: *The Rescuer; The Valachi Papers.*

SHIRLEY MAC LAINE—actress. Motion pictures: *Sweet Charity; The Apartment; Irma La Douce; Woman Times Seven.*

JOHN MAGUIRE—named president, State University of New York at Old Westbury (fall 1970). Permanent trustee, Martin Luther King Memorial Center; editorial board member, *Christianity and Crisis.* Former associate professor of religion, Wesleyan University.

FRANK MANKIEWICZ—syndicated columnist. Latin America regional director, Peace Corps, Washington (1964–1966); press secretary to Robert F. Kennedy (1966–1968).

BURKE MARSHALL—deputy dean, Yale Law School. Assistant Attorney General, civil-rights division, U.S. Justice Department (1961–1965); senior vice president, IBM Corporation (1969–1970).

GEORGE MC GOVERN—Senator from the State of South Dakota.

JOHN MC HUGH—patrolman, Philadelphia police force.

ROBERT MC NAMARA—president, World Bank. Director, Ford Motor Company (1957–1961); Secretary of Defense (1961–1968).

JAMES MEREDITH—attorney; lecturer; stockbroker. First Negro graduate, University of Mississippi.

JOSEPH MOHBAT—reporter, Associated Press.

CLARK MOLLENHOFF—former deputy counsel to President Richard M. Nixon. Reporter, Washington bureau, Cowles publications (1950–1969).

ROBERT MORGENTHAU—U.S. Attorney, Southern District, New York (1961–1970).

BILL MOYERS—publisher, *Newsday* (1967–1970); deputy director, Peace Corps (1961–1963); special assistant to President Lyndon B. Johnson (1963–1967).

DANIEL P. MOYNIHAN—former Assistant for Urban Affairs to President Richard M. Nixon; director, Joint Center for Urban Studies, Massachusetts Institute of Technology, and Harvard. Assistant Secretary of Labor (1963–1965). Co-author of *Beyond the Melting Pot.*

GENEVIEVE MURPHY — housewife, Elizabeth, New Jersey.

RICHARD NEUSTADT—director, Institute of Politics, John Fitzgerald Kennedy School of Government, Harvard University. Consultant to President John F. Kennedy (1961–1963). Author of *Presidential Power.*

JACK NEWFIELD—reporter, the *Village Voice.* Author: *A Prophetic Minority; Robert Kennedy: A Memoir.*

MICHAEL NOVAK—associate professor of philosophy and theology, State University of New York at Old Westbury. Author of *The Experience of Nothingness.*

ANGELA NOVELLO—secretary to the United States Ambassador to Denmark. Personal secretary to Robert F. Kennedy (1957–1968).

LAWRENCE F. O'BRIEN—Democratic National Chairman. Special assistant to President John F. Kennedy (1961–1963) and President Lyndon B. Johnson (1963–1965); Postmaster General of the United States (1965–1968); campaign director, Kennedy-Johnson (1960), Johnson-Humphrey (1964), Robert F. Kennedy presidential campaign (1968), Humphrey-Muskie (1968).

KENNETH O'DONNELL—designated Democratic candidate for Governor of Massachusetts (1970); vice president, Responsive Environment Corporation. White House aide to President John F. Kennedy (1960–1963).

FRED PAPERT—president, Papert, Koenig, Lois, Inc. Advisory consultant to Robert F. Kennedy, senatorial campaign (1964) and presidential campaign (1968).

JAY PATTON—grade-school student, Wilmington, Delaware.

GEORGE PLIMPTON—author: *Paper Lion; Out of My League; The Bogey Man.* Editor: *The Paris Review; American Literary Anthology; Writers at Work.*

DAVE POWERS—administrator, John F. Kennedy Museum, Boston. White House aide to President John F. Kennedy (1960–1963).

CHARLES QUINN—television news correspondent; political reporter.

WILLIAM RICHARDS II—reporter, the *Daily Journal,* Elizabeth, New Jersey.

STEVE RITNER—law student, American University, Washington, D.C. Resident of Wilmington, Delaware.

JOHN ROONEY—funeral director, Rooney Funeral Home, New York.

FRANKLIN D. ROOSEVELT, JR.—attorney. President, Roosevelt Automobile Company and Fiat-Roosevelt Motors. U.S. Representative, New York (1949–1954); Under Secretary of Commerce (1963).

CORNELIUS RYAN—author: *The Longest Day; The Last Battle.*

PIERRE SALINGER—president, Gramco Development Corporation and Fox Overseas Corporation. Press secretary to President John F. Kennedy (1961–1963) and President Lyndon B. Johnson (1963–1964); press adviser, Robert F. Kennedy presidential campaign (1968).

HARRISON SALISBURY—assistant managing editor, the New York *Times.* Author: *The 900 Days; War Between Russia and China.*

ROBERT SCHEER—author of *How The United States Got Involved in Vietnam;* co-author of *Cuba: Tragedy in Our Hemisphere.* Editor of *Eldridge Cleaver* (The Post-Prison Memoirs of Eldridge Cleaver). Editor, *Ramparts* magazine (1964–1969).

ARTHUR SCHLESINGER, JR.—Schweitzer professor of humanities, City University, New York. Special assistant to President John F. Kennedy (1961–1963). Author: *The Politics of Upheaval; A Thousand Days: John F. Kennedy in the White House; The Age of Jackson; The Age of Roosevelt.*

MARIAN SCHLESINGER—painter, journalist.

HERB SCHMERTZ—attorney. Manager, corporate planning, Mobil Oil Corporation. Advance man, Robert F. Kennedy presidential campaign (1968).

BUDD SCHULBERG—author: *What Makes Sammy Run; The Disenchanted; The Harder They Fall; On the Waterfront; Sanctuary V.* Founder, Douglass House Watts Writers Workshop, Inner City Cultural Center and Douglass House Foundation.

ADALBERT DE SEGONZAC—Washington correspondent, *France-Soir.*

JOHN SEIGENTHALER—editor, *Nashville Tennessean.* Administrative assistant to Robert F. Kennedy, U.S. Justice Department (1961).

BARBARA SHALVEY—researcher-interviewer. Campaign worker, Robert F. Kennedy senatorial campaign (1964).

WALTER SHERIDAN—NBC correspondent. Special assistant to the Attorney General, U.S. Justice Department (1961–1964); campaign aide, Robert F. Kennedy presidential campaign (1968).

WILLIAM J. SHIELDS—supervisor, passenger-train operation, Penn Central Railroad.

ALEX SMITH—advance man, John F. Kennedy presidential campaign (1960); volunteer worker, Robert F. Kennedy presidential campaign (1968).

PETER SMITH—attorney. Campaign aide, Robert F. Kennedy senatorial campaign (1964); legislative associate, Robert F. Kennedy (1965–1968); campaign aide, Robert F. Kennedy presidential campaign (1968).

CHARLES SPALDING—investment banker, Lazard Frères. Campaign aide, John F. Kennedy presidential campaign (1960) and Robert F. Kennedy presidential campaign (1968).

SAUL STEINBERG—artist. Author: *The Labyrinth; The New World; Le Masque.*

ELIZABETH STEVENS (Mrs. George Stevens, Jr.).

GEORGE STEVENS, JR.—director, American Film Institute. Director,

361

Motion Picture Service, USIA (1962–1967).

JIM STEVENSON—cartoonist-reporter, *The New Yorker*.

JOHN STEWART—folk singer, song writer. Collector, contemporary folk songs, John Fitzgerald Kennedy Library; member, Kingston Trio.

GENERAL MAXWELL D. TAYLOR—president, Institute for Defense Analysis. Military representative to President John F. Kennedy (1961–1962); chairman, Joint Chiefs of Staff (1962–1964); United States Ambassador to Vietnam (1964–1965); special consultant to the President (1965–1969).

FELICIA TEDESCHI—high-school student, Elizabeth, New Jersey.

ANDREAS TEUBER—instructor in philosophy, Institute of Politics, John Fitzgerald Kennedy School of Government, Harvard University, and Massachusetts Institute of Technology. Special assistant, Eugene McCarthy presidential campaign (1968).

JAMES C. THOMSON, JR.—assistant professor of history and research fellow, Institute of Politics, John Fitzgerald Kennedy School of Government, Harvard University. Member, National Security Council (1964–1966).

JOSÉ TORRES—columnist, the New York *Post*. Light-heavyweight boxing champion (1965–1966).

DICK TUCK—aide, John F. Kennedy presidential campaign (1960), Robert F. Kennedy senatorial campaign (1964), Robert F. Kennedy presidential campaign (1968).

JOSEPH TYDINGS—Senator from the State of Maryland.

JESSE UNRUH—Democratic candidate for Governor of California (1970).

Former speaker, California Assembly.

JEAN STEIN VANDEN HEUVEL—journalist, interviewer.

WILLIAM VANDEN HEUVEL—attorney. Special assistant to Robert F. Kennedy, U.S. Justice Department (1962–1964); vice president, New York Constitutional Convention 1967). Author (with Milton Gwirtzman) of *On His Own: RFK, 1964–1968*.

ADAM WALINSKY—attorney. Democratic candidate for Attorney General of New York (1970); attorney, U.S. Justice Department (1963–1964); speechwriter and legislative aide to Senator Robert F. Kennedy (1964–1968).

GILLIAN WALKER—theatrical producer. Associated with National Educational Television. Associate producer, Circle in the Square, New York (1965–1969) and Ford's Theatre, Washington, D.C. (1968–1969).

WILLIAM WALTON—artist. Chairman, U.S. Commission on Fine Arts; trustee, Kennedy Memorial Library.

THEODORE WHITE—historian. Author: *Thunder Out of China; The Mountain Road; Caesar at the Rubicon; The View From the Fortieth Floor; The Making of the President*.

JIM WHITTAKER—manager, Recreational Equipment Company Inc. First American to climb Mount Everest (1963); leader, Mount Kennedy expedition (1965); Washington State Chairman, Kennedy for President (1968).

TOM WICKER—columnist; associate editor, the New York *Times*. Author of *Kennedy Without Tears*.

ROGER WILKINS—officer in charge, Social Development, the Ford Foundation. Director CRS, U.S. Justice Department (1966–1969).

HOSEA WILLIAMS—director, voter registration and political education, Southern Christian Leadership Conference. Former aide to Martin Luther King, Jr.

MILLIE WILLIAMS—instructor, United States Research and Development Corporation. Staff member, Robert F. Kennedy Senate office (1966–1968).

HARRIS WOFFORD—president, Bryn Mawr. Special assistant to President John F. Kennedy (1961–1962); associate director, Peace Corps (1964–1966); president, State University of New York at Old Westbury (1966–1970). Co-editor, *Report of the U.S. Commission on Civil Rights.*

SYLVIA WRIGHT—reporter, *Life* magazine.

ADAM YARMOLINSKY—profesor of law, Harvard University; member, Institute of Politics, John Fitzgerald Kennedy School of Government, Harvard University. Special Assistant Secretary of Defense (1961–1964); deputy Assistant Secretary of Defense, international security affairs (1965–1966).

THE REVEREND ANDREW J. YOUNG—designated Democratic candidate for Congress, Fulton County, Georgia (1970). Former executive vice president, Southern Christian Leadership Conference; permanent board member, Martin Luther King Memorial Center; chairman, governing council, Institute of Nonviolence and Social Change.

Index

DATE DUE

NOV 0 5 1996